Organizational Improvisati

CW00348607

The relatively new field of organizational improvisation is concerned with the pressures on organizations to react continually to today's ever-changing environment.

Organizational improvisation has important implications for such subjects as product innovation, teamworking and organizational renewal, and this new book brings together some of the best and most thought-provoking papers published in recent years.

The ten articles featured illustrate the development of the concept, from its jazz-based origins to its contemporary application within specific organizational fields.

Organizational improvisation is now emerging as one of the most important areas of organizational science, and this book provides a comprehensive collection of works, showing both the theoretical underpinnings and illustrating the practical application of these concepts in real organizations.

Ken N. Kamoche is Associate Professor at City University of Hong Kong. His research has appeared in various journals, and he has published two previous books, *Sociological Paradigms and Human Resources*, and *Understanding Human Resource Management*.

Miguel Pina e Cunha is Assistant Professor at the Faculdade de Economia, Universidade Nova de Lisboa. He researches, and has been widely published, in the fields of organizational change and improvisation.

João Vieira da Cunha is a PhD student at the MIT Sloan School of Management. His research has been published in leading journals such as the *Journal of Organizational Change Management* and the *International Journal of Management Reviews*.

Organizational Improvisation

Edited by
**Ken N. Kamoche, Miguel Pina e Cunha
and João Vieira da Cunha**

London and New York

First published 2002
by Routledge
11 New Fetter Lane, London EC4P 4EE

Simultaneously published in the USA and Canada
by Routledge
29 West 35th Street, New York, NY 10001

Routledge is an imprint of the Taylor & Francis Group

© 2002 Selection and editorial matter, Ken N. Kamoche, Miguel Pina e
Cunha and João Vieira da Cunha; individual chapters, the contributors.

Typeset in Baskerville by Wearset Ltd, Boldon, Tyne and Wear
Printed and bound in Great Britain by TJ International Ltd, Padstow,
Cornwall

British Library Cataloguing in Publication Data
A catalogue record for this book is available from the British Library

Library of Congress Cataloging in Publication Data
A catalog record for this book has been requested

ISBN 0-415-26175-9 (hbk)
ISBN 0-415-26176-7 (pbk)

Contents

Illustrations

Tables

Contributors

Frank J. Barrett Naval Postgraduate School, Monterey.
David T. Bastien University of Wisconsin–Eau Claire.
Shona L. Brown McKinsey and Company.
Mary M. Crossan University of Western Ontario.
João Vieira da Cunha Massachusetts Institute of Technology.
Miguel Pina e Cunha University Nova de Lisboa.
Kathleen M. Eisenhardt Stanford University.
Mary Jo Hatch University of Virginia.
Todd J. Hostager University of Wisconsin–Eau Claire.
Ken N. Kamoche City University of Hong Kong.
Wanda J. Orlikowski Massachusetts Institute of Technology.
Anne S. Miner University of Wisconsin–Madison.
Christine Moorman Duke University.
Marc Sorrenti Good impressions.
Karl E. Weick University of Michigan.

Acknowledgments

The editors and publishers would like to thank the following for permission to use copyright material.

Sage Publications for Bastien D.T. and T.J. Hostager, 'Jazz as a process of organizational innovation', *Communication Research*, 1988, vol. 15, 582–602.

Elsevier Science for Crossan, M. and M. Sorrenti, 'Making sense of improvisation', *Advances in Strategic Management*, 1996, vol. 14, 155–80.

Hatch, M.J. for 'Exploring the empty spaces in jazz: how improvisational jazz helps redescribe organizational structure', *Organization Studies*, 1999, vol. 20, 75–100.

Blackwell for Cunha, M.P., J.V. Cunha and K.N. Kamoche, 'Organizational improvisation: what, when, how and why', *International Journal of Management Reviews*, 1999, vol. 1, 299–341.

Institute for Operations Research and the Management Sciences for Weick, K.E., 'Improvisation as a mindset for organizational analysis', *Organization Science*, 1998, vol. 9, 543–55; Barrett, F.J., 'Creativity and improvisation in jazz and organizations: implications for organizational learning', *Organization Science*, 1998, vol. 9, 605–22; Orlikowski, W.J., 'Improvising organizational transformation over time: a situated change perspective', *Information Systems Research*, 1996, vol. 7, 63–92.

Instituto Superior de Psicologia Aplicada for Weick, K.E., 'The aesthetic of imperfection in orchestras and organizations', *Readings in Organization Science*, 1999, 541–63.

Administrative Science Quarterly for Brown, S.L. and K.M. Eisenhardt, 'The art of continuous change: Linking complexity theory and time-based evolution in relentlessly shifting organizations', *Administrative Science Quarterly*, 1997, vol. 38, 628–52.

American Marketing Association for Moorman, C. and A.S. Miner, 'The convergence of planning and execution: Improvisation in new product development', *Journal of Marketing*, 1998, vol. 62, 1–20.

Cordon Art for Metamorphosis II.

The editors would like to thank Catriona King and Gavin Cullen for their help and assistance.

1 Introduction and overview

Ken N. Kamoche, Miguel Pina e Cunha and
João Vieira da Cunha

The chapters in this volume are part of an emergent discipline of organizational analysis which we believe now fully deserves the attention of organization theorists and practitioners. This emergent paradigm is in part an attempt to grapple with the complexities of a rapidly changing world and the need to look beyond the traditional sources of competitive advantage. The complexity of organizations indeed continues to keep theorists busy as they strive to tackle the perennial problem of how to design efficient and viable organizations and how best to respond to or anticipate new environmental challenges. These efforts have seen developments in a number of fields, from transaction cost economics (Williamson, 1979) to institutional theory (Meyer and Rowan, 1977) and the resource-based view of the firm (Barney, 1991; Grant, 1991).

Organizational improvisation is one of the more recent theoretical developments, and one which is only now beginning to capture the imagination of organization theorists. Improvisation has variously been described as the merging of planning and action, the realization of action as it unfolds, thinking and acting extemporaneously and so forth. Improvisation has slowly begun to generate some interest amongst researchers. Some people are drawn to it because it seems to offer novel interpretations of organizational action; others are no doubt curious about its potential contribution to our understanding of concepts like creativity, innovation, structure and so forth. Some are probably familiar with the manifestations of improvisational behaviour in other fields such as the arts and are interested to know how lessons from these fields can, if at all, be transferred to the field of organization studies. All these and many others are legitimate concerns. They are also to be expected in a field which is still in an embryonic stage.

Our purpose is to shed some light on these questions as well as to offer a sense of direction as to how research in organizational improvisation might proceed. We believe that improvisation is a central feature of organizational reality and indeed a definitive feature of the way we go about our day-to-day activities. Improvising takes place in much of what we do: from holding conversations to making fairly important decisions that have a fundamental bearing on our very existence. This reality is enacted in our personal lives as well as in the organizational context. There has been a growing awareness in recent years that the concept of improvisation constitutes a new opportunity to explore the nature of organizations. Indeed many researchers have been trying to understand the meaning of improvisation, the manifestations of improvisational behaviour, and the circumstances under which improvisation happens. Cunha *et al.* (this volume, Chapter 12) have attempted to convey a sense of these efforts.

As noted above, organizational improvisation is still in its earlier stages of development and much remains to be done before the full contribution of this research paradigm to organization science can be fully appreciated. It is with this in mind that we offer this volume of some of the most salient contributions to this emergent field. There are of course many other papers which constitute the growing corpus of knowledge on the phenomenon of organizational improvisation. We hope, however, that the few we have selected will together point to new directions for research into a field which we feel is ripe for further enquiry.

In the sections below we delve into the jazz-based literature to determine the extent to which the jazz metaphor has continued to inform the debate on organizational improvisation. We then identify what this debate means for an important aspect of organizing: structure. The discussion then turns to organizational change and how this debate relates to improvisational action. The following section proceeds to locate the nature and role of improvisation within the context of rapid change in an increasingly turbulent business world. We conclude this chapter with a look at what improvisation means within the socio-cultural context insofar as improvised action is about getting things done by people. Throughout this discussion we endeavour to illustrate the contributions the chapters in this volume make to these important themes.

Lessons from jazz

The field of organizational improvisation has drawn heavily from jazz music. This was probably inevitable given the accessibility of the jazz metaphor and more importantly, the fact that jazz seems to be one of the more salient phenomena in which improvisation has been developed to a high level of sophistication. Crossan and Sorrenti (this volume, Chapter 3) have also identified the importance of improvisational theatre, e.g. the *Commedia dell'arte* form that emerged in Western Europe in the sixteenth century. Theorists have continued to show a healthy predilection to draw from unusual sources in their efforts to advance theory via metaphor. This quest for metaphorical explication in part represents a concern to design new approaches to tackle intractable organizational problems.

The quest to improve organizational effectiveness has seen scholars delve into metaphorical arenas as diverse as the symphony orchestra (e.g. Kanter, 1989; Sayles, 1964) and war (e.g. Hou *et al.*, 1991). This tendency is particularly notable in strategic management where competitive pressures require organizations to be constantly on the look out for new ways to compete and to discover new sources of 'competitive advantage'. While we do not conceive of improvisation merely as a metaphor, we recognize that its contribution to organization science will be judged, *inter alia, vis-à-vis* other metaphors and certainly in terms of its 'value-added' as a metaphor. In this regard it is helpful to gain some understanding of the nature of jazz improvisation, to appreciate its constitutive features, the implications of its essentially processual and emergent nature, as well as its limitations in assessing organizational action.

In the performing arts like jazz, improvisation refers to composing and performing in the same moment, i.e. realizing a musical performance without the benefit of deliberate planning about how each note will be executed, the order and flavour of each solo, the direction the performance will take, how long it will last, etc. With these definitions in mind, the thought of people improvising action might at first glance appear far-fetched given the structural nature of many organizations coupled with the fact that many managers have a preference for order and stability. In particular this appears even more far-fetched when the observer's frame of reference is the field of performing arts like jazz and theatre. Surely, managers and employees cannot be compared with musicians and actors! On closer scrutiny, however, it becomes evident that there are lessons that organizations could learn from the performing arts as well as from other aspects of human endeavour.

It should be pointed out, however, that the apparent absence of structure in the improvised arts does not imply chaos, randomness or disorder, and as Hatch (this volume, Chapter 5) cautions, it is not simply about making it up as you go along. Some of the lessons derivable from the arts have been articulated by a number of authors in this emergent literature. Some of these insights are discussed in a number of the contributions in this volume. Improvisation has been developed to a high level of sophistication in performing arts like jazz music and this is probably one of the manifestations of improvisational behaviour that many readers will be familiar with. But as some scholars have argued, the inspiration to improvise can come from any number of sources. Similarly, there is much to be gained from exploring the potential contribution of a wide range of metaphors and analytical perspectives.

Following Weick's (1992) suggestion of a jazz band as a prototype organization, Barrett (this volume, Chapter 7) demonstrates how jazz improvisation can offer useful lessons as to how organizations can be designed for maximum learning and innovation. The rationale for this exercise is partly based on Barrett's contention that the things that managers and jazz musicians do are not all that dissimilar: they have to continuously invent novel responses without following a predetermined script and with little certainty as to the outcomes of their actions. The consequences of their actions are unfolding as the actions themselves are being enacted; and the actions are directed at a specific audience, which could be jazz enthusiasts or in the case of managers – in our view – customers, employees, investors and other stakeholders.

Barrett then proceeds to detail a number of characteristics which contain real lessons for managerial action. These include 'provocative competence' in order to instigate a departure from routines and recipe behaviour, treating errors as a source of learning, and alternating between soloing and supporting in order to give everyone room to think, enhance learning and distribute the leadership task. In his work on the aesthetics of imperfection following Gioia (1988), Weick (this volume, Chapter 8) elaborates the significance of a mindset which is appreciative of the failures that occur in the process of making genuine efforts to innovate. Such failure becomes normalized as an inevitable aspect of improvisation and the stigma usually associated with failure is eradicated. According to Weick, with an aesthetics of imperfection, errors are thus treated as opportunities for further learning rather than threats.

In an analysis which clearly demonstrates the nature and implications of composing and performing contemporaneously, Bastien and Hostager (this volume, Chapter 2) present a case study of a process through which a jazz band engages in a performance in front of an audience without the benefit of a rehearsal or sheet music. Their work is a rare effort to analyse an improvised jazz performance *in situ* and draw lessons for organizational action (see also Bastien and Hostager, 1992). The authors argue that the process of jazz improvisation is self-consciously spontaneous, creative and expressive, it is a social process and a collective approach to the process of innovation. These characteristics are clearly not alien to what we see in organizations. Bastien and Hostager identify specific musical structures and social practices which for them constitute the *structural conventions* in the jazz process. These include the cognitively held rules for creating new musical ideas, such as those for chords and chordal progressions, the song, behavioural norms and communicative codes.

In the field of product innovation, Kamoche and Cunha (2001) have drawn from jazz to isolate social and technical characteristics that they then apply to the product innovation process. These structures are based on Bastien and Hostager's structural conventions of the jazz process. These characteristics include trust, communicative codes, performative competence, experimentation, frequent refashioning in the light of new information, audience/customer response and so forth. For Hatch (this volume, Chapter 5), jazz offers some very useful lessons as a vehicle to achieve a redescription of organizational structure which is *performative*, thus concerned with sensemaking, realizing action and 'the process of becoming'. As such, organizational structure is not perceived merely as a state or an outcome, but a set of performance practices or processes.

With this re-interpretation and application of metaphor, Hatch demonstrates how jazz musicians alter the structural foundations of their performance by sustaining and creatively engaging the ambiguity inherent in the potential for multiple interpretations. This has important implications for organizations. It opens up the possibility of organizational members redefining the structures with which they operate rather than be held hostage by them. We note that social interaction and the fluidity of cultures together constitute a form of ambiguity which is constantly being refashioned through processes of sense-making, communications, leadership, and power. In this context, organizational members have access to opportunities to redefine and reinterpret social relations, the organization of work as well as their identities. Jazz musicians redefine the structure as they enact the definitive features of an improvisational performance such as 'soloing' (taking the lead), 'comping' (offering harmonic and rhythmic support to the temporary leader), listening and responding to the cues and ideas from others, and so forth.

We can begin to anticipate the application of these metaphorical contributions in activities like teamwork which involve collaboration, in particular where such collaboration requires high degrees of creativity and autonomy such as product innovation. Important features include extensive information-sharing and communications and a culture that actively fosters idea-generation (e.g. Brown and Eisenhardt, this volume, Chapter 10; Hutchins, 1991; Moorman and Miner, this volume, Chapter 11; Nonaka and Takeuchi, 1995; Tatikonda and Rosenthal, 2000). Similarly, the idea of constantly engaging and redefining the existing structures can be pursued on the basis of using real-time information flows and market intelligence that are fed into the design and development processes to respond to customer needs (e.g. O'Connor, 1998; Veryzer, 1998).

While these ideas open up new ways of conceptualizing and using structure, many issues still need to be addressed before the lessons from jazz improvisation can become more widely accepted. For example, to what extent can organizations allow ordinary members to retain tacit or implicit structures without the fear of compromising managerial control, quality or customer service? In spite of all the talk about empowerment today, will managers permit employees to redefine rules and norms and trust employees to retain these 'in their heads' as jazz musicians retain the tune and play around it without explicitly articulating its every constitutive melodic, harmonic or rhythmic structure? Do managers have enough faith in the organizational culture's ability to nurture this ability to internalize the structure? Developments in surveillance and peer pressure (e.g. Barker, 1993; Sewell, 1998) suggest that the challenges are enormous but not insurmountable.

Nevertheless, we argue that many manifestations of organizational action and forms of organizing are analogous with the emergent action more often associated with the performing arts. This is so if we roll back the assumptions underpinning cognitive rationality and begin to look more closely at how people actually solve problems, discover new ways to handle unanticipated occurrences, respond to technological, cultural and competitive challenges while developing their learning capabilities. While jazz certainly offers useful lessons, it is worth recalling that, in fact, there are plenty of opportunities for people to improvise outside of the performing arts and certainly within organizations where impromptu action has to be taken. In his assessment of improvisation as a mindset, Weick (this volume, Chapter 4) identifies a number of other non-jazz settings in which improvisation takes place. These include ordinary activities like cooking, competing, travelling, the acquisition and use of language, therapy and so forth. In fact, according to Bateson (1989), the very nature of human existence is a continuing process of improvisation as we compose our lives.

Toward a minimal structure of organizing

The emergence of the improvisational paradigm has less to do with merely exploring new metaphors than finding new ways to address real organizational challenges as well as filling gaps that existing methods of apprehending organizational reality have not fully addressed. Indeed one of the underlying rationales for improvisation has to do with dissatisfaction with the enduring conception of structure. The organization theory literature has from the very beginning concerned itself with the question of structure, with writers like Burns and Stalker (1961) proposing the dichotomy of organic and mechanistic, which has led researchers to try to determine the 'right' amount of structure, or to specify the structural forms appropriate for certain environments.

Distinctions such as organic and mechanistic may not always be all that clear cut. In fact, as Brown and Eisenhardt (this volume, Chapter 10) found out, successful firms seemed to achieve a viable balance where some aspects like meetings, priorities and responsibilities were fairly well structured while flexibility was realized through extensive communication and freedom to improvise current products. They suggest the notion of 'semi-structure' to capture this phenomenon. Similarly, in Kamoche and Cunha's (2001) improvisational model of new product development, specified elements of social and technical structures are clearly defined and rather than constrain action, actually serve as a template through which innovative action is accomplished. This template thus serves as a 'minimal structure'.

Similarly, drawing from jazz improvisation, Barrett (this volume, Chapter 7) suggests the need for structures that are minimal, non-negotiable, tacitly accepted and which would not need to be constantly articulated. March (1991) argues that organizational adaptive processes must maintain an appropriate balance between 'exploration' and 'exploitation'. The former includes, for example, search, variation, experimentation and innovation, while the latter refers to refinement, efficiency and implementation. In new service development, Edvardsson *et al.* (1995) emphasize the need to combine systematic modelling and fortuity. These examples illustrate the need to strike a balance between structure and flexibility. In product innovation such a balance takes on new meaning as a synthesis (e.g. Tatikonda and Rosenthal, 2000).

In jazz music, songs play an important role in keeping the musicians focused while permitting them the flexibility they need to improvise around its harmonic, melodic and rhythmic structures. As Eisenberg (1990) points out, the process of 'jamming' (whether in jazz or sports) provides a minimal view of organizing which at once sets out minimal commonalities and elaborates possibilities for further innovation. Finding an organizational equivalent of a minimal structure is no easy task. Various authors have suggested using credos, mission statements, product prototypes and so forth. These structures create a shared sense of orientation. They help focus action on the things that really matter while allowing individual members and teams to introduce variation within the zones of manoeuvre defined by the minimal structures inasmuch as the structures are not there to constrain but rather to facilitate innovative action. A structure such as a mission statement or product prototype thus sets out the scope available for members to align their activities with the organizational objectives. It can also signal important changes so that members stay attuned in the same way that the bassist or any member of a band might signal new directions.

For Hedberg *et al.* (1976) such structures are essential in helping organizations avoid future problems by keeping processes dynamically balanced. The need to maintain some sort of minimal structure is particularly vital when people find themselves in highly turbulent environments and potentially disastrous circumstances. For example, Weick (1993) demonstrates how improvising action as well as maintaining a basic structure saved lives in a tragic forest fire. In the ensuing collapse of all order and the role system that previously constituted the formal structure, one firefighter was able to survive by improvising an action which entailed the unusual step of starting a fire to fight the approaching blaze and thus create a safe buffer zone. This is likened to the art of bricolage whereby the bricoleur uses whatever materials are on hand in a creative way to achieve outcomes, in this case survival. Two other firefighters survived by sticking together and sustaining intersubjectivity through the interaction brought about by partnership. Thus when formally constituted structures begin to fall apart and threaten to become untenable, the need to fall back on basic structural elements like trust, leadership, competence and creativity intensifies.

Realizing organizational change

When the concept of 'change management' first took root, change was treated as a deliberate intervention by specified change agents who set out to design and implement new strategies and operational procedures in order to enhance organizational functioning. These deliberate, systematic and well-planned efforts to institute change have found expression in a large number of literatures, ranging from organization development (e.g. Porras and Robertson, 1992) to total quality management (e.g. Deming, 1982; Oakland, 1989), and more recently, business process re-engineering (e.g. Hammer and Champy, 1993).

While some researchers recognize that even planned, strategic change has a processual and emergent character (e.g. Pettigrew and Whipp, 1991), there is still an underlying assumption in the change management literature that change is top-down and executive-driven. Those affected by the change, including ordinary employees, are often treated as passive implementers of initiatives they have played no role in formulating. With the onset of re-engineering, many of these passive implementers were quickly turned into victims of retrenchment and downsizing. To the extent that change management is now very much associated with downsizing and reductions in headcounts. Concerns have been raised not just about the ability of organizations to tap into the talents of employees in accomplishing change, but also about the effect on learning. If employees are afraid of falling victim to the next round of retrenchment, conformity and work-to-rules might seem a more sensible and safer option except where innovativeness and deviance are not only encouraged but rewarded.

If the accomplishment of change is treated as a managerially-driven strategic initiative based on rational planning and accommodating little or no deviation from standard procedures, spontaneity is lost. Yet, the potential robustness of concepts like fortuity, serendipity and unplanned experimentation appear to expose the gaps in these traditional forms of organizing. Mintzberg and Water's (1985) work on 'emergent strategy', Quinn's (1982) 'logical incrementalism', and Miller's (1993) 'architecture of simplicity', are examples of this critique, which we find relevant here. This line of thinking goes some way toward restoring a sense of proactivity in individuals (and teams) and the potential for experimentation outside the often rigid structures of planned organizational change. We consider this proactivity and initiative-taking to be consistent with the impetus of improvisation.

While allowing for incremental change, the 'punctuated equilibrium' school of thought holds that change is episodic and radical (e.g. Gersick, 1988, 1991; Romanelli and Tushman, 1994). Punctuated equilibrium – a concept derived from natural history – is characterized by a sequence of actions interspaced with inertial movements. This raises important questions about the suitability of clearly defined structures for certain group and organizational activities. However, while this model continues to generate a great deal of interest, it also seems to be at odds with the reality of many firms today for whom radical change is not an episodic deviation from long periods of stability but a definitive feature of the way they compete (e.g. Brown and Eisenhardt, this volume, Chapter 10). Orlikowski (this volume, Chapter 9) makes a similar point by arguing that this model is based on the assumption of stability and a preferred state of equilibrium (assumptions it shares with the 'planned change' and the 'technological imperative' perspectives). These perspectives are clearly untenable in circumstances where stability and equilibrium are neither achievable nor realistic. Their ability to foster and sustain a climate of continuous and spontaneous change characterized by experimentation and trial and error is questionable.

Orlikowski's 'situated change perspective' is an exciting way of researching organizational transformation which is enacted subtly and gradually but with significant consequences for the organization of work, as social actors engage in ongoing improvisation to make sense of challenges and problems that arise on a continuing basis. Constant re-invention and organizational renewal through *ad hoc* adaptation rather than systematic planning and dramatic managerial intervention are being increasingly recognized as realistic descriptions of the way much of organizational change and transformation are achieved today.

Applying trial-and-error with new techniques and solutions to unfamiliar and emergent problems is an improvisational technique often associated with situations involving high risks and potential disaster. Examples include the rescue of Appollo XIII by NASA scientists (Lovell and Kluger, 1995), and the rescue of a ship by crew members following the failure of the navigation system (Hutchins, 1991), or escape from a forest fire (Weick, 1993). Organizational reality is, however, characterized by numerous examples of less dramatic and more ordinary forms of adaptation in which social actors are engaged in an ongoing process of problem-solving, re-definition of problems, communication, re-adjustment of frames of reference, con-flict-resolution, variation of procedures and so forth, while in the process accomplishing emergent, yet deep-seated change. We see such sensemaking as a central feature of what it means to improvise action in organizational settings.

Managing in a turbulent world

Change in organizations and in particular in the organization of work is not always easy to anticipate, let alone plan for. The vicissitudes of the world economy, especially those that struck Asia in the late 1990s, demonstrated the potential magnitude of environmental turbulence and the resultant, extremely far-reaching, consequences. Economies like those of Thailand and South Korea which, in the 1980s and early 1990s, came to epitomize the 'Asian economic miracle', found themselves rocked by collapsing currencies, capital flight, business closures, high unemployment and an unprecedented degree of economic volatility. Aspiring 'tigers' like Malaysia and Indonesia saw economic collapse accompanied by political and social instability.

Even the more stable economies like Hong Kong and Singapore experienced a high degree of volatility, reductions in incomes and a rise in unemployment. This sort of turbulence has forced organizations to re-invent themselves by cultivating flexibility and innovativeness. Managers in the region have been forced to abandon the assumption of stability and to acknowledge that a state of equilibrium is not only ethereal but in reality a liability which breeds complacency and does little to foster innovativeness.

Models predicated on the assumption of predictability and stability are becoming increasingly obsolete in the highly turbulent world we live in today. Rapid techno-logical change, intensified competitive forces, the vicissitudes of globalization including recent turbulence in the financial markets have all combined to radically change the business environment to such an extent that continuous change has become a permanent phenomenon with organizations having to constantly reinvent themselves (e.g. Eisenhardt, 1989; D'Aveni, 1994; Chakravarthy, 1997; Rajaram and Fitzgerald, 2000). Some aspects of this phenomenon have been captured in the notion of 'hyper-competition' whereby slow-moving, stable entities are being transformed into highly adaptable entities that are constantly searching for unusual modes of competition and discovering new sources of competitive advantage (e.g. D'Aveni, 1994).

Discovering or inventing new ways to compete also involves radically changing management styles and attitudes as well as transforming the processes of product development and service delivery. In industries characterized by hyper-competition, where action has to be made without the benefit of systematic planning and highly structured decision processes, traditional methods of management become not only inadequate but a threat to organizational survival. In product innovation, such situations demand flexible, extemporaneous actions by agile management (Thomke and Reinertsen, 1998).

In their analysis of improvised jazz performances, Bastien and Hostager found such performances to be characterized by a high degree of task uncertainty. Musicians in turn learn to cope with this turbulence by inventing task structures to manage the turbulence and facilitate innovation. They argue further that the social structures which constrain behaviour in jazz as well as in business involve relatively informal norms and codes. They propose the notion of 'centring' as a strategy for coping with change and turbulence. This is a collective process in which innovation begins with a centre that consists of a shared understanding (e.g. a song familiar to all) from which the social actors can then determine how to adopt new ideas, achieve variation and incrementally move into new and unfamiliar task environments. Essentially this defines a minimal structure which allows the organizational members to determine where to go next, how to handle the emergent turbulence and achieve organizational renewal.

Turbulent industries are proving to be fertile ground for empirical investigations into the emergence and success of improvisation. Brown and Eisenhardt's (this volume, Chapter 10) chapter is set in the high-velocity computer industry. The authors argue that this setting is attractive precisely because of its extraordinary rate of change. Coping with the continuous changes in a highly turbulent industry becomes a major factor in competitive success. In a previous contribution, Eisenhardt and Tabrizi (1995) demonstrate the effectiveness of an experiential approach involving improvisation to product development in the computer industry.

In a similar vein, Moorman and Miner's chapter (this volume, Chapter 11) chapter examines the incidence and effectiveness of improvisation in product development when firms face environmental turbulence. Without discounting the value of planning, they point to the irony in much of the current work on product innovation which treats planning as the norm while acknowledging the increasingly dynamic nature of business environments (see also Wind and Mahajan, 1997). Moorman and Miner set out to examine, *inter alia*, whether environmental turbulence increased the incidence of improvisation and the likelihood that improvisation would generate effective products and processes in new product development. They found that turbulence increases the incidence of improvisation, and that in high turbulence environments, improvisation improves design effectiveness but not market effectiveness. However, when turbulence is high, the improvisation–cost-efficiency relationship is weaker. These results have important implications for the adoption of an improvisational approach in turbulent environments. It cannot be taken for granted that improvisation will always be successful. There is evidently a need for more research to determine the circumstances under which improvisation is both feasible and desirable.

Spontaneity, culture and concerted action

The famous distinction between deliberate and emergent strategies (Mintzberg and Waters, 1985) has important implications for the enactment of improvisational activity as defined here. As we have argued above, the idea that organizational action – in particular that relating to change management – based on *a priori* planning and follows a systematic and well-choreographed text is increasingly being challenged. Emergent strategies on the other hand, as the name suggests, evolve organically as the reality unfolds, and the resultant change comes about without having been anticipated.

The foregoing has important implications for the management of emergent action and the dynamics of spontaneity. As organizational improvisation continues to gain currency, researchers will need to demonstrate how this phenomenon advances our understanding of actions and behaviours that are emergent, spontaneous and creative. With a definition of improvisation and intuition guiding action in spontaneous ways, Crossan and Sorrenti (this volume, Chapter 3) have identified how improvisation enhances our understanding of the management of spontaneity. Their analysis sheds new light on how improvisation facilitates the accomplishment of experimental learning and highlights the ubiquity of improvisation in organizations. For them, improvisation is not merely something that managers revert to when planning breaks down, but an important facet of management which plays a critical role in organizational learning and strategic renewal.

In fact for many managers, improvisation is a legitimate and widely accepted way to manage. In this regard, Aram and Walochik (1996) found that Spanish managers displayed a consistent preference for improvisational action, represented in informality, flexibility, spontaneity and relatively low reliance on organizational systems and procedures. There are, of course, many researchers over the years who have highlighted this informal, fragmented and spontaneous aspect of managerial work and behaviour (e.g. Mintzberg, 1980; Stewart, 1998). There are not many, so far, who have specifically addressed the nature and incidence of *improvisation* in such behaviour. Aram and Walochik attribute this apparent Spanish preference for improvisation to the Spanish culture which they argue is characterized by informality, individualism, independence, spontaneity and is epitomized in the 'spirit of the legionnaire'. Their respondents also reported negative consequences of improvisation, such as ill-advised, impulsive decision-making, conflicts, stunted opportunities to grow the business beyond the informal and owner-centred style into a more decentralized organization, and so forth.

Clearly, the role of culture is one that opens up exciting opportunities for further research. Are some cultures more prone to improvisation than others? Are there some cultural attributes which lend themselves more easily to improvisational behaviour? In what cultural environments is improvisation likely to thrive? The importance of creating a culture supportive of innovation is now widely acknowledged (e.g. Perry, 1995; Zien and Buckler, 1997). Thus, to the extent that improvisation is about experimentation and exploration, an 'innovative culture' which fosters entrepreneurialism and inventiveness would appear to be essential. As many authors have observed, the experimental nature of improvisation implies a high potential for error and misjudgment; Zien and Buckler (1997) found that among highly innovative companies a hundred investigations for every market success was a common rule of thumb. Managers wishing to foster improvisation might therefore generate cultures and design human resource practices which have a high tolerance for failure, and help to bring out people's creativity.

We conclude this section with a brief mention of Howard Becker's (1986) thoughts on how people engage in concerted activities. Becker offers the concept of 'culture' to explain the phenomenon of concerted activity and draws insights from his own experience of playing improvised music (including jazz) with complete strangers. This idea of achieving a level of cohesiveness amongst people engaged in a social activity – or, in the language of jazz improvisation, 'finding the groove' – is a powerful vehicle for generating and sharing knowledge and a sense of shared reality. Creating a sense of shared reality is a difficult and challenging task, and one which is complicated further by the diverse backgrounds, frames of reference, belief systems and attitudes that characterize organizational contexts today.

Becker argues that people may have to negotiate when events are not fully or even partly covered by already shared understandings. More importantly, they may need to improvise when dealing with unfamiliar situations or when their modes of interaction cannot easily be reconciled by standard recipes. What we are seeing in the contributions in this volume and in the overall emergent literature on organizational improvisation is a questioning of standard recipes not merely in unfamiliar situations but increasingly in situations in which we previously believed we had a sense of shared reality.

References

Aram, J.D. and Walochik, K. (1996) Improvisation and the Spanish manager. *International Studies of Management and Organization*, 26: 73–89.

Barker, J.R. (1993) Tightening the iron cage: concertive control in self-managing teams. *Administrative Science Quarterly*, 38: 408–38.

Barney, J. (1991) Firm resources and sustained competitive advantage. *Journal of Management*, 17: 99–120.

Bateson, M.C. (1989) *Composing a life.* New York: Atlantic Monthly.

Becker, H.S. (1986) *Doing things together: selected papers.* Evanston, IL: Northwestern University Press.

Burns, T. and Stalker, G.M. (1961) *The management of innovation.* London: Tavistock.

Chakravarthy, B.S. (1997) A new strategy framework for coping with turbulence. *Sloan Management Review*, Winter: 69–82.

D'Aveni, R. (1994) *Hypercompetition: managing the dynamics of strategic maneuvering.* New York: Free Press.

Deming, W.E. (1982) *Quality, productivity and competitive position.* Cambridge, MA: MIT Center for Advanced Engineering Study.

Edvardsson, B., Haglund, L. and Mattsson, J. (1995) Analysis, planning, improvisation and control in the development of new services. *International Journal of Service Industry Management*, 6: 24–35.

Eisenberg, E. (1990) Jamming: transcendence through organizing. *Communication Research*, 17: 139–64.

Eisenhardt, K.M. (1989) Making fast strategic decisions in high velocity environments. *Academy of Management Journal*, 32: 543–76.

Eisenhardt, K.M. and Tabrizi, B.N. (1995) Accelerating adaptive processes: product innovation in the global computer industry. *Administrative Science Quarterly*, 40: 84–110.

Gersick, C.J.G. (1988) Time and transition in workteams: toward a new model of group development. *Academy of Management Journal*, 31: 9–41.

Gersick, C.J.G. (1991) Revolutionary change theories: a multilevel exploration of the punctuated equilibrium paradigm. *Academy of Management Review*, 16: 10–36.

Gioia, T. (1988) *The imperfect art.* New York: Oxford University Press.

Grant, R.M. (1991) The resource-based theory of competitive advantage: implications for strategy formulation. *California Management Review*, 33: 493–505.

Hammer, M. and Champy, J. (1993) *Reengineering the corporation.* New York: HarperCollins.

Hedberg, B., Nystrom, P. and Starbuck, W. (1976) Camping on seesaws: prescriptions for a self-designing organization. *Administrative Science Quarterly*, 21: 41–65.

Hou, W.C., Sheang, L.K. and Hidajat, B.W. (1991) *Sun Tzu: war and management.* Singapore: Addison-Wesley.

Hutchins, E. (1991) Organizing work by adaptation. *Organization Science*, 2: 14–39.

Kamoche, K. and Cunha, M.P. (2001) Minimal structures: from jazz improvisation to product innovation. *Organization Studies*, 22.5.

Kanter, R.M. (1989) *When giants learn to dance.* New York: Simon & Schuster.

Lovell, J. and Kluger, J. (1995) *Apollo XIII.* New York: Simon & Schuster.

March, J.G. (1991) Exploration and exploitation in organizational learning. *Organization Science*, 2: 71–87.

Meyer, J.W. and Rowan, B. (1977) Institutionalized organizations: formal structure as myth and ceremony. *American Journal of Sociology*, 83: 340–463.

Miller, D. (1993) The architecture of simplicity. *Academy of Management Review*, 18: 116–38.

Mintzberg, H. (1980) *The nature of managerial work.* Englewood Cliffs, NJ: Prentice-Hall.

Mintzberg, H. and Waters, J.A. (1985) Of strategies: deliberate and emergent. *Strategic Management Journal*, 6: 257–72.

Nonaka, I. and Takeuchi, H. (1995) *The knowledge creating company.* New York: Oxford University Press.

O'Connor, G.C. (1998) Market learning and radical innovation: a cross case comparison of eight radical innovation projects. *Journal of Product Innovation Management*, 15: 151–66.

Oakland, J.S. (1989) *Total quality management.* Oxford: Butterworth-Heinemann.

Perry, S.T. (1995) How small firms innovate: designing a culture for creativity. *Research-Technology Management*, 38: 14–17.

Pettigrew, A. and Whipp, R. (1991) *Managing change for competitive success.* Oxford: Blackwell.

Porras, J.I. and Robertson, P.J. (1992) Organizational development: theory, practice and research, in M.D. Dunnette and L.M. Hough (eds) *Handbook of Industrial and Organizational Psychology.* Palo Alto: Consulting Psychologists Press.

Quinn, J.B. (1982) *Strategies for change: logical incrementalism.* Homewood, IL. Richard D. Irwin.

Rajaram, V. and Fitzgerald, E. (2000) Firm capabilities, business strategies, customer preferences, and hypercompetitive arenas. *Competitiveness Review*, 10: 56–82.

Romanelli, E. and Tushman, M.L. (1994) Organizational transformation as punctuated equilibrium: an empirical test. *Academy of Management Journal*, 37: 1141–66.

Sayles, L. (1964) *Managerial behaviour: administration in complex organizations.* McGraw-Hill.

Sewell, G. (1998) The discipline of teams: the control of team-based industrial work through electronic and peer surveillance. *Administrative Science Quarterly*, 43: 397–428.

Stewart, R. (ed.) (1998) *Managerial work.* Aldershot: Ashgate.

Tatikonda, M. and Rosenthal, S.R. (2000) Successful execution of product development projects: balancing firmness and flexibility in the innovation process. *Journal of Operations Management*, 18: 401–25.

Thomke, S. and Reinertsen, D. (1998) Agile product development: managing development flexibility in uncertain environments. *California Management Review*, 41: 8–30.

Veryzer, R.W. (1998) Discontinuous innovation and the new product development process. *Journal of Product Innovation Management*, 15: 304–21.

Weick, K.E. (1992) Agenda setting in organizational behavior. *Journal of Management Inquiry*, 1: 171–82.

Weick, K.E. (1993) The collapse of sensemaking in organizations: the Mann Gulch disaster. *Administrative Science Quarterly*, 38: 628–52.

Williamson, O.E. (1979) Transaction cost economics: the governance of contractual relations. *Journal of Law Economics*, 22: 233–61.

Wind, J. and Mahajan, V. (1997) Issues and opportunities in new product development: an introduction to the special issue. *Journal of Marketing Research*, 34: 1–12.

Zien, K.A. and Buckler, S.A. (1997) Dreams to market: crafting a culture of innovation. *Journal of Product Innovation Management*, 14: 274–87.

2 Jazz as a process of organizational innovation

David T. Bastien and Todd J. Hostager

Jazz is more than just a style of music that is captured in our collections of records, tapes, and compact discs. It is a celebration of the process of creating music, a form of musical innovation that engages performers as active composers in the collective invention, adoption, and implementation of new musical ideas. As a process of organizational innovation, jazz addresses some central concerns of organizations and their managers. First, jazz is self-consciously spontaneous, creative, and expressive. It is fundamentally concerned with *inventiveness* as an expected mode of thought and behavior. Second, jazz is most typically a social process, involving a group of inventive musicians. Jazz enables individual musicians to coordinate the innovation process so that they achieve a credible and aesthetically pleasing *collective* outcome. The jazz process is built on the assumption that each individual musician is simultaneously and consciously adapting to the whole, supporting the other players, and mutually influencing the outcome. Jazz is thus a truly collective approach to the entire process of innovation, for it requires that the invention, adoption, and implementation of new musical ideas by individual musicians occurs within the context of a shared awareness of the group performance as it unfolds over time.

Jazz is produced through a theory of music and a set of known social practises, both of which enable inventive and integrated performances. As with all of the arts, jazz is also an industry and a profession. Those practitioners who work at jazz as a full-time profession learn the theories and practices more fluently than practitioners who work at it on a part-time basis. Studying how adroit jazz professionals successfully manage the coordination of an inventive performance ought to provide insight into at least one way of managing the process of organizational innovation.

In this article, we examine the jazz process by analyzing a concert in which four musicians accomplished a group performance without the benefit of rehearsal or the guidance of sheet music. By focusing on the process involved in this type of performance, our study differs from prior social scientific investigations of jazz in two important regards. First, previous studies (e.g. Bougon, Weick, and Binkhorst, 1977; Voyer and Faulkner, 1986a, 1986b) focused on a different type of group jazz performance, in which (a) rehearsal is a means of working out an authoritative version of a musical innovation prior to group performance, (b) sheet music is a mechanism of constraint on innovation during performance, and (c) group performance largely consists of the reproduction of previously innovated musical ideas for an audience. Our study instead examines a group performance in which musical invention, adoption, and implementation are collectively determined directly in front of an audience without rehearsal or sheet music.

The second difference between our study and previous investigations is in our use of a "process research" perspective as opposed to a "variance research" perspective (Rogers, 1983, p. 194). Previous studies advanced our understanding of group jazz performance by establishing a map of the perceived causal relationships between such variables as (a) satisfaction with the rehearsal, (b) time spent rehearsing, and (c) the quality of the performance. Our study, however, seeks to advance understanding of group jazz performance by establishing a basic understanding of the "time-ordered sequence of a set of events" (Rogers, 1983, p. 194) in the musical performance.

We begin with an overview of the methods used to generate data in our study, which include a videotape of the performance and observations made by participants in the performance. We then briefly describe the known structural conventions through which the jazz process occurs. Next, we use these structural conventions to interpret the case study data and to identify two basic patterns for organizational innovation in the jazz process. We probe further into the first pattern by adopting Poole's Multiple Sequence Model (1983) as an analytic device for tracking cognitive and behavioral components of the jazz process in, and across, time. This analysis highlights the crucial roles of shared information, communication, and attention in the jazz process. Next, we examine the second pattern in greater detail and identify a basic strategy that enables musicians to invent and coordinate increasingly complex musical ideas. Finally, we close with implications of our findings for organizational innovation in contexts beyond those of group jazz.

Methods

Our case study consists of a jazz concert that was produced by Bob DeFlores and Maytime Productions and performed on June 29, 1985, in Saint Paul, Minnesota. The data for the present study reside in three sources: (a) a videotape of the concert, (b) our written notes of one participant's observations during a review of the videotape, and (c) written observations made by the other participants, based on their review of the videotape and their reading of a case study report that we wrote about the jazz concert.

Arranging and videotaping the concert

As students of organizational innovation, we were fortunate to happen upon the videotaped record of a jazz performance that embodied a process of collective musical innovation. The advent of a relatively inexpensive and unobtrusive videotaping technology allows researchers such as ourselves to obtain a fairly complete record of complex behavioral events as they unfold across time in particular organizational contexts. Videotaped data facilitate process research by enabling us to better track events in, and across, time.

The conditions for the jazz concert and the production of the videotape were established by Bob DeFlores and Maytime Productions. Four musicians were selected by the procedures, each according to his general level of professional competence and, in particular, to his ability to play traditional jazz songs (i.e. "standards"). Four participants were invited and received monetary compensation for playing the concert: Bud Freeman on tenor saxophone, Art Hodes on piano, Biddy

Bastien (the father of one of the authors) on bass, and Hal Smith on drums. As a group, they represented over 200 years of individual professional experience, although they had no professional experience in playing together as a quartet. Because they had not played together as a quartet, they constituted a "zero-history" group (Bormann, 1975), a group that attempts to accomplish a task collectively without the benefits bestowed by a history of working together.

Although the producers did not conceive of their actions as those of social scientists, the conditions they established for the concert can be viewed as a set of controls for a collective musical innovation task: zero-history, no rehearsal, and no sheet music. In bringing such a group together under these circumstances, DeFlores and Maytime Productions planned a performance in which the entire process of musical invention and integration took place in front of an audience. Arrangements were made with K-TWIN, a video production company, to videotape the entire performance.

Participant observations on the videotape and the written case

Upon obtaining a copy of the videotape, we arranged to have one of the participants (Biddy Bastien) view the videotape and make observations about the performance for us. We instructed Bastien to point out and explain the important organizing and communicative behaviors displayed by all four participants as the performance unfolded. On the basis of his observations, we then drafted a written case of the jazz concert, which we provided with the videotape to the other three participants for their observations. The participant observation data were a valuable source of insight for us. Many understandings of the jazz process discussed herein were either explicitly contained in, or directly stimulated by the participant observations. This data source was especially valuable for our description of the structural conventions in jazz.

Structural conventions in the jazz process

Jazz is a process of musical innovation in which a group of performers collectively invents new musical ideas, adopts some of these ideas, and implements the adopted ideas by incorporating them into their performance and by using them as bases for further musical invention. As a collective approach to the process of innovation, jazz specifies a turbulent (Emery and Trist, 1975) task environment for individual musicians, a complex field for interaction in which individuals are simultaneously required to invent new musical ideas and to adapt their playing to that of the collectivity. Turbulence in this environment not only results from the dynamic process of individual invention; turbulence also arises from the dynamic process of coordinating invention. Moreover, these dynamic processes are not independent of one another. The invention of musical ideas affects and is affected by the adoption and implementation of musical ideas. The inherent turbulence in this jazz process produces uncertainty for performers insofar as each musician cannot fully predict the behavior of the other musicians or, for that matter, the behavior of the collectivity.

How is it possible for musicians to manage these dynamic processes and produce an inventive and integrated musical outcome? The answer lies in two sets of structural conventions contained in the jazz profession: musical structures and social practices. These structures serve to constrain the turbulence of the jazz process by specifying particular ways of inventing and coordinating musical ideas. By imposing particular limitations on the range of potential musical and behavioral choices available to performers, these structural conventions also serve as "information" that reduces individual uncertainty (Rogers, 1983, p. 6). Paradoxically, these structures enable collective musical innovation by constraining the range of musical and behavioral choices available to the players (see Appendix).

Musical structures

The structural conventions specified by jazz music *theory* consist of the cognitively held rules for generating, selecting, and building upon new musical ideas, including rules for proper chords, chordal relationships, and chordal progressions. Musical innovation in jazz is thus neither entirely random nor entirely determined: new musical ideas are invented, adopted, and implemented through rules for musical grammar, much as our everyday discourse is generated through grammatical conversational rules (see Clark *et al.*, 1981). A second type of musical structure – a *song* – is often employed in group performance. As with music theory, songs can be viewed as cognitively held rules for musical innovation. Songs are more concrete and limiting musical structures than jazz theory in that they embody particular patterns of chords and chordal progressions. However, songs allow for inventive variations on such core musical patterns as (a) time, (b) chords and chordal progressions, (c) phrasing, (d) chorus length, and (e) levels of embellishment (complexity). When a particular song is called in a group jazz performance, musicians who know the song have immediate information concerning these and other musical patterns. This information reduces their uncertainty about the collective task and enables them to focus on producing the coordinating inventive variations on musical themes contained in the song. Group jazz based on chordal theory is a type of group jazz performance that does not rely on songs to facilitate invention and coordination. Most group jazz does rely on the musical structures contained in both music theory and songs. Both of these structures were used in the concert that we examined (our appendix contains a more technical and detailed discussion of musical structures).

Social practices

Social practices, including both *behavioral norms* and *communicative codes*, are a second source of constraint on the jazz process. These unwritten structural conventions are contained in the profession of jazz and are passed on through various socialization practices. *Behavioral norms* are shared expectations about appropriate behavior (Mitchell, 1978). Behavioral norms facilitate integration among the musicians. Examples of behavioral norms in jazz are the following:

1   The nominal leader of the group decides and communicates each song and the key in which it is to be played.
2   The soloist determines the style (time, level of complexity, etc.), and the other musicians are expected to support this determination.

3   At one point or another during the performance, each musician gets an opportunity to be the soloist (i.e. the dominant voice that is supported by the others).
4   The chorus is the basic unit of soloist control, unless otherwise specified by the nominal leader (see Appendix).

Each of these norms specifies a particular qualification to the collective or consensual character of group jazz. The first norm indicates an authoritarian function of the nominal leader in determining a particular musical/task structure – a song – through which individual musicians produce an inventive and coordinated performance. The second, third, and fourth norms indicate an authoritarian function that is sequentially shared among all performers; every musician gets to play the role of a leader at some point in the jazz process.

A second type of social practice structure, *communicative codes*, consists of behaviors that are intended to be communicative and that rely on the arbitrary assignment of meaning to behavior, with the arbitrary assignment agreed upon by a community of code users. These codes include (a) lexical items, or words and phrases of distinct meaning in the profession, and (b) nonverbal codes that have become a tradition in the profession (e.g. turning to an individual, eye contact at particular points in the performance, hand signals, changing the volume of one's playing). Codes are vehicles through which musicians communicate about their performance while it is occurring. They are designed to enable clear communication among the performers while remaining relatively unobtrusive to the viewing audience.

Taken together, jazz music theory, songs, and social practices impose structural constraints on the process of collective innovation, constraints that enable inventive and integrated group jazz performances. Next we interpret the case study data in terms of these structural conventions and identify basic patterns in the jazz process of organizational innovation.

Basic patterns of events in the group jazz performance

Prior to the actual performance, the four musicians had very little time to discuss what would happen. In the discussion that did occur backstage, the following agreements were reached:

1   Freeman (the nominal leader) would call the songs and their keys.
2   The songs called by Freeman would be standards, songs presumably known to most jazz players.
3   Each song would begin with a piano introduction by Hodes, after which Freeman would play the melody and then a few choruses of inventive solo on tenor sax. Next, Hodes would take a chorus or two of inventive solo. Following Hodes, either Freeman would pick up the lead again or Bastien on bass and Smith on drums would alternate on four- or eight-bar "breaks" (i.e. inventive solos in four- or eight-bar lengths).
4   There would be no dragging (i.e. no gradual slowing of tempo).

All four of these agreements reduced the uncertainty of the musicians by providing them with information regarding what to expect and how to behave during the concert. The first agreement cemented a shared understanding that this behavioral norm would be in effect during the performance and reinforced the use of cognitively held information on the level of social practice structures. The information reduced some of the uncertainty for the players, who now knew that Freeman would call the songs and that they should pay attention to him at particular times during the concert. The second agreement also reduced the uncertainty of the musicians by informing them that Freeman would invoke shared musical/task structures – songs known by all four players – on which they would inventively vary, using jazz music theory generative rules. Like the first agreement, the third agreement added to the shared information contained on the level of social practice structures. This agreement reduced at least two sources of uncertainty by providing musicians with information that (a) they would all get a chance to solo during the performance, and (b) they could expect to solo only at particular times during the performance. Like the second agreement, the fourth agreement also added information about musical structures. The musicians now shared an understanding that, regardless of the tempo specified by a particular song, they were not to gradually slow this tempo over the course of the song.

When the players reached their places on stage, Freeman called the first song, "Sunday." This rather simple song has a musical/task structure that specified a relatively limited range of musical choices for the performers. As agreed, the song began with a piano introduction by Hodes. Freeman followed Hodes with a solo on tenor sax. Each musician knew that Freeman would follow Hodes and would play the melody and a few choruses of inventive solo. Toward the end of Freeman's solo, we observed two forms of communicative behavior by Freeman, behavior that signaled to the rest of the musicians that he was relinquishing the lead to Hodes. One such behavior was the music theoretical cue of "winding down" the solo: Freeman signaled the end of his solo by directing his musical invention toward the full resolution of the current chord (see Appendix).

The other communicative behavior was a nonverbal visual cue that Freeman directed at Hodes; shortly (a beat or two) before the end of his solo. Freeman looked at Hodes in order to signal the end of his solo. Both behaviors accessed shared, cognitively held information on the social practice level by signaling that Freeman was indeed giving up the lead according to group expectations. Toward the end of Hodes's solo, Freeman became more active physically, and this activity appeared to focus the attention of the entire group on the change that was forthcoming. At the end of Hodes's solo, Freeman directed a nonverbal communicative behavior – a questioning look – to Bastien and Smith. This behavior accessed information on the social practice level and, congruent with the preconcert agreement, provided Bastien and Smith with an opportunity to take the lead. Both Bastien and Smith responded to Freeman by nodding in the affirmative. The end of the song was verbally cued by Freeman's use of the code "going out."

Following a long bit of banter with the audience, Freeman called the second song, "You Took Advantage of Me." This song had more potential for inventive variation than did "Sunday." As in the first song, the musicians paid a great deal of attention to the soloist. During his solo, Hodes introduced a bass line that was unexpected by Bastien, but because of the heightened attention among group members to the soloist, Bastien readily picked up the change and followed it. Freeman continued to use visual cues to underscore changes in the soloist, looking at the coming soloist and nodding at him. Freeman also used verbal cues to heighten attention at change points and to cue particular behavior patterns. For example, Freeman looked at Smith and called a chorus of "fours." At the end of Smith's chorus, Freeman said "again," indicating to Smith and the rest of the group that Smith would play a second chorus.

The third song, "Misty," allowed for a great deal of inventive variation, particularly in the use of embellished, complex chordal progressions. Despite this opportunity to extend the group's musical inventiveness radically in the direction of greater complexity, Freeman and Hodes chose to stick with simple variations during their solos. This behavior cemented an understanding among the performers on the level of musical structure, an understanding that, from a music theory standpoint, the group would constrain their musical invention to relatively unembellished, simple ideas, regardless of the level of potential embellishment in a particular song.

The first set was finished by a fourth and fifth song, a Hodes solo piece and an early thirties standard. During the fourth song, Hodes used a hand sign – two fingers – to signal a change from 4/4 to 2/4 time. Hodes had used 2/4 time in a previous solo, and his use of the hand sign reinforced an understanding among the other musicians that he preferred to play in this meter during his solos, despite a preference among the others for 4/4 time during their solos. The fifth song was characterized by patterns established in the earlier songs, including unembellished musical invention and Freeman's use of verbal codes to signal his approval of their playing.

The second set began in a less uncertain and turbulent social task environment than did the first set, because musicians could rely on their knowledge of the precedents and preferences worked out in the first set. Because everything was relatively new and unpredictable during the first set, constant visual attention was required of the musicians. During the second set, there was a marked shift from the constant visual attention of the first set to a more selective attention. In the second set, attention was high around the points of potential change by the soloist, but dropped off noticeably between these points. Because they could rely on a greater pool of shared information, musicians could better predict upcoming changes in soloists as well as the preferred patterns of musical invention for each soloist. Due to this phenomenon, Freeman was able to extend his solo by an additional chorus on one song in the second set. He recognized that the attention of the others was focused on him in anticipation of a potential change while they waited for his signals. When Freeman did not cue a change, the others simply followed him into a third chorus of his solo.

The third and final set began in an even less uncertain and turbulent social task environment for the performers. Having two sets of shared performance history to rely on, the group became increasingly adventurous in their invention from the standpoint of musical theory. For the final part of the concert, the group dropped its use of song structures and relied solely on music theory and shared performance history to invent an entirely new song, "Twin Cities Blues."

In terms of cognition and behavior, we found at least two basic patterns of events in this case study of collective musical innovation:

1. During the first set, musicians displayed a great deal of attention to each other, with particular emphasis on the soloist and the nominal leader (Freeman), who

actively solicited the attention of the musicians during points of potential change in soloists. Freeman's communicative behavior at these points helped to coordinate the group during actual changes by managing attention (Van de Ven, 1986) and by invoking cognitively held norms for behavior. As the concert progressed, this cycle of cognition and behavior became ingrained as shared information among the group members. Attention clearly became more selective among the musicians, for now they could better predict when and to whom they should pay attention. In the latter part of the concert, heightened attention occurred only around points of potential change in the soloist. Freeman found that he no longer had to work at soliciting attention during these points of change and could instead focus on communicating his preferences to the group. Throughout the performance, points of potential change were specified as shared information on two cognitive levels – musical and social practice structures – and were invoked through nonverbal and verbal behavior. As the jazz performance proceeded and a shared social task history was established, information was added on these cognitive levels. This information reduced the uncertainty and turbulence of the jazz process and allowed the musicians to become more selective in their attention.

2. The performance began, with Freeman calling songs of limited potential for musical complexity/embellishment and with players inventing simple/unembellished musical ideas. As the concert progressed, Freeman called songs with greater potential for musical complexity, and the jazz players, building on the musical ideas invented during earlier songs, invented more complex musical ideas. Importantly, however, the group did not radically increase the complexity of the ideas it invented from song to song, despite the fact that such increases were allowed by the song structures. Instead, the group established a shared understanding that musical invention would be constrained to simple variations on core musical patterns contained in each song structure (that is, simple relative to the complexity allowed by this structure). By using this strategy for musical invention, the group relied on its history of collectively invented musical ideas to explore a new song and creatively extend its repertoire of invented idea in the direction of greater complexity. Indeed, the concert culminated in a social task with a great deal of potential for musical complexity: the invention of an entirely new song.

Tracking cognition and behavior in the group jazz performance

Poole (1983) developed a multiple sequence model to relate different aspects of social task processes. This model suggests portraying group processes as a set of parallel strands or tracks of activity as they emerge over time. Each track represents a different aspect of the process and concerns a different level of data. One of the strengths of this approach is that it allows the analysis of relationships within and across levels. We adapted Poole's approach to our present purposes by designating three tracks to represent the cognitive and behavioral components of change events in the jazz concert: (a) *musical structure*, including cognitively held structural conventions as specified by music theory and by songs, (b) *social structure*, involving cognitively held norms for behavior and communicative codes, and (c) *communicative behavior*, consisting of nonverbal and verbal signs.

In his multiple sequence model, Poole (1983) introduced the concept of breakpoints – points in time when changes occur across all tracks – and found that the direction and basic nature of group activity changed at these points. The break-point concept is important to the present study, in that it provides means of analyzing changes in group activity in terms of their cognitive and behavioral components. Figure 2.1 portrays the multiple sequence tracking for the first three songs of the jazz concert. As shown by the musical structure track, from a music theory standpoint changes in group activity (e.g. changes in soloists) could occur at almost any point during the song on a note-by-note basis, but would most likely occur at the beginnings of bars and phrases.

The level of social structure is shown in the second track that portrays the change event potentials specified by behavioral norms and by the preconcert agreements. Information at this level is more specific as to when the musicians can expect changes to occur; according to the norms of the profession, changes will occur at the ends of choruses. Moreover, the preconcert agreements provided the four musicians with an even greater level of detailed information by specifying who would solo at what point in time and for how many choruses. The social structure imposes even greater constraints on individual and group behavior than does the musical structure.

The level of communicative behavior, shown in the third track, indicates that actual changes in the group task were invoked less frequently than allowed by the change event potentials contained in the musical and social structure. What the three tracks reveal is a basic pattern of increasing constraints on individual and group behavior. As we descend from the level of musical structure to the level of social structure to the level of actual communicative behavior, each level further limits the range of behavioral choices available to the jazz performers and thereby enables coordinated musical invention by reducing uncertainty among the players.

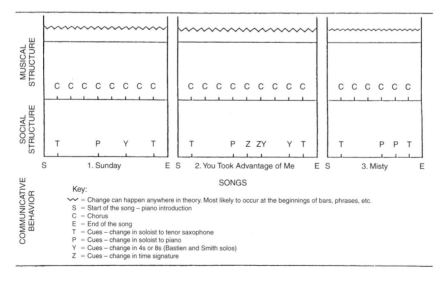

Figure 2.1 Multiple sequence tracking of musical structure, social structure, and communicative behavior for the first three songs in the concert.

Perhaps more important, however, are the revelations (a) that all changes in group activity that occurred during the song were invoked by some form of communicative behavior and (b) that these changes occurred only at the times of change potential that were specified by the musical and social structures. The multiple sequence tracking of a song shows that the potential for change must exist on the levels of musical and social structure before change can be considered and acted on by the players. Moreover, in order for an actual breakpoint or change event to occur, change potentials contained in the shared knowledge of musical and social structure must be explicitly invoked by coded communication among the individual performers. This redundancy across cognitive and behavioral components of the change event is important, for it captures the attention of individual musicians and enables them to enact changes in unison.

Over the course of the concert, preferred patterns of change became ingrained as shared information on both musical and social structure levels. Relying on this information, the musicians could better predict when and to whom they should pay attention. For example, at one point of potential change during the third song, Hodes looked at the drummer and bassist and communicated a change in time from 4/4 to 2/4. These players were able to pick up and enact this change because, based on the pattern established in the previous two songs, they knew that they should pay attention to Hodes at this particular point in the song. When Hodes again switched to 2/4 time in a subsequent solo, this pattern was reinforced as shared information on musical and social structure levels, enabling the other musicians to better predict what was going to happen during Hodes's solos.

One important implication flowing from the multiple sequence tracking concerns a relationship between individual knowledge of music theory and social practices and the overall knowledge level of the group. Because the group jazz process relies on *shared* musical and social knowledge, the total knowledge that is usable by the entire group can only equal or slightly exceed the knowledge of the least informed (i.e. the least competent) member of the group. In the concert of study, all four musicians were highly competent in music theory and social practices and shared a knowledge of standard jazz songs. We predict that groups that include musicians of very different knowledge bases will either produce jazz that is not well integrated or will perform at a level roughly equivalent to that of the least competent member.

Centering as a basic strategy for organizational innovation

The second pattern we identify in the case study is a particular strategy for achieving even greater constraint on musical invention (and hence easier coordination) through choice of repertoire or songs. Freeman began the concert by calling a relatively simple song that contained a limited potential for musical variation. By choosing such a song at the outset, Freeman specified a relatively placid environment for musical invention: a territory in which the musicians tested simple variations on simple core musical patterns in a relatively predictable and certain social task setting. These variations were either rejected or adopted. If adopted, they were implemented through repetition and were used as bases for further variation. One way of conceiving this collective process of inventing, adopting, and implementing musical ideas is as a "centering strategy." As represented in Figure 2.2a, the jazz

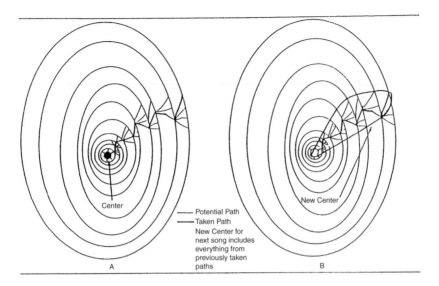

Figure 2.2 The centering strategy for organizational innovation.

musicians began with a center that consisted of shared information regarding jazz music theory, song structures, behavioral norms, and communicative codes. This center of shared information specified potential paths of musical invention for the musicians, who then selectively invented ideas along some of these paths. The group, in turn, then selectively adopted some of these ideas/paths and implemented them into organizational practice as shared bases for further musical invention. As represented in Figure 2.2b, the center of shared knowledge was extended outward by incorporating all of the ideas/paths implemented in the previous songs and the group became capable of inventing and coordinating more complex musical variations.

This phenomenon allowed Freeman confidently to lead the group in the direction of greater inventive complexity as the jazz concert progressed. With each successive song, the group relied on its ever-increasing center of shared information to invent and integrate increasingly complex musical ideas. Indeed, this strategy allowed the group to extend its center of shared information to the extent that it could successfully accomplish an immensely complex task: Unguided by an existing song structure, the group invented and coordinated an entirely new song. The centering strategy can be a successful method for incrementally moving a group or organization into new and unknown social task environments.

Implications for understanding the organizational innovation process

As in group jazz, the social task environment for many modern organizations is basically turbulent and only marginally predictable; situations such as mergers, acquisitions, divestitures, joint ventures, entries into new markets, and development of new industries entail considerable turbulence and uncertainty for organization members (Van de Ven *et al.*, 2000). Individuals in these organizational circumstances face uncertainty similar to that experienced by jazz players during a collectively improvised performance. We saw that jazz musicians rely on two types of structural conventions to constrain their behavior, reduce uncertainty, and diminish turbulence. The level of musical structure specifies particular limitations on the musical choices available to the players. Similarly, task structures in business, (such as formally specified and coded constraints like legislation, industry regulation, governmental mandates, technical theories, organizational mission statements, strategic plans, policies, and procedures) specify particular limitations on behavioral choices available to organization members. In both jazz and business, the social level of structural constraints on behavior involves relatively informal norms and codes that concern interpersonal relations and communication.

In the present case study information on the level of social structure mediates between task structure and behavior. Social structure is, in jazz and business, essential for innovation in organizations. This level informs the players of potential changes in the nature of the innovation activity and the probability that changes will occur. Moreover, we found that social task processes in general are critically reliant on shared knowledge. This evidence implies that social tasks involving individuals of different knowledge bases will be problematic. Lastly, we identified a successful strategy for moving an organization into new, unknown territory. This case study shows that a centering strategy can be effective in accomplishing this goal, for it allows organization members to accommodate a new and unknown social task environment gradually and transform it into an old, known environment. Indeed, Bastien (2000) observed this phenomenon in a corporate acquisition, where centering was effectively used as a strategy for managing the disjunctive change felt by the organization. Kanter (1985) also discussed the strategy of centering as a technique for managing change.

Consistent with these findings, we anticipate that communication and management researchers will be able (a) to isolate certain of the operative task and social structures in cases of organizational innovation, (b) to track these structures and communicative behavior across time, (c) to identify breakpoints in the process of innovation, and (d) to generate additional data concerning the shared knowledge hypothesis and centering strategy. We believe that this line of research holds promise for increasing our knowledge of organizational innovation, knowledge that can be used to critique instances of socially improvised task activity, instruct individual players in task and social structures, and to train players in necessary attention and communication skills.

The history of jazz has been recorded in such a way that we primarily remember great individual musicians and we think of their contributions as solely owned. A more complete review of the history of jazz would reveal that the great contributions to the art form (and indeed the great individuals) were realized in a social and professional context. Lester Young's contribution, for example, would not have been realized outside of a context in which he *and* his supporting players were all thoroughly competent in the structural knowledge and processual skills of the jazz profession. An overemphasis on individual expression and creativity occurred during the past 25 years or so in the jazz profession, an emphasis that leads us to forget the extent to which jazz is inherently and fundamentally a collective activity. The present study emphasizes a more balanced approach to understanding and managing organizational innovation, one in which individual invention is embedded in a collective context and is inseparable from the inventive and integrative activity of the entire group. Great jazz and great advances in the art have not been achieved by stars against a placid background. Rather, greatness in jazz resulted from a constellation of cooperatively improvising artists, each of whom has a chance to shine as a star.

Appendix

A technical overview of musical structures in jazz

Jazz chordal theory is a variant of general chordal theory and is concerned with various arithmetic relationships and sequences. Jazz theory enables the production of inventive and coordinated musical outcomes through the spontaneous and creative use of generative rules that specify particular ways of inventing and coordinating musical ideas. Although this approach to music theory is unique in Western music, there are similar approaches to music theory in Eastern music (notably, the raga music of India). The technical overview that follows is an extremely simplified representation of musical structures in jazz, intended as an introductory illustration of these structures.

In the jazz theory of music generation, an octave is divided into 12 evenly spaced intervals, each of which is given a letter name: C, D flat, D, E flat, E, F, G flat, G, A flat, A, B flat, and B. This array of 12 notes is called a *chromatic scale*. Major and minor scales, however, are the compositional basis of most jazz. These are specific sequences of an uneven division of the octave into 8 intervals. For instance, a C Major scale contains only the following intervals: C D E F G A B C. In other words, in a major scale, the second, fourth, seventh, and eleventh intervals are skipped. In minor scales, a different pattern of skipping chromatic tones is used to achieve the scale. Jazz has traditionally relied on four scales, although others are sometimes employed: major scales, minor scales, dominant seventh scales, and minor seventh scales. All four employ the same logic of selecting 8 unequal intervals from a 12-tone chromatic scale, but the sequences are different in each of the scales.

A chord is a specific sequence of tones within a major or minor scale, further eliminating some notes. For instance, a C Major chord (called a *triad*, in this case) includes only the first, third, and fifth interval in a C Major scale (C E G). Chords in each of the scale families can be embellished through the addition of further tones from the scale. For example, a C6 chord is the major triad (C E G) plus the sixth interval of the C Major scale (A).

Either embellishments resolve to a specific following chord, or they do not resolve at all (i.e. they are terminal, signaling the end of a phrase). This characteristic of chordal embellishments allows musicians to take many different theoretical paths within the same basic chord.

In jazz theory, a song is principally a sequence or progression of chords. Often these are repeating short sequences, with AABA sequences being the most common. Here a sequence of chords is established (the A sequence), played through a second time (A*A*), followed by a different sequence of equal length (AA*B*), and finally repeated (AAB*A*). The AABA sequence is called a *chorus*. In general, songs prescribe only basic chord families and not specific embellishments, leaving embellishment choices up to the musicians.

The melody of a song is composed of notes contained within the chords of the progression, as are all of the notes played by the musicians who provide the background that supports the melody. For example, if a saxophonist is playing the melody and is backed up by a bassist, pianist, and drummer, all four will be playing notes that are different and yet congruent with the chordal structure of the song. The relationship between melody and accompaniment is complicated by the concept of embellishment, however, and when one musician plays notes from a specific embellished chord, the others must pick up that embellishment if the performance is to sound good or integrated. Finally, the dominant or lead voice is called the soloist, despite the fact that often the other musicians are still playing and providing background support to the soloist.

Acknowledgement

We gratefully acknowledge the assistance of Bob DeFlores, Maytime Productions (Dr. Sheldon Pinsky and Arlene Fried), and K-TWIN in securing access to the videotaped data for the present study. Maytime Productions is a nonprofit corporation created to promote and preserve the enjoyment and understanding of jazz as a living American art form. We are especially indebted to the four musicians – Hal Smith and Biddy Bastien, and the late Bud Freeman and Art Hodes – for their performance and for their willingness to be studied. Without the generous contributions of all of these individuals, the present study could not have been carried out. We acknowledge the assistance and encouragement of the late Dr. Reginald T. Buckner, who organized the conference at which an earlier version of this article was presented. We also extend our appreciation to Dr. Mary L. Nichols for including an earlier version of this article in the discussion paper series of the Strategic Management Research Center (University of Minnesota). This article benefited from the helpful comments and suggestions of Everett M. Rogers, Andrew H. Van de Ven, and an anonymous reviewer.

References

Bastien, D.T. (2000). Communication, conflict, and learning in mergers and acquisitions. In A.H. Van de Ven, H.L. Angle, and M.S. Poole (Eds), *Research on the management of innovation* (Vol. 1, chap. 11). Cambridge, MA: Ballinger.

Bormann, E.G. (1975). *Discussion and group methods* (2nd ed.). New York: Harper & Row.

Bougon, M., Weick, K. and Binkhorst, D. (1977). Cognition in organizations: An analysis of the Utrecht Jazz Orchestra. *Administrative Science Quarterly, 22,* 606–639.

Clark, V.P., Escholz, P.A. and Rosa, A.F. (1981). *Language: Introductory readings* (3rd ed.), New York: St. Martin's.

Emery, F.E. and Trist, E.L. (1975). *Towards a social ecology: Contextual appreciations of the future in the present.* London: Plenum.

Kanter, R.M. (1985). *The change masters: Innovations for productivity in the American work place.* New York: Simon & Schuster.

Mitchell, T.R. (1978). *People in organizations: Understanding their behavior.* New York: McGraw-Hill.

Poole, M.S. (1983). Decision development in small groups: III. A multiple sequence model of group decision development. *Communication Monographs, 50,* 321–341.

Rogers, E.M. (1983). *Diffusion of innovations* (3rd ed.). New York: Free Press.

Van de Ven, A.H. (1986). Central problems in the management of innovation. *Management Science, 32*, 590–607.

Van de Ven, A.H., Angle, H.L. and Poole, M.S. (Eds) (2000). *Research on the management of innovation* (Vols. 1 and 2). New York: Oxford University Press.

Voyer, J.J. and Faulkner, R.R. (1986a). Cognition and leadership in an artistic organization. *Proceedings of the National Academy of Management* (pp. 160–164). Chicago: Darby Press.

Voyer, J.J. and Faulkner, R.R. (1986b). *Strategy and organizational cognition in a simple professional bureaucracy*. Unpublished manuscript, Rutgers University, Newark, NJ.

3   Making sense of improvisation

Mary Crossan and Marc Sorrenti

The phone rings. You answer. You respond.

"You" may be a CEO being presented with an investment opportunity, a customer service representative hearing from an irate customer, or a sales manager receiving an order. Whether you are responding to a phone call, a knock at the door, or a chance meeting in the hall, spontaneous activities permeate your day. In his study of CEOs, Mintzberg (1973, p. 36) observed that over 90 percent of their verbal contacts were *ad hoc*. The sheer number of spontaneous actions within organizations would seem to imply that improvisation is a well-studied topic in management literature. However, improvisation has received minimal attention from management theorists and practitioners. In part, this is due to the assumption that there is no skill or quality to improvisation, or at least none that can be taught. A related problem is that improvisational action is often considered inferior to planned action; one reverts to improvisation only when planning breaks down. However, Mintzberg has described the pitfalls of planning concluding that planning tends to "undermine both creativity and strategic thinking ... discouraging truly novel ideas in favor of extrapolation of the status quo, or marginal adaptation" (1994, p. 158).

We assert that there is a skill to improvisation, and that the quality of improvisational action varies. Furthermore, improvisation is an important facet of management, and a critical part of organizational learning and strategic renewal. This paper begins with a brief description of improvisation, followed by a discussion of the link between improvisation and organizational learning. A simple categorization is applied to the management literature on improvisation from which a framework is developed to delve more deeply into the richness of the topic. Finally, implications for researchers and managers are presented.

Defining improvisation

Although Mintzberg documented the *ad hoc* nature of managerial action, we must ask whether all *ad hoc* action is improvisational. The short answer is "no." That actions are *ad hoc* or spontaneous is only one dimension of improvisation. The second dimension is that actions are guided by intuition. We put forth the following definition of improvisation: *intuition guiding action in a spontaneous way*. Naturally, there are degrees of intuition and spontaneity of action, but we can depict high and low levels of each, as shown in Figure 3.1.

Returning to the phone vignette presented at the outset, we know that each of

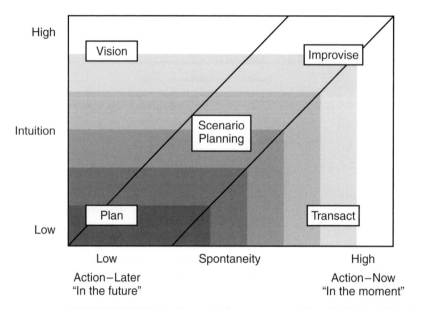

Figure 3.1 Positioning improvisation.

the three scenarios, as well as many others we could conjure up, are *ad hoc* or spontaneous in nature. There is no time to plan, we answer the phone and respond. It is interesting to note, however, that we can convert a spontaneous situation into one which is less spontaneous by negotiating some time before giving the response, as many will do with a phone call. The CEO presented with an investment opportunity may want to check with others before committing resources. However, in many instances, time is the scarce resource. Failing to respond in the moment may result in a lost opportunity. The CEO may lose the investment opportunity if swift action is not taken. On the other hand, the customer service representative who can provide an immediate response to the irate customer may help to improve the customer's view of the company. The sales manager who is able to commit to the customer over the phone may secure the order. Therefore, while we may be able to negotiate more time, a cost may result from our delay.

Degree of spontaneity is only one dimension of improvisation. The second dimension is the degree to which intuition guides action. Many spontaneous responses are fairly routine in nature, with relatively little or no intuition applied. The customer service representative may simply follow a set of procedures for dealing with the irate customer. The sales manager may simply offer a quote to the customer placing an order, based on a formula established by others who have determined the appropriate costs and margins. On the other hand, the response may be fairly intuitive with no set standard, policy, or procedure to rely on. The sales manager may need to make an immediate commitment with only an intuitive feeling for whether the company has the capability and capacity to produce the product at a particular price.

To clarify what we mean by intuition, we concur with Behling and Eckel who suggest that intuition is "choices made without obvious formal analysis" (1991,

p. 47). However, as Behling and Eckel pointed out, there are many further interpretations of this broad definition. More specifically, we support the view that intuition is an unconscious process based on distilled experience.

This emphasis on the unconscious process underscores the creative quality of intuition which is not bound by the necessity of fully articulating our thought process or rationale. The emphasis on distilled experience supports Simon's view of intuition as "analysis frozen into habit and into the capacity for rapid response through recognition" (1989, p. 38). Intuition as distilled experience recognizes that the quality of intuitive response depends upon the expertise or patterns of experience in a particular domain. Cappon distinguishes between intuition as "negative energy" or the potential stored in the batteries of the collective memory, versus that which is discharged as "positive energy" through words, numbers, drawings, and actions (1994, p. 15). We view distilled experience as the negative energy or potential, and the unconscious process as the means of tapping that energy.

There are other definitions of improvisation which we drew on, but could not fully support, including the notion that intuition incorporates creation and execution at the same time (Solomon, 1986); is imagination guiding action in an unplanned way (Chase, 1988); and is the ability to "make do" with available resources (Weick, 1993a). We concluded that the degree to which action is guided by intuition was more precise than either creation or imagination; and that the degree of spontaneity was a more accurate reflection of the process than either an "unplanned way" which begs the question – what is planning?, or "at the same time" which is too limiting. That improvisation is about "making do with available resources" is assumed by the spontaneous dimension of our definition, since it represents the context for action.

The two dimensions of improvisation as demonstrated in Figure 3.1 help to distinguish different types of organization activities. For example, the "transact" and "improvise" modes run the risk of being lumped together if we fail to consider the intuitive nature of the actions. As well, what we have referred to as "vision" may be confused with "improvise" if we focus solely on the intuitive dimension, but fail to consider the time orientation of the action. We use vision to underscore the future orientation of this mode of operating. Where intuition has some currency is in the mode of operating where executives brainstorm about the future. Distinguishing vision from planning on the basis of intuition is consistent with Mintzberg, who stated that: "Visionary leaders likewise integrate decisions, in their cases informally, or if you prefer intuitively. Yet to encompass their behavior under the planning label would again seem to broaden it beyond reasonable (and current) usage" (1994, p. 12).

We have positioned "scenario planning" in the middle since it is a methodology that attempts to draw the future into the present. "Using scenarios is rehearsing the future. You run through the simulated events as if you were already living them. You train yourself to recognize which drama is unfolding. That helps you avoid unpleasant surprises, and know how to act" (Schwartz, 1991, p. 200). At the same time, the creation of scenarios blends elements of planning and visioning. Schwartz defines scenarios as "a set of organized ways for us to dream effectively about our own future" (1991, p. 4).

It is important to note that our definition of improvisation is neutral with respect to performance. Improvisation is not necessarily good. There is variability in both the quality of improvisational action and its suitability under various conditions. However, we believe that a better understanding of improvisation will enable us to enhance the quality of action.

In summary, improvisation is an important facet of organizational life. Mintzberg (1973) has established the pervasiveness of spontaneous action. Stalk (1988) has focused on the importance of "time" as a competitive advantage, which suggests that the need for spontaneous action may become even more prevalent. Simon (1989) and Agor (1989) have summarized the arguments regarding the prevalence and importance of intuition, and Simon argues for the importance of the intersect between spontaneity and intuition: "Every manager needs also to be able to respond to situations rapidly, a skill that requires the cultivation of intuition and judgment over many years of experience and training" (1989, p. 38).

Improvisation and organizational learning

In our view organizational learning requires organizations to plan, vision, scenario plan, transact, and improvise. But of these five activities, we seem to know less about how to improvise effectively. In part this is because intuition has largely been neglected by organizational learning researchers. In our research we have argued that any theory of organizational learning needs to explain where new insights and ideas for the improvement of current practice originate (Crossan, Lane, and White, 1996). We include intuiting as one of the four "I's" of organizational learning, with the other three being interpreting, integrating, and institutionalizing. However, as we have defined it, intuition on its own is not improvising. Intuition becomes improvisation when it is applied to action in a spontaneous way. The dimension of spontaneity has been equally neglected. We must keep in mind that it is not simply organizational learning that will create competitive advantage, but the *rate* of organizational learning.

The intersection between intuition and spontaneity melds together cognition and action. And the link between cognition and action (behavior) is an important facet of organizational learning (Crossan, Djurfeldt, Lane, and White, 1995). At the simplest level we can think of individual learning as a combination of changes, or lack thereof in cognition and behavior, as depicted in Figure 3.2. Clearly, where there is no change in either cognition or behavior there is "no learning," and where an individual has undergone changes in both there is "integrated learning."

Much of our attention in learning has been directed toward "anticipatory learning" where changes in cognition precede changes in behavior. Unfortunately, many cognitive changes never manifest themselves in behavioral change because other beliefs override or "block" the situation. And as Festinger (1957) and Heider (1958) noted, our thoughts and actions seek a balanced state. As a result the tension or lack of balance may resolve itself into the "no learning" quadrant.

Similarly, while organizations have often "forced" behavioral changes on employees, these changes often only endure while the force (policy, rule, norm, threat) is in place. There has been less attention given to "experimental learning" where changes in behavior precede changes in cognition. The likelihood that the new behaviors will prompt changes in cognition is supported by a mind-set that suspends judgment while trying out new behaviors. One route to experimental learning is through improvisation. Given the subconscious nature of intuition, action precedes understanding with improvisation. We act, and then make sense of it afterward.

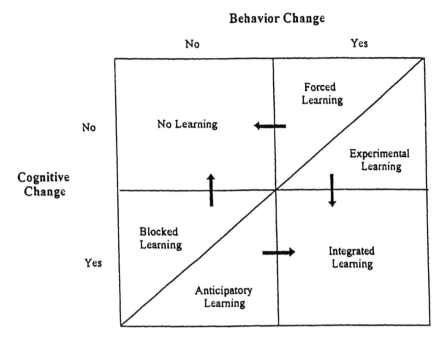

Figure 3.2 Cognition–Behavior Link.

It is interesting to note that the scenario planning methodology attempts to: "suspend our disbelief in all the futures: to allow us to think that any one of them might take place. Then we can prepare for what we don't think is going to happen" (Schwartz, 1991, p. 203). The challenge in scenario planning is to create the suspension of disbelief in the absence of action. The more real the scenarios and the more "in the present" they appear to be, the greater the likelihood that they will capture the imagination of the participants. Role playing is used extensively in scenario planning to help simulate future states.

Although we have focused on the individual level, neither organizational learning nor improvisation is limited to the individual. Improvisation is particularly instructive in developing our understanding of the cognition-action linkage at the group level since it focuses on the nature of relationships and interactions required to be collectively spontaneous. It also serves as a useful way to think about how organization structures and systems impact the flexibility and spontaneity of organizations. In talking about the fallacy of detaching thought from action, Mintzberg concludes:

> while thinking must certainly precede action, it must also follow action, close behind, or else run the risk of impeding it! Formal planning poses the danger of distancing that connection and therefore discouraging action. That is why, at least under difficult conditions, planning may be better conceived as an interpreter of action than a driver of it, and why action itself may be driven by thinking of a less formalized and more involved nature
>
> (1994, p. 294).

Improvisation literature

Given the lack of theory on improvisation in management, we are not surprised that the literature tends to fall into two camps: one that "describes" organizational process as improvisational, and one that "prescribes" organizations as more improvisational. There is also a sharp distinction between literature which examines improvisation at the organizational level and literature which examines it at the individual and group levels. However, given the sparsity of literature on the individual and group levels, we have condensed them under a behavioral heading, as illustrated in Figure 3.3.

Organizational–descriptive approaches

The descriptive literature that deals with improvisation at the organization level relates primarily to the emergent or incremental nature of strategy. In general, literature within this category is presented in contrast with traditional approaches to organizational strategy that emphasize planning methods and the prediction and control of future environments.

The concept of emergent strategy is well established in management theory (Mintzberg, 1988). Mintzberg suggests that only a portion of any strategic activity is executed according to plan. The planned or intended strategy has some unrealized components, which are discarded or neglected when they are no longer appropriate. The remaining portion of the intended strategy is the deliberate strategy, or the activity that takes place because of some prepared plan. New strategic components that emerge from the actions taken are then incorporated into the organization's strategy, creating a realized whole. The emergent nature of strategy is what we refer to as improvisation. Mintzberg (1994) argues that all strategic activity involves some blend of intended and emergent strategy.

Pascale (1984) provides a vivid example of improvisation in a description of Honda's penetration into the North American motorcycle market. A Boston Consulting Group (BCG) study cited by Pascale suggested that Honda had redefined the American motorcycle market with an emphasis on small motorcycles, which, because of their success in Japan, afforded Honda the advantage of high volumes and low production costs. The BCG study makes the claim that Honda's

	Descriptive	*Prescriptive*
Organizational	Observation of organizational strategy's improvisational or unplanned nature—strategy as process, often created and implemented simultaneously	Tools which position improvisation as an instructive way of looking at organizational strategy and design—improvisation as an alternative metaphor for organizations
Individual/Group Behavioral	Observations of patterns of improvised managerial behavior	The development of improvisational skills to enhance the quality of managerial decisions

Figure 3.3 Distinctions in management literature on improvisation.

competitive advantage in the market was the result of a premeditated and methodical plan.

In fact, as Pascale points out from interviews with the six Honda executives who were given the responsibility for the launch, the introduction of highly popular small motorcycles which "transformed the market" was a reluctant step taken by the Honda team. Production problems with the larger machines, combined with some pedestrian interest in the small machines the Honda executives had brought over for their own use, combined to make the introduction of small motorcycles the only viable alternative for Honda. In four years Honda had established a market share of 63 percent of the American motorcycle market.

While the eventual outcome may have an elegant logic in retrospect, we must not confuse the original intention with the logic of the outcome. Weick (1969) cites that much of our social understanding is derived from retrospective sense-making; as the BCG study suggests, the motivation to establish retrospective logic may overwhelm our sense that actions are not always the result of preconceived planning.

The example of the development of the "Post-it Note" by the Minnesota Mining and Manufacturing Company (3M) (Peters and Waterman, 1982) provides another example of improvisation. The technology used in the product was the result of failed product development. The adhesive 3M was attempting to develop required a great deal of bonding, and a failed experiment produced the adhesive now used in the Post-it Note product. The "failed" adhesive could be removed from paper products without tearing the paper, a remarkable achievement in its own right. But by the standards of the intended outcome, the adhesive was an abject failure. By recognizing the opportunity, 3M transformed the office supplies market and introduced a product that is now common in offices worldwide.

In recognizing that the strategy of organizations is often shaped in some way by reactions to unpredictable events, researchers have also found that top executives tend to deal with these unpredictable situations in a logically incremental fashion (Quinn, 1978). Decisions are improvised within the constraints of the organization's structures and systems, and according to the political behavior of the individuals involved. The premise is that these emergent activities acquire the logic of the organizational systems, subsystems, and structures. Quinn's observation is that a significant portion of organizational strategic direction is affected by these improvised increments or responses to opportunities.

The central argument in these examples is that strategies are often not a successful series of decisions derived from premeditated actions. Rather, they evolve from the day-to-day actions of a variety of individuals in a spontaneous and often intuitive fashion. The common element is that strategy is a learning process which demands that strategic opportunities which arise over the course of implementation are not always predictable; and that competitive advantage and success often arise out of an organization's ability to see these opportunities, use them, and capitalize on them. They are examples of organizations creating and revising their strategies in response to the moment. They are observations of organizational improvisation.

Behavioral–descriptive approaches

While the previous examples indicate that organizational strategy may operate in a way that allows a certain degree of flexibility to take advantage of opportunities, organizational action is the culmination of individual actions. Barnard (1938) was among the first to articulate the view that the softer, more intuitive side of management activity is a crucial element to successful managerial decisions. Mangham and Pye (1991) report that a large percentage of the actions taken by top executives rely, to a large degree, on the judgment of the executives, in union with their analytical skills. Although Mintzberg (1973) identified that managers spend very little time on planned activities, his observations about what they did pertained more to the roles they adopted than the managerial characteristics associated with the activity. He did note, however, that the activities could be characterized by their brevity, variety, and fragmentation.

The ability to act spontaneously is perhaps most commonly observed when the opportunity for analysis is removed because of extremely critical time pressures. Situations of crisis requiring immediate action without the benefit of prior analysis provide a useful look at improvised behavior. Several studies (Kreps, 1991; Bosworth and Kreps, 1986; Powers, 1981; Weick, 1993a) have indicated that improvised behavior is useful in times of crisis or disaster. Disasters have the effect of legitimizing the improvisation of roles (Powers, 1981; Blumer, 1963) and of presenting events which could not have been predicted, making improvised behavior a necessary complement to disaster planning (Kreps, 1991; Bosworth and Kreps, 1986). Weick (1993a) positions the skill of improvisation as a factor in maintaining conditions of order in environments that appear chaotic. In these cases the researchers see planning as a facilitating framework which, combined with improvisational skills, assists adaptation. Therefore, we need not see structure as conflicting with our ability to adapt to changing circumstances.

An example of improvisation being useful in periods of crisis is examined in detail by Weick (1993a). In a depiction of a documented prairie fire disaster that killed several firefighters, Weick examined the actions of one of the survivors. This survivor devised a way out of an approaching fire by building an escape fire in front of himself, and then lying in the ashes and allowing the approaching blaze to pass over him. The solution he devised had not been previously learned – he simply incorporated information that he already knew, and created a solution which matched the circumstances. Those who did not survive relied on their instinctual flight response and ran away, later to be engulfed in the quickly approaching flames. Weick's assertion is that an individual used to routinely drawing order out of chaos is flexible enough to deal with these situations calmly. He calls this activity "bricolage" – making do with the materials that are available to create solutions that are required in the moment. As noted in our definition of improvisation, we assume that individuals must make do with available resources if they are to act "in the moment." In the case of crisis the scarcity of other resources, not just of time, provides the context around which intuitive insights to "make do" with the resources must be developed.

The behavioral/descriptive studies have characterized the fragmented and brief nature of managerial activity, as well as the use of judgment and intuition as critical aspects of management. Crisis situations have provided an opportunity to either observe or reflect on improvisation.

Organizational–prescriptive approaches

Even though improvised action exists within organizations, managers often have difficulty viewing actions as something other than a series of rational, planned decisions. Management literature that deals with organizational improvisation in a prescriptive way has concentrated on new operating metaphors that help alter managers' paradigms. Although there has been controversy on the use of metaphors to advance organizational theory (Pinder and Bourgeois, 1982; Bourgeois and Pinder, 1983; Morgan, 1983), we support the case made by Morgan (1980, 1983), Weick (1991), and Tsoukas (1991) that metaphors help to provide meaning through the elaboration of patterns of insight. Even the opponents of the use of metaphors have recognized their value in the early stages of research (Pinder and Bourgeois, 1982).

There are only a few articles in the management domain that take a prescriptive orientation to improvisation at the organizational level (Perry, 1991, 1994; Weick, 1993b; Crossan *et al.*, 1996). Perry (1991) presents the view that organizational strategy may be seen through the lens of jazz improvisation. His central premise is that organizations might be better off if they started to conduct themselves with the sense of flexibility and environment negotiation that jazz improvisation implies. This approach might make organizations more responsive to customer needs, thus affording competitive advantage. He proposes that such flexibility might occur as a result of the application of two processes: vision-based improvisation, in which actions are improvised within a given strategic intent; or opportunity-based improvisation, in which actions are improvised to find the maximum number of strategic possibilities (reliant on lateral thinking, described by De Bono, 1973). Further, he suggests that organizations, rather than choosing between one approach or the other, will likely employ some combination of the two.

We have contrasted traditional theater with improvisional theater to highlight the differences between the two forms (Crossan *et al.*, 1996). Traditional theater begins with a script which dictates the direction and life of the performance. The director ensures that the script is faithfully delivered and selects a group of actors to fulfill prescribed roles which are well defined and, largely, unalterable. Sets are constructed to provide the necessary locale and atmosphere for the script and finally, costumes are designed to provide further clarity and focus. In contrast, improvisation uses no script, sets, props, or costumes. Where the traditional play operates by necessity on focus, control, and a predetermined environment, improvisation is flexible, open, and unpredictable. In traditional theater planning is the cornerstone to a successful performance as the acts are orchestrated, the interactions are rehearsed, and the script, director, and actors control the environment. In improvisation actions are spontaneous, and the audience fuels the actors.

An analogy can be made between traditional theater and business. A business operates under an overall corporate strategy and set of policies (script). This blueprint determines the plot, or the nature of the business in terms of goals, products, markets, and competitive advantage. Organizational structures delineate the functions and interactions of employees (actors), whose role it is to operate within that strategy as specialists confined to a specific function. The CEO (director) plays an integral role in ensuring that the strategy unfolds as intended. Assets (sets) and, in some cases, uniforms (costumes) facilitate the delivery of the strategy. Many businesses tend to operate like a play, emphasizing planning and control. However, such organizations may need to become more improvisational if they do not want to fold in the same manner plays do when they have finished their run. They may learn from the jazz analogy, which demonstrates how improvisation actually builds on traditional structures. We conclude that good improvisation relies on the traditional technical skills gained through practice.

Weick (1993b) advances a metaphor of organizational design as improvisation, as he systematically attempts to break down the architectural metaphor prevalent in approaches to organizational design. He presents the notion that the design is a function of the negotiated actions of its members, and that the design of an organization is in a constant state of change. His metaphor presents an alternative viewpoint to the predominating theory that organizational structures exist on paper or within organizational charts.

These metaphors are particularly valuable since they highlight that there are varying degrees of quality to improvisational activity; there is good and bad improvisation, and it is a skill that can be learned. They also suggest how improvisation may be improved, by highlighting the individual and group behaviors which support it. Some of these behaviors are explored in the following section.

Behavioral–prescriptive approaches

Given the dearth of descriptive literature on improvisational behavior, it is not surprising that there is a lack of prescriptive literature. What little there is comes from two sources. The first offers prescriptions from theatrical improvisation; the second presents prescriptions from the management domain concerning various components of improvisation, including intuition and creativity.

We reviewed the literature on theatrical improvisation and worked with the Second City Improvisation group to understand the characteristics of good improvisation (Crossan *et al.*, 1996). It is important to note that there are characteristics of good improvisational process, but that such a process does not necessarily yield positive results. However, a good process will enhance the likelihood of a positive outcome. Although good improvisation is ultimately judged by audience response, the participants themselves know when they are creating a good improv set. The stories and actions flow seamlessly and effortlessly with creative narrative lines that unfold in unexpected directions. A number of factors contribute to good improvisation. Some of the salient points are that good improvisation arises when the actors let the environment shape them rather than trying to shape the environment, and when they take incremental steps rather than big leaps in the development of the story line. As individuals they focus on spontaneity and right-brain thinking. As a group they stress trust, friendship, and reciprocity. Overall, good improvisation involves making mistakes, which requires an environment that is receptive to people taking risks, perhaps looking silly, and possibly making errors.

Instances of improvisation being used as a prescriptive technique are limited, though there are reports that improvisional theater techniques are helpful in advancing the behavioral flexibility required in disaster situations (Callahan, 1986). Although this evidence is largely anecdotal, it suggests that building skill in improvisation aids in the development of confidence in drawing order out of chaotic situations.

There is literature that does not directly address the concept of improvisation but deals with prescriptive measures to the challenge of rapidly changing environments, which yields important insights about some of the salient components of improvisation, including the development of intuitive or creative abilities (see Agor, 1986, 1989; Johnson and Daumer, 1993), and the development of team skills or listening skills. Consistent with the prescriptive/organizational literature, the behavioral literature suggests that good improvisation carries the individual responsibility to prepare diligently and to enhance the technical skills that make the improvised action possible and effective.

Improvisational framework

To synthesize the literature on improvisation we need a means to link the descriptive and prescriptive literature, and the individual/group behavioral literature with the organizational literature. The ultimate link will be a theory. For a moment we will present some components of improvisation in the form of a framework that helps to link the various literatures. In doing so we will move outside the management domain to incorporate literature on improvisation in the arts. At the individual level we have determined that intuitive insight and technical ability are critical characteristics; at the group level we need to consider group dynamics; and at the organizational level we must examine the structure that defines improvisational action. Motivation, awareness, and understanding is, ultimately, an individual phenomenon, but is directly affected by the structure of the situation as discussed below.

As an overview we have recognized varying degrees of structure imposed on situations which tend to heighten or dampen improvisational action. We consider external structure a limiting factor in that it establishes the boundaries of appropriate actions. The other factors are enhancing factors, suggesting that an increase in any of these factors increases the number of choices from which we may select appropriate actions. We propose that a key factor enhancing improvisation is the awareness, understanding, and motivation to improvise. The quality of the improvised actions depends, however, on the intuitive and technical ability of the participants and their ability to interact as a group. Creative and innovative ideas and solutions place pressure on the external structure to expand and include them. This situation is prevalent in music, when previously uncharted musical territory is explored; initially, no audience finds it appealing. Over time, if sense may be made of the music, the external structure of musical appropriateness is expanded. This is a slow process. It is noteworthy that the quality of creative action is always judged by the rules of the external structure, but that the forces at play in creative idea generation place outward pressure on the structure. Figure 3.4 illustrates this point graphically.

Enhancing factor: intuitive insight

Given our definition of improvisation, intuition surfaces as a key characteristic and serves three critical functions in the process of improvisation. First, it facilitates the

External Structure

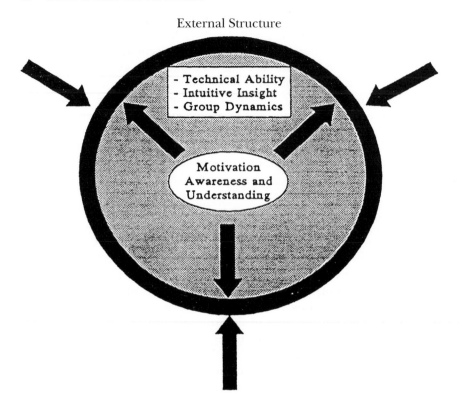

Figure 3.4 Improvisation framework.

identification of a range of possible creative solutions. Second, it aids in the selection of the appropriate solution from the range of possibilities. And perhaps of most importance, the subconscious processing of ideas enables extremely rapid responses.

Some researchers have cited the development of intuitive ability as a determining factor in the achievement of appropriate decisions in the absence of full analytical information (Agor, 1986; Mintzberg, 1976). They view intuition as an enhancement of analytic skills rather than a replacement, their assumption being that the analytical information might be available at some point in time, but time factors do not permit full analysis. Further, Barnard (1938) and Mangham and Pye (1991) refer to judgment as a necessary characteristic of successful executives. In a study of master chess players, Simon (1989) explores the notion of expert intuition, or the condition that high levels of expertise and experience impose on the speed of decision making. The ability that experts possess to quickly discern appropriate actions within a given structure is governed by their intuitive ability to recognize patterns and act appropriately, based on experience that suggests proper and improper courses of action.

This "expert" intuition is a useful frame in that it allows for the discussion of the selection among choices within the external structure imposed. While Simon does not discuss the process through which the expertise is developed, it is clear that experience alone does not produce the eventual expert level of competency.

Rather, the ability to recognize patterns that are either appropriate or not appropriate combines with previous experience to accumulate a knowledge base from the current experience. Therefore, we may assume that chess masters possess the capability of learning from their experience and avoiding inappropriate actions.

Likewise, the ability of the musical improviser to use evaluative judgment to discern appropriate choices from the range that arises from his or her intuition is a crucial quality of successful musical improvisation (Zinn, 1981). In particular, Zinn presents the development of the evaluative judgment as the more difficult, and more valuable skill for the improviser.

Mintzberg (1976) presents these skills of pattern recognition as skills generally handled by the right hemisphere of the brain, and postulates that most managers are conditioned to utilize the left hemisphere, responsible for linear, analytical thinking. His belief that the right hemispheric functions might be improved is consistent with the literature on artistic improvisation (Johnstone, 1981; Spolin, 1983; Chase, 1988). Intuitive ability and creativity may be enhanced under the proper conditions, and the development of intuitive skills is a reversal of conditioning processes that discourage us from seeing possibilities within given situations.

While the ability to recognize the range of choices within the external structure relies on the development of expert intuition, other forms of intuitive development are necessary for the generation of insights that push the limits of the external structure. It is recognized in forms of artistic expression that individuals who are able to expand the range of creative possibilities must venture outside familiar territory. Simon's chess master example supposes that the structure of the "game" is fixed at all times: the rules are fixed, and the environment is knowable. We can apply this example to management function. In some organizations an appropriate response to the organization's external environment is that the rules of the game are relatively fixed, and that expert intuition, or judgment, is an invaluable resource. If, however, an organization experiences an unexpected alteration in its environment, the ability of its members to adjust to new environmental conditions is crucial. In fact, in this case, reliance on expert intuition may be more of a hindrance than a benefit.

Several definitions of intuition refer to activities lying outside the bounds of the rapid processing of experience information. De Bono (1973) refers to the process as lateral thinking, Behling and Eckel (1991) call it entrepreneurial intuition, and Morgan (1993) coins the term "imaginization." Whatever the label, the important point is that an organization's view of its external environment is often inconsistent with that reality and, therefore, the ability to venture outside the perceived structure is a fruitful exercise. We should note that a distinction is made between the external structure imposed by the organization on the individual, and the external structure imposed by the environment on the organization. These distinctions may be artificial, but individuals should recognize when these two structures are inconsistent with one another, and have the ability to determine the appropriate structure within which a range of possibilities may be generated.

Mintzberg (1976) cautions that intuitive or systematic thinking must be articulated through some translation into linear order. Weick (1969) further suggests that this order is imposed through action and retrospection. Improvisation improves an individual's ability to evaluate intuitive insights and to develop skills both in considering a complete range of creative possibilities and in determining appropriate action. It also provides the instant translation of intuitive insights into logical linear processes. In this respect it is the marriage of left and right hemispheric brain functions, and affords the maximum utilization of intuitive thought.

It is clear that intuitive skills are a necessary component in the improvisational process, and that an increase in intuitive ability affords an individual a critical tool in allowing decision making to take place. However, if the quality of improvised action is important, the ability to generate a full range of possibilities is paramount, and depends on what the individual is capable of executing.

Enhancing factor: technical ability

Two of the most profound insights from the prescriptive literature on jazz improvisation are that there are varying degrees of improvisational quality; and that good improvisation builds on a well-developed foundation of traditional skills in the domains in which it is applied, whether it be theater, music, or management. Whereas intuition might be appropriately termed a cognitive skill affecting the ability of the performer to develop and sort out choices, technical skill affords the performer a finite number of choices. The higher the technical skill, the greater the degree of choice.

In the realm of music, Zinn (1981) has made a distinction between noncontrolled and controlled improvisation. Improvisation that is performed with a lack of musical knowledge or physical technique is noncontrolled. In evolving to controlled improvisation the musician acquires both knowledge and technical abilities, and along with them the ability to transform them into "logical musical conclusions."

At its most rudimentary level improvisation may involve a haphazard series of utterances that may appear to make no sense. This type of improvisation is demonstrated by an infant learning to speak or, in some situations, by someone attempting to learn music by first experimenting and becoming comfortable with his or her instrument (Chase, 1988). This type of improvisation embodies the earliest stages of the acquisition of technical skill. We should note that some researchers view the acquisition of knowledge through experience and experimentation as a prerequisite to the acquisition of technical skill. This theory suggests that improvisation begets skill, which affords more choice, which in turn affects the complexity and quality of improvised activity.

From a management perspective a variety of skills could facilitate improvisation. These include the specialized skills to perform a particular job such as engineering, computer programming, or teaching, or the more general skills of listening, speaking, leadership, followership, and social interaction.

Enhancing factor: group dynamics

While the complexity of any improvised action is dependent on the individual characteristics described earlier, improvised action occurs within the framework of social interaction. The nature of this interaction has a bearing on both the number of creative possibilities generated by the individuals and the negotiation of choices among the individuals.

Both Johnstone (1981) and Spolin (1983) suggest that theatrical improvisation depends on the resolution of the question of individual status. While Johnstone holds the view that differences in status must be used to a degree in forming the theatrical product, Spolin views the attempt to garner status as destructive to the improvisational process. Whatever their specific views on the status of performers, they agree on a fundamental underlying premise: that in theatrical improvisation "blocking," or the systematic discouragement of the ideas of a person in the group, is counterproductive to the creative process. Spolin suggests that the competitive frame that accompanies a need for high status has an eventual result of discouraging the status, and thus the inputs, of others.

Blocking involves the imposition of some form of evaluative judgment on the actions of another by saying "no." Johnstone (1981) further points out that a preference for saying "no" is rewarded by the safety that statement affords; those that prefer to say "yes" are rewarded by the adventures they have. Improvisation, then, is a process of determining possibilities, often within groups. The state which allows for the generation of ideas without apparent penalty is the preferred state because it allows optimization of possibilities.

In jazz improvisation the status of the individuals within the group may depend on their levels of technical skill or inventive capacity. During an improvised passage a negotiation process determines which of the ideas being presented is the strongest one. The competitive framework within which this creation process operates suggests that players with lower status must be willing to have their ideas compete with those of higher status players, to maximize the range of creative choice.

The process of negotiation required in both theater and jazz improvisation relies in large measure on the quality of attention that the individuals pay to the process of creation. While this attentiveness and concentration may be required in individual forms of improvisation, the need is heightened with the addition of individuals to a group. The larger the group, the more complex the process of negotiation becomes, and the more sophisticated the individuals' listening skills must be. Dean (1989) suggests that the improviser first learns to develop musical creation as an individual, then as a soloist within a group, and then as a group improviser. The skills required become more complex along the progression because they require heightened senses of listening to the inputs from the other players.

Spolin (1983) illustrates this need by her insistence that students in improvisational theater employ a point of concentration often involving one or more of the senses. Her premise is that improvisation is a complete interaction of an individual with his or her environment, and that an integral part of the environment includes the other members of the group, and their inputs. The point of concentration allows them to take in these inputs and make sense of them. The negotiation that occurs within a group, then, is less a product of competitive fights for status, than the attentive selection of the appropriate direction based on the best available inputs of the participants.

Because this negotiation takes place instantly there is a requirement of the individuals within an improvising group to be in a behavioral condition which allows this negotiation to take place. One of the primary aspects of this condition is a state of awareness and attention to the surroundings.

Since much improvisational activity occurs at the intuitive level, a climate of friendship and trust governs the situation rather than a climate of professionalism and logic. The absence of such an improvisational climate may be the greatest barrier to improvisation.

The limiting factor: external structure

All forms of improvisation occur within some form of external structure. Weick (1969) points out that all enacted activity must be interpreted with some form of grammar that produces sense out of previously equivocal displays of information.

The earliest documented form of Western theatrical improvisation provides some insight here. *Commedia dell'arte* was among the first sources of popular drama in Western Europe around the middle of the sixteenth century. It traditionally involved troupes of actors who would perform a standard set of characters that were common to the form. As a result, most troupes would have the same set of characters, with which audiences would have some familiarity. Actors would perform *all'improviso*, and appear to be producing the plot development while they were performing (Frost and Yarrow, 1990). Pietropaulo (1989) reports that the spontaneity in these performances was limited. Characters were relatively fixed, in that each actor often performed the same role throughout his or her career, while learning appropriate ranges of responses to given situations. Thus, any situation presented allowed a fixed number of standard possibilities from which they could choose a response appropriate to the setting. The improvisation in this case was bounded by an elaborate structure which limited the number of creative options with which the actors could work. Within the structure the number of choices was sufficient to produce different end products with each performance.

The technique used in *commedia dell'arte* of selecting from a finite range of choices is referred to in music as *aleatoric* (derived from the Latin for "dice") (Dean, 1989). While this form of improvisation restricts the musical improviser's choices, other structural factors contain the creative possibilities of the performer. One is musical style, which although a highly subjective area, governs the "feel" of the music. As such, it is doubtful that Gregorian Chant, performed in its familiar form, would represent jazz music. The concerto cadenza developed in the eighteenth and nineteenth centuries allowed a display of spontaneous technical virtuosity on the part of a solo performer, but these improvisations were contained within the style of the composition that was being presented (Dean, 1989).

Other elements restricting creative choice are the instruments, which afford only certain types of sound to the performers, and, in Western music, the 12-tone scale, which divides the octave into 12 equal parts. Although some forms of Eastern music have much finer divisions of the octave, these also govern the style of the music and the range of choices accordingly.

In theatrical forms of improvisation the basic structure imposed on the product likewise may vary. Spolin (1983) suggests that the goal of the improvisation is to "solve the problem" put forward to the actors in a situation. The practice of ad-libbing typically occurs within traditional forms of theater when rehearsed elements are forgotten or upset. The spontaneous action that takes place must be sufficient to get the performance "back on track" and, as such, must be performed within the confines of the character's personality and the direction of the dramatic action. Improvisational sketches often employ some form of dramatic structure (which may be as simple as a beginning and an ending).

In organizations the external structure is similarly a series of constraints that limit the available actions from which members may choose in a given moment. This is consistent with Simon's (1992) view that organizations impose a bounded rationality on the actions of individuals within them. It is also consistent with the notions of strategy as logical incrementalism (Quinn, 1978) and as emergent (Mintzberg, 1988). The Mintzberg (1975) study of managerial activity and the explanation (Mintzberg, Raisinghani, and Theoret, 1976) of the structure of unstructured decisions indicate that any spontaneous action within an organization is to some degree bounded by the constraints of what makes sense within an organization.

Mintzberg presents research which shows that "the analytic approach to problem solving produced the precise answer more often, but its distribution of errors was quite wide. Intuition, in contrast, was less frequently precise but more consistently close" (1994, p. 327). Different structures will provide differing degrees of tolerance for error.

This is not an argument that all actions make sense to an organization, but rather that the degree of structure imposed on a set of actions limits the choices available for appropriate action, and that the appropriateness or quality of the action is measured against the structure itself. Weick (1969) makes the point that actions taken allow sense-making to occur; without action there is nothing to judge, and nothing to interpret, and therefore a maximum degree of ambiguity.

Enhancing factor: motivation, awareness, and understanding

At the outset of this paper we suggested that there was a planning bias that impeded both the study and application of improvisation. The absence of an improvisational climate may be largely the result of a lack of awareness and understanding of improvisation, and hence the absence of motivation to engage in a new and different way of doing things. As Claxton (1984) described, there are four barriers to individual learning: the desire to be competent, comfortable, consistent, and confident. The "4 Cs" become an even greater barrier in improvisation given the spontaneous and intuitive nature of the action. To engage in improvisation an individual must be personally motivated to risk the "4 Cs."

Extending Johnstone's (1981) observations about improvisation to an organizational level we suggest that organizations which embrace a planning orientation are rewarded by the control, comfort, and apparent safety it affords; organizations that embrace an improvisational orientation are rewarded by the adventures they have. An adventurous orientation is quite different from a control orientation, and making the adjustment requires different mind-sets and skill sets. Without an awareness of the need for improvisation, or an understanding of what it entails, there will be little motivation to engage it.

Although "motivation" has been presented as a separate dimension from the limiting factor of "structure," it is not surprising that the two are tightly coupled. We would expect that a structure that limits improvisation will not yield a high level of motivation to engage in it. Harper (1989, p. 114) discussed the use of intuition at NASA:

> NASA executives knew that situations could arise that may not have preformu-
> lated answers or when time would be short, and the astronauts would have to

make decisions without the benefit of computer simulations or additional studies. In these situations their intuitive skills would have a significant influence on the mission's success and their personal safety. NASA officials knew intuition is like a parachute. You hope it will not be used, but when all the sophisticated systems cannot help you, it's nice to have around.

Under ordinary conditions the structure of the situation at NASA rules out improvisation. However, when the systems break down, as we saw with Apollo 13, there is both motivation and structure to improvise.

Research and managerial implications

Although there are many research implications we would like to focus on three areas of improvisation: (1) what we should study; (2) where we should study; and (3) how we should study. We shall also extend these implications about research on improvisation to organizational learning.

What we should study in improvisation

In this burgeoning field of research there is ample opportunity for development in a variety of areas. Our use of the term "should" is stronger than we might like, but points in the direction of some salient research needs and opportunities which arise from this paper. The five implications regarding improvisation follow the flow of the paper. The first is the need to engage in a dialogue about the definition of improvisation. We have focused on spontaneity and intuition as two defining dimensions. We have found these dimensions to be particularly useful in distinguishing improvisation from other activities in organizations such as planning, visioning, and transactional activities which have not been formerly teased apart.

Every definition, however, makes certain assumptions, elevates some aspects, and even discounts others. For example, we have assumed that in order to act spontaneously we must make do with available resources, which is a central feature of Weick's (1993a) definition. Elevating, rather than assuming, the aspect of resources in the definition will turn the spotlight of research in a slightly different direction. This is quite appealing in the case of crisis where the challenge for intuition is to make creative use of the available resources. However, it may be misleading in other circumstances where the only scarce resource is time. We have also assumed multiple levels of analysis in our definition: individual, group, and organizational. Whether it is productive to make this explicit is not clear. Our bias in these early stages of theoretical development is to simplify the definition, with elaboration developing through discussion. This does, however, require researchers to engage in greater inquiry to understand; they cannot simply rely on their own interpretation of the definition. Although we have been quite thoughtful about the definition presented here, there is a need and opportunity for researchers to engage in a dialogue about the definition of the phenomenon.

Engaging in a dialogue about definition will help the research community articulate the meaning of improvisation, and will help to avoid the pitfall of overreliance on metaphor that Pinder and Bourgeois (1982) have raised. However, getting locked into definitional debates is another potential pitfall. On a parallel front, there is an opportunity to begin to formulate a bridge between the descriptive and prescriptive perspectives through the development of theory. We have advanced several characteristics as a step in this direction. We need to question whether there are other critical characteristics that we need to consider, as well as to generate a better understanding of the characteristics presented here. In understanding these characteristics we have a tremendous opportunity to tap into other literature bases to augment the theoretical development. For example, we have identified technical skill as an important characteristic. As we develop a better understanding of the kind of technical skills required to improvise, we will be able to tap into research on communication and leadership, for example. Pursuit of theory will also help to sharpen the definition of improvisation.

Each of the characteristics we have advanced represents an opportunity for future research. However, there are two that are particularly thorny: motivation and structure. We describe them as thorny because they embody what we think are some of the most difficult issues about improvisation: When should individuals, groups, and organizations engage in improvisation? Why do they engage in it? Why don't they engage in it? Although presented as two separate areas for future research, motivation and structure are tightly intertwined, as discussed in the body of this paper. Future research needs to address the types of structures in which improvisation flourishes, when it works, and when it does not. The NASA example provides a glimpse of the boundaries dividing improvised, planned, and transactional behavior. Although motivation will be tied to structure, there are individual elements related to psychological dimensions such as the "4 Cs" that warrant examination. That there is a planning bias that impedes improvisation is a fundamental question that researchers need to address.

Although it seems premature to seek to understand the link between improvisation and performance before we have either defined the concept or developed a theory, we assert that by seeking to understand when improvisation works and when it does not, we will be in a better position to develop a useful theory. If we can talk about the quality of improvisation in the arts, how do we determine the equivalent in management?

Our intent in this section has not been to constrain the direction of future research, but to identify a few areas of productive research that arise from the concepts presented in this paper.

Where we should study improvisation

We would like to advocate a broad range of opportunities for research. There is still much to be gained by examining improvisation in the arts where it has had a long tradition. As a research community we have borrowed well from the arts, but we believe we can learn even more by studying improvisation outside of the management domain.

Following in the Mintzberg tradition we have a strong bias to study the phenomenon "where it lives" as well. Observation of improvisation in organizations will help to clarify definition, characteristics, performance-related issues, and metaphor translation. However, this type of field research poses challenges in delineating between transactional and improvisational actions which do not exist in the arts, for example, where it is clearer that the jazz or theater improv group is improvising.

However, studying organizations in the early stages of development may yield more improvisational behavior.

Organizations that deal with crisis on a regular basis present another opportunity to target improvisation. Although we may feel like ambulance chasers, hospital emergency rooms, fire stations, and lifeguard operations, for example, present us with opportunities to observe improvisation in real time, and to extract reflections from participants about the nature of improvisation.

Finally, we can work in the laboratory to advance our understanding of improvisation through simulations, and controlled experiments. This type of work may be particularly valuable in examining the effectiveness of intervention techniques, such as individual or group training in improvisation.

How we should study improvisation

The foregoing discussion about what we should study, and where we should study it, leads to our advocation that the methodology should fit the research issue. We should use a variety of methodologies from participant observation and field-based research, to survey methodology, to experimental laboratory work. However, the employment of a variety of methodologies creates a challenge for integration. The pursuit of diverse methodologies creates a higher need for well-articulated concepts that build on one another in order to form a foundation for theoretical integration.

We will suggest one unusual approach to research on improvisation – that researchers should experience it in the context of a group that makes improvisation their profession, such as a theater group. Unfortunately many of us do not possess the musical skill to experience musical improvisation, but we all have the minimum level of communication skills to participate in theater improvisation. Applying our own understanding of improvisation we believe that it is by doing that we will understand.

Implications for organizational learning

Others in this volume will have articulated important research implications for organizational learning. However, by examining improvisation as a facet of organizational learning, we would like to raise three key implications. The first is that the application of intuition to action in a spontaneous way has been a neglected area of organizational learning, and there is much to be explored in this area. In these closing statements we will provoke thinking by suggesting that what many researchers and practitioners seek as they latch on to organizational learning, is an understanding of what seems to be the mysterious process of developing unique interpretations in a rapidly changing environment. In reading this description of improvisation some might actually equate improvisation with the domain of organizational learning – a conclusion that leads us to the second implication.

Learning is not synonymous with improvisation. We see improvisation as one facet of organizational learning along with a variety of others, including planning, visioning, scenario planning, and transacting. Organizational learning depicts organizational transformation using a learning lens which serves to elevate the cognitive-behavior interface. Organizational learning involves both the intuitive and spontaneous aspects of the creation of new insights, and the institutionalization of those insights in systems, structures, and procedures.

Finally, we have emphasized that there are varying degrees of quality of improvisation: there is good improvisation and there is bad improvisation (and everything in between). The same may be said for organizational learning. Every organization learns, and that learning is not necessarily productive. We do not adorn either improvisation or organizational learning with a halo. We do suggest, however, that they are processes that can be managed to enhance their effectiveness.

Management implications

Although this paper has adopted a theoretical orientation we would like to conclude with some managerial implications. We have identified the prevalence and importance of improvisation, and have suggested that individuals and organizations may have a planning bias that impedes improvisation. At a minimum we hope this paper raises managers' awareness of improvisation and the potential biases that may exist. Equipped with an understanding of its importance, managers might open their organizations to researchers who will want to study improvisation "where it lives." Finally, managers may want to heed the same advice given to researchers. One of the best ways to begin to understand improvisation is to experience it.

Conclusion

Improvisation is a part of daily organizational life, and a vital aspect of organizational learning. Sometimes it is done well; sometimes it is done poorly. However, we know very little about what characteristics separate the two extremes. In this paper we have tried to move a step forward in clarifying some terminology, presenting some research, and identifying some critical qualities of improvisation. The tradeoff between prudence and exploration will continue to vex organizations caught in turbulent environments. It is clear that improvisation is, and will continue to be, a thorny area for management theorists and practitioners. We are excited about the opportunities presented by the study of improvisation as an area of research, the opportunity it provides in informing the larger body of research on organizational learning, and its potential for management. As a research area it is not without the challenges and complexity that are familiar to the researcher of organizational learning. Our ability to draw on the practice of improvisation in the arts provides us with a better understanding of the complexity, and in our minds, keeps the challenge within our grasp.

References

Agor, W. (1986, Winter). The logic of intuition: How top executives make important decisions. In *Organizational Dynamics*, 5–18.

Agor, W. (Ed.) (1989). *Intuition in organizations: Leading and managing productively*. Newbury Park: Sage.

Barnard, C. (1938). *The functions of the executive*. Cambridge, MA: Harvard University Press.

Behling, O. and Eckel, N. (1991). Making sense out of intuition. *Academy of Management Executive*, 5 (1), 46–54.

Blumer, H. (1963). Collective behaviour. In A.M. Lee (Ed.), *Principles of sociology* (pp. 167–222). New York: Barnes and Noble.

Bosworth, S.L. and Kreps, G.A. (1986, October). Structure as process: Organization and role. *American Sociological Review.*

Bourgeois, W. and Pinder, C. (1983). Contrasting philosophical perspectives in administrative science: A reply to Morgan. *Administrative Science Quarterly, 28,* 608–613.

Callahan, M.R. (1986, December). Art imitates worklife: The world according to PACT. *Training and Development Journal,* 56–59.

Cappon, D. (1994). *Intuition and management: Research and application.* Westport, CT: Quorum Books.

Chase, M.P. (1988). *Improvisation: Music from the inside out.* Berkeley: Creative Arts.

Claxton, G. (1984). *Live and learn: An introduction to the psychology of growth and change in everyday life.* Hampton and Row Publishers.

Crossan, M., Djurfeldt, L., Lane, H.W. and White, R.E. (1995). Organizational learning: Dimensions for a theory. *International Journal of Organizational Analysis, 3* (4), 337–360.

Crossan, M., Lane, H.W., Klus, L. and White, R.E. (1996). The improvising organization: Where planning meets opportunity. *Organization Dynamics, 24* (4), 20–35.

Crossan, M., Lane, H.W. and White, R.E. (1996). Organizational learning: Toward a unifying framework. Working paper, the University of Western Ontario, London, Ontario.

Dean, R. (1989). *Creative improvisation: Jazz, contemporary music and beyond.* England: Milton Keynes.

De Bono, E. (1973). *Lateral thinking: Creativity step by step.* New York: Harper and Row.

Festinger, L. (1957). *A theory of cognitive dissonance.* Stanford, CA: Stanford University Press.

Frost, A. and Yarrow, R. (1990). *Improvisation in drama.* London: Macmillan.

Gridley, M.C. (1991). *Jazz styles: History and analysis.* Englewood Cliffs, NJ: Prentice Hall.

Hamel, G. and Prahalad, C.K. (1989, May–June). Strategic intent. *Harvard Business Review,* 63–76.

Harper, S.C. (1989). Intuition: What separates executives from managers. In W. Agor (Ed.), *Intuition in organizations: Leading and managing productively* (pp. 111–124). Newbury Park, CA: Sage.

Heider, F. (1958). *The psychology of interpersonal relations.* New York: John Wiley and Sons.

Johnson, P. and Daumer, C.R. (1993, Summer). Intuitive development: Communication in the nineties. *Public Personnel Management,* 257–268.

Johnstone, K. (1981). *Impro-improvisation and the theatre.* London: Methuen.

Kreps, G.A. (1991). Organizing for emergency response. In T. Drabek (Ed.), *Emergency management – policies and practices for local government.* Washington, DC: International City Management Association.

Mangham, I.L. and Pye, A. (1991). *The doing of managing.* Oxford: Basil Blackwell.

Mintzberg, H. (1973). *The nature of managerial work.* New York: Harper & Row.

Mintzberg, H., Raisinghani, D. and Theoret, A. (1976, June). The structure of unstructured decision processes. *Administrative Science Quarterly,* 246–274.

Mintzberg, H. (1975, July–August). The manager's job: Folklore and fact. *Harvard Business Review.*

Mintzberg, H. (1976, July–August). Planning on the left side and managing on the right. *Harvard Business Review.*

Mintzberg, H. (1988). Opening up the definition of strategy. In H. Mintzberg, J.B. Quinn and R.M. James (Eds), *The strategy process: Concepts, contexts, and cases* (pp. 13–20). Englewood Cliffs, NJ: Prentice Hall.

Mintzberg, H. (1994). *The rise and fall of strategic planning.* New York: The Free Press.

Morgan, G. (1980). Paradigms, metaphors, and puzzle solving. *Organization Theory, Administrative Science Quarterly, 25,* 605–622.

Morgan, G. (1983). More on metaphor: Why we cannot control tropes in administrative science. *Administrative Science Quarterly, 28,* 601–607.

Morgan, G. (1993). *Imaginization: The art of creative management.* Newbury Park, CA: Sage.

Pascale, R.T. (1984). Perspective on strategy: The real story behind Honda's success. *California Management Review, 26* (3), 47–72.

Perry, L.T. (1991, Spring). Strategic improvising: How to formulate and implement competitive strategies in concert. *Organizational Dynamics,* 51–64.

Perry, L.T. (1994, Summer). Real time strategy: Improvising team based planning for a fast changing world. *Organizational Dynamics,* 76–77.

Peters, T. and Waterman, R. (1982). In search of excellence. New York: Harper and Row.

Pietropaulo, D. (1989). *The science of buffoonery: Theory and history of the commedia dell'arte.* Ottawa: Dovehouse.

Pinder, C. and Bourgeois, V.W. (1982). Controlling tropes. *Administrative Science Quarterly, 27,* 641–652.

Powers, C. (1981, July). Role imposition and role improvisation: Some theoretical principles. *The Economic and Social Review,* 287–299.

Quinn, J.B. (1978, Fall). Strategic change: Logical incrementalism. *Sloan Management Review,* 7–21.

Schwartz, P. (1991). *The art of the long view.* New York: Doubleday Currency.

Simon, H.A. (1989). Making management decisions: The role of intuition and emotion. In W. Agor (Ed.). *Intuition in organizations: Leading and managing productively* (pp. 23–39). Newbury Park, CA: Sage.

Simon, H.A. (1992). *Economics, bounded rationality, and the cognitive revolution.* Aldershot, England: Edward Elgar.

Solomon, L. (1986). Improvisation II. *Perspectives in new music, 24,* 224–235.

Spolin, V. (1983). *Improvisation for the theatre,* Evanston, IL: Northwestern University Press.

Stalk, G. (1988, July–August). Time – the next source of competitive advantage. *Harvard Business Review,* 41–51.

Tsoukas, H. (1991). The missing link: A transformational view of metaphors in organizational science. *Academy of Management Review, 16* (3), 566–585.

Weick, K. (1969). *The social psychology of organizing.* Reading, MA: Addison-Wesley Publishing.

Weick, K.E. (1991). Theory construction as disciplined imagination. *Academy of Management Review, 14* (4), 516–531.

Weick, K.E. (1993a, Dec). The collapse of sensemaking in organizations: The Mann Gulch disaster. *Administrative Science Quarterly,* 628–652.

Weick, K.E. (1993b). Organizational redesign as improvisation. In G.P. Huber and W.H. Glick (Eds), *Organizational change and redesign: Ideas and insights for improving performance* (pp. 346–379). New York: Oxford University Press.

Zinn, D. (1981). *The structure and analysis of the modern improvised line volume 1: Theory.* New York: Excelsior Music Publishing.

4 Improvisation as a mindset for organizational analysis

Karl E. Weick

The emphasis in organizational theory on order and control often handicaps theorists when they want to understand the processes of creativity and innovation. Symptoms of the handicap are discussions of innovation that include the undifferentiated use of concepts like flexibility, risk, and novelty; forced either-or distinctions between exploration and exploitation; focus on activities such as planning, visioning, and strategizing as sites where improvements are converted into intentions that await implementation; and reliance on routine, reliability, repetition, automatic processing, and memory as the glue that holds organization in place. Since the term "organization" itself denotes orderly arrangements for cooperation, it is not surprising that mechanisms for rearranging these orders in the interest of adaptation, have not been developed as fully. (See Eisenberg (1990) for an important exception.) That liability can be corrected if we learn how to talk about the process of improvisation.

Thus, the purpose of this essay is to improve the way we talk about organizational improvisation, using the vehicle of jazz improvisation as the source of orienting ideas. I start with two brief descriptions of the complexity involved when musicians compose in the moment. Then I review several definitions intended to capture holistically what is happening when people improvise. Next, I take a closer look at selected details in improvisation, namely, degrees of improvisation, forms of improvisation, and cognition in improvisation. These understandings are then generalized from jazz to other settings such as conversation, therapy, and relationships of command. I conclude with implications for theory and practice.

Descriptions of jazz improvisation

Here are two accounts of what happens when order and control are breached extemporaneously in jazz performances, and a new order created.

> The sense of exhilaration that characterizes the artist's experiences under such circumstances is heightened for jazz musicians as storytellers by the activity's physical, intellectual, and emotional exertion and by the intensity of struggling with creative processes under the pressure of a steady beat. From the outset of each performance, improvisers enter an artificial world of time in which reactions to the unfolding events of their tales must be immediate. Furthermore, the consequences of their actions are irreversible. Amid the dynamic display of imagined fleeting images and impulses – entrancing sounds and vibrant feel-

ings, dancing shapes and kinetic gestures, theoretical symbols and perceptive commentaries – improvisers extend the logic of previous phrases, as ever-emerging figures on the periphery of their vision encroach upon and supplant those in performance. Soloists reflect on past events with breathtaking speed, while constantly pushing forward to explore the implications of new outgrowths of ideas that demand their attention. Ultimately, to journey over musical avenues of one's own design, thinking in motion and creating art on the edge of certainty and surprise, is to be "very alive, absolutely caught up in the moment."

(Berliner 1994, p. 220)

While they are performing their ideas, artists must learn to juggle short- and intermediate-range goals simultaneously. To lead an improvised melodic line back to its initial pitch requires the ability to hold a layered image of the pitch in mind and hand while, at the same time, selecting and performing other pitches. The requirements of this combined mental and physical feat become all the more taxing if, after improvising an extended phrase, soloists decide to manipulate more complex material, developing, perhaps, its middle segment as a theme. In all such cases, they must not only rely on their memory of its contour, but their muscular memory must be flexible enough to locate the segment's precise finger pattern instantly within their motor model of the phrase.

(Berliner 1994, p. 200)

Attempts to capture definitionally what is common among these examples have taken a variety of forms.

The word improvisation itself is rooted in the word "proviso" which means to make a stipulation beforehand, to provide for something in advance, or to do something that is premeditated. By adding the prefix "im" to the word proviso, as when the prefix "im" is added to the word mobile to create immobile, improvise means the *opposite* of proviso. Thus improvisation deals with the unforeseen, it works without a prior stipulation, it works with the unexpected. As Tyler and Tyler (1990) put it, improvisation is about the un-for-seen and unprovided-for which means it "is the negation of foresight, of planned-for, of doing provided for by knowing, and of the control of the past over the present and future" (p. x).

Some descriptions of improvisation, often those associated with jazz, describe this lack of prior stipulation and lack of planning as composing extemporaneously, producing something on the spur of the moment. Thus, we have Schuller's (1968, p. 378) influential definition that jazz involves "playing extemporaneously, i.e. without the benefit of written music ... (C)omposing on the spur of the moment." Schön describes this extemporaneous composing in more detail as "on-the-spot surfacing, criticizing, restructuring, and testing of intuitive understandings of experienced phenomena" while the ongoing action can still make a difference (1987, pp. 26–27).

I have found it hard to improve on the following definition, which is the one that guides this essay: "Improvisation involves reworking precomposed material and designs in relation to unanticipated ideas conceived, shaped, and transformed under the special conditions of performance, thereby adding unique features to every creation" (Berliner 1994, p. 241).

It is also possible to highlight definitionally, sub-themes in improvisation. Thus, one can focus on order and describe improvisation as "flexible treatment of pre-planned material" (Berliner 1994, p. 400). Or one can focus on the extemporaneous quality of the activity and describe improvisation as "intuition guiding action in a spontaneous way" (Crossan and Sorrenti 1996, p. 1) where intuition is viewed as rapid processing of experienced information (p. 14). Attempts to situate improvisation in organization lead to definitions such as the Miner *et als* (1996) suggestion that improvisation consists of deliberately chosen activities that are spontaneous, novel, and involve the creation of something while it is being performed (pp. 3–4).

While it is tempting to adopt these compressed themes in the interest of economy, we may be better served as theorists if we retain the larger and more complex set of options and see which subsets are most useful to explain which out-croppings. For example, spontaneity and intuition are important dimensions of improvisation. Yet, in a rare outspoken passage, Berliner argues as follows.

> [T]he popular definitions of improvisation that emphasize only its sponta-neous, intuitive nature – characterizing it as the 'making of something out of nothing' – are astonishingly incomplete. This simplistic understanding of improvisation belies the discipline and experience on which improvisers depend, and it obscures the actual practices and processes that engage them. Improvisation depends, in fact, on thinkers having absorbed a broad base of musical knowledge, including myriad conventions that contribute to formulat-ing ideas logically, cogently, and expressively. It is not surprising, therefore, that improvisers use metaphors of language in discussing their art form. The same complex mix of elements and processes coexists for improvisers as for skilled language practitioners: the learning, the absorption, and utilization of linguistic conventions conspire in the mind of the writer or utilization of linguistic con-ventions conspire in the mind of the writer or speaker – or, in the case of jazz improvisation, the player – to create a living work.
>
> (Berliner 1994, p. 492)

What Berliner makes clear is that the compression of experience into the single word "intuition" desperately needs to be unpacked because it is the very nature of this process that makes improvisation possible and separates good from bad impro-visation.

Similarly, Berliner is worried lest, in our fascination with the label "spontaneous," we overlook the major investment in practice, listening, and study that precedes a stunning performance. A jazz musician is more accurately described as a highly dis-ciplined "practicer" (Berliner 1994, p. 494) than as a practitioner.

Reminders that we should take little for granted in initial studies of improvisation seem best conveyed by more complex definitions that spell out what might be taken for granted. In the following section, I will suggest three properties of improvisation that may be especially sensitive to changes in other organizational variables. The implied logic is that changes in these variables affect the adequacy of improvisation which in turn affects adaptation, learning, and renewal.

Degrees of improvisation

To understand improvisation more fully, we first need to see that it lies on a continuum that ranges from "interpretation," through "embellishment" and "variation" ending in "improvisation" (Lee Konitz cited in Berliner 1994, pp. 66–71). The progression implied is one of increased demands on imagination and concentration. "Interpretation" occurs when people take minor liberties with a melody as when they choose novel accents or dynamics while performing it basically as written. "Embellishment" involves greater use of imagination, this time with whole phrases in the original being anticipated or delayed beyond their usual placements. The melody is rephrased but recognizable. "Variation" occurs when clusters of notes not in the original melody are inserted, but their relationship to that original melody is made clear. "Improvisation" on a melody means "transforming the melody into patterns bearing little or no resemblance to the original model or using models altogether alternative to the melody as the basis for inventing new phrases" (Berliner 1994, p. 70). When musicians improvise, they "radically alter portions of the melody or replace its segments with new creations bearing little, if any, relationship to the melody's shape" (Berliner 1994, p. 77). To improvise, therefore, is to engage in more than paraphrase or ornamentation or modification.

With these gradations in mind it is instructive to re-examine existing examples of improvisation to see whether they consist of radical alterations, and new creations. Miner *et al.* (1996, pp. 9–14) describe several instances of organizational improvisation and the verbs they use suggest that their examples fit all four points on the continuum. Thus, they describe improvisations during new product development that consists of a "shift" in a light assembly (interpretation); a "switch" in a product definition or "adding" a light beam source (embellishment); "altering" the content of a prior routine or "revising" a test schedule (variation); and "creating" an internal focus group or "discovering" a way to do a 22-second information search in 2 seconds (improvisation). If my attempt to assign the Miner *et al.* (1996) verbs to Konitz's four categories is plausible, then it suggests several things. First, activities that alter, revise, create, and discover are purer instances of improvisation than are activities that shift, switch, or add. Second, activities toward the "interpretation" end of the continuum are more dependent on the models they start with than are activities toward the improvisation end. As dependency on initial models increases, adaptation to more radical environmental change should decrease. Third, as modifications become more like improvisations and less like interpretations, their content is more heavily influenced by past experience, dispositions, and local conditions. When people increasingly forego guidance from a common melody, they resort to more idiosyncratic guidance. It is here where differentials in prior experience, practice, and knowledge are most visible and have the most effect. Fourth, the stipulation that people deliberately act extempore should be easier to execute if they stick closer to a guideline than if they depart radically from it. Thus, interpretation and embellishment should be initiated more quickly under time pressure than is true for variation and improvisation. Deliberate injunctions to be radically different may falter if they fail to specify precisely what the original model is, in what sense it is to remain a constraint, and which of its properties are constants and which are variables. These questions don't arise in the three approximations to improvisation represented by interpretation, embellishment, and variation.

The point is, deliberate improvisation is much tougher, much more time consuming, and places higher demands on resources, than does deliberate interpretation. If deliberateness is a key requirement for something to qualify as organizational improvisation, and if we construe improvisation in the sense used by Konitz, then full-scale improvisation should be rare in time-pressured settings. But, if it could be accomplished despite these hurdles, then it should be a substantial, sustainable, competitive advantage.

Fifth, and finally, any one activity may contain all four gradations, as sometimes happens in jazz.

> Over a solo's course, players typically deal with the entire spectrum of possibilities embodied by these separable but related applications of improvisation. At one moment, soloists may play radical, precomposed variations on a composition's melody as rehearsed and memorized before the event. The very next moment, they may spontaneously be embellishing the melody's shape, or inventing a new melodic phrase. There is a perpetual cycle between improvised and precomposed components of the artists' knowledge as it pertains to the entire body of construction materials. . . . The proportion of precomposition to improvising is likewise subject to continual change throughout a performance.
>
> (Berliner 1994, p. 222)

Re-examination of the Miner *et al.* (1996) examples suggests that some involve the entire spectrum of improvisation and others do not. For example, when design engineers tackled the problem of flawed filters at Fast Track, they improvised a new feature, reworked the assemblies, shifted how lights were to stand, changed the formal technical features, and added a light beam source. The intriguing possibility is that full spectrum improvisation like this has different properties than simple stand-alone improvisation. Full spectrum improvisation makes fuller use of memory and past experience, can build on the competencies of a more diverse population, is more focused by a melody, and may be more coherent. If this is plausible then it should be more persuasive, diffuse faster, and be more acceptable since a greater variety of people within the firm can understand how it has developed. Furthermore, they are able to recognize some of its pre-existing components. It is also possible that the smooth versus sudden changes celebrated by those who invoke the concept of punctuated equilibrium are simply manifestations of full spectrum (smooth) or solitary (sudden) improvisation.

The point of all this is that we may want to be stingy in our use of the label improvisation and generous in our use of other labels that suggest approximations to improvisation. When we focus on approximations, we focus both on connections to the past and on the original model that is being embellished. The spectrum from interpretation to improvisation mirrors the spectrum from incremental to transformational change. It becomes less common in organizations than we anticipated, but its antecedents become clearer as do its connections with themes of order and control.

Forms of improvisation

These connected themes of order and improvisation become even clearer when we look more closely at the object to which the process of improvisation is applied. As bassist-composer, Charles Mingus, insisted, "you can't improvise on nothing; you've gotta improvise on something" (Kernfeld 1995, p. 119). This is the same Mingus who once actually reduced a promising young saxophonist to tears before an audience, with his running commentary of "Play something different, man; play something different. This is jazz, man. You played that last night and the night before" (Berliner 1994, p. 271). The ongoing tension to "improvise on something" but to keep the improvisations fresh is the essence of jazz. That tension may be weaker in non-musical organizations where routine embellishment of routines is sufficient and expected and where surprise is unwelcome. But, whether embellishment is major or minor, improvisation involves the embellishment of something.

In jazz, that "something" usually is a melody such as originated in African-American blues and gospel songs, popular songs, ragtime piano and brass-band marches, Latin American dances, or rock and soul music (Kernfeld 1995, p. 40). What is common to these melodies is form imposed by a sequence of harmonic chords and a scheme of rhythm. Other objects available for embellishment that are more common to organizations range from routines and strategic intent (Perry 1991), to a set of core values, a credo, a mission statement, rules of engagement, or basic know-how. Gilbert Ryle (1979) argued that virtually all behavior has an *ad hoc* adroitness akin to improvisation because it mixes together a partly fresh contingency with general lessons previously learned. Ryle describes this mixture as paying heed. Improvisation enters in the following way.

> (T)o be thinking what he is here and now up against, he must both be trying to adjust himself to just this present once-only situation *and* in doing this to be applying lessons already learned. There must be in his response a union of some Ad Hockery with some know-how. If he is not at once *improvising* and improvising *warily*, he is not engaging his somewhat trained wits in a partly fresh situation. It is the pitting of an acquired competence or skill against unprogrammed opportunity, obstacle or hazard. It is a bit like putting some *new* wine into *old* bottles.
>
> (Ryle 1979, p. 129)

Thus, improvisation shares an important property with phenomena encompassed by chaos theory (e.g. McDaniel 1996, Stacey 1992), namely, origins are crucial small forms that can have large consequences (e.g. cracks in shoulder bones determine hunting success among Naskapi Indians (Weick 1979, pp. 262–263)). Melodies vary in the ease with which they evoke prior experience and trigger generative embellishments. Some melodies set up a greater number of interesting possibilities than do other melodies. The same holds true for organizational "melodies" such as mission statements, which range from the banal to the ingenious and invite well-practiced or novel actions on their behalf.

While improvisation is affected by one's associates, past experiences, and current setting, it is also determined by the kernel that provides the pretext for assembling these elements in the first place. These pretexts are not neutral. They encourage some lines of development and exclude other ones. And this holds true regardless of the improviser. While it is true that a masterful musician like tenor saxophonist, Sonny Rollins, can find incredible richness in mundane melodies such as "Tennessee Waltz" and "Home on the Range," it is equally true that these melodies themselves unfold with unusual progressions relative to the standard jazz repertory (e.g. "I Got Rhythm"). It is the capability of these progressions to challenge and evoke, as well as the competence of the performer, that contribute to improvisation. It is easy to overlook the substantive contribution of a melody because it is so small and simple. It's important to remember that a melody is also an early and continuing influence.

The important point is that improvisation does not materialize out of thin air. Instead, it materializes around a simple melody that provides the pretext for real-time composing. Some of that composing is built from precomposed phrases that become meaningful retrospectively as embellishments of that melody. And some comes from elaboration of the embellishments themselves. The use of precomposed fragments in the emerging composition is an example of Ryle's (1979) "wary improvisation" anchored in past experience. The further elaboration of these emerging embellishments is an example of Ryle's opportunistic improvisation in which one's wits engage a fresh, once-only situation. Considered as a noun, an improvisation is a transformation of some original model. Considered as a verb, improvisation is composing in real time that begins with embellishments of a simple model, but increasingly feeds on these embellishments themselves to move farther from the original melody and closer to a new composition. Whether treated as a noun or a verb, improvisation is guided activity whose guidance comes from elapsed patterns discovered retrospectively. Retrospect may range back as far as solos heard long before or back only as far as notes played just this moment. Wherever the notes come from, their value is determined by the pattern they make *relative to* a continuing set of constraints formed by melody. The trick in improvisation is, as Paul Desmond put it, to aim for "clarity, emotional communication on a not-too-obvious level, form in a chorus that doesn't hit you over the head but is there if you look for it, humor, and construction that sounds logical in an unexpected way" (Gioia 1988, p. 89).

Cognition in improvisation

As this more detailed picture of improvisation begins to emerge, there is a recurring implication that retrospect is significant in its production. In jazz improvisation people act in order to think, which imparts a flavor of retrospective sensemaking to improvisation. Ted Gioia puts it this way: unlike an architect who works from plans and looks ahead, a jazz musician cannot "look ahead at what he is going to play, but he can look behind at what he has just played; thus each new musical phrase can be shaped with relation to what has gone before. He creates his form retrospectively" (Gioia 1988, p. 61). The jazz musician, who creates form retrospectively, builds something that is recognizable from whatever is at hand, contributes to an emerging structure being built by the group in which he or she is playing, and creates possibilities for the other players. Gioia's description suggests that intention is loosely coupled to execution, that creation and interpretation need not be separated in time, and that sensemaking rather than decision making is embodied in improvisation. All three of these byproducts of retrospect create a different understanding of organized action than the one we are more accustomed to where we commonly look for the implementation of intentions, the interpretation of prior creations, and for decisions that presume prior sensemaking.

When musicians describe their craft, the importance of retrospect becomes clear, as these excerpts make clear.

> After you initiate the solo, one phrase determines what the next is going to be. From the first note that you hear, you are responding to what you've just played: you just said this on your instrument, and now that's a constant. What follows from that? And then the next phrase is a constant. What follows from that? And so on and so forth. And finally, let's wrap it up so that everybody understands that that's what you're doing. It's like language: you're talking, you're speaking, you're responding to yourself. When I play, it's like having a conversation with myself.
>
> (Max Roach cited in Berliner 1994, p. 192)

> If you're not affected and influenced by your own notes when you improvise, then you're missing the whole essential point.
>
> (Lee Konitz cited in Berliner 1994, p. 193)

> When I start off, I don't know what the punch line is going to be.
>
> (Buster Williams cited in Berliner 1994, p. 218)

The importance of retrospect for improvisation imposes new demands that suggest why organizational improvisation may be rare. To add to a store of ironies that are beginning to accumulate, not only is improvisation grounded in forms, but it is also grounded in memory. Forms and memory and practice are all key determinants of success in improvisation that are easy to miss if analysts become preoccupied with spontaneous composition. Implied in each musician's account is the relationship that "the larger and more complex the musical ideas artists initially conceive, the greater the power of musical memory and mental agility required to transform it" (Berliner 1994, p. 194).

To improve improvisation is to improve memory, whether it be organizational (Walsh and Ungson 1991), small group (Wegner 1987), or individual (Neisser and Winograd 1988). To improve memory is to gain retrospective access to a greater range of resources. Also implied here is the importance of listening *to oneself* as well as to other people. Prescriptions in organizational studies tout the importance of listening to others (e.g. the big news at GE is that Jack Welch discovered ears) but miss the fact that good improvisation also requires listening to one's own comments and building on them.

The reader is referred back to the description of composing in the moment on p. 543 that starts "while they are performing," to see again how important memory is to improvisation. This importance is reflected in formal jazz study.

> In one class, a teacher arbitrarily stopped the solos of students and requested that they perform their last phrase again. When they could not manage this, he chastised them for being "like people who don't listen to themselves while they speak." Aspiring improvisers must cultivate impressive musical recall in both aural and physical terms if they are to incorporate within their ongoing conversation new ideas conceived in performance.
>
> (Berliner 1994, p. 200)

Viewed through the lens of retrospect, jazz looks like this.

> The artist can start his work with almost random maneuver – a brush stroke on a canvas, an opening line, a musical motif – and then adapt his later moves to this initial gambit. A jazz improviser, for example, might begin his solo with a descending five-note phrase and then see, as he proceeds, that he can use this same five-note phrase in other contexts in the course of his improvisation.
>
> This is, in fact, what happens in Charlie Parker's much analyzed improvisation on Gershwin's "Embraceable You." Parker begins with a five-note phrase (melodically similar to "you must remember this" phrase in the song "As Time Goes By") which he employs in a variety of ingenious contexts throughout the course of his improvisation. Parker obviously created his solo on the spot (only a few minutes later he recorded a second take with a completely different solo, almost as brilliant as the first), yet this should not lead us to make the foolish claim that his improvisation is formless.
>
> (Gioia 1988, p. 60)

Viewed through the lens of retrospect, larger issues look like this. If events are improvised and intention is loosely coupled to execution, the musician has little choice but to wade in and see what happens. What will actually happen won't be known until it is too late to do anything directly about it. All the person can do is justify and make sensible, after the fact, whatever is visible in hindsight. Since that residue is irrevocable, and since all of this sensemaking activity occurs in public, and since the person has a continuing choice as to what to do with that residual, this entire scenario seems to contain a microcosm of the committing forces that affect creative coping with the human condition (Weick 1989). Small wonder that Norman Mailer, in his famous essay "The White Negro," described jazz as "American existentialism."

This simple exposition of degrees of improvisation, forms for improvisation, and cognition in improvisation does not begin to exhaust the dimensions of jazz improvisation that are relevant for organizational theory. Other potential themes of interest might include the ways in which "mistakes" provide the platform for musical "saves" that create innovations (e.g. Berliner 1994, p. 191, 209, 210–216; Weick, 1995); skills of bricolage that enable people to make do with whatever resources are at hand (Harper 1987, Levi-Strauss 1966, Weick 1993); and social conventions that complement structures imposed by tunes (Bastien and Hostager, 1992).

Non-jazz settings for improvisation

What I have tried to show so far is that descriptions of composing on the spur of the moment, and attempts to portray this process definitionally and dimensionally, comprise a language that allows analysts to maintain the images of order and control that are central to organizational theory and simultaneously introduce images of innovation and autonomy. The ease with which improvisation mixes together these disparate images of control and innovation (Nemeth and Staw 1989) becomes even clearer if we look at other settings where improvisation seems to occur.

A swift way to see the potential richness of improvisation as a metaphor is simply to look in the index of Berliner's (1994) authoritative volume under the heading, "Metaphors for aspects of improvisation" (p. 869). In his analyses Berliner finds that jazz improvisation is likened to cuisine, dance, foundation building, a game of chess, a journey, landing an airplane, language, love, marriage, preparing for acting, painting, singing, sports, and acting like a tape recorder (some drummers "are like tape recorders. You play something and then they imitate it"; p. 427). By a process of backward diagnosis, we therefore expect to find improvisation where people cook, move, construct, compete, travel, etc.

Perhaps the setting that most resembles jazz improvisation, at least judging from its frequency of mention, is language acquisition and use (e.g. Ramos 1978, Suhor 1986). Jazz musician Stan Getz describes improvisation as a way of conversing.

> It's like a language. You learn the alphabet, which are the scales. You learn sentences, which are the chords. And then you talk extemporaneously with the horn. It's a wonderful thing to *speak* extemporaneously, which is something I've never gotten the hang of. But musically I love to talk just off the top of my head. And that's what jazz music is all about.
>
> (Maggin 1996, p. 21)

An example of the easy movement that is possible between the two domains is Berliner's equating of improvisation with rethinking.

> The activity [of jazz improvisation] is much like creative thinking in language, in which the routine process is largely devoted to rethinking. By ruminating over formerly held ideas, isolating particular aspects, examining their relationships to the features of other ideas, and, perhaps, struggling to extend ideas in modest steps and refine them, thinkers typically have the sense of delving more deeply into the possibilities of their ideas. There are, of course, also the rarer moments when they experience discoveries as unexpected flashes of insight and revelation.
>
> Similarly, a soloist's most salient experiences in the heat of performance involve poetic leaps of imagination to phrases that are unrelated, or only minimally related, to the storehouse, as when the identities of formerly mastered patterns melt away entirely within new recombinant shapes.
>
> (Berliner 1994, pp. 216–217)

Discussions of improvisation in groups are built on images of call and response, give and take (Wilson 1992), transitions, exchange, complementing, negotiating a shared sense of the beat (see Barrett's (1998) discussion of groove), offering harmonic possibilities to someone else, preserving continuity of mood, and cross-fertilization. In jazz, as in conversation, self-absorption is a problem. Wynton Marsalis observed that in playing, as in conversation, the worst people to talk to and play with are those who, "when you're talking, they're thinking about what they are going to tell you next, instead of listening to what you're saying" (Berliner 1994, p. 401). What is also striking about jazz conversation, as with conversations in other settings, is the many levels at which they function simultaneously. Thus, jazz improvisation involves conversation between an emerging pattern and such things as formal features of the underlying composition, previous interpretations, the player's own logic, responsiveness of the instrument, other musicians, and the audience.

Managerial activities, which are dominated by language and conversation, often become synonymous with improvisation. Thus, we find Mangham and Pye (1991) proposing close parallels between improvisation and organizing. Here is what they observe in top management teams.

> Our respondents assert that they learn what they are about in talking to and trusting their colleagues, that they often recognize and develop their own views in the very process of seeking consensus, that talking to others heightens their awareness, sharpens their focus. But they also assert that they are in command, that they do plan and shape the future with clear intent, that they know where it is they are heading.
>
> (p. 77)

Like jazz musicians, managers simultaneously discover targets and aim at them, create rules and follow rules, and engage in directed activity often by being clearer about which directions are not right than about specified final results. Their activity is controlled but not predetermined (Mangham and Pye 1991, p. 79).

Here is how Mangham and Pye make sense of what they observe.

> What we are proposing is that in their daily interactions our managers, no less than managers elsewhere, sustain appreciative systems or improvise readinesses which reflect their values and beliefs which, in turn, are likely to be influenced by and to influence received ideas about the doing of organizing. We hold that much of the doing of organizing is either a matter of running through a *script* or an instance of *improvisation*, and that both of these activities relate to readings which have reference to appreciative systems which are, in turn, reflections of deeply held beliefs and values.
>
> (Mangham and Pye 1991, p. 36)

What Mangham and Pye (1991) make clear is that managing shares with jazz improvisation such features as simultaneous reflection and action (p. 79), simultaneous rule creation and rule following (p. 78), patterns of mutually expected responses akin to musicians moving through a melody together (p. 45), action informed by melodies in the form of codes (p. 40), continuous mixing of the expected with the novel (p. 24), and the feature of a heavy reliance on intuitive grasp and imagination (p. 18). These managers are not just Herbert Simon's (1989) chess grandmasters who solve problems by recognizing patterns. And neither are jazz musicians. They are that, but more. The more is that they are also able to use their experience of "having been there" to recognize "that one is now somewhere else, and that that 'somewhere else' is novel and may be valuable, notwithstanding the 'rules' which declare that one cannot get here from there" (Mangham and Pye 1991, p. 83).

Daft and Weick (1984) suggest that when managers deem an environment to be unanalyzable, they seek information by means of strategies that are "more personal, less linear, more *ad hoc* and improvisational" (p. 287). Sutcliffe and Sitkin (1996) have argued that total quality interventions basically involve what they call a "redistribution of improvisation rights." [See also Wruck and Jensen (1994, p. 264) on allocation of decision rights to initiation, ratification, implementation, and monitoring.] Successful quality management occurs when people are newly authorized to paraphrase, embellish, and reassemble their prevailing routines, extemporaneously. Furthermore, they are encouraged to think while doing rather than be guided solely by plans. Thus, when a firm "disseminates improvisation rights" it tends to encourage the "flexible treatment of preplanned material," which means that quality improvement and jazz improvisation are closely aligned.

Improvisation is common in public-sector organizations and occurs often on the front-line, as Weiss (1980, p. 401) suggests.

> Many moves are improvisations. Faced with an event that calls for response, officials use their experience, judgment, and intuition to fashion the response for the issue at hand. That response becomes a precedent, and when similar questions come up, the response is uncritically repeated. Consider the federal agency that receives a call from a local program asking how to deal with requests for enrollment in excess of the available number of slots. A staff member responds with off-the-cuff advice. Within the next few weeks, programs in three more cities call with similar questions, and staff repeat the advice. Soon what began as improvisation has hardened into policy.
>
> (p. 401)

Improvisation also occurs in settings as disparate as psychotherapy, medical diagnosis, and combat.

Improvisation is the heart of psychotherapy. Thus, it is not surprising to find that one of the most prominent and original jazz pianists, Denny Zeitlin, is also a practicing psychiatrist who sees patients approximately 30 hours per week (Herrington 1989). Kenney (1990, p. 1) describes the parallels between therapy and improvisation.

> Given the unpredictable nature of a client's communication, the therapist's participation in the theatrics of a session becomes an invitation to improvise. In other words, since the therapist never knows exactly what the client will say at any given moment, he or she cannot rely exclusively upon previously designed lines, pattern, or scripts. Although some orientations to therapy attempt to shape both the client and therapist into a predetermined form of conversation and story, every particular utterance in a session offers a unique opportunity for improvisation, invention, innovation, or more simply, change.
>
> (Keeney 1990, p. 1)

If therapy is viewed as improvisation, then therapies are viewed as songs. The song can be played exactly as scored or with improvisation, but one would not expect an improvisational therapist to play only one song over and over anymore than one would expect a jazz musician to play only one song throughout a lifetime.

Improvisation sometimes lies at the heart of medical diagnosis as well, but only when practitioners jettison narrow versions of decision rationality in favor of improvisation. Starbuck (1993) suggests that good doctors do not base their treatments on diagnosis. They leave diagnosis out of the chain between symptoms and treatment because it discards too much information and injects random errors. There are many more combinations of symptoms than there are diagnoses, just as there are many more treatments than diagnoses.

> (T)he links between symptoms and treatments are not the most important keys to finding effective treatments. Good doctors pay careful attention to how patients respond to treatments. If a patient gets better, current treatments are heading in the right direction. But, current treatments often do not work, or they produce side-effects that require correction. The model of symptoms-diagnoses-treatments ignores the feedback loop from treatments to symptoms, whereas this feedback loop is the most important factor.
>
> (Starbuck 1993, p. 87)

The logic can be applied to academic research.

> Academic research is trying to follow a model like that taught in medical schools. Scientists are translating data into theories, and promising to develop prescriptions from the theories. Data are like symptoms, theories like diagnoses, and prescriptions like treatments. Are not organizations as dynamic as human bodies and similarly complex? Theories do not capture all the information in data, and they do not determine prescriptions uniquely. Perhaps scientists could establish stronger links between data and prescriptions if they did not introduce theories between them. Indeed, should not data be results of prescriptions? Should not theories come from observing relations between prescriptions and subsequent data?
>
> (Starbuck 1993)

Starbuck reminds us that, when faced with incomprehensible events, there is often no substitute for acting your way into an eventual understanding of them. How can I know what I am treating until I see how it responds? To organize for diagnosis is to design a setting that generates rich records of symptoms, a plausible initial treatment, alertness to effects of treatments, and the capability to improvise from there on. Theories, diagnoses, strategies, and plans serve mostly as plausible interim stories that mix ignorance and knowledge in different patterns.

Isenberg (1985, pp. 178–179), following the work of Bursztjahn *et al.* (1981), has also discussed what he calls treating a patient empirically. Like Starbuck, he notes that a diagnosis, if it is inferred at all, occurs retrospectively after the patient is cured. Isenberg then generalizes this medical scenario to battlefield situations. This application fleshes out a much earlier statement by Janowitz (1959, p. 481) that a combat soldier is not a rule-following bureaucrat who is "detached, routinized, self-contained: rather his role is one of constant improvisation. . . . The impact of battle destroys men, equipment, and organization, which need constantly and continually to be brought back into some form of unity through on-the-spot improvisation." For Isenberg, the parallel between empirical medicine and empirical fighting is that in both cases

> tactical maneuvers (treatment) will be undertaken with the primary purpose of learning more about (diagnosing) the enemy's position, weaponry, and strength, as well as one's own strength, mobility, and understanding of the battlefield situation. . . . Sometimes the officer will need to implement his or her

solution with little or no problem definition and problem solving. Only after taking action and seeing the results will the officer be able to better define the problem that he or she may have already solved!

(pp. 178–179)

The steady progression from jazz to other sites where improvisation is plausible culminates in the idea that living itself is an exercise in improvisation. People compose their lives, as Mary Catherine Bateson (1989) suggests in this composite description.

> I have been interested in the arts of improvisation, which involve recombining partly familiar materials in new ways, often in ways especially sensitive to context, interaction, and response.... (The idea of life as an improvisatory art) started from a disgruntled reflection on my own life as a sort of desperate improvisation in which I was constantly trying to make something coherent from conflicting elements to fit rapidly changing settings.... Improvisation can be either a last resort or an established way of evoking creativity. Sometimes a pattern chosen by default can become a path of preference.... Much biography of exceptional people is built around the image of a quest, a journey through a timeless landscape toward an end that is specific, even though it is not fully known.... (These assumptions are increasingly inappropriate today because) fluidity and discontinuity are central to the reality in which we live. Women have always lived discontinuous and contingent lives, but men today are newly vulnerable, which turns women's traditional adaptations into a resource.... The physical rhythms or reproduction and maturation create sharper discontinuities in women's lives than in men's, the shifts of puberty and menopause, of pregnancy, birth, and lactation, the mirroring adaptations to the unfolding lives of children, their departures and returns, the ebb and flow of dependency, the birth of grandchildren, the probability of widowhood. As a result, the ability to shift from one preoccupation to another, to divide one's attention, to improvise in new circumstances, has always been important to women.

(pp. 2, 3, 4, 5, 6, 13)

The newfound urgency in organizational studies to understand improvisation and learning is symptomatic of growing societal concerns about how to cope with discontinuity, multiple commitments, interruptions, and transient purposes that dissolve without warning. To understand more about improvisation undoubtedly will help us get a better grasp on innovation in organizations. That's important. But it is not nearly as important as is understanding how people in general "combine familiar and unfamiliar components in response to new situations, following an underlying grammar and an evolving aesthetic" (Bateson 1989, p. 3). To watch jazz improvisation unfold is to have palpable contact with the human condition. Awe, at such moments, is understandable.

Implications for theory

While several implications for organizational theory have already been mentioned, I want to suggest some of the richness implicit in improvising by brief mention of its relation to postmodern organizational theory and to paradox.

The idea of improvisation is important for organizational theory because it gathers together compactly and vividly a set of explanations suggesting that to understand organization is to understand organizing or, as Whitehead (1929) put it, to understand "being" as constituted by its "becoming." This perspective, found in previous work by people such as Allport (1962), Buckley (1968), Follett (1924), Mangham and Pye (1991), Maruyama (1963), Mintzberg and McHugh (1985), and Weick (1969, 1979) has been newly repackaged as the "unique intellectual preoccupation of 'postmodern' organizational theorists" (Chia 1996, p. 44). Thus, we find people talking once more about the ontology of becoming, using images already familiar to process theorists and musicians alike, images such as emergence, fragments, micro-practices that enact order, reaccomplishment, punctuation, recursion, reification, relations, transcience, flux, and "a sociology of verbs rather than a sociology of nouns" (Chia 1996, p. 49). If theorists take improvisation seriously, they may be able to give form to the idea of "becoming realism" (Chia 1996) and add to what we already know.

They may, for example, be able to do more with the simultaneous presence of seeming opposites in organizations than simply label them as paradoxes. There is currently an abundance of conceptual dichotomies that tempt analysts to choose between things like control and innovation, exploitation and exploration, routine and nonroutine, and automatic and controlled, when the issue in most organizations is one of proportion and simultaneity rather than choice. Improvisation is a mixture of the precomposed and the spontaneous, just as organizational action mixes together some proportion of control with innovation, exploitation with exploration, routine with nonroutine, automatic with controlled. The normally useful concepts of routine (Gersick and Hackman 1990, Cohen and Bacdayan 1994) and innovation (Amabile 1988, Dougherty 1992) have become less powerful as they have been stretched informally to include improvisation. Thus, a routine becomes something both repetitious and novel, and the same is true for innovation. A similar loss of precision [Reed (1991) refers to it as a "rout"] has occurred in the case of decision making where presumptions of classical rationality are increasingly altered to incorporate tendencies toward spontaneous revision. Neither decisions nor rationality can be recognized in the resulting hodgepodge. What is common among all of these instances of lost precision is that they attempt to acknowledge the existence of improvisation, but do so without giving up the prior commitment to stability and order in the form of habit, repetition, automatic thinking, rational constraints, formalization, culture, and standardization. The result, when theorists graft mechanisms for improvisation onto concepts that basically are built to explain order, is a caricature of improvisation that ignores nuances highlighted in previous sections. These caricatures leave out properties of organizational improvisation such as the tension involved in mixing the intended and the emergent and the strong temptation to simplify in favor of one or the other; the possibility that order can be accomplished by means of ongoing ambivalent mixtures of variation and retention that permit adaptation to dynamic situations; the chronic temptation to fall back on well-rehearsed fragments to cope with current problems even though these problems don't exactly match those present at the time of the earlier rehearsal; the use of emergent structures as sources for embellishment which enables quick distancing from previous solutions; the close resemblance between improvising and editing; the sensitivity of improvisation to originating conditions;

and the extensive amount of practice necessary to pull off successful improvisation. The remedy would seem to lie in a variety of directions such as positing routines, innovation, and decision making as inputs to improvisation akin to melodies (e.g. people improvised on this routine); treating improvisation as a distinct form of each (e.g. this routine was executed improvisationally); treating each of the three as a distinct way to engage in organizational improvisation (e.g. routinizing of improvisation); and, treating improvisation as a stand alone process like the other three consisting of a fixed sequence of conceiving, articulating, and remembering.

Implications for practice

The concept of improvisation also engages several concepts in mainstream organizational practice and likewise suggests ways to strengthen them. For example, if time is a competitive advantage then people gain speed if they do more things spontaneously without lengthy prior planning exercises (Crossan and Sorrenti 1996, p. 4). To do more things spontaneously is to become more skilled at thinking on your feet, a skill that is central in improvisation even though it is not given much attention in accounts of managerial action. Improvisation has implications for staffing. Young musicians who are laden with technique often tend to be poor at improvisation because they lack voices, melodies, and feeling (Berliner 1994, p. 792, ftn. 17; Davis 1986, p. 87), which sounds a lot like the liability that corporations associate with newly minted MBAs. The remedy for students is to mix listening with history, practice, modeling, and learning the fundamentals, which can be tough if they are driven, instrumental, in a hurry, and have little sense of what they need to know. The irony is that it is this very haste which dooms them to be a minor player who sounds like every other technique-laden minor player, none of whom have much to say.

If we treat the preceding description of improvisation as if it contained the shell of a set of prescriptions for adaptive organizing, then here are some possible characteristics of groups with a high capability for improvisation:

1　Willingness to forego planning and rehearsing in favor of acting in real time;
2　Well developed understanding of internal resources and the materials that are at hand;
3　Proficient without blueprints and diagnosis;
4　Able to identify or agree on minimal structures for embellishing;
5　Open to reassembly of and departures from routines;
6　Rich and meaningful set of themes, fragments, or phrases on which to draw for ongoing lines of action;
7　Predisposed to recognize partial relevance of previous experience to present novelty;
8　High confidence in skill to deal with nonroutine events;
9　Presence of associates similarly committed to and competent at impromptu making to;
10　Skillful at paying attention to performance of others and building on it in order to keep the interaction going and to set up interesting possibilities for one another.
11　Able to maintain the pace and tempo at which others are extemporizing.

12   Focused on coordination here and now and not distracted by memories or anticipation;
13   Preference for and comfort with process rather than structure, which makes it easier to work with ongoing development, restructuring, and realization of outcomes, and easier to postpone the question, what will it have amounted to?

Limits to improvisation

If theorists conceptualize organizations as sites where the activity of improvisation occurs, this may offset their tendency to dwell on themes of control, formalization, and routine. It may also help them differentiate the idea of "flexibility," which tends to be used as a catchall for the innovative remainder. Nevertheless, there are good reasons why the idea of improvisation may have limited relevance for organizations. If organizations change incrementally – punctuations of an equilibrium seldom materialize out of thin air without prior anticipations – then those incremental changes are more like interpretation and embellishment than variation or improvisation. Thus, even if organizations wanted to improvise, they would find it hard to do so, and probably unnecessary. Improvisation in one unit can also compound the problems faced by other units to which it is tightly coupled. Furthermore, bursts of improvisation can leave a firm with too many new products and processes to support (Miner *et al.* 1996, p. 26).

The intention of a jazz musician is to produce something that comes out *differently* than it did before, whereas organizations typically pride themselves on the opposite, namely, reliable performance that produces something that is standardized and comes out the same way it did before. It is hard to imagine the typical manager feeling "guilty" when he or she plays things worked out before. Yet most jazz musicians perform with the intention of "limiting the predictable use of formerly mastered vocabulary" (Berliner 1994, p. 268). Parenthetically, it is interesting to note that the faster the tempo at which a musician plays, the more likely he or she is to fall back on the predictable use of a formerly mastered vocabulary. It is difficult to be affected by one's own newly created notes when musical ideas have to be conceived and executed at $8\frac{1}{2}$ eighth notes per second (tempo of one quarter note $= 310$). At extremely fast tempos there is no choice but to use preplanned, repetitive material to keep the performance going. This suggests that there are upper limits to improvisation. If this is true then high-velocity organizations (Eisenhardt 1989) – which resemble jazz ensembles in many ways – become especially interesting as sites where the increasing tempo of activity may encourage, not improvisation, but a sudden reversion back to old ideas that have no competitive edge. A key issue in high-velocity organizations is just how much of a constraint velocity really is. Recall that in the case of jazz improvisation, creative processes continually struggle under the unrelenting demands of a steady beat. In jazz improvisation, deadlines are reckoned in seconds and minutes whereas high-velocity organizations deal with deadlines reckoned in hours and days. While it is true that pressure is pressure, it is also true that at some speeds memory plays an increasingly large role in the product produced. This suggests that high-velocity organizations may have more latitude for improvisation than do jazz ensembles, but only up to a point. High velocity organizations may be vulnerable in ways similar to those described by Starbuck and Milliken (1988) and Miller (1993). Success encourages simplification, more risk taking, less slack, and accelerated production, all of which shrink the time available for adaptive improvisation and force people back on older ideas and away from the very innovating that made them successful in the first place.

Even if organizations are capable of improvisation, it is not clear they need to do it. One of the realities in jazz performance is that the typical audience is none the wiser if a musician makes a mistake and buries it, plays a memorized solo, solves a tough problem, inserts a clever reference to a predecessor, or he is playing with a broken instrument and working around its limits. If composing in real time is difficult and risky, and if the customer is unable to appreciate risk taking anyway, then the only incentives to take those risks lie with one's own standards and with fellow musicians. Those incentives may be sufficient to hold sustained improvisation in place. However, most organizations may not reward originality under the assumption that customers don't either. If we add to these characteristics the fact that the musical consequences in a jazz performance are irreversible whereas managers try never to get into anything without a way out, and the fact that musicians love surprises but managers hate them, then we begin to see that improvisation may be absent from the organizational literature, not because we haven't looked for it, but because it isn't there.

My bet is that improvising is close to the root process in organizing and that organizing itself consists largely of the embellishment of small structures. Improvising may be a tacit, taken-for-granted quality in all organizing that we fail to see because we are distracted by more conspicuous artifacts such as structure, control, authority, planning, charters, and standard operating procedures. The process that animates these artifacts may well consist of ongoing efforts to rework and reenact them in relation to unanticipated ideas and conditions encountered in the moment. In organizing as in jazz, artifacts and fragments cohere because improvised storylines impose modest order among them in ways that accommodate to their peculiarities. Order through improvisation may benefit some organizations under some conditions and be a liability under other conditions. These contingencies need to be spelled out. But so too does the sense in which improvisation may be part of the infrastructure present in all organizing.

Conclusion

A final sense in which jazz improvisation mirrors life is captured in an entry from Norman Mailer's journal dated December 17, 1954 (source of this quotation is unknown).

> Jazz is easy to understand once one has the key, something which is constantly triumphing and failing. Particularly in modern jazz, one notices how Brubeck and Desmond, off entirely on their own with nothing but their nervous system to sustain them, wander through jungles of invention with society continually ambushing them. So the excitement comes not from victory but from the effort merely to keep musically alive. So, Brubeck, for example will to his horror discover that he has wandered into a musical cliché, and it is thrilling to see how he attempts to come out of it, how he takes the cliché, plays with it, investigates it, pulls it apart, attempts to put it together into something new and sometimes

succeeds, and sometimes fails, and can only go on, having left his record of defeat at that particular moment. That is why modern jazz despite its apparent lyricalness is truly cold, cold like important conversations or Henry James. It is cold and it is nervous and it is under tension, just as in a lunch between an editor and an author, each makes mistakes and successes, and when it is done one hardly knows what has happened and whether it has been for one's good or for one's bad, but an "experience," has taken place. It is also why I find classical music less exciting for that merely evokes the echo of a past "experience" – it is a part of society, one of the noblest parts, perhaps, but still not of the soul. Only the echo of the composer's soul remains. And besides it consists too entirely of triumphs rather than of life.

Life in organizations is filled with potential inventions that get ambushed when people slide into old clichés. Pulling oneself out is tense work. It can be cold work. Occasionally there is triumph. Usually, however, as people at Honda put it, "A 1 per cent success rate is supported by mistakes made 99 per cent of the time" (Nonaka and Takeuchi 1995, p. 232). Jazz improvisation, itself built of "moments of rare beauty intermixed with technical mistakes and aimless passages" (Gioia 1988, p. 66), teaches us that there is life beyond routines, formalization, and success. To see the beauty in failures of reach is to learn an important lesson that jazz improvisation can teach.[1]

Note

1   This essay expands on themes mentioned in my brief remarks in Vancouver on August 8, 1995 (e.g. "defining characteristics of improvisation," "examples of improvisation in non-musical settings") and it retains all specifics used to ground those themes (e.g. Pyle and Gioia on adroit *ad hoc* action, Mingus on melodies, Keeney on psychotherapy, and Mailer on society's proneness to ambush invention). These expansions are a perfect example of "reworking precomposed material in relation to unanticipated ideas" conceived *during* the writing itself, which is simply another way of saying, it is an exhibit of improvisation.

References

Allport, F. H. 1962. A structuronomic conception of behavior: Individual and collective. *Journal of Abnormal and Social Psychology*. 64 3–30.

Amabile, T. M. 1988. A model of creativity and innovation in organizations. *Research in Organizational Behavior*. 10 123–167. JAI, Greenwich, CT.

Barrett, Frank. 1998. Creativity and improvisation in jazz and organizations: Implications for organizational learning. *Organization Science*. 95 605–622.

Bastien, D. T., T. J. Hostager. 1992. Cooperation as communicative accomplishment: A symbolic interaction analysis of an improvised jazz concert. *Communication Studies*. 43 92–104.

Bateson, M. C. 1989. *Composing a Life*. Atlantic Monthly, New York.

Berliner, Paul F. 1994. *Thinking in Jazz: The Infinite Art of Improvisation*. Univ. of Chicago, Chicago, IL.

Buckley, W. 1968. Society as a complex adoptive system. W. Buckley, ed., *Modern Systems Research for the Behavioral Scientist*. Aldine, Chicago, IL. 490–513.

Bursztjahn, H., A. Feinbloom, R. Hamm, A. Brodsky. 1981. *Medical Choices, Medical Chances*. Dell, New York.

Chia, R. 1996. The problem of reflexivity in organizational research: Towards a postmodern science of organization. *Organization.* 3 31–59.

Cohen, M. D., P. Bacdayan. 1994. Organizational routines are stored as procedural memory: Evidence from a laboratory study. *Organization Science.* 5 554–568.

Crossan, M., M. Sorrenti. 1996. Making sense of improvisation. Unpublished manuscript. Univ. of Western Ontario.

Daft, R., K. Weick. 1984. Toward a model of organizations as interpretation systems. *Academy of Management Review.* 9 284–295.

Davis, F. 1986. *In the Moment.* Oxford, New York.

Dougherty, D. 1992. Interpretive barriers to successful product innovation in large firms. *Organization Science.* 3 179–202.

Eisenberg, E. 1990. Jamming! Transcendence through organizing. *Communication Research.* 17 2 139–164.

Eisenhardt, K. M. 1989. Making fast strategic decisions in high-velocity environments. *Academy of Management Journal.* 32 543–576.

Follett, M. P. 1924. *Creative Experience.* Longmans, Green, New York.

Gersick, C. J. G., J. R. Hackman. 1990. Habitual routines in task-performing groups. *Organizational Behavior and Human Decision Processes.* 47 65–97.

Gioia, T. 1988. *The Imperfect Art.* Oxford, New York.

Harper, D. 1987. *Working Knowledge.* Univ. of Chicago Press, Chicago, IL.

Herrington, B. S. 1989. Merging of music, psychiatry yields richly composed life. *Psychiatric News.* April 7. 16.

Isenberg, D. J. 1985. Some hows and whats of managerial thinking: Implications for future army leaders. J. G. Hunt and J. D. Blair, eds, *Leadership on the Future Battlefield.* Pergamon-Brassey's, Washington, DC. 168–181.

Janowitz, M. 1959. Changing patterns of organizational authority: The military establishment. *Administrative Science Quarterly.* 3 473–493.

Keeney, B. P. 1990. *Improvisational Therapy.* Guilford, New York.

Kernfeld, B. 1995. *What to Listen for in Jazz.* Yale Univ., New Haven, CT.

Levi-Strauss, C. 1966. *The Savage Mind.* Univ. of Chicago, Chicago, IL.

Maggin, D. L. 1996. *Stan Getz: A Life in Jazz.* Morrow, New York.

Mangham, I., A. Pye. 1991. *The Doing of Managing.* Blackwell, Oxford, UK.

Maruyama, M. 1963. The second cybernetics: Deviation-amplifying mutual causal processes. *American Scientist.* 51 164–179.

McDaniel, Reuben R., Jr. 1996. Strategic leadership: A view from quantum and chaos theories. W. J. Duncan, P. Ginter, L. Swayne, eds, *Handbook of Health Care Management.* Blackwell, Oxford, UK.

Miller, D. 1993. The architecture of simplicity. *Academy of Management Review.* 18 116–138.

Miner, A. J., C. Moorman, C. Bassoff. 1996. Organizational improvisation in new product development. Unpublished manuscript. University of Wisconsin, Madison, WI.

Mintzberg, H., A. McHugh. 1985. Strategy formation in an adhocracy. *Administrative Science Quarterly.* 30 160–197.

Neisser, U., E. Winograd, eds. 1988. *Remembering Reconsidered: Ecological and Traditional Approaches to the Study of Memory.* Cambridge University, Cambridge, UK.

Nemeth, C. J., B. M. Staw. 1989. The tradeoffs of social control and innovation in groups and organizations. L. Berkowitz, ed., *Advances in Experimental Social Psychology.* 22 175–210. Academic, San Diego, CA.

Nonaka, I., H. Takeuchi. 1995. *The Knowledge-creating Company.* Oxford, New York.

Perry, L. T. 1991. Strategic improvising: How to formulate and implement competitive strategies in concert. *Organizational Dynamics.* 19 4 51–64.

Ramos, R. 1978. The use of improvisation and modulation in natural talk: An alternative approach to conversational analysis. N. K. Denzin, ed., *Studies in Symbolic Interaction.* 1 319–337. JAI, Greenwich, CT.

Reed, M. 1991. Organizations and rationality: The odd couple. *Journal of Management Studies.* 28 559–567.

Ryle, G. 1979. Improvisation. G. Ryle, ed., *On Thinking.* Blackwell, London, UK. 121–130.

Schön, D. A. 1987. *Educating the Reflective Practitioner.* Jossey-Bass, San Francisco, CA.

Schuller, G. 1968. *Early Jazz.* Oxford, New York.

Simon, H. A. 1989. Making management decisions: The role of intuition and emotion. W. H. Agor, ed., *Intuition in Organizations.* Sage, Newbury Park, CA. 23–29.

Stacey, R. D. 1992. *Managing the Unknowable.* Jossey-Bass, San Francisco, CA.

Starbuck, W. H. 1993. "Watch where you step!" or Indiana Starbuck amid the perils of academe (Rated PG). A. G. Bedeion, ed., *Management Laureates.* 3 65–110. JAI, Greenwich, CT.

—— F. Milliken. 1998. Challenger: Fine tuning the odds until something breaks. *Journal of Management Studies.* 25 319–340.

Suhor, C. 1986. Jazz improvisation and language performance: parallel competitiveness. *ETC.* 43 4 133–140.

Sutcliffe, K. M., S. Sitkin. 1996. New perspectives on process management: Implications for 21st century organizations. C. Cooper, S. Jackson, eds, *Handbook of Organizational Behavior.* Wiley, New York.

Tyler, S. A., M. G. Tyler. 1990. Foreword. B. P. Keeney, ed., *Improvisational Therapy.* ix–xi. Guilford, New York.

Walsh, J. P., G. R. Ungson. 1991. Organizational memory. *Academy of Management Review.* 16 57–91.

Wegner, D. M. 1987. Transactive memory: A contemporary analysis of the group mind. B. Mullen, G. R. Goethals, eds, *Theories of Group Behavior.* 185–208. Springer-Verlag, New York.

Weick, K. E. 1969. *The Social Psychology of Organizing.* Addison-Wesley, Reading, MA.

—— 1979. *The Social Psychology of Organizing.* 2nd edn. Addison-Wesley, Reading, MA.

—— 1989. Organized improvisation: 20 years of organizing. *Communication Studies.* 40 241–248.

—— 1993. Organizational redesign as improvisation. G. P. Huber, W. H. Glick, eds, *Organization Change and Redesign.* Oxford, New York, 346–379.

—— 1995. Creativity and the aesthetics of imperfection. C. M. Ford, D. A. Gioia, eds, *Creative Action in Organizations.* 187–192. Sage, Thousand Oaks, CA.

Weiss, C. H. 1980. Knowledge creep and decision accretion. *Knowledge: Creation, Diffusion, Utilization.* 1 381–404.

Whitehead, A. N. 1929. *Process and Reality.* Macmillan, New York.

Wilson, R. C. 1992. Jazz: A metaphor for high-performance teams. J. A. Heim, D. Compton, eds, *Manufacturing Systems.* 238–244. National Academy Press, Washington, D.C.

Wruck, K. H., M. C. Jensen. 1994. Science, specific knowledge, and total quality management. *Journal of Accounting and Economics.* 18 247–287.

5 Exploring the empty spaces of organizing

How improvisational jazz helps redescribe organizational structure

Mary Jo Hatch[1]

Introduction

As businesses become more adaptable and flexible in response to shifting demands and opportunities in their globalizing markets, traditional understandings of organizational structure are breaking down. At first, this breakdown was described in terms of the organization chart; relationships were too multidimensional to be represented by drawing them in a two-dimensional frame, or they changed so frequently that making a chart seemed pointless. When old structural notions collapsed further, this change was communicated with terms such as outsourcing, de-layering, de-differentiation and re-engineering. Now, concepts such as networks and virtual organizations are challenging traditional notions of organization itself. However, like a collapsing star that forms a black hole, the collapsing notion of organizational structure does not disappear. Its absence is felt as an empty space that attracts. For instance, some organization members speak of a frustrating and perpetual lack of communication and coordination and a commensurate loss of control and identity; they may even become nostalgic and personify their emptiness as the 'absent leader'. Others experience empty space as freedom to create something new.

When a concept such as organizational structure no longer suits our descriptive or analytical purposes (e.g. because it is too static to help us understand organizations described by terms such as 'adaptable', 'flexible' and 'virtual'), it is generally acceptable to replace it with another, better formulated concept. The trouble is, for the time being anyway, nothing better has come along. In fact, work by Rorty (1989) suggests the wisdom of admitting that the search for a final set of concepts is endless. Instead, Rorty advocates redescription, a constant recycling of old concepts using new (even contradictory) language for the sake of replacing a worn out vocabulary with a new one. In Rorty's (1989) words:

> The method is to redescribe lots and lots of things in new ways, until you have created a pattern of linguistic behavior which will tempt the rising generation to adopt it, thereby causing them to look for appropriate new forms of nonlinguistic behaviour, for example, the adoption of new scientific equipment or new social institutions.

Rorty (1989: 9) further explains that the method does not involve arguing against old vocabularies, but rather trying 'to make the vocabulary that I favor look attractive by showing how it may be used to describe a variety of topics'. Although Rorty focuses on what redescription implies for the emergence of a new kind of human being (the liberal ironist), I will merely borrow his method in order to recycle the concept of organizational structure so as to fit it within the emerging vocabulary indicated in the opening paragraph. To do this, I will use metaphor, which Rorty (following Hesse 1980 and Davidson 1984) offers as a vehicle of redescription.

It is important to acknowledge that I am by no means the first person to attempt to reconceptualize organizational structure (nor am I likely to be the last). The most influential of these attempts to date has been made by Anthony Giddens and his followers who proposed and developed structuration theory (e.g. Giddens 1979, 1984; Ranson *et al.* 1980; Pettigrew 1987; Reed 1997). However, their work stays firmly rooted in the 'old' vocabulary of modernist sociology and organization theory, while I shall attempt to position organizational structure within an emerging vocabulary sometimes linked to postmodern theory (e.g. Cooper and Burrell 1988; Gergen 1992; Hassard 1996a). While there are points of connection that might be established between structuration theory and the metaphoric approach I adopt, I leave these comparisons for future consideration (which I will touch upon in the conclusion).

Following Rorty, I will use a metaphorical approach. Morgan (1986) suggested that metaphor engages and involves a broader experience base than do other approaches to theorizing, in that metaphor works with the total imagination of the theorist. That is, metaphor does not simply operate within the analytical range of imagination (where Giddens and his followers focus), but calls on emotional and aesthetic capacities as well. Rorty (1989: 17) explains how metaphor contributes to an emerging vocabulary:

> we need to see the distinction between the literal and the metaphorical in the way Davidson sees it: not as a distinction between two sorts of meaning, nor as a distinction between two sorts of interpretation, but as a distinction between familiar and unfamiliar uses of noises and marks [i.e. words]. The literal uses of noises and marks are the uses we can handle by our old theories ... Their metaphorical use is the sort which makes us get busy developing a new theory.

In this essay, I use the case of jazz music, or more explicitly, improvisational jazz performance, as a perhaps unlikely, but nonetheless valuable, metaphor for the purpose of redescribing organizational structure. This metaphor is unlikely in that jazz is more often noted for its lack of structure, but it is precisely this paradox that suggests the jazz metaphor as a valuable tool of redescription. That is, it is the uneasy relationship between structure, jazz, and the musicians who perform it that makes this metaphor both so unfamiliar and so promising in the context of the emerging vocabulary that redescription serves. I say this because contradiction, paradox and suspicion of structures (as totalizing agents) are all part of postmodern organization theory which regularly contributes to the emerging vocabulary of organization studies (e.g. Reed and Hughes 1992; Hassard and Parker 1993; Boje *et al.* 1996; Burrell 1997).

As my use of metaphor fits Rorty's notion of redescription rather than description, please bear in mind that I am not trying to suggest that jazz and organization are equivalent. My thesis is that orienting ourselves to organizational structure along the lines of the way jazz musicians orient to their structures in performing jazz could help us to generate a redescription of organizational structure that is compatible with the emerging vocabulary of organization studies. Thus my use of the jazz metaphor to redescribe organizational structure is performative; it calls upon engagement, or rather re-engagement, with organizational practices and processes, as will be explained below. Furthermore, because my approach is pragmatic/ hermeneutic rather than analytic, it will have to be demonstrated rather than explained. Thus, in this essay, I will invoke my understanding of a jazz-like appreciation of structure and then transfer this appreciation, via metaphoric redescription, to the concept of organizational structure. In doing this, I shall attempt to make the redescription 'look attractive' by showing how it relates to a variety of topics including ambiguity, emotion and time, all of which are part of the emerging vocabulary of organization studies and to each of which, I claim, the jazz metaphor makes an imaginative contribution.

All that jazz

There are many aspects of jazz. In this section, I will describe only those that have stood out in my mind as being directly related to structure either in jazz theory or in the context of the history of jazz performance. The material on jazz presented below is derived from a combination of three sources. First, I am married to a jazz musician (drummer and songwriter), and much of my understanding of jazz was formulated as I listened to and watched jazz being performed, and talked to jazz musicians before and after my husband's rehearsals and gigs. Second, and as a direct effect of the first, I have had the privilege of tutelage by Danish jazz master Per Goldschmidt whose lifelong exposure to organizational sociology (his father and stepfather were both sociologists) rendered his font of knowledge about jazz more easily accessible to me. Third, the rich development of the improvisation metaphor in organization studies (e.g. Bastien and Hostager 1988, 1992; Weick 1989, 1993, 1998; Eisenberg 1990; Crossan and Sorrenti 1997; Hatch 1997; Barrett 1998), as well as the extensive jazz literature (especially Berliner 1994), provided support and further inspiration to the points I will make below.

I recognize that many readers will have limited knowledge of jazz, so jazz needs to be described in enough detail to permit redescribing organizational structure using the terms of jazz. Those readers who have performed as jazz musicians may find my descriptions unnecessarily long-winded, and at the same time incomplete. I acknowledge that attempts to describe what is largely tacit knowledge are unsatisfactory when compared with lived experience. Nonetheless, I believe I have gained much insight and understanding from this metaphor without the benefit of actually playing jazz. As most readers will probably be in a similar position, my descriptions are meant to share my understanding and the potential of this metaphor with them. If you do play jazz, you can develop this metaphor on your own: my comments here are merely offered to inspire you to do so.

Structure in jazz

The structure of jazz provides the material idea upon which jazz musicians improvise. Improvisation, in turn, constitutes the distinguishing feature of jazz. To put this another way, jazz is distinguished from other genres of music (e.g. classical, rock) in the improvisational use it makes of structure. As I will tell it below, jazz musicians use structure in creative ways that enable them to alter the structural foundations of their playing. My development of the jazz metaphor will bring out this paradoxical quality of jazz along with a few other points that I will then relate to the emerging vocabulary of organization studies. In order to accomplish this, we need to begin with some basics.

Heads, tunes and improvisation

Jazz performances are structured around the playing of tunes which themselves are loosely structured via partial musical arrangements called heads. The head of a tune defines, at a minimum, a chord sequence, a basic melodic idea, and usually an approximate tempo. Jazz musicians can play a head in any key, using a variety of rhythms and altered harmonies that the musicians introduce during the performance of the tune. Improvisation centres around the head, which is usually played through 'straight' (without much improvisational embellishment) at the beginning of the tune, then improvised upon, and finally returned to and played again as the ending. The head gets a tune started by suggesting a particular rhythm, harmony and melody. The tune is then built from this starting point via improvisation within which different interpretations of the initial idea are offered and new ideas and further interpretations can be explored.

Although the head is normally only played explicitly at the beginning and end of a tune, the structure contained in the head is implicitly maintained throughout. To understand how this works, hum the melody of the head to yourself over and over throughout a tune and you will instantly recognize its presence as the musicians improvise in its absence. In fact, jazz musicians often keep the head in their heads (i.e. in their audile imagination) as they play, and use it, not only as an improvisational focal point, but to keep track of where they are in the song temporally, harmonically and melodically.

Soloing, comping and fours

Soloing provides a mechanism for a given musician to take the lead in introducing new ideas that carry the tune along after the head has been played. This role is passed around among the players (sometimes the order of soloing is agreed upon in advance, sometimes it is worked out as the musicians play). While one musician solos, others may accompany them (a practice known as comping), providing rhythmic or harmonic support to the soloist's improvisation, and occasionally offering (or feeding) the soloist ideas which may or may not be incorporated into the solo.

Soloists encourage the exchange of ideas by leaving space in their playing for other musicians to make suggestions, for instance they may leave gaps between their melodic phrases, or play their chords ambiguously by leaving out certain notes that would distinguish one chord from one or two others. Of course, they do not explicitly think, 'Okay, now I will leave a space for someone else to fill'. Space-making and filling are more spontaneous than this. Jazz musicians listen to the playing of the other musicians and, in listening, spaces are created and filled by a logic that emerges as part of the interaction of the musicians. This simultaneous listening and playing produces the characteristic give and take of live jazz improvisation and also provides the conditions for conflict that can introduce the unexpected that inspires performance excellence, but also risks disaster.

The swapping back and forth of roles between soloists and those comping can perhaps best be seen in a practice known variously as trading, taking, or swapping fours (or as just plain fours), sometimes indicated on stage by one of the musicians holding up four fingers. In fours, jazz musicians take turns playing four bar solos in rapid succession (usually the drummer takes four bars between each of the other musicians) creating an intense exchange of musical ideas and sound.

Listening and responding

Listening plays a major role in improvisational jazz. It is so important because the openness of jazz structure (e.g. subtlety, implicitness and ambiguity) means that the predictability of others' playing is at a minimum, and the chances for conflict (e.g. undesired disharmonies, rhythmic disagreements) are extremely high. However, rather than constraining or even thwarting good performance, these conflicts can challenge the musicians to make sense out of unexpected sound patterns. Accomplished jazz musicians know that mistakes are defined by their context, so, if someone plays a 'wrong' note, changing the context can save the situation and, in the best cases, produces a novel idea. Incorporating the unexpected is essential to great jazz improvisation. Of course, as jazz musicians become experienced, their capacity to anticipate the moves of others grows along with their ability to respond to unexpected moves. Thwarting the anticipatory expectations of those they play with becomes an important mechanism for keeping the jazz 'alive'.

Ideally, each musician listens to all the other players all the time they are performing a tune. Nevertheless, many musicians freely admit that they reach this ideal only once in a while, primarily when they achieve peak moments of jazz performance. At other times, the musicians will concentrate on listening to one or two of the other players intensely, often shifting their focus from one player to another as the tune develops. Thus, in any tune, the likelihood is that at least somebody is listening and responding to each player who is contributing. Of course, the best listening and responding involves noticing how others are listening and responding to you. All other factors held constant, the greater the interpenetration of listening and responding, the better the music sounds, and it is this auditory interpenetration that, in part, structures the performance of a tune.

Groove and feel

If a band is to achieve peak performance on a given tune, the musicians must find the groove. A jazz performance is said to be 'in the groove' when the jazz is played well and thus is very satisfying. Groove helps the musicians play together and know where notes and accents belong – it allows them to feel the structure of the tune inside themselves, which is what is required for them to depart from predictable patterns. For instance, rhythmically, groove involves 'locking in' which means the musicians (especially the drummer and bass player) agree where the beat is. Once the groove is found, the drummer or bass player can play ahead of, or behind, the beat to create tension by either pushing the tune forward or holding it back, ever so slightly. Without a strong sense of the groove, the practice of playing ahead or behind the beat would lead to rushing or dragging, but with groove, this practice heightens the emotional content of the performance and helps give the music a distinctive feel (which, in this case, is due to the relative placement of notes).

Jazz musicians use feel, not only in conjunction with rhythm, but also in relation to the harmonic and melodic structures of jazz. For instance, pitch, timbre, and melody can create tension and release independently or in combination with playing ahead or behind the beat. Furthermore, context (e.g. how the musicians and their audience relate to each other and the situation they are in at the time a tune is performed) contribute to making the feel of a tune different every time it is played. Together, groove and feel contribute mightily to the emotional and aesthetic appeal of the playing and encourage the audience to share in the music by feeling what the musicians feel. When groove and feel are fully embodied (creating music that literally and physically moves the listener), a sense of communion occurs among those present (present both physically, and in the sense of being aware of what is going on, i.e. listening).

Parallels between jazz and the emerging vocabulary of organization studies

Table 5.1 summarizes the basic points about jazz introduced thus far and offers some parallels with the emerging vocabulary of organization studies. For instance, developing the capacity to switch between the roles of leading and supporting is a skill associated with successful teamwork and collaboration. The jazz metaphor suggests listening for soloing, comping and trading fours in everyday team interactions, and perhaps assessing the extent to which those roles are adequately fulfilled and to whether switches between them are being smoothly performed (e.g. Are solos interesting? Are those providing the comping contributing to the soloist's ideas or are they interfering with the soloist's ability to express him or herself? Do players know when to take a solo? Do they know when and how to end one?). These issues can be further elaborated by thinking about listening and responding. Are interactions between organizational members openings for new ideas and opportunities for accommodating them? These questions are closely associated with sense-making in organizations (Weick 1995) and might be usefully related to organizational talk (e.g. Boden 1994) and the strategy process (e.g. Mintzberg *et al.* 1976; Pettigrew and

Table 5.1 Parallels between jazz and the emerging vocabulary of organization studies.

Jazz	Descriptions	Emerging vocabulary
Soloing	Taking the lead	Teamwork
Comping	Supporting others' leads	Collaboration
Trading fours	Switching between leading and supporting	
Listening	Opening space for others' ideas	Sense-making
Responding	Responding to and accommodating others' ideas	Strategy process
Groove and feel	Emotional tension and release	Organizational
	Resonance of embodied sound	culture and identity
	Communion among players and audience members	

Whipp 1991). Likewise, groove and feel align with organizational culture and identity in their similar emphases on emotional and aesthetic aspects of organizational life (e.g. Alvesson 1990; Gagliardi 1990, 1996; Hatch 1993; Schultz 1992; Hatch and Schultz 1997).

Although simple analogies to current interests in organization studies place the jazz metaphor in a parallel relationship to the emerging vocabulary of organization studies, we want much more insight and involvement from a metaphoric approach than this set of new terms standing alone can offer. To be of value, the jazz metaphor must make an original contribution to our understanding. In Rorty's terms, it must substantially revise our current vocabulary *and* the descriptions they uphold. Can the jazz metaphor accomplish this? I believe it can, or that *we* can, via the use of the jazz metaphor, as I will attempt to show below.

However, before we leave the simple analogy level, notice that the process of redescription has already begun. For instance, look at column 1 of the table and notice the emphasis on sensory and sensual engagement that permeates the jazz metaphor. Listening is obviously connected to hearing, but the musicality of all aspects of the metaphor goes much further, inviting us to *hear and feel* organizing, to listen for and move to its rhythms, harmonies and melodies. This is in contrast to previous approaches to organizational structure that are generally not sensual but rather analytical, orienting our minds to aspects of organizing but generally not engaging our bodies or their sensory capacities. The jazz metaphor encourages us to think about organizational structure with our ears and to engage our bodies and emotions in the process. This sensory and emotional engagement relates to another important feature of jazz – it is *played*.

Jazz happens. It is an activity, not just an abstract category. As an activity, jazz is something to be entered into, participated in, experienced. Via the jazz metaphor, organization can also be imagined as an activity to be entered into, participated in and experienced, and the jazz metaphor encourages us to do so. When engaged in this way, imagining organizational structure extends us well into the arena of activity. Here we find another similarity to organization studies – jazz is focused on performance. However, the jazz metaphor turns traditional organizational interpretations of performance in new directions by suggesting that organizational structure should be redescribed in performative terms (i.e. structure not as a state or outcome, but as a set of performance practices or processes). To develop the performative aspects of the jazz metaphor let us move on to the matter of how musicians use their structures when they play jazz.

How jazz musicians use their structures: the empty spaces of jazz

If we wanted to be more jazz-like in our appreciations of organizational structure, where would we begin? I believe the key to metaphoric redescription using jazz as the vehicle lies in appropriating the ways in which jazz musicians orient themselves toward and use their structures. Notice that I have moved beyond the usual question 'what structure should/do we use' and focused instead on the question 'how should/do we use our structure?'. This is an important linguistic move, because it takes structure out of the domain of states of being and repositions it as a part of the process of becoming. This reorientation invites activity and constitutes engagement or, to use more performative terms, it activates and engages.

In the most general terms, instead of trying to find ways to express their structures explicitly, jazz musicians constantly make structure implicit and discover what they are able to express – it is a structure that supports, but does not specify. For example, as we saw above, finding the groove permits jazz musicians to internalize a tune's rhythmic, harmonic and melodic structure, which frees them from playing it explicitly. Not playing the head, while improvising on it, is another example of the implicitness of structure in jazz.

You should understand that jazz musicians do not need or even want to play their structures explicitly. For example, jazz musicians avoid playing 'one' (especially the first downbeat of the first measure of a section of music), even though, if they did not know where one was, they would be lost and would find it impossible to play together (this is one common condition for a 'crash' or 'trainwreck' where the musicians so interfere with one another that they cannot go on playing the tune, or, even if they are able to cover up and go on playing, the tune is considered a disaster according to every criterion of acceptable jazz performance).

Likewise, jazz musicians do not accept their structures as given. They believe that the appropriate attitude to structure is one of finding out what you can get away with. Thus, jazz musicians interpret their structures as loosely as possible, maximizing ambiguity and the potential for interpretive multiplicity. Much of the looseness attributed to jazz is imparted by this orientation toward structure. The erroneous impression that jazz is simply 'made up as you go along' is the result of the freedom granted by implicit structures (i.e. structure that is not played explicitly but is nonetheless present in the minds, emotions and bodies of the players). The freedom imparted by not having to play structural features means that the musician can play around them, and this encourages creativity (Eisenberg 1990). That is, *not* playing structures creates space to improvise and this produces the framebreaking attitude that creativity theorists argue provokes the creative imagination (e.g. Adams 1990). It also inspires innovation and change. In jazz terms, however, notice how framebreaking means using the frame to step outside the frame.

To see this more clearly, *we* need to step out of the frame of playing a jazz tune and take a broader perspective on how jazz has changed over the course of its history. As Per Goldschmidt explained it to me, jazz was born along with Ragtime music in the late 1800s, and from there it moved to New Orleans style, Swing and Be-Bop, to Modern and Free jazz. If you study the history of these jazz styles, you will notice a sequence in which the structure of a previous period is repeatedly brought into question, where jazz musicians, in trying to say something new, move away from increasingly familiar structures of past and current styles, until something recognizably different emerges.

Take the case of rhythm. Rhythmically, traditional European music is played on the 1st and 3rd beats of a four count measure, while Ragtime music emphasizes the 2nd and 4th beats of the measure. As the emphasis moves from 1 and 3, to 2 and 4 you get the Ragtime, jazzy feel. As jazz developed further down this path, musicians started playing rhythms in between all four beats, shifting the rhythm from a quarter to an eighth note (i.e. triplet) feel, and later still to a 16th note feel, first giving us Dixieland and Swing styles, and then Be-Bop and Modern jazz. A similar thing happened harmonically. In each stylistic phase of development, jazz musicians played outside familiar harmonic structures until they moved so far outside that some other structure had to be inferred. Critics and other commentators on the jazz scene interpreted these rhythmic and harmonic shifts as recognizable new styles, which they labelled New Orleans, Swing, Be-Bop and Modern, until, with Free jazz, structure became so subtle as to be practically undetectable to any but the most sophisticated listener, including many traditional jazz musicians. In fact, some see Free jazz as an attempt to play without any structure at all, though even the most free jazz needs a little structure to permit the musicians to orient themselves to each other within the tune.

To put this historical view in processual terms, as each use of structure is challenged by playing outside or between the anticipated notes, harmonies and beats of an existing form, new forms of jazz are created which redefine expectations and thus present new opportunities (new empty spaces) for thwarting them. Thus, the practices of jazz (e.g. soloing, comping, trading fours, listening and responding, finding the groove, playing the head, improvising) fill the empty spaces in the structure of jazz as it is currently constituted, and as this happens, the structure of jazz itself is transformed. Put another way, the improvisational practices of jazz constitute the conditions of its own structural transformation, even as the structures of jazz provide the starting point for improvisation. In this way, playing what is not explicated by one structure permits the creation of another, not unrelated to the first, but rather displaying both continuity and discontinuity with it. In other words, structure used in improvisational ways provokes innovation that radically alters ideas about what structure 'is' in both a material and ontological sense.

Jazz musicians do not simply use structure to organize themselves, they play their structures implicitly by explicitly *not* playing them and in doing so *play with* their structures in the dual senses of interacting with structure and altering it via improvisation. By putting structure on a performative basis (playing along with it interactively), jazz musicians are able to alter their structures radically in the historical sense of creating a discontinuity with the past, but they do this only by building on the continuity of the past that is expressed as the structure they do not play. The continuity in their heads (the structure of the tune) inspires the discontinuity on their lips and in their fingers (improvisation) as they go about transforming jazz as an idiom of musical expression.

To summarize, structure is not sacred to the jazz musician, it serves its own alteration. Thus, it is not static, it is dynamic, and, in this sense, structure has a complex relationship to time: it is simultaneously continuous and discontinuous with the past. Furthermore, as jazz musicians use it, structure is subtle, implicit and largely unheard except in silent accompaniment to what is played out loud; it exists more as an absence than as a presence. In addition, for the jazz musician, structure is interpretively open and often ambiguous, which means that, on any particular occasion, a tune can be taken in multiple directions; the directions in which it will be taken are only decided in the moment of playing and will be redetermined each time that tune is played. Finally, structure has emotional qualities that allow musicians and their audiences to communicate outside intellectual consciousness, such as via groove and feel. Thus, a jazz-like view is one in which structure has ambiguity, emotionality and temporality, qualities that are as likely to be found in the absences of structure (i.e. its empty places) as in its presence. All of these themes can be identified in the emerging vocabulary of organization studies which has, oddly enough, 'discovered' them through an almost jazz-like process of playing in the empty spaces of organization theory, as will be pointed out below.

The empty spaces of organizing: redescribing organizational structures in tune with the jazz metaphor

What if we were to view organizational structure as ambiguous, emotional and temporal (or temporary)? Recently, explorations in and of organizations have started separately down each of these paths. While there are certainly differences between these lines of research, I will now relate each, via the jazz metaphor, to the concept of organizational structure as I would recommend it be redescribed. I do this to engage the redescription of organizational structure offered by the jazz metaphor with the emerging vocabulary of organization studies and to further demonstrate their mutual resonance. This section of the paper addresses the questions: What might a jazz-like orientation towards organizational structures sound like? How might we engage with our organizational structures as jazz musicians engage with theirs?

The ambiguity of structure

As was explained above, the empty places of the structure of a tune produce ambiguity. This openness (or lack of closure) in structure permits any of the musicians to take the tune in a variety of directions, which, if played well, contribute innovation to the history of jazz and create momentary pleasure for both audience members and performers. In this jazz-based view, structuring occurs in what is not specified in the sense that the unspecified is an ambiguity that can be creatively interpreted to produce innovation. In jazz, ambiguity explains nothing, it is a part of the structure of tunes and its function lies in licensing jazz musicians to perform creatively. Although ambiguity in tune structures can be interpreted in ways that bring the musicians into conflict with each other, this conflict is not seen as detrimental to performance, but rather as inviting reinterpretation of the context within which meaning is made.

In organization theory, ambiguity was first conceptualized in relation to organizational decision making and choice. March and Olsen's (1976) theory of organizational ambiguity specified four forms of ambiguity: the ambiguity of intention (e.g. ill-defined preferences or multiple and conflicting goals), the ambiguity of understanding (e.g. multiple interpretations of intentions and feedback), the ambiguity of history (e.g. difficulty understanding what happened and why), and the ambiguity of organization (e.g. due to frequent reorganizations). Thus, March and Olsen conceptualized ambiguity in relation to the empty spaces left by goal incongruence, disagreement on methods or explanations, and by organizational change. However, whereas March and Olsen theorized ambiguity as part of the explanation for the limits of rationality in organizational choice processes, the jazz metaphor encourages us to reinterpret these empty spaces as opportunities to improvise.

Interestingly, in his discussion of ambiguity and choice in organizations, March (1976: 76–78) described play, not in the musical sense, but rather as a 'strategy for suspending rational imperatives toward consistency' which serve the purpose of helping organizations to discover new goals. For March (1976: 77), 'playfulness allows experimentation'. He went on to explain:

A strict insistence on purpose, consistency, and rationality limits our ability to find new purposes. Play relaxes that insistence to allow us to act 'unintelligently' or 'irrationally', or 'foolishly' to explore alternative ideas of possible purposes and alternative concepts of behavioral consistency.

When March's ideas about play are linked to the performativity of the jazz metaphor, two ideas are suggested. First, March clarifies at least one contribution the jazz metaphor can make to our redescribed notion of organizational structure – in its playfulness, the jazz-inspired version of structure offers a route to creativity in defining new organizational purposes and goals. The jazz metaphor in turn offers imagination for how to explore alternative purposes along the lines of jazz improvisation, that is, by subjecting ideas to soloing, comping, trading fours, listening and responding. Furthermore, via its emphasis on sensory and bodily engagement, the jazz metaphor suggests how improvisation in organizational decision making can happen other than in a purely intellectual (e.g. rational) way. Good decision making with respect to creatively defining new goals and purposes, like good jazz performance, will require groove and feel.

March's ideas about the links between playfulness and the definition of new goals for organizations introduces the issue of the strategic use of ambiguity. Eisenberg (1984) addressed this issue, describing the benefits of strategic ambiguity in terms of what he called unified diversity. Eisenberg (1984: 230) claimed that people in organizations do not always promote correspondence between their intentions and the interpretations given to their messages. At times, they purposefully omit contextual cues to allow for multiple interpretations by others. In his view, organizational structures are at least partly defined in terms of tensions (e.g. between centralization and decentralization) and ambiguity helps construct and maintain these tensions by allowing 'for multiple interpretations while at the same time promoting a sense of unity'. The task for leaders, in Eisenberg's view, is to find 'a level of abstraction at which agreement can occur', where ambiguity 'foster[s] agreement on abstractions without limiting specific interpretations' (1984: 231). Imai *et al.* (1988) give several examples of the strategic use of ambiguity in the management of new product development teams in Japanese companies, such as the case of Honda's development of the City car. In this case, Imai *et al.* (1988: 528) report, top managers only instructed the team of young designers 'to create a radically different concept of what a car should be like', and to develop 'the kind of car that [you], the young, would like to drive'.

Eisenberg's analysis of strategic ambiguity in organizations is similar to the case of jazz musicians who each make their own distinctive contributions based on their interpretations and ideas, while at the same time making enough reference to structure to permit their efforts to form the unity that is a tune. However, my view of ambiguity in structure is not as strategic as is Eisenberg's; it focuses on how ambiguity achieves both unity and diversity by emphasizing the possibilities inherent in an ambiguous structure and the dual role of that structure to: (1) support multiple and diverse contributions and (2) provide enough unity to support the interpretation of the varied contributions of several players as a single tune, or, in the case of organizations, to support the interpretation of the contributions of various organizational members as a single performance. This view is supported by Meyerson's (1991) study of ambiguity in hospital social work.

Meyerson (1991) related ideas about ambiguity to organizational culture in her study of the experiences of hospital social workers who described their normal worklife as highly ambiguous. Meyerson observed that, in her sample, social workers shared a common orientation and overarching purpose, faced similar problems and had comparable experiences, yet this shared culture accommodated different beliefs and incommensurable technologies, implied different solutions to common problems, and supported multiple and sometimes conflicting meanings. She concluded that the effective performance of hospital social work depends upon the acceptance and use of ambiguity, which she claimed could be supported or not by the organizational cultures to which social workers belonged, with support leading to lower levels of psychological burnout.

Feldman (1991) offered case-based illustrations of March and Olsen's (1976) theory of organizational ambiguity. In particular, Feldman's illustrations of the ambiguity of intention and understanding in the U.S. Department of Energy presented the dark side of using ambiguity strategically for the purpose of maintaining unified diversity, as Eisenberg advocates. For instance, in showing how ambiguous goals and multiple interpretations conspired against effective action and undermined organizational self-esteem, Feldman suggested the cultural limits of strategic manoeuvring via ambiguous expression, limits that are overlooked by Eisenberg's more prescriptive approach. Thus, along with Meyerson's study, Feldman's work points to the importance of considering cultural context in studies of the ambiguity of organizational structures and practices.

Organizational ambiguity in the broad sense of support for multiple goals and interpretations permits the maintenance of vital organizational tensions such as between centralization and decentralization. Application of the jazz metaphor suggests how the ambiguity of organizational structure accommodates and may even nurture these tensions. Jazz musicians recognize ambiguities as empty spaces into which they can insert their ideas and have influence on the way a tune is being played at any given moment. Ambiguity allows musicians to play the same tunes, but simultaneously to personalize and make new every tune they play, each time they play it. Ambiguity in organizational structures, viewed in this way, works similarly by allowing organizational members to replay organizational values and competencies in personalized ways that offer the opportunity for creativity and innovation within a cultural context that provides coherence. However, remember the caveats offered by Meyerson and especially by Feldman: the interpretation given to the strategic use of ambiguity may be an important consideration; ambiguity read as an opening to improvise (e.g. the Honda City Car case, the supportive social work culture) may be very different relative to ambiguity interpreted as a leader's refusal to take a solo when it comes his or her way (e.g. Feldman's Department of Energy examples). Using ambiguity effectively requires an engaged ability to listen and respond, as the jazz metaphor makes plain.

The emotionality of structure

Perhaps the biggest empty space in our prior conceptualizations of organizing has been emotion. Although organizational structures are based in human relationships, manners and other organizational actors have often tried to remove emotion from these relationships, suggesting that emotions are inappropriate to the workplace because they interfere with rational decision making. Hopfl and Linstead (1997: 5) trace the avoidance and devaluation of emotions in organizational discourse to Weber's suggestion that elimination of the irrational and emotional is one of the chief contributions of bureaucracy to capitalism. Although Weber himself merely reported that this aspect of bureaucracy was interpreted as a virtue (he never said by whom), his writings on bureaucracy have been interpreted by rationalist organization theorists and managers as a pillar of support for anti-emotionalism. However, a growing number of organizational scholars and researchers believe that we have been too unsympathetic (*sic*) in our understanding of the emotional aspects of organizational relationships (e.g. Hochschild 1983; Rafaeli and Sutton 1989; Albrow 1992; Fineman 1993; Ashforth and Humphrey 1995). These researchers make many points about the value and role of emotions, for example in learning and change processes, and for purposes of developing organizational citizenship, commitment and involvement.

Few studies of emotion in organizations have examined structural questions, though Hochschild's (1983) highly influential work in this field described emotional labour in terms of 'feeling rules'. The study of jazz undertaken above, however, suggests a different aspect of structure as emotion. This aspect involves thinking of organizational structure in terms, not of rules, but of communication. If emotion can be communicated, and there is much social-psychological evidence that it can be, then emotion may contribute structurally to organizations by organizing relationships. Put a little differently, the feelings organization members have orient them to one another in particular ways, and these orientations are part of what constitutes an organization's structure as patterns of interaction and relationship.

Positioning structure within the emotional realm recognizes frequently ignored communication channels that offer an important complement to rational means of structuring organizational relationships. For instance, the importance of emotional structuring in organizations becomes clear in the context of de-layering. As influence and persuasion replace authority as avenues for getting things done in de-layered organizations, relationships shift away from their former dependence on rationality towards emotional bases such as liking and interpersonal attraction. However, the importance of the emotional aspects of structure is perhaps even more significant at the level of interactions than at the level of relationships. This would be particularly true for organizations that depend upon the constant reconfiguration of project teams or that indulge in temporary alliances, networks or other highly flexible, new organizational forms.

The jazz metaphor suggests that whenever we interact, communication rests as heavily upon emotional and physical feeling as it does on the intellectual content of the messages involved. I came to view structure in emotional terms when I tried to imagine the organizational equivalent of groove and feel in music. Groove and feel in jazz terms involve making structural aspects of performance (e.g. tempo and rhythm) implicit, which jazz musicians accomplish by rendering them subjects of their emotions and physical bodies (i.e. by literally feeling tempo and rhythm in an emotional and physical sense). Just as jazz musicians assign tempo and rhythm to the emotional realm and communicate on this basis to one another as they improvise (even when they have never played together before), workers may equally depend upon their ability to emotionally communicate as they coordinate their efforts for organizational achievement in the context of temporary teams or fluid networks. In this regard, Eisenberg (1990: 145–146) made the important point that emotional communication does not necessarily depend upon self-disclosure, but rather is an intimacy based in shared action. That is, we are as capable of using our emotions to form working relationships as we are of using them to form friendship or familial relationships, and this capacity can extend to those with whom we have no relationship at all apart from the opportunity to act together at a particular moment in time.

The link to action brings us once again to the theme of the performative aspects of jazz. According to Csikszentmihalyi (1990), peak performance in many fields of endeavour, including athletics and music, is accompanied by a subjective state of flow in which performers experience absorption into the moment, lose their sense of self and situation, and achieve effortless performance. Csikszentmihalyi's descriptions of flow remind me of jazz musicians' discussions of rhythm and harmony, and of groove and feel, not just as material features of jazz music, but as something jazz musicians internalize and embody in the context of performing a tune. Rhythm, harmony, groove and feel have emotional and aesthetic dimensions, and when these aspects of work processes are engaged we may likewise find the experience of flow that Csikszentmihalyi claims constitutes peak performance.

The jazz metaphor further suggests that flow can be communicated between those who are working closely together. As rhythm, harmony, groove and feel create a communion between musicians, audiences and musical experience, so flow permits an emotional form of communication to occur between co-workers (this could be part of what Gersick, 1994, referred to by her concept of 'entrainment', though she did not explicitly discuss entrainment in terms of emotion or flow). In other words, appreciating the groove and feel of work processes may harmonize bodies in a communal rhythm of work that contributes to peak collaborative performance.

If work processes have rhythm, harmony, groove and feel, then the jazz metaphor suggests developing emotional and bodily sensitivity to work. One place to look for evidence of the effectiveness of such a strategy might be the outdoor development programmes in which many organizations have invested considerable time and money (Dainty and Lucas 1992). Such programmes (e.g. the corporate development unit of Outward Bound) claim to make organizational members more aware of the physical and emotional dimensions of the work that they perform in their organizations. The contributions of such programmes can be perhaps better understood using concepts such as rhythm, harmony, groove and feel that are connected by the jazz metaphor to concerns for entrainment and flow. That is, team members who are in touch with their bodies and emotions may be better able to develop rhythm, harmony, groove and feel in their work processes which will enhance communication and the collaborative potential of their teamwork.

The temporality of structure

Time is another empty space in our organizational theorizing recently exposed by a small group of organizational researchers and made a part of the emerging vocabulary of organization studies. According to these researchers (e.g. Jaques 1982; Dubinskas 1988; Gherardi and Strati 1988; Hassard 1991, 1996b), the issue of time in organizations is many-sided and can be related to phenomena ranging from scheduling, cyclical events and developmental cycles, to organizational histories, scenarios for contemplating the future, and corporate vision. Most of these researchers describe two aspects of time that I find to be particularly relevant to my rendition of the jazz metaphor for organizational structure: tempo, and the relationship between past, present and future.

Tempo

In his introduction to a compilation of four ethnographies focused on the uses and meanings of time in high technology companies, Dubinskas drew on Bourdieu (1977) to explain the issue of tempo in relation to the strategic manipulation of time. Dubinskas (1988: 14) wrote:

> the setting of tempo, the stretching of boundaries, the rushing and relaxing of schedules, and the celebration of passages. This artful manipulation of time is part of the practical and intentional reconstruction of orderliness. The ability or power to exercise this art skilfully, in a recognizably patterned but not rigidly rule-bound way, is a key to the process of building effective social relations.

Bourdieu (1977: 7) offered several examples of manipulating tempo in strategically organizing action, including:

> holding back or putting off, maintaining suspense or expectation, or on the other hand, hurrying, hustling, surprising, and stealing a march, not to mention the art of ostentatiously giving time ('devoting one's time to someone') or withholding it ('no time to spare').

The strategic manipulation of time in the sense of setting and monitoring the pace of work is often claimed as the rightful (if much contested) domain of management (e.g. Taylorism, Fordism). Nevertheless, as Gersick found in her studies of group projects (1988, 1989) and a venture capital backed start-up firm (1994), there is a pattern to the pacing of work in project teams. Gersick reported that the groups she studied worked slowly up to a critical point about mid-way through their 'life', after which, the pace increased in response to a growing sense of urgency to complete by an explicit deadline. Thus, in her study, Gersick made sense of time in relation to targets and deadlines that were externally imposed upon the groups that she observed.

The jazz metaphor provides an alternative interpretation of Gersick's half-life phenomenon. It suggests that different work processes, like different jazz tunes, may have an inherent tempo and, when played at this tempo, they 'feel right'. Instead of the tempo changing at the midpoint of a project, as Gersick claimed, perhaps the intensity of involvement, like the crescendo that builds up towards the end of a well-performed jazz tune, alters the internal perception of time, such that one is left with an impression of a faster pace.

The difference in interpretation is also important because, if tempo is a feature of structure in organizing, as it is in music, then changing tempo can lead to great difficulties of coordination. A strong leader, of course, like an orchestra conductor, can direct a group to alter its tempo to great effect. However, if a group is using tempo to organize itself, like a jazz band does, then respecting the tempo of a work process may be critical to achieving high performance levels because it is used to coordinate activities in the absence of a fixed leadership role. Perhaps it is even because they are tuned-in to tempo that groups such as jazz bands are able to change roles as needed for attaining peak levels of performance. In such cases, rather than a leader-driven performance, the tempo itself carries performance along.

Years of talk about diminishing product lead times have left the impression with many managers that processes can be 'played' at any tempo, and that faster is better. This reinforces images of project leaders as drivers of performance along the lines of the orchestral model. On the other hand, if what is required is intensity of involvement rather than actual speed, then the image of driving is wrong. Unlike urgency, which comes from external pressures, intensity comes from within, so influence over it will likewise need to be located there. This suggests that, in the improvisation mode at least, team members (including whoever is taking the lead at a particular moment) need to be driven rather than driving. Their fully engaged listening and responding will help to bring the group's performance together, the intrinsic satisfactions of which will give the greatest chance of achieving peak performance levels.

This discussion indicates one of the limits of the jazz metaphor. Although some work processes may be better regarded as requiring interplay and intensity disciplined by a steady beat or tempo, others may fit the orchestral model of a strong leader directing the tempo. To use the jazz metaphor to the full effect requires distinguishing between situations demanding creativity or flexibility and those in which well-accepted work processes simply have to be completed faster. When creativity or flexibility are required, using analogies to jazz performance in respect to building intensity can be a useful way to achieve transition out of the traditional mindset of directive leadership focused on communicating urgency and increasing pace.

In the context of performing a jazz tune, musicians build intensity from the structure of their playing. They generally begin with a round of open solos in which players work out some of their ideas in relation to the head and to what other soloists and those comping have introduced up to that point in the tune. The initial round of solos may be followed by multiple rounds of fours. Here the intensity usually increases due to the rapid succession of solos and to the more intertwined listening and responding called forth from the musicians. As anticipation builds in relation to how well the players are interacting with one another's ideas, the intensity grows until it spills into and forms the final part of the tune – the ending. Endings involve all the musicians playing at once, now hopefully completely engaged in listening and responding, but also drawing on the ideas they laid down at earlier points in the tune. Intensity peaks as all of these ideas are layered together making a final collaborative statement that finds it conclusion by once again playing the head, but this time the head is played with all that has just happened still hanging in immediate memory leaving, in a well-played tune at least, a sense of completion.

Notice two things in this notion of layering to achieve an ending. First, layering is the linguistic equivalent of everyone talking at once, except that, in jazz, this simultaneity is synchronized by the structure developed via improvising around a previous structure. The organizational equivalent would be everyone doing their job at once such that ideas and skills come together in an intense moment of interactivity which has the potential to inform and inspire each participant in a different, albeit synchronized, way. Here space becomes a consideration in that one wonders whether synchronicity can be achieved when performers are separated by physical distances. In addition to a view of time as a point at which performance can come together (i.e. the ending), a second aspect of time suggests how the present can extend over, reach into, or otherwise connect the past and future. This idea can be seen above in the ambiguous status of the head played as either a beginning or as an ending of a tune. In this regard, notice particularly how endings set up expectations of again playing this (or another) tune by concluding with a beginning.

Past, present and future

As described above, the playing of heads in jazz gives both a starting point, and a place to return to, making it possible to create an ending that acknowledges the beginning. Gherardi and Strati (1988: 159) frame a similar aspect of organizational time as 'the activity of the organizational actors themselves, who see key events as being bounded by a beginning and an end'. Those structured points of beginning and ending provide reference to where we have been in the historical past, but also serve as leaping off points that carry us into the future when the present performance will be part of history. Thus, for jazz musicians, the playing of a tune is the connecting point between past, present and future just as a tune's head is the connecting point between its beginning and ending.

In performance, in the strict present of playing jazz, the past has not simply passed. It is re-played, and thus re-established in the present by the musicians and audience members. For example, those tunes that are played most frequently, comprise a collective memory that jazz musicians hold in common, known as jazz standards (e.g. Billie Holiday's 'God Bless the Child', Duke Ellington's 'Take the A Train', Thelonius Monk's 'Round Midnight', A.C. Jobim's 'The Girl From Ipanema', Miles Davis' 'All Blues', Chick Corea's 'Spain'). Playing the head of a jazz standard is likely to evoke memories that link past and present for both musicians and their audiences. Citation, in which jazz musicians play famous solos, phrases or styles associated with other (often more famous) musicians, likewise links the past with the present. Playing heads and citing are practices that allow musicians to incorporate the ideas of those who have had an influence on jazz, but who are not present on stage. These ideas and memories enrich the present moment and imbue it with the emotionally attractive forces of recognition and continuity with the past. Notice, however, how different memories of a particular tune are brought together in the instant of playing it *this time*. The specific memories invoked are shaped by the possibilities presented by these musicians and this audience in the present moment.

As the past is invoked with the playing of a head, so too is anticipation of the improvising to come, thus the future is invited into the present via expectation created by recollection of similar experiences in the past. These expectations and recollections of musicians and audience members fill the venue of performance with a commingling of time past and time future, memory and anticipation. Thus, time past and time future merge in their influence on time present, which is occasioned by the performance of tunes in a celebration of what Ricoeur (1984: 9, citing Augustine) referred to as the threefold present (i.e. the present of the past, the present of the present, and the present of the future). In this way, associations to a tune are spread out in past time and brought forward in their connection with 'the present of the present', to borrow Ricoeur's phrase. Furthermore, anticipating this can draw future time into the present moment, where it can raise expectations and magnify intensity.

In a temporally sensitive view of organizational structure, the dialectic of past, present and future is similarly compelling. As organizations perform, their memories (institutionalized in the artifacts, norms and customs of organizational culture) are invoked by cultural practices such as storytelling, joking, or other forms of symbol manipulation in much the same way that memories pervade the jazz musician's playing of a tune when past performances are invoked through the playing of heads or the use of citation. Likewise, memories of the organization's past colour present attentions and thereby shape the future via their capacity to stimulate expectations and anticipations that further influence attention, thereby creating a commingling of past and future in the threefold present.

To return again to the theme of performance, if past experience is construed as supporting an expectation of peak performance, the chances of peak performance are enhanced. Invoking past occasions when such achievement was realized reminds us of this potential, and thereby serves a motivational or inspirational role. If expectations are negative, of course, a depressing effect will occur. Either way, emotionally charged memories are likely to set up expectations. Such connections are often interpreted in rather simplistic terms, suggesting to many managers an image of leadership as cheerleading. The jazz metaphor suggests recognizing how the memories and expectations of organizational actors intersect at any given moment to structure the emotional and temporal dimensions of work and organizing in such a way as to influence action. If one wants to have an effect on organizational outcomes, the jazz metaphor suggests that one must enter the process, which means direct engagement in the threefold present of performing. Only through personal engagement can the hermeneutic of memory, attention and expectation be activated, and even then, influence will likely only be in proportion to the degree of emotional/aesthetic involvement of those engaged in the process. Notice how disengaged leadership does not prevent the process from taking place, it only locates the process within a set of actors who are emotionally and aesthetically disconnected from those who hope to influence them.

Summary

To summarize, structure is temporal in the sense that it has tempo and takes place over time, but also in the sense that it constitutes temporal experiences in the commingling of past, present and future in the threefold present. Via recollection, structure evokes emotional connections with the past which, in anticipation, can cast emotional anchors into the future raising both expectations for and the intensity of the present moment. However, the meanings and experiences invited by the temporality and emotionality of structure are perpetually ambiguous, riddled with the empty spaces that continuously present new opportunities for structural change via engagement in the play of performance. Thus, we find but one of myriad ways to redescribe structure as simultaneously ambiguous, emotional and temporal using the jazz metaphor.

Conclusion

My reason for exploring the jazz metaphor in this essay was to investigate the potential for redescription that Rorty (1989) claimed on behalf of the metaphoric approach. My reason for choosing the jazz metaphor was partly its unfamiliarity within the discourse of structure (which Rorty claimed is essential for redescription), and partly its richness, which I associated with a variety of aspects of organizing appearing within the emerging discourse of organization studies (especially ambiguity, emotionality and temporality). In developing the redescription, I followed Rorty's advice not to try to argue against the old vocabulary, but rather to engage with a new one. However, now it is time to break the silence between redescription and 'the old vocabulary' because some readers will want to know what the benefit of the metaphoric approach is relative to other recent reconceptualizations of organizational structure, especially those provided by Giddens and his followers.

First let me reiterate that the claimed benefit of metaphoric redescription is that it facilitates escaping the clutches of worn out vocabularies. Other approaches to reconceptualizing organizational structure, by remaining entrenched in old metaphors such as those of the machine, the organism and the system, do not offer an equal possibility to construct a new vocabulary in Rorty's terms. By the same token, I mean nothing sacred by the jazz metaphor. It worked to help me reconceptualize organizational structure in terms compatible with the emerging vocabulary of organization studies, and so I offer it to you on that basis. It is the redescription process that matters, however, not the metaphor *per se*. In fact, if the jazz metaphor works well, it too will need replacement, because in time it will become literal rather than metaphoric, as Davidson (1984) explained, and will lose its power to inform and inspire.

Some may want to argue that all that I have said about organizational structure can be said (or even has been said) by those less ambitious of breaking free from old vocabularies. I suspect that those who say this are appropriating what I have offered back into an old vocabulary. To be as precise as I can be, I do not find in earlier reconceptualizations of organization structure the emotional and aesthetic dimensions of structure emphasized by the jazz metaphor. One could say that these dimensions are present in all conceptualizations in a latent form, but my response is that the metaphoric approach taps that latency.

It is my view that there are boundaries of experience that the less figurative language of literal (minded) science cannot easily cross. The metaphoric approach penetrates these boundaries. Thus, my claim for the contribution of this essay is that the metaphoric nature of the method employed contributes something unique. In the specific case of the jazz metaphor, it contributes imagination for the redescribed concept in that it helps us to hear, feel and engage with, rather than simply think about, our organizational structures. I claim that this element of appreciation is lacking in previous attempts to reconceptualize organizational structure and that, therefore, the metaphoric approach contributes distinctive value (though the jazz metaphor does not necessarily contribute greater value than that which other metaphors bring). What I am arguing is that we need to go beyond reconceptualization – or perhaps to go before it – to redescribe organizational structure as a means to connect with a new vocabulary for organizational theorizing that embraces emotional and aesthetic appreciation as well as analytical rigour.

Following jazz practice, let me now return to my starting point and re-state the observation that organizational structure itself has become an absence in our discourse. The move I made in recovering the concept via metaphoric redescription is a continuation of the move that led to its abandonment in the first place, that is, the move of making and filling empty spaces. This paper is not intended to put an end to this process of making and filling empty spaces, but rather to celebrate it for the sake of engaging in the ever emerging discourse of organization studies. Thus, this paper has not been about doing something never done before, but about doing something worth doing again. It is about weaving past and future together to find expressions of identity and being that are not mere repetitions of the past, but which continuously reinvent the present in relation to both past and future. Redescription is an important part of this unending process, and the development of the jazz metaphor in this essay is my contribution to this enterprise.

The jazz metaphor, like any other metaphoric approach, has limitations. In developing and applying a metaphor, it is easy to become so caught up in similarities between vehicle and target that differences are ignored. There are certain aspects of organizational structure that are ignored by the jazz metaphor. The most obvious of these, pointed out earlier, is that many aspects of organizing are routine and do not require improvising. Here, perhaps another metaphor (e.g. orchestral conducting) would be more useful. The analysis provided in this paper suggests that the jazz metaphor is likely to be most valuable in situations demanding creativity and flexibility, where improvisation is a benefit to performance.

Please be aware that I do not offer the jazz metaphor as a new root metaphor for the field of organization studies. It is, in Rorty's terms, but a "passing theory", a tool for keeping thought moving in a way that only temporarily suits our purposes and imaginations. I believe it is but one among a variety of metaphoric opportunities. What is important is what we *do* with our metaphors, as Rorty (1989) and Davidson (1984), among others, have explained. In this case, I used the jazz metaphor to bring out temporal, emotional and ambiguous aspects of organizational structure as a concept to guide both thinking and organizing. Nevertheless, other metaphors in other times and places could have equal or greater value.

In the end, my development of the jazz metaphor is more a demonstration of Rorty's (1989) redescription than an offer of a new metaphor for organization studies, but what is more, the paper engages the practices it describes. In it, there have been solos and there has been comping, a give and take between the ideas I was trying to express and ideas taken from the emerging vocabulary of organization studies. Furthermore, this tune has been played before, and this rendition contains references to the responses of earlier audiences (reviewers' suggestions, and comments by those who have come to talks I have given on the jazz metaphor) in the form of my responses to their responses which are embedded in this text. Successive readings can continue this process to exhaustion. But each time the paper is read, if I achieve my ambition to have you listen and respond, there will be the chance of developing a groove and feel that permits us to communicate beyond the normal intellectual channels by engaging emotional and aesthetic dimensions of our being. This, for me, is where the value of this metaphoric redescription is to be found.

Note

1 I would like to thank Peter Case, Silvia Gherardi, David Wilson and the anonymous *Organization Studies* reviewers who offered insight and made valuable contributions to this paper. Special thanks go to Per Goldschmidt and Doug Conner for their patient development of my understanding and appreciation of jazz and for the inspiration I find in their music.

References

Adams, James L. 1990 *Conceptual blockbusting: A guide to better ideas*, 3rd Ed. Reading, MA: Addison Wesley.

Albrow, Martin 1992 'Sine ire et studio' – or: 'Do organizations have feelings?'. *Organization Studies* 13/3: 313–330.

Alvesson, Matts 1990 'Organization: From substance to image'. *Organization Studies* 11/3: 373–394.

Ashforth, Blake, and Ronald Humphrey 1995 'Emotion in the workplace: A reappraisal'. *Human Relations* 48/2: 97–126.

Barrett, Frank 'Creativity and improvisation in jazz and organizations: Implications for organizational learning'. *Organization Science* 9/5: 605–622.

Bastien, David T., and Todd J. Hostager 1988 'Jazz as a process of organizational innovation'. *Communication Research* 15: 582–602.

Bastien, David T., and Todd J. Hostager 1992 'Cooperation as communicative accomplishment: A symbolic interaction analysis of an improvised jazz concert'. *Communication Studies* 43 (summer): 92–104.

Berliner, Paul F. 1994 *Thinking in jazz: The infinite art of improvisation*. Chicago: University of Chicago Press.

Boden, Deirdre 1994 *The business of talk: Organizations in action*. Cambridge: Polity Press.

Boje, David M., Robert P. Gephart, Jr., and Tojo Joseph Thatchenkery, editors 1996 *Postmodern management and organization theory*. Thousand Oaks, CA: Sage.

Bourdieu, Pierre 1977 *Outline of a theory of practice*. Cambridge: Cambridge University Press.

Burrell, Gibson 1997 *Pandemonium: Towards a retro-organization theory*. London: Sage.

Cooper, Robert, and Gibson Burrell 1988 'Modernism, postmodernism, and organizational analysis: An introduction'. *Organization Studies* 9/1: 91–112.

Crossan, Mary, and Marc Sorrenti 1997 'Making sense of improvisation'. *Advances in Strategic Management* 14: 155–180.

Csikszentmihalyi, Mihaly 1990 *Flow: The psychology of optimal experience*. New York: Harper and Row.

Dainty, Paul, and Donna Lucas 1992 'Clarifying the confusion: A practical framework for evaluating outdoor development programmes for managers'. *Management Education and Development* 22/2: 106–122.

Davidson, Donald 1984 'What metaphors mean' in *Inquiries into truth and interpretation*. D. Davidson, 245–264. Oxford: Oxford University Press.

Dubinskas, Frank A., editor 1988 *Making time: Ethnographies of high-technology organizations*. Philadelphia: Temple University Press.

Eisenberg, Eric M. 1984 'Ambiguity as strategy in organizational communication'. *Communication Monographs* 51: 237–242.

Eisenberg, Eric M. 1990 'Jamming: Transcendence through organizing'. *Communication Research* 17/2: 139–164.

Feldman, Martha 1991 'The meanings of ambiguity: Learning from stories and metaphors' in *Reframing organizational culture*. P.J. Frost *et al.* (eds), 145–156. Newbury Park, CA: Sage.

Fineman, Stephen, editor 1993 *Emotion in organizations*. London: Sage.

Gagliardi, Pasquale 1990 'Artifacts and pathways and remains of organizational life' in *Symbols and artifacts: Views of the corporate landscape*. Pasquale Gagliardi (ed.), 3–38. New York: Aldine de Gruyter.

Gagliardi, Pasquale 1996 'Exploring the aesthetic side of organizational life' in *Handbook of organization studies*. S.R. Clegg, C. Hardy and W.R. Nord (eds), 565–580. London: Sage.

Gergen, Kenneth 1992 'Organisation theory in the post-modern era' in *Rethinking organisations: New directions in organisation theory and analysis*. M. Reed and M. Hughes (eds), 209–226. London: Sage.

Gersick, Connie 1988 'Time and transition in work teams: Toward a new model of group development'. *Academy of Management Journal* 31: 9–41.

Gersick, Connie 1989 'Marking time: Predictable transitions in task groups'. *Academy of Management Journal* 32: 274–309.

Gersick, Connie 1994 'Pacing strategic change: The case of a new venture'. *Academy of Management Journal* 37: 9–45.

Gherardi, Silvia, and Antonio Strati 1988 'The temporal dimension in organizational studies'. *Organization Studies* 9/2: 149–164.

Giddens, Anthony 1979 *Central problems in social theory: Action, structure and contradictions in social analysis*. London: Macmillan.

Giddens, Anthony 1984 *The constitution of society: Outline of the theory of structuration*. Berkeley: University of California Press.

Hassard, John 1991 'Aspects of time in organization'. *Human Relations* 44/2: 105–125.

Hassard, John 1996a 'Exploring the terrain of modernism and postmodernism in organization theory' in *Postmodern management and organization theory*. D.M. Boje, R.P. Gephardt and T.J. Thatchenkery (eds), 45–59. Thousand Oaks, CA: Sage.

Hassard, John 1996b 'Images of time in work and organization' in *Handbook of organization studies*. S.R. Clegg, C. Hardy and W.R. Nord (eds), 581–598. London: Sage.

Hassard, John, and Martin Parker 1993 *Postmodernism and organizations*. London: Sage.

Hatch, Mary Jo 1993 'The dynamics of organizational culture'. *Academy of Management Review* 18/4: 657–693.

Hatch, Mary Jo 1997 'Jazzing up the theory of organizational improvisation'. *Advances in Strategic Management* 14: 181–191.

Hatch, Mary Jo, and Majken Schultz 1997 'Relations between organizational culture, identity and image'. *European Journal of Marketing* 31: 356–365.

Hesse, Mary 1980 'The explanatory function of metaphor' in *Revolutions and reconstructions in the philosophy of science*. Mary Hesse. Bloomington, IN: Indiana University Press.

Hochschild, Arlie Russell 1983 *The managed heart*. Berkeley, CA: University of California Press.

Hopfl, Heather, and Stephen Linstead 1997 'Learning to feel and feeling to learn: emotion and learning in organizations'. *Management Learning* 28: 5–12.

Imai, Ken-Ichi, Ikujiro Nonaka, and Hirotaka Takeuchi 1988 'Managing the new product development process: How Japanese companies learn and unlearn' in *Readings in the management of innovation*, 2nd Edn. M.L. Tushman and W.L. Moore (eds), 337–381. Cambridge, MA: Ballinger.

Jaques, Elliott 1982 *The form of time*. New York: Crane Russak.

March, James G. 1976 'The technology of foolishness' in *Ambiguity and choice in organizations*. J.G. March and J.P. Olsen (eds), 69–81. Bergen, Norway: Universitetsforlaget.

March, James G., and Johan P. Olsen 1976 'Organizational choice under ambiguity' in *Ambiguity and choice in organizations*. J.G. March and J.P. Olsen (eds), 10–23. Bergen, Norway: Universitetsforlaget.

Meyerson, Debra 1991 'Normal' ambiguity?' in *Reframing organizational culture*. P.J. Frost *et al.* (eds), 131–144. Newbury Park, CA: Sage.

Mintzberg, Henry, Duru Raisinghani, and Andre Theoret 1976 'The structure of unstructured decision processes'. *Administrative Science Quarterly* 21: 246–275.

Morgan, Gareth 1986 *Images of organization*. Newbury Park: Sage.

Pettigrew, Andrew M. 1987 'Context and action in the transformation of the firm'. *Journal of Management Studies* 24: 649–670.

Pettigrew, Andrew M., and Richard Whipp 1991 *Managing change for competitive success*. Oxford: Basil Blackwell.

Rafaeli, Anat, and Robert Sutton 1989 'The expression of emotion in organizational life' in *Research in organizational behavior*, Vol. 11. L.L. Cummings and B.M. Staw (eds), 1–42. Greenwich, CT: JAI Press.

Ranson, Stewart, Bob Hinings, and Royston Greenwood 1980 'The structuring of organizational structures'. *Administrative Science Quarterly* 25: 1–17.

Reed, Michael I. 1997 'In praise of duality and dualism: Rethinking agency and structure in organizational analysis'. *Organization Studies* 18/1: 21–42.

Reed, Michael I., and Michael Hughes, editors 1992 *Rethinking organisations: New directions in organisation theory and analysis*. London: Sage.

Ricoeur, Paul 1984 *Time and narrative*, Vol. 1. Chicago: University of Chicago Press.

Rorty, Richard 1989 *Contingency, irony and solidarity*. New York: Cambridge University Press.

Schultz, Majken 1992 'Postmodern pictures of organizational culture'. *International Studies of Management and Organization* (Summer): 15–35.

Weick, Karl E. 1989 'Organized improvisation: 20 years of organizing'. *Communication Studies* 40: 241–248.

Weick, Karl E. 1993 'Organizational redesign as improvisation' in *Organizational change and redesign: Ideas and insights for improving performance*. G.P. Huber and W.H. Glick (eds). 346–379. New York: Oxford University Press.

Weick, Karl E. 1995 *Sensemaking in organizations*. Newbury Park: Sage.

Weick, Karl E. 1998 'Improvisation as a mindset for organizational analysis'. *Organization Science* 9/5: 540–555.

6 Organizational improvisation

What, when, how and why

Miguel Pina e Cunha, João Vieira da Cunha
and Ken N. Kamoche

Realized organizational strategies and actions, be they a new product development, a major corporate restructuring or entering a new market do not solely depend on the organization's deliberate options and explicit or even implicit intentions. Complexity and chaos theory have shown that, in addition to the unpredictability of the environment (Emery and Trist 1965), organizational actions can have unintended – and unexpected – consequences (Stacey 1996).

In spite of the ineffectiveness of traditional control mechanisms on this emergent share of organizational action, it can have a strong impact on its performance outcomes (Mintzberg and McHugh 1985; Mintzberg and Waters 1982). Therefore, organizations cannot let it go untamed, at the risk of having but little control over the impact of their decisions. Organizational improvisation has been emerging as a possible answer to this challenge by allowing companies to subdue, at least partially, the emergent part of their actions, and even environmental fortuities, to their own will. In this vein, a growing number of organizational researchers are starting to take improvisation seriously and a number of texts on this topic have already been published. None the less, as we will argue later, these texts are still to agree on a sound definition of this concept – let alone any robust findings on its occurrence in organizational settings (Weick 1998).

This chapter is an attempt to fill this gap by drawing on the existing body of literature addressing organizational improvisation in order to present a formal definition of its construct and a comprehensive review of its antecedents, influencing factors and outcomes. To accomplish this goal, we will first outline what has been the recent history of research on organizational improvisation and then address the issues of what this construct means, when it happens, how it is performed and why organizations should do it, while considering the challenges this concept raises for researchers and practitioners alike.

The (short) history of organizational improvisation

A striking characteristic of the literature on organizational improvisation is its low degree of cumulativity, making it difficult to compartmentalize its development, although it has already undergone several stages. In an attempt to tackle this challenge, we divided authors on this topic into two generations, and its conceptual evolution into three stages (see Table 6.1).

First-generation authors ground their study of improvisation in research of this phenomenon in the arts, especially in jazz music, due to improvisation's centrality

Table 6.1 Two generations and three stages of theory development in organizational improvisation.

Theory stage/ author's generation	Main characteristics	Articles
First/first	*Grounds*: Activities where improvisation is standard practice (jazz, improvisational theater). *Goal*: Use these instances as metaphors to present a systematic list of characteristics and facilitators of improvisation that can be transposed to organizational settings.	Barrett (1998); Bastien and Hostager (1988); Eisenberg (1990); Hatch (1999); Kamoche and Cunha (1997, 1998); Meyer (1998); Mirvis (1998); Pasmore (1998); Peplowski (1998); Weick (1993a, 1999)
Second/ second	*Grounds*: Empirical and anecdotal examples of improvisation in organizational settings. *Goals*: Formal definition and characteristics of improvisation in organizational settings.	Crossan *et al.* (1996); Crossan (1997, 1998); Crossan and Sorrenti (1997); Orlikowski (1996); Orlikowski and Hoffman (1997); Moorman and Miner (1995, 1998a, b); Miner *et al.* (1996); Perry (1991); Weick (1993b, s.d.)
Third/first	*Grounds*: Improvisation in jazz. *Goals*: Question current theory on organizational improvisation and fine-tune a formal definition and characteristics of this phenomenon.	Hatch (1997); Hatch (1998); Weick (1998)

in it. Second-generation authors draw on anecdotal and empirical evidence from the business arena to study this phenomenon directly, although occasionally recurring to jazz as a metaphor, although in a much lighter fashion than their first-generation counterparts.

The first stage of theory development in organizational improvisation was, in essence, an attempt, by first-generation authors, to transpose to organizational contexts the characteristics of improvisation and *bricolage* in jazz and improvisational theater, where this phenomenon is the norm. The contributions of this first stage of research on improvisation were, apart from fueling interest in the topic, the translating of jazz performance elements into the organizational arena, and several lists of competencies that organizations should possess to be able to improvise effectively. None of these works, however, systematically discussed the limitations of jazz and improvisational theater as a metaphor for organizational improvisation.

The second stage of development of organizational improvisation departs from the former by taking improvisation away from the arts and into the field. Using anecdotal and empirical evidence (e.g. Crossan and Sorrenti 1997; Moorman and Miner 1995; 1998a,b), emerging second generation authors develop formal definitions of organizational improvisation, show its relevance in current competitive environments and develop and test, mostly by means of grounded theory, propositions that aim at surfacing triggers and elements of this phenomenon in organizational settings. As a consequence, second-stage articles allow improvisation to emerge as a 'proper' research topic and try to build the foundations needed to allow research of a more positivist fashion on it. Additionally, an unidimensional definition of improvisation emerges from these articles, focusing on the temporal distance between conception and execution that seems to be shared by all major authors. However, these still fail to address the limitations of jazz as a metaphor for the occurrence of this phenomenon in organizational settings. Empirical studies are limited to a somewhat small number of triggers and consequences of improvisation, which is still much of an organizational 'black box', allowing for a widening of the ratio between issues for further research and implications for the practice of management.

The third stage of development of the study of improvisation in organizational contexts witnesses a comeback from first-generation authors, which surfaces some critical issues underlying second-stage articles, drawing again heavily on jazz to question some of the outcomes of those articles, especially in what concerns the definition of organizational improvisation, that held a temporal perspective of this phenomenon. These authors deem this definition as too limited to be productive as far as further research goes and to encompass the alleged broadness of this construct (Weick 1998). They fail, however, to provide a new one, limiting themselves to quote from jazz theory (e.g. Weick 1998) or to embellishing second stage definitions (Hatch 1997). Contrary to what has happened in other areas of social research (e.g. Gardner and Rogoff 1990; Leinhardt and Greeno 1986; Machin and Carrithers 1996), organizational scientists, until now, seem to have waived the option of defining and studying improvisation in a way that suits their individual research targets, subjects and methods. Thus, Weick's will of 'not pushing jazz as much as [. . .] pushing improvisation' remains, even in later generations' (Hatch and Weick 1998, 604) texts, a noble yet unfulfilled intention.

What does organizational improvisation mean?

A formal definition

As this short 'history' of organizational improvisation clearly shows, formal definitions of this construct are produced by one of two methods: either 'cutting and pasting' from jazz theory (e.g. Barrett 1998; Bastien and Hostager 1988, 1993a, s.d., 1998a,b; Eisenberg 1990; Erickson 1982; Pasmore 1998; Weick 1999) or by cutting, at the author's convenience, the construct as it has been defined (again) by researchers in jazz improvisation (e.g. Crossan and Sorrenti 1997; Miner *et al.* 1996; Moorman and Miner 1995, 1998a,b), only to deliver 'compressed themes [of improvisation adopted] in the interest of economy' (Weick 1998, 544).

None the less, if we approach this body of literature free of any strings attached to improvisation in jazz, it is possible to find several common threads in it that allow for the building of a sounder definition of organizational improvisation. In doing this, we will split this construct into its two components: the words 'organizational' and 'improvisation'.

Improvisation is *organizational* because it is carried out by an organization and/or its members, in a fashion close to that adopted by Miner *et al.* when stating that 'actions are organizational if they are taken by one or more individuals on behalf of a team, an organization and/or a project' (1996, 5). Therefore, our usage of term 'organizational' departs from prior definitions of this concept that equated 'organizational' with 'collective', which strike us as an oversimplification (e.g. Moorman and Miner 1998b).

Drawing on both the definitions put forth by the various authors on this topic (see Table 6.2) and the critiques issued by third-stage texts, *improvisation* can be defined as the conception of action as it unfolds, drawing on available material, cognitive, affective and social resources.

Organizational improvisation can thus be defined as *the conception of action as it unfolds, by an organization and/or its members, drawing on available material, cognitive, affective and social resources.*

Improvisation and bricolage

This definition integrates the criticisms put forth by third-stage articles and the dominant organizational improvisation literature by explicitly acknowledging the inseparability of the convergence between conception and execution (the first part of the definition) – improvisation, as it is currently defined (e.g. Crossan and Sorrenti 1997; Moorman and Miner 1998a,b) – and the ability to build solutions from *available* (vis-à-vis *optimal*) resources, i.e. *bricolage* (last part of the definition) – the point made by later texts on this phenomenon.

In this manner we propose that the separate treatment that the concepts of improvisation and *bricolage* seem to be receiving from the literature is only apparent. If we look beyond the paragraphs where these authors explicitly state their definition of organizational improvisation, and where *bricolage* is labeled as a construct close to but different from improvisation and transferred to the background of research imperatives, we can see that some authors, from which Weick (e.g. 1993a,b, 1999, s.d.) clearly stands out, use these concepts interchangeably, as synonyms. Moreover, even earlier generation authors on organizational improvisation implicitly acknowledge the linking between these concepts. Eisenberg's definition of improvisation as 'making do with minimal commonalities and *elaborating simple structures in complex ways*' (1990, 154; our emphasis) together with Weick's 'to make something *from whatever materials are currently available*' (s.d.: 21; our emphasis) are only two of the best examples. Improvisation is also present in definitions of organizational *bricolage* (see Table 6.3). Weick's definition of *bricolage* as 'us[ing] whatever resources and repertoire one has *to perform the task one faces*' (1993a, 352; our emphasis) is a good example.

The relationship between improvisation and *bricolage* is made explicit in third stage articles. Hatch (1997), for example, added *bricolage* to Crossan and Sorrenti's temporal definition of improvisation, by rephrasing it from 'intuition guiding action in a spontaneous way' (Crossan and Sorrenti 1997, 156) to 'intuition guiding action *upon something* in a spontaneous *but historically contextualized* way (Hatch 1997, 181; emphasis in the original), and Weick argued that both Crossan and Sorrenti's (1997) and Moorman and Miner's (1998a,b) definitions of improvisation – the two major formal attempts to define this phenomenon in organizational settings – are 'subthemes in improvisation' (1998, 544) and 'compressed themes [adopted] in the interest of economy' (1998, 544). This author goes on to present a definition quoted from Berliner (1994), which includes both the temporal and the '*bricolage*' dimensions of improvisation, bringing back the latter to the foreground of research in this area. Drawing on Weick's comments and recognizing the limits of her definition of improvisation, Crossan states that 'it may be necessary to further unpack the intuitive dimension to ensure that we do not lose sight of the *discipline, practice and*

Table 6.2 Definitions of improvisation across the literature.

Author	Definition	Area
A. Organizational perspectives on improvisation		
A1. Explicitly addressing improvisation		
Barrett (1998)	'fabricating and inventing novel responses without a prescripted plan and without certainty of outcomes; discovering the future that [action] creates as it unfolds' (p. 605)	Management
Bastien and Hostager (1988)	'the invention, adoption and implementation of new [...] ideas by [individuals] within the context of a shared awareness of the group performance as it unfolds over time.' (p. 583)	Organizational innovation
Berkiner (1998)	'becoming acting managers' (p. 583)	Management
Crossan (1997)	'spontaneity of action [with a high] level of intuition.' (p. 39)	General management
Crossan (1998)	'Action [...] taken in a spontaneous and intuitive fashion' (p. 593)	General management
Crossan and Sorrenti (1997)	'intuition guiding action in a spontaneous way' (p. 156)	Organizational learning
Crossan *et al.* (1996)	'mak[ing] decisions and adapt[ing] to changing needs and conditions' (p. 26); '...ideas [...] emerge in new and creative ways not planned by the performer' (p. 28); '...take advantage of the opportunities that present themselves in the moment' (p. 34)	Strategy
Deal and Key (1998)	'From judaism [it] is the blend of *keva*, the planful, and *kavanah*, capturing the moment' (p. 161)	Corporate celebration
Eisenberg (1990)	'making do with minimal commonalities and elaborating simple structures in complex ways' (p. 154)	Communication and management
Eisenhardt (1997)	'organizing in a way such that the actors both adaptively innovate and efficiently execute. [...] creating [...] in real time' (p. 255)	Decision making and strategy
Hatch (1999)	'[to] use structure in creative ways that enable [the] alter[ing] the structural foundations of [performance' (p. 78); 'mak[ing] structure implicit and discover what they are able to express – it is a structure that supports, but does not specify' (pp. 82–83)	Organization
Hatch (1997)	'intuition guiding action upon something in a spontaneous but historically contextualized way' (p. 181)	Management
Hatch (1998)	'playing around and [...] with a structure' (pp. 566–567)	Organization theory
Kamoche and Cunha (1997)	'the ability to compose and perform contemporaneously' (p. 362)	Teamworking

Author	Definition	Area
Kamoche and Cunha (1998)	'the merging of composition and performance, where both happen contemporaneously' (p. 5)	Product innovation
Meyer (1998)	'in the [...] nick of time [...] devising resourceful solutions to intractable problems' (p. 572)	Organization
Mirvis (1998)	'make things up as they go along' (p. 587)	Management
Moorman and Miner (1995)	'extemporaneous and deliberate organizational action' (p. 9)	Marketing
Moorman and Miner (1998a)	'composition converg[ing] with execution' (p. 702)	Organizational memory and innovation
Moorman and Miner (1998b)	'when the composition and execution of an action converge in time' (p. 1)	New product development
Miner *et al.* (1996)	'actions, both spontaneous and novel, that result in the creation of something while actions are unfolding' (p. 3)	New product development
Orlikowski (1996)	'accommodations to and experiments with [...] everyday contingencies, breakdowns, exceptions and unintended consequences' (p. 65)	Technology and change
Orlikowski and Hoffman (1997)	'enacting an ongoing series of local innovations that embellish [a prescripted] structure, respond to spontaneous departures and unexpected opportunities, and iterate or build on each other over time' (p. 13)	Organizational change
Pasmore (1998)	'created in real time.' (p. 6); '...emergent synergy' (p. 6); '...behave in a flexible fashion, but only within the bounds of control provided by a [set of agreements]' (p. 8)	Organization and learning
Peplowski (1998)	'deliberately painting [yourself] into corners just to get out of them' (p. 560)	Management
Perry (1991)	'formulat[ing] and implement[ing] strategies together in real time' (p. 51)	Strategy
Weick (1999)	'[no] distinction [...] between composition and performance, [...] structure from process, plans from implementation, process from product and prospect from retrospect' (p. 6); '...disciplined imagination' (p. 6); '...think[ing] both compositionally and spur of the moment at the same time' (p. 11)	Organizational theory
Weick (1993a)	'processes and designs that are continuously reconstructed' (p. 348); '...a shifting pattern of attention and meaning imposed on an ongoing stream of social activity' (p. 351)	Organization design

Table 6.2 continued.

Author	Definition	Area
Weick (1993b)	'when one organizational order collapses, [and] a substitute [is] invented immediately' (p. 640)	Organization design
Weick (1998)	'deal[ing] with the unforeseen, [working] without prior stipulation, [working] with the unexpected' (p. 544); 'Improvisation involves reworking precomposed material and designs in relation to unanticipated ideas conceived, shaped and transformed under the special conditions of performance, thereby adding unique features to every creation' (p. 544; quoting Berliner [1994: 241])	Organization theory
Weick (s.d.)	'composing extemporaneously, producing something on the spur of the moment' (p. 19); '…thinking and doing unfold[ing] almost simultaneously' (p. 19); '…to make something from whatever materials are currently available' (p. 21)	Risk mitigation

A2. Implicitly addressing improvisation

Author	Definition	Area
Brown and Eisenhardt (1997)	'combin[ing] limited structure with extensive interaction and freedom [to make changes] on current products' (p. 3); '…an organizing strategy of "making it up as you go along"' (p. 15); 'it means creating a product while simultaneously adapting to changing markets and technologies' (p. 15)	Innovation
Brown and Duguid (1991)	'respond[ing] to whatever the situation itself – both social and physical throws at [people], […] build[ing], *ad hoc* and collaboratively, robust models that do justice to particular difficulties in which [people] find themselves.' (p. 47)	Organizational learning
Ciborra (1996)	'efficiently generate new combinations of resources, routines and structures which are able to match the present, turbulent circumstances' (p. 104)	Organization structure
Eisenhardt and Tabrizi (1995)	'rapidly building intuition and flexible options so as to cope with an unclear and changing environment' (p. 88); '…combin[ing] real-time learning through design iterations and testing with the focus and discipline of milestones and powerful leaders' (p. 108)	Innovation
Ellis (1982)	'dealing with […] Issues as [they] came up' (p. 4)	Strategy

Author	Definition	Area
Hutchins (1991)	'[action] emerg[ing] from the interactions among the participants without any explicit planning' (p. 23); '. . . a search in a very complex space for a [task] structure and a social structure that fit each other and that get the job done' (p. 23); '. . . an adaptation process that [takes] place by way of local interactions' (p. 36)	Organizational design
Johnson and Rice (1984)	'the degree to which an innovation is changed by the adopter in the process of adoption and implementation after its original development' (p. 169)	Technology and change
Klein and Dellarocas (1998)	'[the] ability to respond effectively when "exceptions" occur' (p. 1)	Workflow management
Pearson *et al.* (1997)	'efforts to turn around the intensity of a crisis and to keep it from spreading to other, yet uncontaminated parts of the organization and its environment [while it unfolds]' (p. 56)	Crisis management
Slocum *et al.* (1994)	'[doing] anytime, [for] anybody, anywhere and anything' (p. 46)	Strategy and learning

B. Psychological perspectives on improvisation

Berry and Irvine (1986)	'day-to-day cognitive performance' (p. 272)	Cross-cultural cognitive psychology
Gardner and Rogoff (1990)	'adapting planning to [the] circumstances.' (p. 481)	Children's developmental psychology
Scribner (1986)	'mind in action' (p. 15)	Cognitive psychology
Southworth (1983)	'[is] born out of the "now", [it] is likely to be ever changing and may be unconventional' (p. 204)	Therapy

C. Sociological perspectives on improvisation

Machin and Carrithers (1996)	'not hav[ing] a stable response to [external stimuli], but rather [create] different responses according to [. . .] circumstances' (p. 344); 'Embody[ing] different senses of person in different situations.' (p. 345)	Anthropology
Powers (1981)	'the extent to which [meaning is] invented by the people immediately involved in a relationship.' (p. 289)	Sociology
Sharron (1983)	'immediate and spontaneous [. . .] process of creation' (p. 224)	Sociology

Table 6.2 continued.

Author	Definition	Area
D. Other perspectives on improvisation		
Erickson (1982)	'strategically adaptive action' (p. 161); '...locally situated variation around [...] nonlocally prescribed themes' (p. 165); '...making new kinds of sense together in adapting to the fortuitous circumstances of the moment' (p. 166)	Educational psychology
Leinhardt and Greeno (1986)	'making rapid on-line decisions' (p. 75); 'planning and decision making embedded in the performance [of a task]' (p. 76)	Educational psychology
Barrett and Peplowski (1998)	'creating [...] on the spot without a prescripted [...] plan' (p. 558)	Jazz music

Table 6.3 Definitions of *bricolage* across the literature.

Author	Definition	Area
Berry and Irvine (1986)	'someone who works with his hands and uses devious means compared to those of the craftsman' (pp. 271–272; quoting Levi-Strauss, 1966: 16–17)	Cross-cultural cognitive psychology
Moorman and Miner (1998b)	'making do with the materials at hand' (p. 705; quoting Levi-Strauss, 1967: 17)	Organizational learning
Thayer (1988)	'mak[ing] things work by ingeniously using whatever is at hand, being unconcerned about the "proper" tools and resources' (p. 239)	Leadership
Weick (1999)	'build[ing] something that is recognizable from whatever is at hand' (p. 11)	Organizational theory
Weick (1993a)	'a process of sensemaking that makes do with whatever materials are at hand' (p. 351); '...to use whatever resources and repertoire one has to perform whatever task one faces' (p. 352)	Organizational design
Weick (1993b)	'someone able to create order from whatever materials were at hand' (p. 639); 'being able to, usually in the company of similarly skilled people, form the materials or insights [available] into novel combinations' (p. 640)	Organizational structure
Weick (s.d.)	'making do with whatever is at hand, and skill at working in an *ad hoc* manner' (p. 20)	Risk mitigation

experience on which intuition is based' (1998, 593; our emphasis), implicitly admitting a lack of concern for the '*bricolage*' element of improvisation.

From the argument above, we can claim that the definition we put forth renders explicit what has been already stated implicitly ('between the lines') by most authors – that both *bricolage* and improvisation belong to the same construct. Apart from resulting from the uncovering of this common theme among writings on organizational improvisation, there are two major reasons for coupling both concepts.

Firstly, improvisation implies the pre-existence of a set of resources, be it a 'plan of action', knowledge or a social structure, upon which variations can be built (Orlikowski and Hoffman 1997; Weick 1999). Kamoche and Cunha, although they are first-generation authors because of their heavy reliance on the jazz metaphor, presented in a recent article (Kamoche and Cunha 1998), a rationale for the need of a 'minimal structure' in new product development processes to allow a tighter alignment to highly competitive environments, arguing that this was a necessary condition for improvisation (and *bricolage*) to happen.

Secondly, if improvisation means to respond in real time (Crossan and Sorrenti 1997; Moorman and Miner 1998a,b), then it immediately follows that improvisers cannot wait for optimal resources to be deployed and have to tackle the issues at hand with those that are currently available (Weick, s.d.). In fact, although Moorman and Miner (1998a,b) are considered the pioneers as far as empirical research in organizational improvisation goes, in truth there are several earlier empirical studies of this phenomenon, even under the explicit label of 'organizational improvisation' that provided evidence for the co-presence of real-time planning and *bricolage* (e.g. Johnson and Rice 1984; Orlikowski and Hoffman 1997). Most of these articles define improvisation in a fashion close to the one adopted here, as temporal convergence of conception and execution together with *bricolage* (see Table 6.2). Therefore, when improvisation happens then, necessarily, *bricolage* will too.

Inevitably, the previous argument raises an issue of reciprocity: is improvisation present whenever *bricolage* is performed? Formal definitions of *bricolage* as the one presented by Thayer (1988, 239) which states that it means 'making things work by ingeniously using whatever is at hand, being unconcerned about the "proper" tools and resources' does not seem to imply the simultaneity of conception and execution that partially characterizes improvisation. None the less, research on *bricolage* as performed by cognitive scientists and anthropologists seems, as it is the case with organizational theory, to be unable to separate *bricolage* from improvisation (e.g. Berry and Irvine 1986; Scribner 1986), thus making the performance of these two skills temporally coincident. Moreover, it makes sense to claim that *bricolage* only makes sense when having to 'plan in real time'. If time is abundant, it seems only sensible to wait for the 'optimal' resources and optimize their deployment (Pfeffer and Salancik 1978).

In the end, as implied by our definition, *bricolage* and improvisation are two lenses that can be used to look upon a single phenomenon whose real descriptive (and, one is tempted to say, explanatory) power rests in the two being brought together.

Improvisation is . . .

Having addressed the broader issue of the aggregation of *bricolage* and improvisation (defined in temporal terms) under a single construct (that, for the sake of simplicity, we will label 'organizational improvisation'), we now turn to the explanation of the various elements of the definition proposed above.

. . . The conception of action as it unfolds . . .

Improvisation has been formally defined as the convergence between conception and execution (Moorman and Miner 1998a, b). Although third-stage texts deem this definition to be seriously limited (Weick 1998), planning in action is still an important element of improvisation. Partially defining improvisation as 'the conception of action as it unfolds' allows us to focus on three major characteristics of this construct. First and foremost, it means that improvisation is *deliberate*, meaning that it is the result of intentional efforts on behalf of the organization and/or any of its members (Miner *et al.* 1996). Secondly, it means that improvisation is *extemporaneous* – it cannot be planned for (Weick 1990) and often ensues from an attempt to enhance the deliberateness of the emergent part of organizational strategy and action (Crossan and Sorrenti 1997; Mintzberg and McHugh 1985; Perry 1991), although it can also be purposefully triggered (Weick 1993a) (one of the 'teachings' from the jazz metaphor that organizational theory has still to implement). Thirdly it means that improvisation *occurs during action* (Miner *et al.* 1996), meaning that organizational members do not stop to think on what would be the best response to a problem or the best way to take advantage of an opportunity. Instead they develop their response by acting on the problem or opportunity (Weick, s.d.), and can only judge its correctness by hindsight, not by foresight as in traditional planning.

. . . drawing on available material, cognitive, affective and social resources

Here we focus on the '*bricolage*' dimension of improvisation, already explored in detail above. This last part of the definition states that the temporal coincidence of planning and executing improvisational action demands that it is performed with available (*vis-à-vis* optimal) resources, meaning that organizational members must have an intimate knowledge of those resources and must be adroit at working with and combining them (Weick 1993a). In jazz music these resources, apart from the instruments and the affective mood of the group, are mostly enfolded in the score, as the material embodiment of the song. In organizational improvisation, a device such as this has still to be found, although a number of authors has hinted at several alternatives (e.g. Perry 1991; Weick 1999). This definition aims at contributing towards the development of this construct by putting forth a typology of resources upon which individuals, groups and organizations can improvise, that underlies, in a more implicit or explicit fashion, most articles on this topic. We can group these resources under four major categories.

Material resources is a general category that encompasses all those resources that lie 'outside' the individual and the organizational social system. Examples of these resources are information systems, financial resources, buildings and other 'tangible' infra-structures.

Cognitive resources is a category that comprises the set of mental models held by the individual members of the organization. These mental models may be explicit or tacit, and may be acquired both inside and outside the organization. This category is not limited to theories in use but also incorporates espoused theories (Argyris and Schön 1992) because they too come to bear when members conceive in real time, especially in group situations (Harvey 1996; Janis 1971).

Affective resources are an important element of improvisation, yet still a much neglected one in the literature. Eisenberg's (1990) article is one of the best examples of research on this issue, arguing that improvisers' experience, during performance, a feeling of transcendence and emotional interconnectedness, even without prior interaction and self-disclosure. Interestingly enough, recent (and not so recent) group behavior theory also shows that the adequate emotional state can help teams avoid the pitfalls of group deviations (Harvey 1996; Janis 1971; Senge 1990). Hatch (1997) has also referred the importance of 'locking in' a specific emotional state among group improvisers she designates as 'the groove', arguing that this is a necessary condition for improvisation to happen.

Social resources refer to the social structures present among members performing improvisation. These structures include not only formal relationships, but also explicit and tacit rules and informal patterns of interaction. Labeling resources in this category social instead of organizational is a purposeful choice because, as in jazz music, the knowledge and embodiment of these structures may be acquired outside the organization (e.g. skills acquired through professional training). In this case, these structures would then be laid upon each one of the members' experiences in organizational teamwork, in the likeness of what happens in the development of 'swift trust' (Jarvenpaa and Shaw 1998).

Variations of improvisation

Improvisation is usually presented as a phenomenon that can be observed in varying degrees and forms.

Degrees of improvisation

Most authors argue that improvisation can happen in varying degrees. Some authors state that organizational improvisation occurs along a continuum upper-limited by spur-of-the-moment action and lower-limited by entirely planned action (Moorman and Miner 1995, 1998b). Other authors, although still relying on the image of a continuum, posit discrete levels of improvisational activity. Weick (1998), for example, draws on jazz performance, to build a four-level hierarchy. The first level is called 'interpretation', where plans are strictly followed; and then continues to 'embellishment', where the plan is rephrased but still recognizable; and to 'variation', where unplanned actions are inserted while still holding a clear relationship to the original plan. Finally, when radical departures from plans are to be observed, then we are witnessing 'improvisation' (Weick 1998).

The latter approach, however, is still much rooted in musical improvisation – as can be easily inferred from the language used, and provides few clues as to how to proceed when measuring the degree of improvisation in organizational contexts. In this light, the coincidence between those espousing the 'continuum approach' to assess this phenomenon, and those doing empirical research on it, does not appear to be attributable to mere chance (e.g. Miner *et al.* 1996; Moorman and Miner 1998b). Framing this phenomenon in a continuum is thus an option more attuned with organizational (and research) practice than the use of a set of discrete categories with unclear boundaries. Furthermore, although we do not contend that every deviation from a planned course of action should be labeled as improvisational, it seems that treating only radical departures from plans as improvisational is not a wholly tenable position, especially in light of earlier and current research on this phenomenon (e.g. Brown and Eisenhardt 1997; Johnson and Rice 1984; Moorman and Miner 1998a, b; Orlikowski and Hoffman 1997). In fact, equating improvisation with only radical departures would amount to treating it as a punctuated equilibrium phenomenon (Gersick 1991), whereas research on this topic in both organizational and musical/jazz settings (e.g. Berliner 1994; Brown and Eisenhardt 1997; Eisenhardt and Tabrizi 1995; Hatch 1999) shows that the *raison d'être* of improvisation lies in its ability to provoke significant changes by building upon limited variations, in a fashion close to the 'butterfly effect' proposed by chaos and complexity theory (Stacey 1996).

Types of improvisation

Moorman and Miner's research on improvisation in new product development (Miner *et al.* 1996; Moorman and Miner 1998b) uncovered a further set of categories of this phenomenon: collective vs individual; product vs process; and behavioral vs cognitive.

Improvisation is *collective* when it results from the combined effort of several individuals, groups and/or organizations. It is *individual* when it results from the efforts of a single person (Moorman and Miner 1998b).

Product improvisations affect the substantive nature of products and outcomes of the organization and *process* improvisations relate to the 'content, character and sequence of previous routines' (Miner *et al.* 1996, 10).

Finally, *behavioral* improvisation refers to novel actions taken to affect organizational outcomes and *cognitive* improvisation refers to new interpretations of external stimuli (Miner *et al.* 1996; Smircich and Stubbart 1985).

This categorization of organizational improvisation strengthens our argument sustaining its relative underdevelopment in organizational theory. In fact, most of the constructs currently associated with improvisation (see the following section) would be classifiable under these labels. Organizational innovation, for example, can be individual or collective; can focus on a process or a product and can be behavioral or cognitive (Craig and Hart 1992). Therefore, this classification seems to be of little use for the development of organizational improvisation as an independent construct. The building of a useful typology of this phenomenon seems only to be possible through a wide empirical grounding, and not simply by importing traditional categories from other areas of organizational research.

Related constructs

There are several constructs that can be associated with improvisation but that differ from it in important ways. The most commonly addressed in the literature are creativity, adaptation and innovation.

A first and, for the sake of our argument, central difference between these constructs and improvisation lies in the fact that the former are all aimed at pushing variety and at seeking effectiveness, while the latter aims to be a synthesis between those goals and their antithesis – pushing homogeneity and seeking efficiency.

Having performed this first distinction, we will now turn to the relationships between each of these constructs and organizational improvisation.

Creativity, in the organizational arena, refers to 'the creation of a valuable, useful new product, service, idea, procedure, or process by individuals working together in a complex social system' (Woodman *et al.* 1993, 293). Departing from this definition, we can see that this construct shares with improvisation a focus on novelty, but differs from it in the sense that it can result from a plan and that it can be delayed in order to be performed with optimal (*vis-à-vis* available) resources (Amabile 1998). Creativity may be observed during improvisation, when actions are *absolutely* novel (meaning that they didn't exist before). However improvisational performance may only be *relatively* novel, meaning that it had been done before but that it was never (1) used by those undertaking the improvisation and/or (2) in the situation that triggered the improvisation (Moorman and Miner 1998a).

Adaptation refers to the adjustment to external conditions (Campbell 1989). This construct shares with improvisation its focus on changing course of action but, as with creativity, the conception of an adaptation can occur before its implementation (e.g. Hamel and Prahalad 1994; Hammer and Champy 1993). Moreover, adaptation can be timed in order to have all the necessary resources in place when it is implemented, as the organizational metaphors from military war clearly show (Von Clauzewitz 1976). None the less, in highly turbulent environments and/or in highly complex scenarios, adaptation may be limited to be improvisational at the expense of being too late to respond effectively to an external threat (Crossan *et al.* 1996; Perry 1991).

Innovation can be defined as 'the adoption of any device, system, process, problem, program, product or service that is new to the organization' (Dougherty 1996, 424). This construct shares with improvisation its focus on relative (to the organization and/or the situation at hand) novelty but, as with the previous concepts, innovation may be planned and scheduled so that all the necessary resources are in place. In fact, Cooper (1979) provided broad empirical evidence to show that when this is so, innovations tend to perform better on the market. In spite of this, improvisation has been posited as an alternative model of organizational innovation whose growing importance is again due to the quantum changes on competitive landscapes (Bettis and Hitt 1995). However, this model is still in the margins of mainstream new product development research, with few notable exceptions (e.g. Brown and Eisenhardt 1998).

Learning happens when 'forgetting, concealing and silencing hide a new set of continuities and in their place create new categories, different meaning and more organization' (Weick and Westley 1996, 456). Although often a result of improvisation (Moorman and Miner 1995, 1998a), improvisation can occur without learning (e.g. Weick, s.d.) and vice versa (Crossan and Sorrenti 1997). In addition, learning can also result from carefully planned experiments, like those following the scientific method (Gower 1997). Notwithstanding, in highly competitive environments, the rate of learning – which can be increased through the ability to improvise – can be a strong competitive advantage (Crossan and Sorrenti 1997).

Measuring improvisation

Having discussed organizational improvisation, its related constructs and main variations, we now turn to the issue of its measurement.

Our literature review uncovered two studies of improvisation where this construct was formally measured. The most salient one, widely considered the first research of this type conducted on organizational improvisation, is Moorman and Miner's work on the role of memory in new product development (Moorman and Miner 1998b). These authors draw on their definition of improvisation as 'composition converg[ing] with execution' (1998a, 702) to argue that improvisation would best be measured by 'the length of time between the design and execution of an action' (1998a, 716). In fact, when measuring improvisation in an actual research setting, the authors rely on the following measure (Moorman and Miner 1998b, 17):

Seven point semantic differential scale

Rate the action:

- Figured out action as we went along/Action followed a strict plan as it was taken
- Improvised in carrying out this action/Strictly followed our plan in carrying out this action
- Ad-libbed action/Not an ad-libbed action.

Although having some limitations, namely an over-reliance on the subject's perception of improvisation (this is what is *de facto* measured on the two last items) and the restriction of improvisation to its temporal dimension, this approach seems to provide a standardized measure of temporal convergence between planning and execution (Moorman and Miner 1998b) amounting to an 'objective' although partial measure of organizational improvisation.

The second study on this phenomenon is Johnson and Rice's work on 'open technology' implementation processes in organizations (Johnson and Rice 1984), much in the line of Orlikowski's work on technology-facilitated change (Orlikowski 1996; Orlikowski and Hoffman 1997). These authors set out to study a phenomenon they call 'reinvention'; none the less, if we compare their definition with most definitions of improvisation (see Table 6.2), we find that these are just two different labels for the same construct.

Johnson and Rice measured 'reinvention' as 'the number of innovation components over and "above" a standard configuration' (1984, 170). This means that they literally count the variations around what was planned or, to use a jazz metaphor the number of notes played by the musicians that were not a part of the original score of the song. The use of this measurement of improvisation deserves two considerations. First, it takes the convergence of planning deviations and the implementation of those deviations as given – something that does not amount to a serious flaw because the authors explicitly state that the deviations counted are those performed 'in the process of adoption and implementation', meaning those whose conception was very close (or even coincident) to their execution. Secondly, by concentrating on the *content difference* between the planned and the actual performance (instead of the *temporal difference* between both), Johnson and Rice address the issue of how to measure *bricolage*, which we see as an integral part of the improvisation construct. In fact, what the authors are measuring is the organizational/group/individual ability to make the most out of the available structure. In this sense, we argue that being able to make more out of the resources available means performing a higher degree of *bricolage* and, consequently, of improvisation.

Drawing on both measures, but departing from their use in isolation from each other, we argue that *bricolage*, being part of the improvisation construct, should be taken into account when conceiving a way to evaluate the occurrence and incidence of this phenomenon. Therefore, and based on the definition presented above, we propose a measure that takes into account *both* the gap between the conception and execution of the variations around a course of action defined *a priori* in an explicit or implicit manner. This way, before looking for instances of improvisation, the researcher should then be equipped with cognitive maps of what the subjects believe is the 'standard' course of action (e.g. Voyer and Faulkner 1989). Using an image from jazz, what we are arguing is that the measuring of improvisation in a specific performance possesses a higher degree of reliability if the researcher takes with him or her not only a stopwatch, but also a copy of the written score of the 'standard' of the song played in that performance.

When does improvisation happen?

An organization improvises when it faces an occurrence it perceives as unexpected for which it does not possess any kind of preplanned course of action and which is perceived as requiring fast action (Crossan and Sorrenti 1997; Hatch 1997; Moorman and Miner 1995, 1998a,b; Weick 1993a, 1999, s.d.). Thus improvisation arises when *both* (1) a demand for (a) speed and (b) action and (2) an unexpected (and unplanned for) occurrence are perceived by the organization. This raises three major issues: (1) the origin of the demand for action; (2) the origin of the unexpected occurrence; and (3) the origin of the demand for speed.

As we argued while defining organizational improvisation, its practice entails action. This means that, for improvisation to occur, the unexpected event perceived by the organization must be: (1) perceived as important and (2) perceived as within the action span of the organization. It is commonsensical to state that, if an unexpected event is not perceived as important to the organization, then it is unlikely that it will feel motivated to take any action relative to that occurrence. A book publisher would do little to take action in the face of a new entrant in the automobile market; a car manufacturer, facing the same situation, would probably deploy significant resources to do so. In the same vein, an organization will only act upon those events that it perceives as possible objects of its action. Thus, even in the face of an important event, the organization will only improvise if it believes that there is something it can do about it.

The occurrence of an important and 'actionable' phenomenon is not a sufficient condition for improvisation to be triggered, the organization has to perceive this phenomenon as unexpected *and* 'unplanned for' (Miner *et al.* 1996). A lag in demand is both important and 'actionable' but it can be planned for months in advance, such as in the case of seasonal demand cycles. However, the fact that an occurrence is unexpected does not immediately trigger improvisational action, it must be cumulatively 'unplanned for' (Ciborra 1996). This means that the organization/group/individual does not have a predefined script/course of action to handle the event. A loss of cabin pressure, although not being a planned event on a plane trip, is dealt with through highly standardized procedures, designed long before its occurrence.

Unexpected and 'unplanned for' occurrences can happen externally – in the environment – or internally – in the organization. Independently of their locus, the triggers behind these occurrences vary according to the perspective we espouse about reality. We can either believe that (1) reality is objective and exists independently of the subject or that (2) reality is subjective, socially constructed and contingent to the subject (Smircich and Stubbart 1985; Weick 1993a). Each one of these perspectives encompasses several triggers for improvisation, as shown by Table 6.4.

When considering the organization and its environment as objective realities, the need for improvisation arises from an unexpected mismatch between planned for/expected and actual perceived environmental or organizational conditions. This mismatch can be either imposed on the organization or created by it.

When it is imposed it can be traced to one of two sources. Firstly, complexity and the law of small effects (Stacey 1996) can create unanticipated, emergent environmental states, impossible to predict beforehand. Secondly, fortuity or luck can also be responsible for threats or opportunities that, by definition, are impossible to anticipate and that can have a strong impact on the organization (Crossan *et al.* 1996; Moorman and Miner 1995, 1998b; Perry 1991).

When this mismatch is created by the organization, it can be originated either from the creation of a new vision or from a flaw in its mental models.

On the one hand, an organization may be unsatisfied with its present state and create a new vision for itself. By doing this, the organization is articulating a *future* state of reality it wants to achieve, inducing action in its members by making explicit the distance between current reality and vision (Fritz 1989; Senge 1990). This action is partially planned (especially in business organizations), but the emergent part of these changes has been found to be considerable (Mintzberg and McHugh 1985), and answerable by means of improvisation (Crossan *et al.* 1996; Perry 1991).

On the other hand, the organizational members' mental model of themselves and of their relationship with the environment can be flawed (Senge 1990). This can happen because influential actors, factors or relationships are ignored (or relatively irrelevant ones are taken into account), because influential factors or relationships are misconceived and/or because the organization perceives its environment as a series of linear/cause-and-effect relationships when it actually behaves according to systemic/circular ones.

When considering reality to be subjective and socially constructed, improvisation is triggered not by an unexpected mismatch between expectations and *perceived* environmental conditions, but between expectations and *enacted* environmental conditions, which are by definition (Smircich and Stubbart 1985) a responsibility of the organization and its members. In this context, the need for improvisation may arise from the enactment of a new environment by the organization (Crossan and Sorrenti 1997; Perry 1991; Weick 1993a). When the organization enacts a new environment, there is still a mismatch but it is now reversed. The speed and complexity of changes in the organization is higher than those of environmental changes (Weick 1993a) – organizational members are assuming an environment that differs from the one they are currently facing. This mismatch is attenuated and hopefully eliminated by action (and, concurrently, improvisation) performed *within*

Table 6.4 Triggers of organizational improvisation.

Author(s)	Triggers				
	Reality is objective				Reality is subjective
	External causes		Internal causes		
	Complexity	Fortuity/ luck	New vision	Flaw in mental models	Enactment of a new environment
Barrett (1998)	Yes	Yes			
Bastien and Hostager (1988)	Yes	Yes	Yes		Yes
Berkiner (1998)	Yes				Yes
Brown and Duguid (1991)	Yes	Yes	Yes	Yes	Yes
Brown and Eisenhardt (1997)	Yes	Yes			
Ciborra (1996)	Yes	Yes	Yes	Yes	Yes
Crossan and Sorrenti (1997)	Yes	Yes			
Crossan (1997)	Yes	Yes	Yes	Yes	
Crossan (1998)	Yes	Yes			
Crossan et al. (1996)	Yes	Yes		Yes	
Deal and Key (1998)		Yes	Yes		Yes
Eisenberg (1990)	Yes		Yes		
Eisenhardt and Tabrizi (1995)	Yes	Yes			
Eisenhardt (1997)	Yes	Yes	Yes		
Ellis (1982)	Yes	Yes	Yes		
Hatch (1997)		Yes			Yes
Hatch (1998)	Yes				Yes
Hatch (1999)			Yes		Yes
Hutchins (1991)	Yes	Yes	Yes		
Johnson and Rice (1984)	Yes		Yes		Yes
Kamoche and Cunha (1997)	Yes	Yes			
Kamoche and Cunha (1998)	Yes	Yes			
Klein and Dellarocas (1998)	Yes	Yes		Yes	
Meyer (1998)		Yes		Yes	
Miner et al. (1996)	Yes	Yes			
Mirvis (1998)		Yes			Yes
Moorman and Miner (1995)	Yes	Yes			
Moorman and Miner (1998a)	Yes	Yes			
Moorman and Miner (1998b)	Yes	Yes			
Orlikowski and Hoffman (1997)	Yes	Yes			
Orlikowski (1996)	Yes	Yes			
Pasmore (1998)	Yes	Yes			
Pearson et al. (1997)	Yes	Yes		Yes	
Peplowski (1998)			Yes		Yes
Perry (1991)			Yes		Yes
Slocum et al. (1994)	Yes	Yes	Yes	Yes	
Weick (1993a)	Yes	Yes	Yes	Yes	Yes
Weick (1993b)		Yes		Yes	
Weick (1998)		Yes	Yes		Yes
Weick (1999)	Yes		Yes		Yes
Weick (s.d.)		Yes		Yes	Yes

the organization aiming at transforming not itself but the environment. The task the organization faces is then to alter its actual environment to fit its assumed environment (Weick 1993a).

An unexpected and 'unplanned for' event perceived as important is still not enough to amount to a sufficient condition for improvisation to occur, for two main reasons. Firstly, research on the discrepancy between organizational memory and the perception of newness of an occurrence (Miner *et al.* 1996; Moorman and Miner 1998a, b) shows that, it is not only when this discrepancy is very low that improvisation is hindered – this also happens when this discrepancy is very high. The rationale behind this latter phenomenon is mostly grounded in the triggering of defensive routines (Moorman and Miner 1995). When input from the environment is highly dissonant with individual or organizational expectation, this input tends to be ignored (Argyris and Schon 1992). The well-documented examples of long-established market leaders finding their competitive positions brought to close to insignificant levels, such as IBM's stubborn ignorance of the emerging PC market (Hamel and Prahalad 1994) are good examples of this phenomenon. Secondly, the organization has to perceive a need for speedy action. The appearance of a new competitor can be dealt with by devising a careful plan of action, which is by no means an improvisational action, although its trigger is an important, 'actionable', unexpected and 'unplanned for' occurrence. The missing ingredient is speed (Crossan and Sorrenti 1997; Weick 1999). If immediate action is required, then the organization has no choice but to plan as events unfold and to 'make do' with whatever people and resources it has available at that moment – in short, to improvise (Crossan 1998; Moorman and Miner 1998a; Weick 1993b).

This demand for speed can have either an internal or an external origin. No-exceptions milestones, either explicitly articulated or implicitly enforced through leadership are the internal pushes *par excellence* of speedy action in most business organizations (Brown and Eisenhardt 1997; Eisenhardt and Tabrizi 1995). External pulls for speed of action are normally resident in the environment. The faster a competitive environment is – meaning the shorter the time taken by competitors to respond to each other's actions and to environmental variations – the faster the organization must respond to changes – those that lag behind do so at the price of reduced competitiveness (D'Aveni 1995). This means that the higher the speed of the environment framing the organization, the higher the likelihood of it undertaking improvisational activities. This line of reasoning has led several authors to restrict the occurrence of improvisation to turbulent environments. None the less, if we draw on the work of Emery and Trist (1965), we can easily see that this is a somewhat narrow view that can unnecessarily restrict the pool of researchable industries for this phenomenon and, in the same vein, those that can benefit from the lessons learned from this research. In fact, although *turbulent field* environments are fertile soils for improvisation, because of their high level of complexity, those environments that Emery and Trist (1965) label as *disturbed-reactive*, with their emphasis on speed as competitive weapon, are also likely stages for this activity. In fact, the only difference between these two categories of environments resides on the fact that in the latter, complexity is only originated by its players, while in the former, it can be triggered by the environment itself. Notwithstanding, both environments are subject to considerable levels of fortuity and complexity and are thus probable scenarios for organizations to improvise (Weick 1993a).

Finally, it is important to note that a perception of a mismatch between expected and actual reality can be either perceived as a *problem* or as an *opportunity*, thus leading to qualitatively different triggers for improvisation. In the first case, when improvising, the organization is responding to a change in its environment or in itself that is perceived as a threat and that, if no action is taken, can have serious negative effects. The goal is to neutralize the problem in order to get back to 'business as usual' – the organization resorts to negative feedback to maintain its preferred state (Miner *et al.* 1996). In the second case, when improvising, the organization is taking advantage of an internal or external change that is perceived as an opportunity and that, if action is taken, can have positive effects. The goal is to benefit from this change in order to improve the organization's position – the organization resorts to positive feedback to move to a better state (Perry 1991). Improvisation can be framed under both of these labels, but, in the end, as we noted above, it happens whenever an organization faces an occurrence it perceives as unexpected for which it does not possess any kind of preplanned course of action and which is perceived as requiring fast action, this occurrence is perceived as either a problem or an opportunity.

How does improvisation happen?

An unexpected and 'unplanned for' event demanding fast action is not enough to guarantee that organizational improvisation will occur. There are several conditions an organization must meet to be able to improvise, and there are a number of factors that will affect its effectiveness.

The conditions for improvisation to occur can be grouped under the following headers: (1) an experimental culture; (2) a minimal structure; and (3) a low procedural memory (see Table 6.5).

An *experimental culture* results from a set of values and beliefs that promote action and experimentation – as opposed to reflection and planning – as a way of understanding and dealing with reality. The point is (to paraphrase Peters 1992) to replace a 'ready,..., ready, aim, aim,..., aim, fire' approach by a 'fire,..., fire, aim, fire' one. For this to happen, the organization has to, at least, tolerate errors and, ideally, be able to espouse what Weick (1999) calls an 'aesthetic of imperfection'. Those that do, recognize that in turbulent environments it is difficult to survive, let alone prevail, without seriously pursuing innovation. These companies accept the 90%+ failure rates for which innovation is well known in the business arena (Craig and Hart 1992) as the price to pay for the 10% that do succeed and for the learning that ensues (Crossan and Sorrenti 1997). Cultures, in this kind of organization have strong 'pro-innovation' biases and believe that a great plan can only be accomplished from finding an emerging pattern in actions taken in the past, through sensemaking (Weick 1995). To foster such a culture these companies can use two major mechanisms. Firstly, they reward people based on the number of 'competent mistakes' they have made (a competent mistake being one that results from novel ideas and not from flawed execution) (Picken and Dess 1997). Secondly, they can tap the power of symbolic action and stories as third-order controls (Perrow 1986; Weick 1999), by diffusing tales of 'competent mistakes' as role models for the organization's members.

Another value that an organization must espouse for improvisation to occur is

Table 6.5 Organizational conditions for improvisation.

Author(s)	Experimental culture			Minimal structure			Low procedural memory
	Tolerate/ promote mistakes	Promote action	Sense of urgency	Invisible controls	Clear goals	Short term milestones	
Barrett (1998)	Yes	Yes	Yes	Yes	Yes	Yes	Yes
Bastien and Hostager (1988)		Yes		Yes			
Berkiner (1998)	Yes	Yes					
Brown and Duguid (1991)	Yes	Yes	Yes	Yes	Yes	Yes	
Brown and Eisenhardt (1997)		Yes	Yes	Yes	Yes	Yes	
Ciborra (1996)		Yes	Yes		Yes		Yes
Crossan and Sorrenti (1997)	Yes	Yes		Yes			
Crossan (1997)	Yes	Yes	Yes	Yes			Yes
Crossan (1998)	Yes	Yes	Yes	Yes			Yes
Crossan et al. (1996)	Yes	Yes		Yes			
Deal and Key (1998)	Yes	Yes			Yes		
Eisenberg (1990)	Yes	Yes			Yes		
Eisenhardt and Tabrizi (1995)	Yes	Yes	Yes		Yes	Yes	
Eisenhardt (1997)		Yes	Yes	Yes			
Ellis (1982)	Yes	Yes		Yes	Yes		
Hatch (1997)	Yes	Yes		Yes	Yes		
Hatch (1998)	Yes	Yes		Yes		Yes	Yes
Hatch (1999)	Yes	Yes		Yes			
Hutchins (1991)			Yes	Yes	Yes		
Johnson and Rice (1984)	Yes	Yes		Yes	Yes		
Kamoche and Cunha (1997)	Yes	Yes	Yes	Yes			
Kamoche and Cunha (1998)	Yes	Yes		Yes	Yes		
Klein and Dellarocas (1998)	Yes			Yes	Yes	Yes	
Meyer (1998)	Yes	Yes	Yes	Yes	Yes		
Miner et al. (1996)		Yes	Yes		Yes		Yes
Mirvis (1998)		Yes	Yes		Yes		Yes
Moorman and Miner (1995)		Yes			Yes		Yes
Moorman and Miner (1998a)							Yes
Moorman and Miner (1998b)		Yes	Yes				Yes
Orlikowski and Hoffman (1997)	Yes	Yes		Yes	Yes		Yes
Orlikowski (1996)	Yes	Yes		Yes	Yes		Yes
Pasmore (1998)	Yes	Yes		Yes			
Pearson et al. (1997)			Yes	Yes	Yes		
Peplowski (1998)		Yes		Yes	Yes		
Perry (1991)		Yes					
Slocum et al. (1994)		Yes			Yes		
Weick (1993a)	Yes	Yes		Yes	Yes	Yes	Yes
Weick (1993b)		Yes	Yes	Yes	Yes		Yes
Weick (1998)	Yes	Yes	Yes	Yes	Yes	Yes	
Weick (1999)	Yes	Yes		Yes		Yes	
Weick (s.d.)		Yes	Yes	Yes	Yes		Yes

that of urgency. As we argued when discussing the external triggers of improvisation, the occurrence of an unexpected and 'unplanned-for' event is not enough for improvisation to happen. Those that are to tackle this event should feel that it can only be addressed through fast action (Perry 1991). Otherwise they can fall back on planning (because they perceive that they have time to do so) instead of being pushed to compose a course of action in real-time – a process of a far more daunting nature than the former (Eisenberg 1990).

A *minimal structure* refers to the sets of controls employed to accomplish the efficient effectiveness for which improvisation has been touted (Brown and Eisenhardt 1997; Crossan 1998; Orlikowski 1996; Weick 1998). Most authors on improvisation argue that the only kind of integration mechanisms applicable in an organization that aims to improvise are third-order controls, meaning indirect controls that co-ordinate via culture or ideology (Mintzberg 1995; Perrow 1986; Weick 1993a). This argument can be justified by drawing on the work of Dougherty, who has shown the difficulties of pursuing novel actions in organizations stifled by first- (direct supervision) and second- (standardization) order co-ordination mechanisms (Dougherty 1996). However, drawing on recent findings in critical studies of organizational control, we contend that improvisation can happen in environments where first- and second-order mechanisms are abundant. The touchstone of controlling improvisers lies, we argue, not in the degree of obtrusiveness of those mechanisms but in their invisibility. In regard to first-order controls, direct supervision can be 'delegated' from superior to peers, allowing for the maintenance of this type of co-ordination without hampering creativity (Sewell 1998). In jazz improvisation itself, band members are often chosen because of their reputation not among critics but fellow players (Hatch 1999). Second-order controls can be rendered invisible by incorporating them in the production technology itself (be it of tangible goods or services) (Barley and Kunda 1992; Joerges and Czarniawska 1998).

Apart from control mechanisms, a minimal structure needs two further elements to build upon/realize the potential of the feeling of urgency discussed before and to maintain a minimum level of coherence among improvisational action in order to, again, ensure that its promise of efficient effectiveness does not go unfulfilled (Brown and Eisenhardt 1997).

Milestones or action deadlines have been found to be an effective mechanism for holding the momentum/sense of urgency first triggered by an unexpected and 'unplanned-for' event (Gardner and Roggoff 1990). Furthermore, milestones are opportunities to perform a check between current actions and the development of the situation the organization is facing, allowing the detection of any deviations/ misperceptions that need to be corrected (Brown and Eisenhardt 1997). Moreover, milestones are currently set in advance and planned, thus providing a sense of structure/routinization to improvisational activities often perceived to result from chaos and disorder (Eisenhardt and Tabrizi 1995). Finally, milestones serve as moments of feedback as partial stages/steps are concluded and, thus, potentially increase individual motivation – building the momentum and the sense of urgency needed for improvisation to be sustained.

Clearly articulated goals serve the all-important function of ensuring that improvisational activity amounts to the attainment of organizational objectives. Clearly articulated goals perform, in organizational settings, a very similar function to that of the song in jazz improvisation. They are akin to a magnetic field (or a strange attractor, to use complexity theory) that, although not prescribing individual action, is strongly normative in what concerns the results of such action (Weick 1993a). They also contribute to co-ordination among individual members by defining the results of their activity in a similar process to that of standardization of outputs (Mintzberg 1995).

A *low procedural memory/small number of routines* is also a central condition for improvisation. Procedural memory refers to the set of routines one possesses to address the tasks/challenges one faces (Gersick and Hackman 1990). In this light, improvisation appears to only occur when an organization/individual does not have an adequate routine/procedural memory to respond to an unexpected situation (Moorman and Miner 1995). In situations for which an adequate routine does exist, then improvisation will be highly unlikely. This rationale is grounded on the following: firstly it would be inefficient to invest in finding an improvisational course of action when another such as effective is already stored in memory; secondly, these response processes are often unconscious, automatic and often act undetected, lowering the deliberateness of their choice. However, in spite of empirical proof that organizational memory does hinder improvisation (Moorman and Miner 1998b), it is at least theoretically arguable that the opposite is also true. In fact, if we understand routines as grammars (Pentland and Reuter 1994), and knowing that elements in grammars can be combined in endless possibilities, then procedural memory would be the organizational counterpart of the score of a song, which organizational improvisers could embellish/modify at will during action (Moorman and Miner 1998a; Weick 1998). Moreover, there is also empirical evidence that this is so; in a study on improvisation in the computer industry, Brown and Eisenhardt (1995) found that firms with established routines are more likely to improvise than others without.

Our contribution to the untangling of this paradox lies in affirming that, although organizational memory in fact hinders improvisation, this can be severely attenuated if the organization can build the necessary will to depart from current grammatical forms and use their elements to create new routines as action is unfolding (as we will discuss below).

The factors influencing the quality of improvisation fall under the following categories (see Tables 6.6A and 6.6B): (1) leadership; (2) member characteristics; (3) information flow; (4) memory-related factors; (5) organizational configuration; and (6) resources.

These factors differ from those presented above in that they do not determine whether organizational improvisation will happen or not; instead, they affect its extent and quality, when it does.

Leadership is an important factor affecting the degree and effectiveness of organizational improvisation. Authors drawing on the jazz metaphor argue that a 'servant' leadership style (Greenleaf 1977) and a rotating leadership favor wider departures from canonical practice (Bastien and Hostager 1988; Weick 1993b). The rationale for the relevance of a rotating leadership is grounded in contingency leadership theory, which states that, in unexpected and 'unplanned for' situations, a strong leader must emerge, especially when action must be hastened (Fiedler 1965). Although this seems to contradict the need for a rotating leadership, we contend that instead it renders it more pressing. This is due to the growing complexity and interdisciplinary nature of the problems/opportunities organizations face, which calls for different competencies and knowledge (Stacey 1995). Thus, when each member is called to give his/her contribution to the ongoing improvisation, he/she cannot only act as a 'consultant' or 'counselor' but, instead, as a leader because of the coupling of a scarcity of time and an abundance of complexity/need for specialized knowledge (Stacey 1966; Weick 1993a, s.d.). The leadership style of the group's/organization's formal leader is also an important moderator of improvisation. Paralleling our previous discussion of the 'minimal structure' concept, a direc-

Table 6.6A Influencing factors of organizational improvisation.

Author(s)	Leadership		Member's characteristics				Fluid communication
	Rotating leadership	Serving leadership	Skill	Creativity	Diversity	Dealing with affectivity	
Barrett (1998)			Yes	Yes		Yes	Yes
Bastien and Hostager (1988)	Yes	Yes	Yes	Yes			Yes
Berkiner (1998)		Yes		Yes	Yes		
Brown and Duguid (1991)			Yes	Yes	Yes		Yes
Brown and Eisenhardt (1997)	Yes			Yes	Yes		Yes
Ciborra (1996)					Yes		Yes
Crossan and Sorrenti (1997)		Yes	Yes	Yes	Yes		Yes
Crossan (1997)	Yes	Yes	Yes	Yes			Yes
Crossan (1998)	Yes		Yes	Yes	Yes	Yes	Yes
Crossan et al. (1996)	Yes		Yes	Yes	Yes	Yes	Yes
Deal and Key (1998)		Yes		Yes	Yes	Yes	Yes
Eisenberg (1990)	Yes		Yes		Yes	Yes	Yes
Eisenhardt and Tabrizi (1995)	Yes			Yes	Yes		Yes
Eisenhardt (1997)			Yes	Yes			Yes
Ellis (1982)				Yes			
Hatch (1997)		Yes	Yes	Yes	Yes		
Hatch (1998)			Yes	Yes		Yes	Yes
Hatch (1999)		Yes	Yes	Yes		Yes	Yes
Hutchins (1991)	Yes		Yes	Yes			Yes
Johnson and Rice (1984)		Yes	Yes	Yes			Yes
Kamoche and Cunha (1997)	Yes	Yes	Yes	Yes		Yes	Yes
Kamoche and Cunha (1998)	Yes	Yes	Yes	Yes		Yes	Yes
Klein and Dellarocas (1998)				Yes			
Meyer (1998)	Yes		Yes				Yes
Miner et al. (1996)			Yes	Yes			Yes
Mirvis (1998)	Yes						Yes
Moorman and Miner (1995)			Yes				Yes
Moorman and Miner (1998a)			Yes	Yes			Yes
Moorman and Miner (1998b)				Yes			Yes
Orlikowski and Hoffman (1997)			Yes				Yes
Orlikowski (1996)			Yes		Yes		Yes
Pasmore (1998)			Yes	Yes			
Pearson et al. (1997)		Yes	Yes	Yes	Yes		Yes
Peplowski (1998)	Yes	Yes	Yes				Yes
Perry (1991)				Yes	Yes		Yes
Slocum et al. (1994)							Yes
Weick (1993a)	Yes		Yes	Yes			Yes
Weick (1993b)	Yes	Yes	Yes	Yes		Yes	Yes
Weick (1998)			Yes	Yes			Yes
Weick (1999)	Yes	Yes	Yes	Yes	Yes	Yes	Yes
Weick (s.d.)	Yes	Yes	Yes	Yes		Yes	Yes

tive leader would act as a visible and obtrusive control mechanism that would hamper improvisation. None the less, if the elements of the minimal structure above are in place, a directive leader would restrain the span of the risks its followers take, but this would not put in question the occurrence of improvisation (Eisenhardt and Tabrizi 1995; Weick 1993b). A 'servant' leader, however, can have a meaningful positive impact on the quality of organizational improvisation. This kind of leader holds a twofold stewardship: stewardship for followers and

Table 6.6B Influencing factors of organizational improvisation (continued)

Author(s)	Memory-related factors			Organizational configuration			General purpose resources
	Rich declarative memory	Practicing improvisation	Will to depart from memory	Disclosure relationships	Collateral organization	Small groups	
Barrett (1998)	Yes	Yes	Yes			Yes	
Bastien and Hostager (1988)	Yes			Yes		Yes	
Berkiner (1998)	Yes		Yes	Yes			
Brown and Duguid (1991)	Yes	Yes	Yes	Yes	Yes	Yes	
Brown and Eisenhardt (1997)	Yes		Yes				Yes
Ciborra (1996)		Yes	Yes				Yes
Crossan and Sorrenti (1997)	Yes	Yes	Yes			Yes	Yes
Crossan (1997)	Yes	Yes	Yes	Yes		Yes	
Crossan (1998)	Yes	Yes	Yes	Yes		Yes	
Crossan et al. (1996)	Yes		Yes	Yes		Yes	
Deal and Key (1998)	Yes		Yes	Yes			
Eisenberg (1990)	Yes		Yes		Yes	Yes	
Eisenhardt and Tabrizi (1995)	Yes		Yes				Yes
Eisenhardt (1997)	Yes						Yes
Ellis (1982)		Yes	Yes				Yes
Hatch (1997)	Yes					Yes	
Hatch (1998)	Yes	Yes		Yes		Yes	
Hatch (1999)	Yes		Yes				
Hutchins (1991)	Yes	Yes				Yes	Yes
Johnson and Rice (1984)	Yes						Yes
Kamoche and Cunha (1997)	Yes		Yes				
Kamoche and Cunha (1998)	Yes		Yes				
Klein and Dellarocas (1998)			Yes				Yes
Meyer (1998)	Yes			Yes		Yes	
Miner et al. (1996)	Yes		Yes	Yes			Yes
Mirvis (1998)		Yes	Yes	Yes		Yes	
Moorman and Miner (1995)	Yes		Yes		Yes		
Moorman and Miner (1998a)	Yes		Yes				
Moorman and Miner (1998b)	Yes		Yes				
Orlikowski and Hoffman (1997)	Yes		Yes				Yes
Orlikowski (1996)	Yes						Yes
Pasmore (1998)	Yes		Yes				
Pearson et al. (1997)	Yes	Yes	Yes	Yes		Yes	Yes
Peplowski (1998)	Yes						Yes
Perry (1991)	Yes						Yes
Slocum et al. (1994)	Yes		Yes				
Weick (1993a)	Yes	Yes	Yes		Yes	Yes	Yes
Weick (1993b)	Yes	Yes	Yes	Yes		Yes	Yes
Weick (1998)	Yes	Yes	Yes	Yes			
Weick (1999)	Yes		Yes	Yes		Yes	Yes
Weick (s.d.)	Yes	Yes	Yes	Yes		Yes	Yes

stewardship for the purposes of the organization (Greenleaf 1979). Stewardship for followers has two advantages; first it attenuates the negative effects of practicing improvisation (discussed in the next section) (Eisenberg 1990) and, secondly, it allows for more fluid transitions of 'real' (as opposed to 'nominal') leadership within those improvising. Stewardship for organizational objectives builds upon the 'clear goals' element of the minimal structure presented above, strengthening their ability to focus improvisational actions (Bastien and Hostager 1988; Weick 1993a).

Member's characteristics can also have a significative effect over improvisation in organizations. First and foremost, most authors drawing on the jazz metaphor to study organizational improvisation, argue that the level of performative skill that each individual possesses determines his/her ability to pursue improvisational activity that is very distant from organizational routine (e.g. Crossan *et al.* 1996; Weick 1993a, 1999). Moreover, these authors further argue that, when improvisation is a group phenomenon, this group's improvisational performance will be limited by the ability of its least skilled member (Bastien and Hostager 1988; Hatch 1999). The relevance given to skill rests on it being a vehicle for creativity to be put in practice. Thus, individual creativity is also an important trait that an improviser must possess (Crossan 1998; Erickson 1982). Only high levels of individual creativity will allow for radical departures from current organizational practice which, according to Weick, reflect 'purer instances of improvisation' (1998, 545), with lower levels of it resulting in 'variations' or 'embellishments' that still retain much of the original routine/idea and that may not be as effective. This impact of individual creativity is, of course, only possible when what we called 'the conditions for improvisation' (see above) are present (Crossan and Sorrenti 1997). Otherwise, individual creativity will be occulted (Amabile 1998) or worst – it will feed dangerous organizational phenomena such as groupthink (Janis 1971). Another organizational attribute that can do much for the degree of improvisation and its effectiveness is member diversity. Homogeneous organizations are not prone to diverse approaches to solve problems or to reaping opportunities; the same goes for individuals (Hannan and Freeman 1989). Thus, the 'novel' element of organization improvisation will be seriously compromised if the organization does not benefit from a diverse population and it will probably be limited to mere embellishments or small variations upon existing ideas, products, practices and routines (Hatch 1997; Weick 1998, 1999). A final characteristic of individual organizational members relevant to their improvisational accomplishments is their ability to deal with the affective element of their performance, and the extent to which they believe that treating emotion explicitly is valid in organizational settings. Managing one's own affective state is an important element of improvisation because of the anxiety its performance entails. The perception of an absence of structure will more often than not provoke a considerable level of anxiety among those performing it (Barrett 1998; Hatch 1999). If this anxiety is not dealt with, which seldom can be accomplished without rendering it explicit (Kets de Vries and Miller 1984), then it can reduce the distance between canonical and improvisational practice (Amabile 1998; Eisenberg 1990). It can thus be a threat to the effectiveness of improvisation and, in the end, the organization's will – let alone ability – to perform it. Being able to explicitly recognize and discuss their affective state, those who are probable subjects of improvisation can do much for their ability to engage in it, and the results they will obtain from it.

Factors related to the *information flow* are also relevant to determine the degree and quality of improvisational activity within an organization. This set of factors can be divided into (a) factors related to the information flow between the organization and its environment and (b) factors related to the intra-organizational information flows.

Information flows between the organization and its environment determine the appearance or not of improvisation, and were already discussed when we presented the factors triggering organizational improvisation.

Information flows inside the organization can have an important impact on improvisation in organizational settings because of the centrality of fluid communication among those performing it to avoid its falling into random undirected action (Orlikowski 1996), due to the absence of direct co-ordination mechanisms. Fluid communication serves, thus, as an integrating device when individual's performances are co-ordinated through action alone (Bastien and Hostager 1988). If this fluidity is compromised, the perception of an unexpected and unplanned for occurrence may elicit incoherent and – ultimately – ineffective responses from the organization (Moorman and Miner 1998a), because not all of its members will perceive it as such (especially those in roles further away from the market) and because they will know little of others' efforts to address that challenge.

Considering that improvisation both departs from current routines/knowledge and builds on those routines/knowledge, it follows that organizational memory-related factors potentially affect the way improvisation occurs and the quality and magnitude of its effects. Organizational memory can be decomposed into procedural memory – knowledge of action – and declarative memory – knowledge of facts (Anderson 1983). As we argued before, procedural memory relates to the occurrence (or not) of improvisation. Declarative memory is more related to qualitative variations of this phenomenon. Declarative memory plays an important role in the degree of improvisation: the more facts an organization knows, the broader and, arguably, diversified its base for creativity and thus for improvisation (Amabile 1998; Moorman and Miner 1998b; Woodman *et al.* 1993). None the less, it must also be stated that a wide span of declarative memory may slow the speed of improvisation because of the size of the amount of time that individuals must invest to search through all available alternatives (Moorman and Miner 1998a), although one could argue that bounded rationality would act to counter this phenomenon (Simon 1990). Another issue related to organizational memory that has a potential impact on improvisation relates to procedural memory on its performance. Practicing improvisation in a simulated and 'safe' environment, that is to say, in an environment purposely set up for this aim can help individuals build the skills for effective improvisational activity in 'real' situations by building a procedural memory base for this competence (Crossan 1997) and thus allow them to avoid those mistakes that are characteristic of first-time performances. Finally, another competence related to organizational memory resides in the will to depart from that memory. If individuals cling to the organization's procedural memory, as sparse as it might be, then no matter how rich their knowledge base or how significative is their creative potential, they will tend to fall back on pre-existing routines (Crossan *et al.* 1996; Weick 1999). Therefore, organizational members must be able and willing to unlearn their canonical responses in the face of unexpected and 'unplanned for' events if they are to tackle them through improvisation (Weick, s.d.).

Organizational configuration builds upon the minimal structure to enhance the process and outcomes of organizational improvisation. A first and relevant element of an organizational configuration that fosters improvisation is the existence of close and trusting relationships among its members (Crossan *et al.* 1996; Weick, s.d. 1993b). The presence of such relationships builds a 'safety net' for risk taking (Weick 1999), augmenting the degree to which improvisational practice departs from canonical routines. A quick inspection into the literature on organizational improvisation appears to show that this is not a shared perspective among authors (e.g. Bastien and Hostager 1988; Hatch 1999). However, if we look closely we can find that even those who explicitly state that close relationships may hinder improvisational activity are not delving deeply enough into their own empirical observations. Bastien and Hostager's (1988) experiment with four musicians who had never played together before is an example of this. As the authors show, this group started with highly structured songs, allowing for little improvisation, and slowly progressed to more complex ones, where improvisation happened with a much higher frequency. Bastien and Hostager called this a centering strategy that can be described as replacing lowering social uncertainty with growing task uncertainty. Restating their findings, we can say that the musicians only truly improvised (Weick 1998) when they had been able to build a trusting and close relationship among themselves, as far as the situation they were facing allowed it.

Another still significant element of an organizational configuration that fosters improvisation is a collateral structure. Collateral structures are organizational spaces that may come into being either through a deliberate choice of the formal organization or an emergent phenomenon of the informal one, where members are 'relieved' from the impositions of formal/prescribed practices and are able to pursue less canonical ones (Brown and Duguid 1991). These structures have, thus, three main functions: (a) they allow members to build the requisite variety of ideas necessary for improvisation to occur; (b) they serve as an arena where individuals can practice improvisation in a safer environment before performing it in interaction with the market; and (c) they offer a space for improvisation to be performed when the main organization does not possess the conditions we presented before as necessary for this phenomenon to take place (Peters 1992; Weick 1993a). Group size is the final element of the organization's configuration with a potential impact in its ability to improvise. Exceedingly large groups can reduce the difference between routine behavior and improvised behavior (Powers 1981). This happens mainly because a large group of people cannot co-ordinate itself based on mutual adjustment alone (Mintzberg 1991), and then the newly imposed controls would hinder its ability to improvise (Sharron 1983). Moreover, the larger the group the higher the probability of information distortion and the lower the real-time information communication speed, thus the lower the incidence of improvisation (Moorman and Miner 1995).

A final element influencing improvisation is the resources the individual/team/organization possesses to perform it. Specialized and limited purpose resources can thwart improvisation by limiting organizational members' ability to turn their ideas into practice. Conversely, multipurpose resources are flexible enough to be deployed into a variety of uses, even if those uses were never part of the organization's original intentions (or even imagination) for their applicability (Weick 1993a). Thus, resources may affect improvisation through its *bricolage* dimension by augmenting the possible courses of action an organization can take, because of those resources' flexibility. General-purpose resources reduce the number of constraints upon those that are conceiving action as it unfolds, thus augmenting their potential degree of departure from standard practice/ideas and, ultimately, their ability to reach 'purer' forms of improvisation.

Why does improvisation happen?

Organizational improvisation can have both positive and negative outcomes.

Positive outcomes can be grouped under the following categories (see Table 6.7): (1) flexibility; (2) learning; (3) motivation and (4) affective outcomes.

Negative outcomes are (see Table 6.8): (1) biased learning; (2) opportunity traps; (3) amplification of emergent actions; (4) over-reliance on/addictiveness to improvisation; and (5) increased anxiety.

The most attractive and touted outcome of organizational improvisation is, essentially, flexibility (see Table 6.7). Flexibility is a concept close to that of 'adaptation', in the sense that it aims at maintaining a certain degree of fit with the environment by changing the organization to respond to changes in it, but that differs from adaptation because of the velocity that improvisation allows the organization to have when accommodating those changes. Flexibility, then, puts together adaptation to changes in the environment with high speed, thus maintaining the convergence between the fast and the unexpected, characteristic of its triggers.

Learning is a second outcome of improvisation. Organizations that improvise may learn in three ways. First, they can learn how to improvise. Secondly, they can learn through the formalization/routinization of improvisations. Finally, they can learn more about themselves and their environment through the 'action' component of improvisation.

Several authors, especially those drawing from the arts to study improvisation in organizational settings argue that practicing, i.e. performing improvisation routinely, enhances an organization's ability to improvise (e.g. Crossan *et al.* 1996). The rationale behind this argument is that improvisation is a skill on its own (Weick 1999) that cannot be transmitted explicitly through formal knowledge, but that can only be grown through its performance. These authors normally draw on examples from jazz (Weick 1998) and theater (Crossan *et al.* 1996) to show that only through much practice do people acquire considerable adroitness at the skill of improvising. Moreover, other authors (e.g. Bastien and Hostager 1988; Eisenberg 1990; Leinhart and Greeno 1986) have shown that, when improvising, groups start with few and simple variations pursuing progressively a path of increasing task uncertainty, and thus with increasing opportunities (and demands) to improvise. This suggests that, through action – the performance of improvisation – organizational members are able to hone this skill, thus improving their ability to face tasks that require high proficiency in its use, following what Bastien and Hostager have labeled a 'centering strategy'.

The novel ideas that come out when an organization improvises do not necessarily fade away when this improvisation ends. Miner *et al.* (1996) have shown that improvisations in both processes and products are retained and sometimes routinized by the organization in order to enhance future performance. In this sense an improvisation may be rolled out into an organizational innovation if the organi-

Table 6.7 Positive outcomes of organizational improvisation.

Author(s)	Flexibility	Learning	Higher motivation		Affective outcomes	
			To work	To improvise	Transcendence	Team building
Barrett (1998)	Yes	Yes	Yes	Yes	Yes	
Bastien and Hostager (1988)	Yes	Yes				
Berkiner (1998)	Yes	Yes				
Brown and Duguid (1991)	Yes	Yes	Yes	Yes		Yes
Brown and Eisenhardt (1997)	Yes		Yes			
Ciborra (1996)	Yes	Yes	Yes	Yes		
Crossan and Sorrenti (1997)	Yes	Yes	Yes	Yes	Yes	
Crossan (1997)	Yes	Yes	Yes			Yes
Crossan (1998)	Yes	Yes	Yes	Yes		Yes
Crossan *et al.* (1996)	Yes		Yes			
Deal and Key (1998)	Yes	Yes	Yes			Yes
Eisenberg (1990)	Yes					Yes
Eisenhardt and Tabrizi (1995)	Yes	Yes	Yes			
Eisenhardt (1997)	Yes					
Ellis (1982)	Yes	Yes		Yes		
Hatch (1997)	Yes				Yes	Yes
Hatch (1998)	Yes	Yes		Yes	Yes	
Hatch (1999)	Yes	Yes				
Hutchins (1991)	Yes	Yes		Yes		
Johnson and Rice (1984)	Yes	Yes		Yes		
Kamoche and Cunha (1997)	Yes	Yes				
Kamoche and Cunha (1998)	Yes	Yes				
Klein and Dellarocas (1998)	Yes	Yes				
Meyer (1998)	Yes				Yes	
Miner *et al.* (1996)	Yes	Yes		Yes		
Mirvis (1998)	Yes	Yes		Yes		
Moorman and Miner (1995)	Yes	Yes				
Moorman and Miner (1998a)	Yes	Yes				
Moorman and Miner (1998b)	Yes	Yes				
Orlikowski and Hoffman (1997)	Yes	Yes				
Orlikowski (1996)	Yes	Yes		Yes		
Pasmore (1998)	Yes					
Pearson *et al.* (1997)	Yes	Yes				
Peplowski (1998)	Yes		Yes		Yes	
Perry (1991)	Yes	Yes				
Slocum *et al.* (1994)	Yes	Yes				
Weick (1993a)	Yes	Yes				
Weick (1993b)	Yes	Yes				Yes
Weick (1998)	Yes	Yes		Yes	Yes	
Weick (1999)	Yes	Yes	Yes	Yes	Yes	Yes
Weick (s.d.)	Yes	Yes				Yes

zation continues its use after the event that triggered it is no longer present and ends up endorsing it as standard practice, in either an implicit or explicit fashion.

Finally, improvisation, by stressing action as a way to learn about the situation it is currently facing (Weick 1999), and its environment in general allows the organization to fine-tune, and sometimes to alter dramatically the mental models it holds about itself and its surroundings (Weick and Westley 1996). Moreover, improvisation, with its emphasis on experimentation, opens a whole new learning arena to organizations by showing that mistakes and failures are learning opportunities as

Table 6.8 Negative outcomes of organizational improvisation.

Author(s)	Biased learning	Opportunity traps	Amplification of emergent action	Addictiveness to improvisation	Increased anxiety
Barrett (1998)		Yes	Yes		Yes
Bastien and Hostager (1988)		Does not address negative outcomes			
Berkiner (1998)		Does not address negative outcomes			
Brown and Duguid (1991)					Yes
Brown and Eisenhardt (1997)		Does not address negative outcomes			
Ciborra (1996)					Yes
Crossan and Sorrenti (1997)		Does not address negative outcomes			
Crossan (1997)		Does not address negative outcomes			
Crossan (1998)		Does not address negative outcomes			
Crossan et al. (1996)		Does not address negative outcomes			
Deal and Key (1998)		Does not address negative outcomes			
Eisenberg (1990)				Yes	Yes
Eisenhardt and Tabrizi (1995)		Does not address negative outcomes			
Eisenhardt (1997)		Does not address negative outcomes			
Ellis (1982)				Yes	
Hatch (1997)		Does not address negative outcomes			
Hatch (1998)		Does not address negative outcomes			
Hatch (1999)		Does not address negative outcomes			
Hutchins (1991)		Does not address negative outcomes			
Kamoche and Cunha (1997)	Yes	Yes	Yes		Yes
Kamoche and Cunha (1998)	Yes	Yes	Yes		Yes
Klein and Dellarocas (1998)		Does not address negative outcomes			
Meyer (1998)					Yes
Miner et al. (1996)		Yes	Yes	Yes	
Mirvis (1998)					Yes
Moorman and Miner (1995)					Yes
Moorman and Miner (1998a)		Does not state negative outcomes			
Moorman and Miner (1998b)		Does not address negative outcomes			
Orlikowski and Hoffman (1997)		Does not address negative outcomes			
Orlikowski (1996)		Does not address negative outcomes			
Pasmore (1998)		Does not address negative outcomes			
Pearson et al. (1997)		Does not address negative outcomes			
Peplowski (1998)		Does not address negative outcomes			
Perry (1991)		Does not address negative outcomes			
Slocum et al. (1994)		Does not address negative outcomes			
Weick (1993a)		Does not address negative outcomes			
Weick (1993b)		Does not address negative outcomes			
Weick (1998)		Yes			Yes
Weick (1999)		Does not address negative outcomes			
Weick (s.d.)		Does not address negative outcomes			

legitimate (if not even more so) as environmental scanning and other information-generation techniques (Sitkin 1992).

These two consequences, flexibility and learning, when occurring over long periods of time may amount to a seldom discussed outcome of organizational improvisation: changing dramatically the nature of the organization's business portfolio and, sometimes, the organization itself. This statement is grounded in the argument that most organizations do not change in strong and infrequent bursts – as the punctuated equilibrium model contends (Gersick 1991) – but through small and incremental changes that in the long run can have much more significant and discontinuous results than under the former model (Brown and Eisenhardt 1997; DeGeus and Senge 1997; Eisenhardt and Tabrizi 1995). Van de Ven and Poole (1995) have in fact argued that the punctuated equilibrium model is but a particular case of the incremental change model. Therefore, improvisational activities, as modest as they may seem when they occur, can have a *de facto* transformational effect over the organization.

Improvisation in organizations also results in increasing motivation (1) to work and (2) to improvise.

Higher motivation to work (or motivation *strictu sensu*) results, according to Hackman and Oldham's model, from the levels of task variety, task significance, task autonomy, feedback and task identity (Hackman and Oldham 1980). Improvisation, with its emphasis on milestones and its iterative nature (Brown and Eisenhardt 1997; Eisenhardt and Tabrizi 1995) provides high levels of individual feedback, thus contributing to potential increases in individual motivation. Additionally, when improvisational action has performative outcomes that the organization values as positive, improvisation is likely to earn a higher legitimacy as a standard practice, providing that the organizational culture does not over-rationalize this phenomenon as a pre-planned occurrence (Miner *et al.* 1996; Orlikowski 1996). In this way, the organization as a whole may acquire a higher motivation to improvise when facing unexpected events (Eisenberg 1990).

Organizational improvisation may also have affective outcomes. Improvisation, especially when leading to high performance outcomes, may build a feeling of transcendence among its participants (Eisenberg 1990). This feeling of transcendence is the result of being able to tackle a problem or take advantage of an opportunity that is perceived both as important to the organization and difficult to handle by the means of what is often perceived as sheer ingenuity (Barrett 1998) instead of reliance on plans and routines. Moreover, if this experience is not individual but shared, it can foster the building of strong bonds among participants in this process (Powers 1981) without the need for personal disclosure or prior personal relationships (Bastien and Hostager 1988), pushing affectivity from the individual to the group and sometimes even to the organizational level.

Unfortunately, improvisation does not only entail positive results (see Table 6.8). Learning resulting from its occurrence in an organizational setting can be biased (Moorman and Miner 1995). Organizations can, in fact, when formalizing knowledge acquired while improvising, make a 'leap of abstraction' (Senge 1990) and generalize a solution that makes no sense in circumstances other than those where it was first conceived (Moorman and Miner 1998b). Moreover, even if that solution can be generalized, there are no guarantees that it is the most efficient one, and although this can be tackled through post-action reflection, this does not necessarily take place. In this vein, lessons learned from improvisation have the danger of becoming *de facto* organizational 'panda thumbs' (Gould 1980) or, in other words, legitimate but inefficient solutions to a given category of problems.

Another potential negative outcome of organizational improvisation is a phenomenon called the 'opportunity trap'. An organization falls into an opportunity trap whenever it fails to exploit the novel ideas obtained through exploration processes, namely improvisation. This is to say that the organization may take too long to crystallize a new product concept, for example, in order to wait for more and more new ideas to incorporate into the product and – ultimately – fail to introduce the product into the market in a timely fashion and thus fail to reap the benefits of those ideas. In fact, in a recent research on the use of improvisation in new product development, Miner *et al.* found that this was a major concern for managers in companies taking advantage of this phenomenon, and warned about the potential incidence of this conundrum when pursuing this kind of practice.

Another important consequence of improvisation may be labeled as the amplification of emergent actions. In reality, the appeal of improvisation to organizations, especially those inhabiting business environments, is the ability to increase the deliberateness of realized strategies by acting over their emergent component (Mintzberg 1995) in order to render it as deliberate as possible. None the less, these latter attempts will themselves have unintended and unexpected consequences thus amplifying the emergent part of organizational actions (Mintzberg and Waters 1982). Hopefully, this amplification will be more than compensated by the added deliberateness. However, this is not necessarily so, and organizations that rely on improvisation to handle unexpected events may themselves create those events, falling in a never-ending spiral of complexity and deteriorating manageability, in a way close to what happens when a jazz musician cannot find a way to cohere an improvisation around the underlying score of a song.

Over-reliance/addictiveness on improvisation can be another negative consequence of its practice. The rationale underlying this statement parallels the argument put forth before when discussing the increasing of the will to improvise. If this practice continuously produces positive performance effects it may be over-legitimized as the better way to handle all the challenges posed to the group/organization (Miner *et al.* 1996). Moreover, the feeling of transcendence discussed above is indeed powerful and may become addictive to some members of the organization. In either circumstance, individuals may be tempted to face every new challenge by relying on improvisation, when some of them could be tackled in a more efficient manner through planning. In the limit, over-reliance on improvisation destroys the organizational ability to improvise by exploiting to obsolescence and depletion the plans and routines that serve as the 'score' for its practice.

A final negative consequence of organizational improvisation is the increased anxiety and uncertainty faced by its practitioners. The pressure to deliver 'real time' solutions to unexpected and 'unplanned for' problems is not a light endeavor to handle. Not knowing what challenges the organization will face and having but a light and generalized arsenal to tackle them is sure to breed anxiety and uncertainty among its members (Eisenberg 1990). In modern organizations, this phenomenon is amplified because of the lack of prior interaction-based trust due to reliance on fleeting multifunctional teams that more often than not have none or, at best, little history of joint work experience. This hinders the formation of trusting relationships among their members and increases the perception of exposure felt by individuals when improvising (Bastien and Hostager 1988).

Issues for research

The emerging literature on organizational improvisation has been contributing to this concept's legitimization in the organizational research arena. None the less, current literature still suffers from significant weaknesses. Firstly, articles on organizational improvisation are still excessively wedded to jazz theory. Recalling our previous discussion of the evolution of this concept in organizational settings, we can see that later articles on this subject re-center theory development in the improvisational jazz metaphor, after a series of 'non-jazz' articles and even some empirical research. As rich as the jazz metaphor is for understanding improvisation in organizational settings, in its capacity as a metaphor, it has important limitations that should not be ignored – at the price of ultimately hindering theory development (McCourt 1997; Morgan 1997). To paraphrase Weick (1980), jazz threatens to become a blind spot in organizational improvisation theory. Secondly, empirical research on improvisation is still scarce and is mostly based on grounded theory methodology (e.g. Brown and Eisenhardt 1997; Eisenhardt and Tabrizzi 1995; Orlikowski 1996; Orlikowski and Hoffman 1997). There is only one published quantitative study addressing this phenomenon explicitly – Moorman and Miner's (1998a) work on improvisation in new product development, although, as we argued before there are some others that address it in a more implicit manner.

Although apparently in its infancy, organizational improvisation has already raised some relevant issues for organizational theory as a whole.

A first contribution refers to the demystifying of 'pure' organic structures as the 'ideal' form for complex and highly turbulent environments (Lawrence and Lorsch 1967). In fact, improvisation seems to be an effective mechanism for surviving and thriving in such scenarios, and research has shown that improvisation is a highly structured activity (Barrett 1998; Brown and Eisenhardt 1997; Eisenhardt and Tabrizi 1995). Thus, organizations seem to need some structure even in highly volatile environments, although that structure must be qualitatively different from that demanded by more placid competitive contexts.

An unresolved issue in the literature is the need for close relationships between those improvising. Although some authors present them as a 'must' (e.g. Crossan *et al.* 1996), others argue that improvisation can do well without such 'closeness' and that this only accomplishes a reduction in its effectiveness (e.g. Eisenberg 1990). None the less, a closer look at the evidence put forth by those espousing the latter argument shows that what in fact happens is that improvising teams are able to build a proxy for that closeness through what has been labeled a 'centering strategy' (Bastien and Hostager 1988). In this kind of team performance, individuals start with small variations or embellishments on standards or routine/canonical practices and, when social uncertainty is reduced, they pursue wider deviations from those standards, towards achieving purer forms of improvisation (Hutchins 1991; Weick 1998). Looking at other fields of organizational theory inquiry, we can find other mechanisms for replacing this 'closeness', such as the concept of 'swift trust'. Swift trust is a type of trust that derives not from social similarity or from shared history, but that stems from favorable stereotypes of certain categories of people and of a positive attitude towards teamwork (Jarvenpaa and Shaw 1998). This concept is especially relevant in today's global context, in which individuals often find themselves working with people they have never met (and probably will never meet) in situations they have never faced (Bettis and Hitt 1995; Peters 1992) and thus holds a potentially promising contribution for the study of the co-ordination issues that arise when an organization attempts to improvise.

Another area that current research on organizational improvisation has still to address is its relationship with the national culture. Common sense would suggest

Table 6.9 Empirical and metaphorical grounding of texts on organizational improvisation.

Author(s)	Grounding	Area/Subject
Barrett (1998)	Metaphorical	Jazz
Bastien and Hostager (1988)	Empirical	Jazz
Berkiner (1998)	Metaphorical	Jazz
Brown and Duguid (1991)	Empirical	Organizational practice
Brown and Eisenhardt (1997)	Empirical	New product development
Ciborra (1996)	Anecdotal	Organization structure
Crossan and Sorrenti (1997)	Anecdotal	Organizational learning
Crossan (1997)	Anecdotal/ Metaphorical	Management/Improvisational theater
Crossan (1998)	Anecdotal/ Metaphorical	Organizational improvisation/ Improvisational theater
Crossan *et al.* (1996)	Anecdotal/ Metaphorical	Management/Improvisational theater/Jazz
Deal and Key (1998)	Anecdotal	Corporate celebration
Eisenberg (1990)	Metaphorical	Jazz
Eisenhardt and Tabrizi (1995)	Empirical	New product development
Eisenhardt (1997)	Anecdotal	Strategy and decision making
Ellis (1982)	Anecdotal	Business management
Hatch (1997)	Metaphorical	Jazz
Hatch (1998)	Metaphorical	Jazz
Hatch (1999)	Metaphorical	Jazz
Hutchins (1991)	Empirical	Co-ordination
Johnson and Rice (1984)	Empirical	Technology implementation
Kamoche and Cunha (1997)	Metaphorical	Jazz
Kamoche and Cunha (1998)	Metaphorical	Jazz
Klein and Dellarocas (1998)	Anecdotal	Workflow systems
Meyer (1998)	Metaphorical	Jazz
Miner *et al.* (1996)	Empirical	New product development
Mirvis (1998)	Metaphorical	Jazz
Moorman and Miner (1995)	Theoretical	New product development
Moorman and Miner (1998a)	Theoretical	New product development
Moorman and Miner (1998b)	Empirical	New product development
Orlikowski and Hoffman (1997)	Empirical	Technology implementation
Orlikowski (1996)	Empirical	Technology implementation
Pasmore (1998)	Metaphorical	Jazz
Pearson *et al.* (1997)	Anecdotal	Crisis management
Peplowski (1998)	Metaphorical	Jazz
Perry (1991)	Anecdotal	Business strategy
Slocum *et al.* (1994)	Anecdotal	Business management
Weick (1993a)	Metaphorical	Jazz/*bricolage*/theater
Weick (1993b)	Anecdotal	Firefighting
Weick (1998)	Metaphorical	Jazz
Weick (1999)	Metaphorical	Jazz
Weick (s.d.)	Anecdotal	Firefighting

that cultures with high uncertainty avoidance behavior and high power distance would not be very fertile for this type of activity, but only research can tell for sure.

A final issue that has captured the imagination of researchers in organizational settings is the importance that many attach to a 'high level of knowledge' (e.g. Barrett 1998; Crossan *et al.* 1996; Crossan and Sorrenti 1997; Hatch 1997, 1998; Weick 1993a,b, 1998, 1999, s.d.). This, again, seems to result, from these researchers' over-reliance on the jazz metaphor. In jazz, improvisation is a craft only mastered by more senior performers (Berliner 1994), especially because of the dexterity that playing those instruments normally used by jazz musicians requires. Again, if we look beyond jazz improvisation, we can find an adequate substitute for a high level of knowledge – simplicity of instruments. Research on improvisation use in clinical therapy shows that even the mentally challenged can be adroit improvisers, if provided with the proper instruments (e.g. simple drums, rattles) (Southworth 1983). The question remains whether we can equip individuals with 'organizational rattles' instead of 'organizational saxophones' for them to improvise more freely and, perhaps, more effectively.

Issues for practice

Improvisation seems to be an attractive concept for organizations, especially for those in the business arena. First and foremost, it offers a way for them to remain flexible and adaptive in turbulent environments without having to be purely organic or structureless, something that always seems to be an awkward thought for most executives. Secondly, improvisation allows for the co-presence of effectiveness and efficiency. It allows the organization to detect change by exploration and then to take advantage of it – or at least to respond to it by exploitation. Although existing in a latent mode, this result is not easily achieved because of the seductiveness of exploration and innovation (Eisenhardt 1989). None the less, improvisation, because of its high levels of employee involvement and autonomy, is still a daunting image for bureaucratic organizations (Dougherty 1996), where it will probably mostly happen in 'skunkworks' or other informal settings (Peters 1987; Stacey 1996).

There are several items to take into account when an organization aims at becoming more improvisational.

Firstly, the deliberate creation of an organization with improvising capabilities is a difficult task (Miner *et al.* 1996) and it is not much of a fertile ground for serious normative theory. This is because improvisation cannot be applied instantaneously but must be grown (Brown and Eisenhardt 1997), and is more akin to a recipe than to a prescription to be taken at once (Weick 1993a). Thus, the capability to improvise cannot be implemented by a team of consultants but must instead be grown by the organization itself.

Secondly, abandoning stored procedural memory is a difficult task, even for willing individuals, because of several cognitive limitations of the human mind (Senge 1990). However, if this does not happen then improvisation will be more of an espoused theory than an adopted practice in the organization.

Thirdly, multifunctional teams, because they incorporate people from different professional cultures, with different languages and different repositories of knowledge, may render improvisation very hard to perform. This is a worrying issue if we take into account the recent pro-team bias we have witnessed in the practitioner-oriented literature (e.g. Katzenbach and Smith 1992; Peters 1987, 1992).

A final issue concerns the role of the executive/leader as a manager of meaning and as a catalyst for sensemaking (Weick 1993a). When discussing the external triggers of improvisation, we stated that very low levels of discrepancy between expected and actual reality would tend to hinder improvisation (Moorman and Miner 1995). When these levels are low, the organization and its leader do not have much to be concerned about. This is not the case when these levels are high. Dramatic changes in the environment can have drastic effects on a company's performance and ultimate survival while, arguably, the organization will do little to address those changes – a dynamic that can seriously compromise its longevity. In this type of situation, the role of the manager is to frame environmental changes so that they do not trigger defensive routines in the organization's members in order to render it visible, actionable and ultimately resolvable through improvisation.

Conclusion

Literature reviews are often aimed at inscribing some order into the sizeable stream of texts that most topics of research in organizations seem to command these days. Organizational improvisation is one of the youngest members of this area of scientific endeavor, thus a literature seems to make little sense at this point. In our belief, the opposite is true. The path that organizational improvisation seems to be pursuing has two strange attractors, jazz and organizations, and jazz has, to this day, been the most dominant.

Metaphor is an important instrument of knowledge-building, but its use is dangerous when the area of research has passed its birth stage, when there is still no ground for empirical research. After that stage, grounded theory allows for a first set of hypotheses to be built, upon which more qualitative methods will be employed to arrive at increasingly robust findings. Organizational improvisation has already been the subject of grounded theory and even of a limited number of correlational studies. Thus, our first goal in pursuing this review is to argue for metaphor to be gradually replaced by other research methods, fitter to a more mature body of knowledge, as organizational improvisation appears to be nowadays. Furthermore, by adopting a critical stance, we were able to uncover some underlying commonalities among texts addressing this phenomenon that were yet to be made explicit. In this vein, we presented an *integrative* (instead of an *alternative*) definition of the organizational improvisation construct and an integrative way of measuring it. An additional contribution was made by distinguishing and categorizing the *necessary conditions* for improvisation to occur and the main *influencing factors* determining its degree, performance and results.

Underlying this review, it is also possible to find an effort to translate what has been written on improvisation, which has been mostly directed to the academic public, in a way that practitioners will feel compelled to consider the importance of, if not to adopt, organizational improvisation as a central competence of those organizations dwelling in turbulent and changing environments. By making this statement we are in no way arguing that improvisation is a panacea and that it will only have positive consequences. The path towards an improvisational organization is laden with much toil, for such a skill cannot be bought from a consulting firm, but must purposefully, and more often than not, slowly be grown by the company itself. Moreover, although in increasingly turbulent environments the call for improvisation is hard to silence, the benefits improvisation yields – better organizational performance and personal feelings of transcendence (Eisenberg 1990) – also have a flip side populated with personal anxiety and ever-lurking unintended organizational consequences. However, in environments characterized by the Red Queen effect (Kauffman 1995), where organizations have to keep running just to stay in the same place, and where organizational researchers must precede them in order to have a meaningful impact, studying and implementing/practicing improvisation may appear, in reality, a most daunting challenge. None the less, it can be a most welcome extra boost to allow organizations (and organizational science) to go a little further and, ultimately, to advance and progress.

References

Amabile, T.M. (1998). How to kill creativity. *Harvard Business Review*, 76(4), 77–87.

Anderson, J.R. (1983). *The Architecture of Cognition*. Cambridge, MA: Harvard University Press.

Argyris, C. and Schön, D.A. (1992). *Theory in Practice: Increasing Professional Effectiveness*. San Francisco: Jossey-Bass.

Barley, S.R. and Kunda, G. (1992). Design and devotion: surges of rational and normative ideology in managerial discourse. *Administrative Science Quarterly*, 37, 363–399.

Barrett, F.J. (1998). Coda: Creativity and improvisation in organizations: implications for organizational learning. *Organization Science*, 9(5), 605–622.

Barrett, F.J. and Peplowski, K. (1998). Minimal structures within a song: an analysis of 'All of Me'. *Organization Science*, 9(5), 558–560.

Bastien, D.T. and Hostager, T.J. (1988). Jazz as a process of organizational innovation. *Communication Research*, 15(5), 582–602.

Berkiner, E. (1998). Working the jazz metaphor: musings driving down I-5 past midnight. *Organization Science*, 9(5), 583–585.

Berliner, P.F. (1994). *Thinking in Jazz: The Infinite Art of Improvisation*. Chicago: University of Chicago Press.

Berry, J.W. and Irvine, S.H. (1986). Bricolage: savages do it daily. In Steinberg, R.J. and Wagner, R.K. (eds). *Practical Intelligence: Nature and Origins of Competence in the Everyday World*. Cambridge, UK: Cambridge University Press, pp. 271–306.

Bettis, R.A. and Hitt, M.A. (1995). The new competitive landscape. *Strategic Management Journal*, 16, 7–19.

Brown, J.S. and Duguid, P. (1991). Organizational learning and communities-of-practice: toward a unified view of working, learning and innovation. *Organization Science*, 2(1), 40–57.

Brown, S.L. and Eisenhardt, K.M. (1995). Product development: past research, present findings and future directions. *Academy of Management Review*, 20, 343–378.

Brown, S.L. and Eisenhardt, K.M. (1997). The art of continuous change: linking complexity theory and time-paced evolution in relentlessly shifting organizations. *Administrative Science Quarterly*, 42, 1–34.

Campbell, D. (1989). An introduction to nonlinear dynamics. In Stein, D.L. (ed.). *Lectures in the Science of Complexity*. Redwood, CA: Addison-Wesley, pp. 3–105.

Ciborra, C.U. (1996). The platform organization: recombining strategies, structures and surprises. *Organization Science*, 7(2), 103–118.

Cooper, R.G. (1979). The dimensions of industrial new product success and failure. *Journal of Marketing*, 43(3), 93–103.

Craig, A. and Hart, S. (1992). Where to now in new product development research. *European Journal of Marketing*, 26(11), 2–49.

Crossan, M.M. (1997). Improvise to innovate. *Ivey Business Quarterly*, 62(1), 37–42.

Crossan, M.M. (1998). Improvisation in action. *Organization Science*, 9(5), 593–599.

Crossan, M.M. and Sorrenti, M. (1997). Making sense of improvisation. *Advances in Strategic Management*, 14, 155–180.

Crossan, M.M., White, R.E., Lane, H.W. and Klus, L. (1996). The improvising organization: where planning meets opportunity. *Organizational Dynamics*, 24(4), 20–35.

D'Aveni, R.A. (1995). Coping with hypercompetition: utilizing the new 7-S's framework. *Academy of Management Executive*, 9(3), 45–57.

Deal, T.E. and Key, M.K. (1998). *Corporate Celebration: Play, Purpose and Profit at Work*. San Francisco: Berrett-Koehler.

DeGeus, A. and Senge, P. M. (1997). *The Living Company*. Cambridge, MA: Harvard Business School Press.

Dougherty, D. (1996). Organizing for innovation. In Clegg, S.R., Hardy, C. and Nord, W.R. (eds). *Handbook of Organization Studies*. Thousand Oaks: Sage, pp. 424–439.

Eisenberg, E.M. (1990). Jamming: transcendence through organizing. *Communication Research*, 17(2), 139–164.

Eisenhardt, K.M. (1997). Strategic decision making as improvisation. In Papadakis, V. and Barwise, P. (eds). *Strategic Decisions*. Norwell, MA: Kluwer, pp. 251–257.

Eisenhardt, K.M. (1989). Making fast strategic decisions in high-velocity environments. *Academy of Management Journal*, 32, 543–576.

Eisenhardt, K.M. and Tabrizi, B.N. (1995). Accelerating adaptative processes: product innovation in the global computer industry. *Administrative Science Quarterly*, 40, 84–110.

Ellis, R.J. (1982). Improving management response in turbulent times. *Sloan Management Review*, 23(2), 3–11.

Emery, F. and Trist, E. (1965). The causal texture of organizational environments. *Human Relations*, 18, 21–32.

Erickson, F. (1982). Classroom discourse as improvisation: relationships between academic task structure and social participation structure in lessons. In Wilkinson, L.C. (ed.). *Communicating in the Classroom*. New York: Academic Press, pp. 153–181.

Fiedler, F.E. (1965). The contingency model. In Proshansky, H. and Seidenberg, B. (eds), *Basic Studies in Social Psychology*. New York: Holt, Rinehart and Winston.

Fritz, R. (1989). *The Path of Least Resistance: Learning to Become the Creative Force in Your Life*, 2nd edition. New York: Fawcett Columbine.

Gardner, W. and Rogoff, B. (1990). Children's deliberateness of planning according to task circumstances. *Developmental Psychology*, 26(3), 480–487.

Gersick, C.J.G. (1991). Revolutionary change theories: a multilevel exploration of the punctuated equilibrium paradigm. *Academy of Management Review*, 32, 274–309.

Gersick, C.J. and Hackman, J.R. (1990). Habitual routines in task performing groups. *Organizational Behavior and Human Decision Processes*, 47, 65–97.

Gould, S.J. (1980). *The Panda's Thumb*. New York: W.W. Norton.

Gower, B. (1997). *Scientific Method: A Historical and Philosophical Introduction*. New York: Routledge.

Greenleaf, R.K. (1979). *Servant Leadership: A Journey into the Nature of Legitimate Power and Greatness*. New York: Paulisi Press.

Hackman, J.R. and Oldham, G.R. (1980). *Work Redesign*. Reading, MA: Addison-Wesley.

Hamel, G. and Prahalad, C.K. (1994). *Competing for the Future: Breakthrough Strategies for Seizing Control of your Industry and Creating the Markets of Tomorrow*. Boston: Harvard Business School Press.

Hammer, M. and Champy, J. (1993). *Reengineering the Corporation: A Manifesto for a Business Revolution*. London: Nicholas Brealy.

Hannan, M.T. and Freeman, J. (1989). *Organizational Ecology*. Cambridge, MA: Harvard University Press.

Hatch, M.J. (1997). Jazzing up the theory of organizational improvisation. *Advances in Strategic Management*, 14, 181–191.

Hatch, M.J. (1998). The Vancouver Academy of Management jazz symposium: jazz as a metaphor for organizing in the 21st century. *Organization Science*, 9(5), 556–568.

Hatch, M.J. (1999). Exploring the empty spaces of organizing: how improvisational jazz helps redescribe organizational structure. *Organization Studies* 20(1), 75–100.

Hatch, M.J. and Weick, K.E. (1998). Critical resistance to the jazz metaphor. *Organization Science*, 9(5), 600–604.

Harvey, J. (1996). *The Abiline Paradox and other Meditations on Management*. San Francisco: Jossey-Bass.

Hutchins, E. (1991). Organizing work by adaptation. *Organization Science*, 2(1), 14–39.

Janis, I. (1971). Groupthink. *Psychology Today*, (November), 271–279.

Jarvenpaa, S.L. and Shaw, T.R. (1998). Swift trust in global virtual teams. Unpublished manuscript. University of Texas at Austin.

Joerges, B. and Czarniawska, B. (1998). The question of technology, or how organizations inscribe the world. *Organization Studies*, 19(3), 363–385.

Johnson, B.M. and Rice, R.E. (1984). Reinvention in the innovation process: the case of word processing. In Rice, R.E. (ed.). *The New Media*. Beverly Hills: Sage, pp. 157–183.

Kamoche, K. and Cunha, M.P. (1997). Teamwork, knowledge-creation and improvisation. Proceedings from the international workshop on teamworking (pp. 358–374). Nottingham, UK: University of Nottingham.

Kamoche, K. and Cunha, M.P. (1998). From jazz improvisation to product innovation. Unpublished manuscript. City University of Hong Kong.

Katzenbach, J.R. and Smith, D.K. (1992). *The wisdom of teams: Creating the high performance organization*. Cambridge, MA: Harvard Business School Press.

Kauffman, S.A. (1995). Escaping the red queen effect. *The McKinsey Quarterly*, (1), 119–129.

Kets de Vries, M.F. and Miller, D. (1984). *The Neurotic Organization*. San Francisco: Jossey-Bass.

Klein, M. and Dellarocas, C. (1998). A knowledge based approach to handling exceptions in workflow systems. Unpublished Manuscript. Massachussets Institute of Technology.

Lawrence, P.R. and Lorsch, J.W. (1967). *Organization and environment*. Cambridge, MA: Harvard University Press.

Leinhardt, G. and Greeno, J.G. (1986). The cognitive skill of teaching. *Journal of Educational Psychology*, 78(2), 75–95.

Machin, D. and Carruthers, M. (1996). From interpretative communities to communities of improvisation. *Media, Culture & Society*, 18, 343–352.

McCourt, W. (1997). Discussion note: Using metaphors to understand and to change organizations: A critique of Gareth Morgan's approach. *Organization Studies*, 18(3), 511–522.

Meyer, A. (1998). Antecedents and consequences: Organizing for improvisation: The backstage story of the Vancouver jazz concert. *Organization Science*, 9(5), 569–576.

Miner, A., Moorman, C. and Bassoff, P. (1996). Organizational improvisation in new product development. Unpublished manuscript.

Mintzberg, H. (1995). The structuring of organizations. In H. Mintzberg, J.B. Quinn and S. Goshal (eds). *The strategy process: European edition* (pp. 350–371). Hertfordshire, UK: Prentice Hall Europe.

Mintzberg, H. and McHugh, A. (1985). Strategy formation in an Adhocracy. *Administrative Science Quarterly*, 30, 160–197.

Mintzberg, H. and Waters, J.A. (1982). Tracking strategy in an entrepreneurial firm. *Academy of Management Journal*, 25, 465–499.

Mirvis, P.H. (1998). Variations on a theme: Practice improvisation. *Organization Science*, 9(5), 586–592.

Moorman, C. and Miner, A. (1995). Walking the tightrope: Improvisation and information in new product development. (Report No. 95–101). Cambridge, MA: Marketing Science Institute.

Moorman, C. and Miner, A. (1998a). The convergence between planning and execution: Improvisation in new product development. *Journal of Marketing*, 62, 1–20.

Moorman, C. and Miner, A. (1998b). Organizational improvisation and organizational memory. *Academy of Management Review*, 23(4), 698–723.

Morgan, G. (1997). *Images of organization.* Newbury Park, CA: Sage.

Orlikowski, W.J. (1996). Improvising organizational transformation over time: A situated change perspective. *Information Systems Research,* 7(1), 63–92.

Orlikowski, W.J. and Hofman, J.D. (1997). An improvisational model for change management: The case of groupware technologies. *Sloan Management Review,* 38(2), 11–21.

Pasmore, W.A. (1998). Organizing for jazz. *Organization Science,* 9(5), 562–564.

Pearson, C.M., Clair, J.A., Misra, S.K. and Mitroff, I.I. (1997). Managing the unthinkable. *Organizational Dynamics,* 25(2), 51–64.

Pentland, B.T. and Reuter, H.H. (1994). Organizational routines as grammars of action. *Administrative Science Quarterly,* 39, 484–510.

Peplowski, K. (1998). The process of improvisation. *Organization Science,* 9(5), 560–561.

Perry, L.T. (1991). Strategic improvising: How to formulate and implement competitive strategies in concert. *Organizational Dynamics,* 19(4), 51–64.

Perrow, C. (1986). *Complex Organizations,* 3rd edition. New York: Random House.

Peters, T.J. (1987). *Thriving on Chaos: Handbook for a Management Revolution.* New York: Alfred A. Knopf.

Peters, T.J. (1992). *Liberation Management: The Necessary Disorganization for the Nanosecond Nineties.* New York: Alfred A. Knopf.

Pfeffer, J. and Salancik, G.R. (1978). *The External Control of Organizations: A Resource Dependence Perspective.* New York: Harper & Row.

Picken, J.C. and Dess, G.G. (1997). Out of (strategic) control. *Organizational Dynamics,* 25(1), 35–47.

Powers, C. (1981). Role-imposition or role-improvisation: some theoretical principles. *The Economic and Social Review,* 12(4), 287–299.

Scribner, S. (1986). Thinking in action: some characteristics of practical thought. In Steinberg, R.J. and Wagner, R.K. (eds). *Practical Intelligence: Nature and Origins of Competence in the Everyday World.* Cambridge, UK: Cambridge University Press, pp. 13–30.

Senge, P.M. (1990). *The Fifth Discipline: The Art and Practice of the Learning Organization.* London: Century Business.

Sewell, G. (1998). The discipline of teams: the control of team-based industrial work through electronic and peer surveillance. *Administrative Science Quarterly,* 43, 397–428.

Sharron, A. (1983). Time and space bias in group solidarity: action and process in musical improvisation. *International Social Science Review,* 58(4), 222–230.

Simon, H.A. (1990). Invariants of human behavior. *Annual Review of Psychology,* 41, 1–21.

Sitkin, S.B. (1992). Learning through failure: the strategy of small losses. In Staw, B.M. and Cummings, L.L. (eds). *Research in Organizational Behavior,* vol. 14. Greenwich. CT: JAI Press, pp. 231–266.

Slocum, J.W. Jr, McGill, M. and Lei, D.T. (1994). The new learning strategy: anything, anytime, anywhere. *Organizational Dynamics,* 22(2), 33–47.

Smircich, L. and Stubbart, C. (1985). Strategic management in an enacted world. *Academy of Management Review,* 26, 724–736.

Southworth, J.S. (1983). Improvisation for nonmusicians: a workshop approach. *Journal of Creative Behavior,* 17(3), 195–205.

Stacey, R.E. (1996). *Complexity and Creativity in Organizations.* San Francisco: Berrett-Koehler.

Thayer, L. (1988). Leadership/communication: a critical review and a modest proposal. In Goldhaber, G.M. and Barnett, G.A. (eds). *Handbook of Organizational Communication.* Norwood, NJ: Alex, pp. 231–263.

Van de Ven, A.H. and Poole, M.S. (1995). Explaining development and change in organizations. *Academy of Management Review,* 20(3), 510–540.

Von Clauzewitz (1976). *On War.* New Jersey: Princeton University Press.

Voyer, J.J. and Faulkner, R.R. (1989). Organizational cognition in a jazz ensemble. *Empirical Studies of the Arts,* 7(1), 57–77.

Weick, K.E. (1980). Blind spots in organizational theorizing. *Group and Organization Studies,* 5(2), 178–188.

Weick, K.E. (1993a). Organizational redesign as improvisation. In Huber, G.P. and Glick, W.H. (eds). *Organizational Change and Redesign.* New York: Oxford University Press, pp. 346–379.

Weick, K.E. (1993b). The collapse of sensemaking in organizations: the Mann Gulch disaster. *Administrative Science Quarterly,* 38, 628–652.

Weick, K.E. (1995). *Sensemaking in Organizations.* Thousand Oaks, CA: Sage.

Weick, K.E. (1998). Introductory essay: improvisation as a mindset for organizational analysis. *Organization Science,* 9(5), 543–555.

Weick, K.E. (1999). The aesthetic of imperfection in organizations. In Cunha, M.P. and Marques, C.A. (eds). *Readings in Organization Science.* Lisbon: ISPA.

Weick, K.E. (s.d.). Tools and tragedies in wildland firefighting: barriers to risk mitigation. Unpublished manuscript. University of Michigan.

Weick, K.E. and Westley, F. (1996). Organizational learning: affirming an oxymoron. In Clegg, S.R., Hardy, C. and Nord, W.R. (eds). *Handbook of Organization Studies.* Thousand Oaks: Sage, pp. 440–458.

Woodman, R.W., Sawyer, J.E. and Griffin, R.W. (1993). Toward a theory of organizational creativity. *Academy of Management Review,* 18(2), 293–321.

7 Creativity and improvisation in jazz and organizations

Implications for organizational learning

Frank J. Barrett

> I wake to sleep and take my waking slow. I learn by going where I have to go.
>
> Theodore Roethke, poet

> We must simply act, fully knowing our ignorance of possible consequences.
>
> Kenneth Arrow, economist

> I think the fear of failure is why I try things ... if I see that there's some value in something and I'm not sure whether I deserve to attempt it, I want to find out.
>
> Keith Jarrett, jazz pianist

At the dawn of the twenty-first century, we are in the midst of a revolution that has been called variously the post-industrial society (Bell 1973), the third wave (Toffler 1980), the information revolution (Naisbitt 1983), and the post-capitalist society (Drucker 1993). We do not yet perceive the entire scope of the transformation occurring, but we know that it is global, that it is based on unprecedented access to information, and that since more people have access to information than ever before, that it is potentially a democratic revolution. Perhaps the management of knowledge development and knowledge creation is becoming the most important responsibility for managers as we enter the twenty-first century. Indeed, ideas generated by various streams and movements, including sociotechnical design, total quality management, re-engineering, remind us that the fundamental shift we are experiencing involves empowering people at all levels to initiate innovative solutions in an effort to improve processes.

Given the unprecedented scope of changes that organizations face and the need for members at all levels to be able to think, plan, innovate, and process information, new models and metaphors are needed for organizing. Drucker has suggested that the twenty-first century leader will be like an orchestra conductor. However, an orchestral metaphor – connoting pre-scripted musical scores, single conductor as leader – is limited, given the ambiguity and high turbulence that many managers experience. Weick (1992) has suggested the jazz band as a prototype organization. This paper follows Weick's suggestion and explores the jazz band and jazz improvising as an example of an organization designed for maximizing learning and innovation. To help us understand the relationship between action and learning, we need a model of a group of diverse specialists living in a chaotic, turbulent environment; making fast, irreversible decisions; highly interdependent on one another to interpret equivocal information; dedicated to innovation and the creation of novelty. Jazz players do what managers find themselves doing: fabricating and inventing novel responses without a prescripted plan and without certainty of outcomes; discovering the future that their action creates as it unfolds.

After discussing the nature of improvisation and the unique challenges and dangers implicit in the learning task that jazz improvisers create for themselves, I will broadly outline seven characteristics that allow jazz bands to improvise coherently and maximize social innovation in a coordinated fashion. I also draw on my own experience as a jazz pianist. I have played with and lead combinations of duos, trios, and quartets in addition to touring in 1980 as pianist with the Tommy Dorsey Band under the direction of trombonist Buddy Morrow. I will explore the following features of jazz improvisation.

1   Provocative competence: Deliberate efforts to interrupt habit patterns.
2   Embracing errors as a source of learning.
3   Shared orientation toward minimal structures that allow maximum flexibility.
4   Distributed task: continual negotiation and dialogue toward dynamic synchronization.
5   Reliance on retrospective sense-making.
6   "Hanging out": Membership in a community of practice.
7   Taking turns soloing and supporting.

Finally, I will suggest implications for organizational design and managing for learning.

The nature of improvisation

There is a popular misconception that jazz players are inarticulate, untutored geniuses, that they have no idea what they are playing as if picking notes out of thin air. As biographies of jazz players and studies of jazz have shown, the art of jazz playing is very complex and the result of a relentless pursuit of learning and disciplined imagination. Since (until recently) there have been no conservatories or formal schools of jazz instruction, veteran jazz players are highly committed to self-renewal, having had to create their own learning opportunities.

Jazz improvisers are interested in creating new musical material, surprising themselves and others with spontaneous, unrehearsed ideas. Jazz differs from classical music in that there is no clear prescription of what is to be played. From the Latin "improvisus," meaning "not seen ahead of time," improvisation is "playing extemporaneously . . . composing on the spur of the moment" (Schuller 1989, p. 378). Given the highly exploratory and tentative nature of improvisation, the potential for failure and incoherency always lurks just around the corner. Saxophonist Paul Desmond said that the improviser must "crawl out on a limb, set one line against another and try to match them, bring them closer together" (Gioia 1988, p. 92). Jazz saxophonist Steve Lacy discusses the excitement and danger inherent in improvisation and likens it to existing on the edge of the unknown.

> I'm attracted to improvisation because of something I value. There is a freshness, a certain quality, which can only be obtained by improvisation, something you cannot possibly get from writing. It is something to do with the "edge."

> Always being on the brink of the unknown and being prepared for the leap. And when you go out there you have all your years of preparation and all your sensibilities and your prepared means but it is a leap into the unknown.
>
> (Bailey 1992, p. 57)

The metaphors of leaping into the unknown, hanging out on a limb, suggesting the exhilarating and perilous nature of engaging in an activity in which the future is largely unknown, yet one in which one is expected to create something novel and coherent, often in the presence of an audience.

Gioia captures a sense of the challenge and difficulty inherent in jazz by considering what practitioners of other art forms would subject themselves to if they relied on improvisation as design.

> If improvisation is the essential element in jazz, it may also be the most problematic. Perhaps the only way of appreciating its peculiarity is by imagining what twentieth-century art would be like if other art forms placed an equal emphasis on improvisation. Imagine T. S. Eliot giving nightly poetry readings at which, rather than reciting set pieces, he was expected to create impromptu poems – different ones each night, sometimes recited at a fast clip; imagine giving Hitchcock or Fellini a handheld motion picture camera and asking them to film something, anything – at that very moment, without the benefits of script, crew, editing, or scoring; imagine Matisse or Dali giving nightly exhibitions of their skills – exhibitions at which paying audiences would watch them fill up canvas after canvas with paint, often with only two or three minutes devoted to each "masterpiece."
>
> (Gioia 1988, p. 52)

Improvisation involves exploring, continual experimenting, tinkering with possibilities without knowing where one's queries will lead or how action will unfold.

Learning to improvise: preparing to be spontaneous

It is worth exploring for a moment the way that jazz musicians learn to improvise in order to gain a deeper understanding of how they think while they are playing. Learning to play jazz is a matter of learning the theory and rules that govern musical progressions. Once integrated these rules become tacit and amenable to complex variation and transformation, much like learning the rules of grammar and syntax as one learns to speak. Jazz players learn to build a vocabulary of phrases and patterns by imitating, repeating, and memorizing the solos and phrases of the masters until they become part of their repertoire of "licks" and "crips." According to trumpeter Tommy Turrentine,

> The old guys used to call those things crips. That's from crippled... In other words, when you're playing a solo and your mind is crippled and you can't think of anything different to play, you go back into one of your old bags and play one of your crips. You better have something to play when you can't think of nothing new or you'll feel funny laying out there all the time.
>
> (quoted in Berliner, 1994, p. 102)

After years of practicing and absorbing these patterns, they train their ears to recognize what phrases fit within different forms, the various options available within the constraints of various chords and songs. They study other players' strategic thought process that guided their solo construction, why they chose certain notes and how their motifs fit the contour of the overall phrasing.

A transformation occurs in the player's development when he or she begins to export materials from different contexts and vantage points, combining, extending, and varying the material, adding and changing notes, varying accents, subtly shifting the contour of a memorized phrase. Combining elements from different musical models, mixing different harmonies and grace notes, extending intervals, and altering chord tones is a metaphorical transfer of sorts (Barrett and Cooperrider 1990), transferring from one context into another to produce something new. By combining, extending, and varying, they breathe life into these forms. The variation could involve something as simple as taking automatic phrases and extending them into new and unfamiliar contexts, such as trying out a phrase over a different chord. Pianist John Hicks recalls experiencing a breakthrough when he combined previously unrelated chords. Saxophonist Lee Konitz attempts to create new substitutions as he plays to enrich the basic harmonic structure of standard songs (Berliner 1994, p. 61).

The aim is to integrate ideas, freeing attention so that players can think strategically about their choice of notes and the overall direction of their solos. Hargreaves *et al.* 1991, p. 53) hypothesize that when improvisers employ automatic thinking[1] to execute patterns, they are free to plan the overall strategy of the piece; they are "aware of playing detailed figures or 'subroutines' at a relatively peripheral or unconscious level, with central conscious control reserved for overall strategic or artistic planning." Saxophonist James Moody practices "trying to play something that you like and being able to put it anywhere you want in a tune" (Berliner 1994, p. 174). Jazz critic Mark Gridley claims that Bill Evans was a master strategist.

> Evans crafted his improvisations with exacting deliberation. Often he would take a phrase, or just a kernel of its character, then develop and extend its rhythms, its melodic ideas, and accompanying harmonies. Within the same solo he would often return to it, transforming it each time. And while all this was happening, he would be considering ways of resolving the tension that was building. He would be considering rhythmic ways, melodic ways, and harmonies, all at the same time, long before the moment that he decided was best for resolving the idea. . . . During Bill Evans's improvisations, an unheard, continuous self-editing was going on. He spared the listener his false starts and discarded ideas. . . . Evans never improvised solos that merely strung together ideas at the same rate they popped into his head. The results of these deliberations could be a swinging and exhilarating experience for the listener, but they reflected less a carefree abandon, than the well-honed craftsmanship of a very serious performer working in the manner of a classical composer. The adjective most frequently applied to his music is "introspective."
>
> (Gridley 1991, pp. 302, 303)

It is uncertain to what degree improvisers go through an "unheard, continuous self-editing," an anticipatory, virtual trial and error as they consider different directions and interpretations of the material. Within a split second, musicians must project images and goals gleaned from some musical model or one they have just heard. Although Gridley theorizes that Bill Evans is thinking fairly far ahead and choosing phrases long before he played it, some musicians seem to be deciding within shorter time spans which notes to play. One player describes the subtle interplay between prehearing, responding, and following an idea, who sees the direction of the phrase that is just ahead of him and likens it to "chasing a piece of paper that's being blow into the wind" (Berliner 1994, p. 190). Others speak of going on automatic pilot while they think of something, repeating a phrase in order to buy time while their imagination wakes up. This no doubt, is one characteristic that distinguishes great soloists: how far ahead they are thinking and strategizing about possible phrases, how to shape the contour of their ideas, how and when to resolve harmonic and rhythmic tension. This points toward a delicate paradox musicians face, a point I will explore below: too much reliance on learned patterns (habitual or automatic thinking) tends to limit the risk-taking necessary for creative improvisation; on the other hand too much regulation and control restrict the interplay of musical ideas. In order for musicians to "strike a groove," they must suspend some degree of control and surrender to the flow of the music.

The previous section addressed the nature of improvisation, the challenging task of playing unrehearsed ideas, the process of developing improvisatory skills and the process of learning the jazz idiom. In the following section, I will outline seven characteristics of jazz improvisation and explore how these features apply in non-jazz contexts.

Seven characteristics of jazz improvisation

1   *Provocative competence: interrupting habit patterns*

Perhaps because of the treachery involved in improvising and the risk of playing something that is incoherent, there is often a temptation to do what is feasible, to play notes that are within one's comfortable range. This is why, as many jazz critics attest, there is a temptation on the part of jazz improvisers to rely on "certain stock phrases which have proven themselves effective in past performance (rather than) push themselves to create fresh improvisations" (Gioia 1988, p. 53). Yet, the art of jazz improvisation demands that the musician create something different. Musicians and critics agree that "musicians who 'cheat' by playing the same or similar solos over and over again are looked down upon by colleagues and fans" (Gioia 1988, p. 52). Saxophonist Ronnie Scott contrasts Oscar Peterson's flawless pre-rehearsed solos with the risk taking of Sonny Rollins, who attempts to transform the harmonic and melodic materials that the tune presents.

> Oscar Peterson is a very polished, technically immaculate, performer, who – I hope he wouldn't mind me saying so – trots out these fantastic things that he has perfected and it really is a remarkable performance. Whereas Sonny Rollins, he could go on one night and maybe it's disappointing, and another night he'll just take your breath away by his kind of imagination and so forth. And it would be different every night with Rollins.
>
> (Quoted in Bailey 1988, p. 51)

Because of the temptation to repeat what they do well rather than risk failure, veteran jazz musicians make deliberate attempts to guard against the reliance on pre-arranged music, memorized solos, or habits and patterns that have worked for them in the past. Keith Jarrett decries those who play overlearned clichés and become imitations of themselves: "The music is struggle. You have to want to struggle. And what most leaders are the victim of is the freedom not to struggle. And then that's the end of it. Forget it!" (Carr 1991, p. 53). Jazz musicians often approach their work with a self-reflexiveness, guarding against the temptation to rely on ingrained habits, so that they don't repeat stock phrases and comfortable solos that contradict the goal of improvisation. Tony Oaxley recalls moments of self critique following performances: "The search was always for something that sounded right to replace the things that sounded predictable and (therefore) wrong (Bailey 1992, p. 89). Jarrett put it succinctly: "I think you have to be completely merciless with yourself" (Bailey 1992, p. 122).

Organization learning theorists have noticed that organizations also are tempted to rely on past successes and repeat stock phrases. Behavior in organizations is based on routines – rules, recipes, practices, conventions, beliefs – in short the response system that encodes activity learned from the past. Ordinary learning in organizations tends to lead to stable routines (March 1991) that perpetuate and become fixed even if they are no longer appropriate or detrimental (Levitt and March 1988), as if they are playing themselves automatically. Even when stimuli change, organizations tend to generate the same responses (Weick 1991). Many routines are automatic and not even accessible to ordinary recollection and analysis, so that individuals and organizations continue them long after actors have ceased to be able to provide an account of their purposes (Cohen 1991). Levitt and March (1988) refer to this as the competency trap: the tendency for an organization to become competent and specialized in a routine that was successful, thereby squelching experimentation (March 1991).

Especially under stressful conditions, such as environmental turbulence, there is a tendency to fall back on habitual responses. In this sense, managers often face the same dilemma that jazz players face: their actions are quite public and therefore stressful; they too are tempted to repeat what they do well rather than risk failure if they should depart from what has been proven to work. As Argyris (1990) has pointed out, the pressure to look competent leads people to defend their actions and reasoning. This regression becomes an obstacle to the questioning of assumptions and considering situations from a fresh perspective that could lead to novel initiatives.

Hedberg writes that organizations and managers can voluntarily switch from routines to a deliberate search for alternative possibilities but this is rare: "learning is typically triggered by problems" (Hedberg 1981, p. 16). Of course, even deliberate search for alternatives might not be sufficient for creation of novelty.

This creates a challenge for jazz players: their purpose, by definition, is to avoid that which is automatic and safe and formulas that simply repeat past success. Some jazz musicians avoid "competency traps" and keep fresh alternatives open by deliberately exploring the limits of their knowledge and comfort level. Herbie Hancock recalls an early moment when he discovered the limits of his knowledge. He remembers being inspired when he heard someone playing a passage that he (Hancock) could not play. For some this might be discouraging. But for Hancock, and most successful jazz musicians, this is the beginning rather than the end of the story.

> I had been a musician all my life, had all this training, played with all these great players, but I knew I could never have created that. And if I can't do it, something is missing – I have to find out how to do it! I've always been like that when I've heard something I liked but I couldn't do. That's how I got into jazz. I heard this guy playing (jazz piano) at a variety show in high school, and I knew that he knew what he was doing, and he was doing it on my instrument – but I had no idea of what was going on. So I wanted to learn how to do it. That's what got me started. In order to do that, you have to know what you don't know.
>
> (Novello 1990, p. 445)

What has not been explored much by learning theorists is managers' consciously "switching cognitive gears" from habitual to active thinking (Louis and Sutton 1991). Hedberg *et al.* (1975) encourage organizations to nurture small disruptions and incremental re-orientations to keep learning processes vital and handicap inferior routines. Incremental experiments sharpen perception and activate thought processes.

Many veteran jazz musicians practice provocative competence; they make deliberate efforts to create disruptions and incremental re-orientations. This commitment often leads players to attempt to outwit their learned habits by putting themselves in unfamiliar musical situations that demand novel responses. Saxophonist John Coltrane is well known for deliberately playing songs in difficult and unfamiliar keys because "it made (him) think" while he was playing and he could not rely on his fingers to play the notes automatically. Herbie Hancock recalls that Miles Davis was very suspicious of musicians in his quartet playing repetitive patterns so he forbade them to practice. In an effort to spur the band to approach familiar tunes from a novel perspective, Davis would sometimes call tunes in different keys, or call tunes that the band had not rehearsed. This would be done in concert, before a live audience. "I pay you to do your practicing on the band stand," Hancock recalls Davis telling them. Keith Jarrett recalls Davis' commitment to "keeping the music fresh and moving" by avoiding comfortable routines. "Do you know why I don't play ballads any more?" Jarrett recalled Davis telling him. "Because I like to play ballads so much" (Carr 1992, p. 53).

Miles Davis not only practiced this provocative competence in live concerts, he also extended this to the recording studio. This is illustrated in a famous 1959 session. When the musicians arrived in the recording studio, they were presented with sketches of songs that were written in unconventional modal forms using scales that were very foreign to western jazz musicians at that time. One song, contained 10 bars instead of the more familiar 8 or 12 bar forms that characterize most standards. Never having seen this music before and largely unfamiliar with the forms, there was no rehearsal. The very first time they performed this music, the tape recorder was running. The result was the album *Kind of Blue*, widely regarded as a landmark jazz recording. When we listen to this album, we are witnessing the musicians approaching these pieces for the first time, themselves discovering new music at the same time that they were inventing it.

What makes a disruption provocative rather than noxious can be gleaned from

Miles Davis' example. First, his interruption was affirmative (Barrett 1995): he held an image of members as competent performers able to meet the demands of a challenging task. He believed in their overall potential and capacity to perform successfully even if they felt uncomfortable (and possibly irritated). In fact, his band members were often able to perform at a higher level. Second, he did more than just disrupt habit patterns: he created alternative pathways for action. He imported new material that opened possibilities and suggested alternative routes for his players. Once the song begins, passivity is not an option: the activity is impersonally structured so that musicians are required to play something, to take some kind of action. Third, the interruption was incremental. These foreign contexts were scaled to be challenging, but not overly disruptive. This suggests the role of leadership in cultivating generative metaphors and seeding suggestive narratives (Barrett and Cooperrider 1990).

Hedberg *et al.* (1976) contend that system designers have weak direct influence on participants' behavior. They suggest that designers reconceive their roles as catalysts for a system's self-design by focusing on third order strategies for carrying out second order learning. Miles Davis had a talent for creating incremental obstacles and nurturing small disruptions that provoked his musicians to experiment with new actions that yielded new levels of creativity. This suggests that managers, like Miles Davis, develop a provocative competence that inspires alternative possibilities, an ability to create anomalies and unconventional obstacles that make it impossible for members to rely on habitual responses and rote thinking.

It would be useful to consider the organizational equivalent of requiring members to abandon overreliance on automatic processing and practicing familiar routines. Clearly this would have implications for dislodging conventional assumptions regarding such conventional practices as job descriptions, performance evaluations, and recruitment. Perhaps this is what W. L. Gore and Associates, the makers of Gore-tex, have in mind by abandoning formal job descriptions or conventional chain of command reporting structures. Reportedly, when a newly hired MBA reported for work one day, Bill Gore, the President and founder advised him to "look around and find something you'd like to do." Such a loosely structured environment makes it more difficult to rely on accepted routines and forces new hires to improvise new actions. Or consider the example of the R & D executive at Sony who, wanting to create a mini compact disc player, was faced with engineers who were convinced the CD technology could not be compacted further. Based on familiar routines, and perhaps enamored of the technology they themselves developed, they could not imagine a smaller alternative. The executive walked into the meeting with a 5-inch block of carved wood and told them that the new CD player needed to be no bigger. The engineers now had novel constraints to work through, a challenging puzzle not unlike the modal sketches that Miles Davis' band found when they walked into the *Kind of Blue* recording session.

This suggests that we expand our definition of leadership to include creating conditions that encourage members to bring a mindfulness to their task that allows them to imagine alternative possibilities heretofore unthinkable. Consider the example of British Airlines which held an off-site workshop for its executives to consider ways to improve customer service for the business class. However, instead of sleeping in regular hotel rooms, one executive had the beds removed and replaced them with airline seats. This no doubt disturbed the taken-for-granted routines, not to mention sleep patterns. Faced with the puzzle of these unexpected constraints, they came up with a number of innovations to improve comfort, including the design of a more comfortable seat that included a footrest. Provocative competence involves creating irregular arrangements that disturb "stock phrases" and comfortable playing, encouraging members to improvise new solutions.

2   Embracing errors as source of learning

If past successes create routines that drive out experimentation in organizations, there is a tendency to construe errors as unacceptable. However, errors are a very important source of learning. Abdel-Hamid and Madnick (1990) discuss the need to learn from failures in the development of new software. The Seifert and Hutchins (1992) study of decision making on a Navy ship demonstrated the learning potential of error-making, how errors serve as an opportunity for receiving feedback and becoming familiar with the wider task environment. As individuals learned through error correction procedures, they came closer to the eventual goal of error-free performance. Jazz bands also embrace errors as source of learning, but for quite different reasons. These studies suggest the value of learning from errors as a way to eliminate them under the assumption that in actual performance, errors are ultimately intolerable. Jazz bands, on the other hand, see errors as inevitable and something to be assimilated and incorporated into the performance.

Since jazz improvisation is a highly expressive art form that leads players to go out "on the edge of the unknown," it is impossible to predict where the music is going to lead. Risky, explorative attempts are likely to produce errors. In fact, jazz improvisers regularly make mistakes, often without the audience's awareness. Often, there are discrepancies between intention and action: sometimes the hands fail to play what the inner ear imagines. Sometimes musicians misinterpret others' cues or simply play the wrong notes.

> Somebody who decides to play jazz for a living knows he will struggle for the rest of his life, unless he opts for predictable and smoothing compromise. Honest jazz involves public exploration. It takes guts to make mistakes in public, and mistakes are inherent. If there are no mistakes it's a mistake. In Keith Jarrett's solo improvisations you can hear him hesitate, turn in circles for a while, struggle to find the next idea. Bird used to start a phrase two or three times before figuring out how to continue it. On the spot. Now. No second draft. It can take a toll night after night in front of an audience that just might be considering you shallow.
>
> (Zwerin 1983, p. 33)

Jazz players are often able to turn these unexpected problems into musical opportunities. Errors become accommodated as part of the musical landscape, seeds for activating and arousing the imagination. Drummer Max Roach sees the value in errors, "if two players make a mistake and end up in the wrong place at the wrong time, they may be able to break out of it and get into something else they might not have discovered otherwise." (Berliner 1994, p. 383). Herbie Hancock recalls playing an obviously wrong chord during a concert performance. Hearing the unexpected combination of notes, Miles Davis used them as a prompt, and rather than ignore the mistakes, played with the notes, embellishing them, using them as a creative departure for a different melody. Any event or sound, including an error, becomes a possible springboard to prime the musical imagination, an opportunity to re-define the context so that what might have appeared an error becomes integrated into a new pattern of activity. Looking backward, the "wrong" notes appear intentional.

Rather than treat an enactment as a mistake to be avoided, often what jazz musicians do is to repeat it, amplify it, develop it further until it becomes a new pattern. Pianist Don Friedman recalls listening to a recording with himself on piano and Booker Little on trumpet. When listening to the recording 20 years later, Friedman discovered that he played a major third in the chord instead of a minor third and Little brilliantly accommodated it, allowing the "wrong note" to shape his solo.

> Little apparently realized the discrepancy during his solo's initial chorus, when he arrived at this segment and selected the minor third of the chord for one of the opening pitches of a phrase. Hearing it clash with the pianist's part, Little improvised a rapid save by leaping to another pitch and resting, stopping the progress of his performance. To disguise the error further, he repeated the entire phrase fragment as if he had initially intended it as a motive, before extending it into a graceful, ascending melodic arch. From that point on, Little guided his solo according to a revised map of the ballad. "Even when Brooker played the melody at the end of the take," observed Friedman with admiration, he varied it in ways "that fit the chord I was playing."
>
> (Berliner 1994, p. 383)

Repeating the phrase with the clashing note, Little made it sound intentional. When errors do happen, rather than search for causes and identify responsibility, musicians treat them impersonally: they make adjustments and continue. In this vein, Weick (1990) cites critic Ted Gioia who calls for a different standard for evaluating performance, an "aesthetic of imperfection." Rather than evaluate the success or failure of individual creations based on some external standard of perfection (such as one might find in the evaluation of a classical musical performance), Gioia calls for the need to evaluate courageous efforts. Such an aesthetic would involve evaluating the entire repertoire of actions that the musician attempted, the beautiful phrases combined with the clunkers that were the result of risky efforts, the same expansive efforts that no doubt produce beautiful passages.

One implication for enhancing innovative action in organizations is to question the way we look at errors and breakdowns. How can people in organizations be expected to attempt something that may be outside of their reach if breakdowns are seen as unacceptable? This would suggest that innovation would be enhanced if organizations resisted the attempts to over-focus on the elimination of error or to see mistakes as character blemishes. Too often managers create monuments to organizational breakdowns through exhaustive search for causes and framing mistakes as unacceptable. This often has the unintended consequence of immobilizing people. Given the nature of knowledge work in the organizations of the future, this suggests that perhaps organizations need to adopt an "aesthetic of imperfection," an acknowledgement that learning is something that often happens by trial and error, by brave efforts to experiment outside of the margin. This would propose a different standard for organizational evaluation: evaluate performances not just on conventional standards of success, but on strength of effort; level of purposeful, committed engagement in an activity; perseverance after an error has been made; passionate attempt to expand the horizon of what had been considered possible. At the very least, it suggests distinguishing between errors that are the result of carelessness and those that are the result of caring deeply about a project.

Similarly, once errors are made, how do managers turn these unexpected events into learning opportunities, as imaginative triggers and prompts for new action? Consider an example from Nordstrom's department store where employees are encouraged to "respond to unreasonable customer requests." Stories circulate about an employee paying a customer's parking ticket when the store's gift wrapping took too long. Such capacity for accommodation and adjustment might be indispensable when attempts at innovation and customer satisfaction do not immediately meet expectation. Rather than simply rewarding managers for "fixing" problems, perhaps organizations should consider the way that managers persevere and make use of mistakes as points of creative departure. An aesthetic of imperfection implies that errors would be framed not so much as character blemishes, but as unavoidable mishaps to be creatively re-integrated as negotiation proceeds.

This also suggests that if organizations advocate *ad hoc* action and serendipitous learning, then there are times when members must be willing to release one another for consequences that they could not predict, for errors of trespassing and over-extension. Hannah Arendt (1958) noted that the one antidote to the predicament of unpredictability is forgiveness. Imagine executives developing an aesthetic of forgiveness, releasing those who make noble efforts, for consequences that could not be foreseen. Otherwise, tightly bound bureaucracies might be necessary to ward off trespassers.

3   Minimal structures that allow maximum flexibility

In an effort to guarantee consistency and efficiency, organizations often attempt to systematically avoid changes and ambiguity through creating standard operating procedures, clear and rationalized goals, and forms of centralized control. Hedberg *et al.* (1976) suggested that organizational processes would be improved if designers create minimal structures that allow diversity and minimize consensus. Similarly, Eisenberg (1990) analyzes jamming in jazz bands and contends that creativity is enhanced when emphasis is placed on coordinating action with minimal consensus, minimal disclosure, and minimal, simple structures. Modest structures value ambiguity of meaning over clarity, preserve indeterminacy and paradox over excessive disclosure. By "making do with minimal commonalities and elaborating simple structures in complex ways," (Eisenberg 1990) players balance autonomy and interdependence.

Jazz improvisation is a loosely structured activity in which action is coordinated around songs. Songs are made up of patterns of melodies and chord changes, marked by sections and phrases. Following Bastien and Hostager (1988) songs are "cognitively held rules for musical innovation" (p. 585). When musicians improvise, it is usually based on the repetition of the song structure. These guiding structures are nonnegotiable, impersonal limitations: musicians do not have to stop to create agreements along the way. The selection of standard tunes and their chord changes embody minimal tacit rules that are rarely articulated. The musicians know the chord changes to "All of Me" or a 12 bar blues, so that often musicians who have never met are able to "jam" and coordinate action. These moderate constraints serve as benchmarks that occur regularly and predictably throughout the tune, signalling the shifting context to everyone. Everyone knows where everyone else is supposed to be, what chords and scales players are obliged to play. These minimal constraints allow them freedom to express considerable diversity. Players are free to transform materials, to intervene in the flow of musical events and alter direction. Once there is a mutual orientation around the basic root movement of the chord patterns, even the basic chords themselves can be altered, augmented or substituted.

Songs impose order and create a continuous sense of cohesion and coordination: all the players know where everyone is at any given moment. Individual players are able to innovate and elaborate on ideas with the assurance that they are oriented to a common place. How can organizations achieve fluid coordination without sacrificing creativity and individual contributions? What would be the equivalent in organizations, of structures that are minimal, non-negotiable, impersonal tacitly accepted rules that do not need to be constantly articulated. Weick (1990) suggests that one organizational equivalent of minimal structure might be credos, stories, myths, visions, slogans, mission statements, trademarks. Organizational slogans, such as Avis's "we try harder" are catchy phrases awaiting embellishment, encouraging individual members to elaborate on their version of the melodic path that fits within the tacit constraints. Organizational stories and myths, such as the Nordstrom's employee who paid a waiting customer's parking ticket, persist as markers to remind and seed other employees to embellish on the melody, initiating unusual actions to satisfy customers.

One counterpart to minimal models in organizations is the design prototype. The prototype is the design pattern upon which engineers model and create variations on basic structures. For example Crick and Watson, credited for discovering the structure of DNA, recall that when they were exploring the molecule, they frequently built and re-built prototypes and copper models even though they knew the models were not completely accurate. The DNA prototypes acted as a minimal structure that provided imaginative boundaries around which they could explore options, a shared orientation that invited them to elaborate upon their ongoing creation. Under traditional norms of organizational design, prototypes are often the exclusive property of design engineers, kept separate from manufacturing, marketing, and other groups, not to mention the customer. As a result, many brilliant designs never get produced, or worse, different engineering groups work on their parts separately, only to discover in the final stages that their contributions, however brilliant and innovative, do not fit together. Often technical disciplines are segmented as knowledge specialists develop ideas at different rates, produce solutions that work well in lab settings, but are difficult to reproduce (Purser and Pasmore 1992).

As Weick (1990) pointed out, organizations pay disproportionate attention to beginnings and endings, but not much attention to ongoing temporal coordination. Many breakdowns in innovation occur because organizations are too segmented. Often members do not share a mutual orientation after a project is launched, so that when someone alters action or changes direction, no one is sure where others are located, and do not find out until it is too late. As a result they either feel too constrained to take creative action, or when they do, they discover too late that it causes problems for others.

But what would be the organizational equivalent of song, a structure in which options are minimally-limited, publicly shared, impersonal, simultaneous, and temporally punctuated? Perhaps one counterpart to a song would be rapid prototyping, regular updating and changing of design prototypes. Such a practice would allow cross-discipline communication so that people could create while knowing how and where their ideas fit into the whole evolving system. Consider an alternative that Kodak initiated when they were developing the Funsaver camera. Rather than working separately, the engineering, manufacturing and marketing departments created a shared work space and collaborated to develop a prototype for the camera. Designers made changes and creative contributions to their individual parts, but would update the schematic for the whole camera. Each morning these individual changes were made public and accessible so everyone saw the results of their joint efforts on an ongoing basis and each knew where everyone else was through each stage of the design. Using computer technology to make these contributions public on a regular basis allows everyone to attune themselves to possible direction, like changing the root movement of the chord. People add variants, like the drummer adding accents, that might inspire creative departures. Rapid prototypes function like the loose framework of the song: they leave a great deal of room to depart and deviate; and yet there is enough structure there to give players enough collective confidence to play together. The temporal updating of the minimal structure notifies everyone where others are in their incremental innovations, like the chord changes of a song, and increases the likelihood that people can achieve a successful joint awareness throughout the life of the project.

4 Distributed task: continual negotiation toward dynamic synchronization

Although there are many players well known for their soloing, in the final analysis, jazz is an ongoing social accomplishment. What characterizes successful jazz improvisation, perhaps more than any factor mentioned thus far, is the ongoing give and take between members. Players are in a continual dialogue and exchange with one another. Improvisers enter a flow of ongoing invention, a combination of accents, cymbal crashes, changing harmonic patterns, that inter-weave throughout the structure of the song. They are engaged with continual streams of activity: interpreting others' playing, anticipating based on harmonic patterns and rhythmic conventions, while simultaneously attempting to shape their own creations and relate them to what they have heard.

Jazz improvisation is an emergent, elusive, vital process. At any moment a player can take the music in a new direction, defy expectations, trigger others to re-interpret what they have just heard. Trumpeter Wynton Marsalis, in terms reminiscent of John Dewey's dictum that genuine learning is by nature a participative, democratic experience, compares improvisation to working out ideas in democratic groups.

> Groups of people can get together and the process of their negotiation can have an integrity, and the fact that they can get together and have a dialogue and work – it's like what the UN does. They sit down, and they try to work things out. It's like any governing body. It's like a wagon train, you know.
>
> (Marsalis and Stewart 1995)

Pianist Tommy Flanagan discusses his duo albums with Hank Jones and Kenny Barron.

> You don't know what the other player is going to play, but on listening to the playback, you hear that you related your part very quickly to what the other player played just before you. It's like a message that you relay back and forth. . . . You want to achieve that kind of communication when you play. When you do, your playing seems to be making sense. It's like a conversation.
>
> (Tommy Flanagan quoted in Berliner 1994, p. 369)

In order for jazz to work, players must develop a remarkable degree of empathic competence, a mutual orientation to one another's unfolding. They continually take one another's musical ideas into context as constraints and facilitations in guiding their musical choices. Saxophonist Lee Konitz discusses the interactive interplay.

> I want to relate to the bass player and the piano player and the drummer, so that I know at any given moment what they are all doing. The goal is always to relate as fully as possible to every sound that everyone is making. . . . but whew! It's very difficult for me to achieve. At different points, I will listen to any particular member of the group and relate to them as directly as possible in my solo.
>
> (Lee Konitz quoted in Berliner 1994, p. 362)

Players are continuously shaping their statements in anticipation of others' expectations, approximating and predicting what others might say based on what has already happened.

Traditional models of organization and group design feature static principles in which fluctuations and change are seen as disruptions to be controlled and avoided. Jazz bands are flexible, self-designed systems that seek a state of dynamic synchronization, a balance between order and disorder (Purser and Pasmore 1992), a "built in instability" (Takeuchi and Nonaka 1986). In jazz, ongoing negotiation becomes very important when something interrupts interactive coherence. Given the possibility of disorientation and miscalculations, they must be able to rely on one another to adjust, to amend direction. Drummer Max Roach recalls a performance of "Night in Tunisia" when the players lost the sense of a common beat.

> When the beat got turned around (in Night in Tunisia), it went for about 8 bars. In such a case, someone has to lay out. You can't fight it. Dizzy stopped first because he heard what was happening quicker than the rest of us, and he didn't know where "one" was. Then it was up to Ray Brown and Bishop and myself. One of us had to stop, so Bishop waved off. Then it was up to Ray Brown and myself to clear it up. Almost immediately, we found the common "one" and the others came back in without the public realizing what had happened.
>
> (Berliner 1994. p. 382)

The example above illustrates the dynamic, flexible potential when a group successfully creates a distributed task. Seifert and Hutchins (1992) refer to the features that make up a distributed task: shared task knowledge, horizon of observation, multiple perspectives. Jazz members are able to negotiate, recover, proceed, adjust to one another because there is shared task knowledge (members monitor progress on ongoing basis), have adequate horizon of observation (they are witnesses to one another's performance); and they bring multiple perspectives to bear (each musical utterance can be interpreted from different points of view).

When the players successfully achieve a mutual orientation to the beat, they develop what they call a "pocket," or some refer to as "achieving a groove." Establishing a groove is the goal of every jazz performance. Groove refers to the dynamic interplay within an established beat. It occurs when the rhythm section "locks in" together, when members have a common sense of the beat and meter. Establishing a groove, however, is more than simply playing the correct notes. It involves a shared "feel," for the rhythmic thrust. Once a group shares this common rhythm, it begins to assume a momentum, as if having a life of its own separate from the individual members. There is a sense that the groove acts as what Winnicot called a "holding environment," a reliable nesting that provides a sense of ontological security, a sense of trust that allows people to take risks and initiate actions.

> When you get into that groove, you ride right on down that groove with no strain and no pain – you can't lay back or go forward. That's why they call it a groove. It's where the beat is, and we're always trying to find that.
>
> (Drummer Charlie Persip in Berliner 1994, p. 349)

> Every musician wants to be locked in that groove where you can't escape the tempo. You're locked in so comfortably that there's no way you can break outside of it, and everyone's locked in there together. It doesn't happen to groups every single night, even though they may be swinging on every single tune. But at some point when the band is playing and everyone gets locked in together, it's special for the musicians and for the aware, conscientious listener. There are the magical moments, the best moments in jazz.
>
> (Franklin Gordon in Berliner 1994, p. 388)

> I don't care what kind of style a group plays as long as they settle into a groove where the rhythm keeps building instead of changing around. It's like the way an African hits a drum. He hits it a certain way, and after a period of time, you feel it more than you did where he first started. He's playing the same thing, but the quality is different – it's settled into a groove. It's like seating tobacco in a pipe. You put some heat on it and make it expand. After a while, it's there. It's tight.
>
> (Saxophonist Lou Donaldson in Berliner 1994, p. 349)

What happens when musicians strike a groove adds a paradoxical dimension to our earlier discussion of attention and cognitive processing. Good improvisers, we said, employ a combination of automatic and controlled cognition. However, this experience of groove that improvisers hope for seems to involve a surrender of familiar controlled processing modes; they speak of being so completely absorbed in playing that they are *not* consciously thinking, reflecting, or deciding on what notes to play, as if they are able to simultaneously be inside and outside of their bodies and minds. Controlled thinking is depicted sometimes as an obstacle, something to develop only to escape.

Herrigel suggests a similar paradox in the practice of archery. Like jazz, the art of archery involves deliberate preparation and active conscious attention (controlled cognition) in disciplined practice; but when the moment comes when one wants the perfect shot, the archer must surrender and let go of conscious striving. At that moment:

> nothing definite is thought, planned, striven for, desired or expected, which aims in no particular direction ... which is at bottom purposeless and egoless ... is therefore ... called "right presence of mind." This means that the mind ... is nowhere attached to any particular place.
>
> (Herrigel 1989, p. 41)

This sense of aimless aiming, a surrender in which "nothing is left of you but a purposeless tension" (Herrigel 1989, p. 35) is similar to the way clarinetist Ken Peplowski describes such peak musical moments.

> When we play at our best, I find many times that I'm not actually thinking about anything and you can actually have a strange experience of going outside of yourself and observing yourself while you're performing. It's very strange. And you can actually listen as you're playing and listen to the rest of the group and you can be completely objective and relaxed. And come to think of it, completely subjective also, because you are reacting to everything else around you.
>
> (Peplowski 1995)

This points to a core paradox at the heart of jazz improvisation: if musicians strive too much to attain this state, they obstruct it. Regulation and control can restrict the interplay of musical ideas. Peplowski goes on to say that what makes this possible are prior intensive practice, learning to master tools skills; but at the moment of leaping into playing, "you're forgetting about all these tools you've learned."

Musicians often speak of such moments in sacred metaphors. They speak of the beauty, the ecstasy, the divine, the transcendent joy, the spiritual dimension associated with being carried by a force larger than themselves. They talk about these moments in language strikingly close to what has been described as an autotelic experience, or flow (Csikszentmihalyi 1990). This research suggests that people are able to attain a state of transcendence when they are absorbed in pursuit of desired activity, they feel like they are being carried away by a current, like being in a flow.

When musicians are able to successfully connect with one another at this level and establish a groove, they sometimes experience an ability to perform beyond their capacity. This dimension is perhaps the most elusive, if vital characteristic of jazz improvisation. Pianist Fred Hersch recalls that playing with bassist Buster Williams inspired him to play differently.

> Buster made me play complex chords like Herbie Hancock sometimes plays – that I couldn't even sit down and figure out now. It's the effect of the moment and the effect of playing with Buster and really hearing everything, hearing all those figures.
>
> (Pianist Fred Hersch in Berliner 1994, p. 390)

And Buster Williams recalls that when playing with Miles Davis, the music took on a life of its own.

> With Miles, it would get to the point where we followed the music rather than the music following us. We just followed the music wherever it wanted to go. We would start with a tune, but the way we played it, the music just naturally evolved.
>
> (Buster Williams in Berliner 1994, p. 392)

Most of our studies of organizational behavior have a rational-cognitive orientation. Organizational learning theories in particular stress rational, adaptive modes of inquiry. Appreciating the interactive complexity involved in jazz improvisation suggests that we pay attention to intuitive and emotional connections between organizational members, the experience of passionate connection that inspire deeper levels of involvement and committed participation. Studies of jazz improvisation suggests that researchers revisit such familiar concepts as empowerment, motivation, and team building, concepts which have been studied almost exclusively from a cognitive and individualistic perspective. The experience of spiritual intimacy, synergy, surrender, transcendence, and flow warrant wider study. Would it not be useful to study the role of supportive relationships in drawing out one another's latent capacities, for example? At the very least, this would suggest a relational view of the learning process, in the spirit of Vygotsky's concept of the zone of proximal development. (Vygotsky 1987)

5   *Reliance on retrospective sense making as form*

Because jazz improvisation borders on the edge of chaos and incoherence, it begs the question of how order emerges. Unlike other art forms and other forms of organized activity that attempt to rely on a pre-developed plan, improvisation is widely open to transformation, redirection, and unprecedented terms. Since one cannot rely on blueprints and can never know for certain where the music is going, one can only make guesses and anticipate possible paths based on what has already happened, meanwhile continue playing under the assumption that whatever has happened must amount to something sensible. Gioia (1988) writes:

> The improviser may be unable to look ahead at what he is going to play, but he can look behind at what he has just played; thus each new musical phrase can be shaped with relation to what has gone before. He creates his form *retrospectively.*
>
> (p. 61)

The improviser can begin by playing a virtual random series of notes, with little or no intention as how it will unfold. These notes become the materials to be shaped and worked out, like pieces of a puzzle. The improviser begins to enter into a dialogue with her material: prior selections begin to fashion subsequent ones as themes are aligned and reframed in relation to prior patterns.

Weick (1993) likens the jazz improviser to Levi-Strauss's (1966) concept of *bricolage*, the art of making usage of whatever is at hand. The bricoleur, like the jazz musician, examines and queries the raw materials available and entices some order, creating unique combinations through the process of working through the resources he/she finds. Weick cites the example of a man in upper state New York who built a tractor from a myriad collection of unrelated junk and diverse parts he had accumulated in his front yard. The jazz musician, like the junk collector, looks over the material that is available at that moment, the various chord progressions, rhythmic patterns, phrases and motives, and simply leaps into the quagmire under the assumption that whatever he is about to play will fit in somewhere. Like the bricoleur who assumes that there must be a tractor somewhere in that pile of junk, the improviser assumes that there is a melody to be worked out from the morass of rhythms and chord changes. As new phrases or chord changes are introduced, the improviser makes connections between the old and new material. In the absence of a rational plan, retrospective sense-making makes spontaneous action appear purposeful, coherent, and inevitable.

Organizations tend to forget how much improvisation, bricolage, and retrospective sense making are required to complete daily tasks. In an effort to control outcomes and deskill tasks, they often attempt to break complex tasks down into formal descriptions of work procedures that can be followed automatically. Following Brown and Duguid (1991), managers wrongly assume that these simple steps reflect the way that work actually gets done. Given that many tasks in organizations are indeterminate and people come to them with limited foresight, members often need to apply resourcefulness, cleverness, pragmatism in addressing concerns. They often have to play with various possibilities, re-combining and reorganizing, to find solutions by relating the dilemma they face to the familiar context that preceded it. In spite of the wish for a rational plan of predictable action, they often must take a look around and act without a clear sense of how things will unfold.

Consider Orr's (1990) study of Xerox's training of service technicians representatives. The trainers, in an effort to downskill the task of machine repair, attempted to document every imaginable breakdown in copiers so that when technicians arrived to repair a machine, they simply looked it up in the manual and followed a pre-determined decision tree to perform a series of tests that dictate a repair procedure. Their premise was that a diagnostic sequence can be devised to respond to the machine's predictable problems. However, the study revealed that no amount of documentation could include enough contextual information necessary to understand every problem. Orr (1990) relays a story of a technical rep confronting a machine with error codes and malfunctions that were not congruent with the diagnostic blueprint. This machine's malfunction did not fit the kind of errors that were documented nor had anything like this problem been covered in his training. Both he and the technical specialist he called in to help were baffled. To simply give up the repair effort and replace the machine would have been a solution, but would have meant loss of face with the customer – an unacceptable solution. After exhausting the approaches suggested by the diagnostic, they attempted to make sense of this anomaly by connecting it to previous experiences and stories they had heard from others' experience. After a five-hour trouble shooting session of trials and errors, they fell upon a solution. Many jobs in organizations require this kind of bricolage – fumbling around, experimenting, patching together an understanding of problems from bits and pieces of experience, improvising with the materials at hand. Few problems provide their own definitive solutions.

Jazz players, junkyard collectors and technical reps find themselves in the middle of messes having to solve problems in situ, creating interpretations out of potentially incoherent materials, piecing together other musicians' playing, their own memories of musical patterns, interweaving general concepts with the particulars of the current situation, creating coherent, composite stories.

6   *Hanging out: membership in communities of practice*

An essential part of learning jazz is becoming a member of the jazz community, "hanging out," learning the code, behaving like one of the members. Learning is not simply a matter of transmitting de-contextualized information from one person to another. Local jazz communities of peers in large metropolitan areas such as Detroit, Chicago, and especially New York have served as informal educational systems for disseminating knowledge. Musicians get together to listen to recordings of great soloists, memorize their solos, play tunes in different tempos and keys until they could find the right feel. They join other musicians, "hanging out" in coffee shops and bars after a performance and exchanging stories. Stanley Turrentine remembers he learned from others by "asking about things I didn't understand." Novices discover they need to learn certain "standard" tunes; they learn appropriate keys and tempos: the norms and conventions of the trade. One young trumpeter even recalls learning how to dress from "hanging out" with Miles Davis (Berliner 1994). Central to learning jazz is the institution of the jam session, in which musicians get together to play extemporaneously. A special fraternity often develops among jazz musicians as they guide each other through various learning experiences, borrowing ideas from one another.

Brown and Druguid (1991), refer to organizations as communities of practices. To foster learning, they contend, organizations must see beyond conventional, canonical job descriptions and recognize the rich practices themselves. In the example of the technical rep above, their successful experience with the recalcitrant machine became part of the technicians' folklore, told and retold during coffee breaks. These stories form a community memory that others could draw upon when facing unfamiliar problems. Essential to organizational learning is access to legitimate peripheral participation (Lave and Wenger 1990), understanding how to function as an insider. This recognizes that learning is much more than receiving abstract, acontextual, disembodied knowledge. It is a matter of learning how to speak the language of the community of practitioners.

This has real consequences for organizations. Consider the case of how a technological change attempted at a manufacturing plant failed because management did not value the communal foundation of learning: useful local innovations were not disseminated, learning from mistakes was limited, and good routines that varied from the officially sanctioned ones were kept unofficial. Learners need access to experienced practitioners, through formal and informal meetings, conversations, stories, myths, rituals, etc.

7   *Alternating between soloing and supporting*

One of the most widespread, yet overlooked, structures in jazz is the practice of taking turns. Jazz bands usually rotate the "leadership" of the band: that is, they take turns soloing and supporting other soloists by providing rhythmic and harmonic background. Such an egalitarian model assures that each player will get an opportunity to develop a musical idea while others create space for this development to occur. In order to guarantee these patterns of mutuality and symmetry, it is necessary that people take turns supporting one another. The role of accompaniment, or "comping" is a very active and influential one: it provides a framework which facilitates and constrains the soloist. In written arrangements, the scored passages often precede the soloist's improvisation and channel, sustain, and embellish it. In a sense the background accompaniment conditions the soloist, organizes the course of the solo through passing chords, leading tones and rhythmic accents.

It is not enough to be an individual virtuoso, one must also be able to surrender one's virtuosity and enable others to excel. In order to "comp" or accompany soloists effectively, jazz musicians need to be very good listeners. They need to interpret others' playing, anticipate likely future directions, make instantaneous decisions in regard to harmonic and rhythmic progressions. But they also may see beyond the player's current vision, perhaps provoking the soloist in different direction, with accents and chord extensions. None of this responsiveness can happen unless players are receptive and taking in one anothers' gestures. If everyone tries to be a star and does not engage in supporting the evolution of the soloist's ideas, the result is bad jazz. When they listen well to others' soloing, they help the soloist reach new heights. Usually we think that great performances create attentive listeners. This notion suggests a reversal: attentive listening enables exceptional performance.

This has considerable implication for organizational learning. In spite of the increasing popularity of empowerment and employee involvement, organizations often have difficulty supporting participation (Pasmore and Fagans 1991). Organizations struggle with finding ways to include voices that traditionally have been silenced. The deceptively simple practice of taking turns creates a mutuality structure that guarantees participation, inclusion, shared ownership without insisting on consensus and its unintentional hegemonic consequences.

Beyond a model for sharing leadership through turn-taking, it also offers a model of followership. Given the complex and systemic nature of problems that cross conventional boundaries, managers, as knowledge specialists, cannot be solo operators: they need one another's expertise and support in order to arrive at novel solutions. The term "job rotation" takes on new meaning when we think about the shifting of leadership and support responsibilities that jazz bands enact. Perhaps organizational innovation would thrive if members were skilled at giving others' room to develop themes, to think out loud and discover as they invent. One suggestion would be to have organizational "jam" sessions in which members take turns thinking out loud while others listen. Recent interest in organizational dialogue (Senge 1990) resemble attempts to include disparate voices that might otherwise become overlooked.

Yet, organizations tend to reward individual performance and achievement rather than supportive behaviors. This emphasis often leads to excessive competition to achieve stardom, efforts to be in unilateral control, efforts to defend one's position against challenges, hesitancy to acknowledge the limits of one's knowledge: all obstacles to the learning process (Argyris 1993). Imagine if such practices were to become more widespread in organizations: employees, managers, and executives evaluated on their capacity to surrender self and ego in effort to support the development of another's idea. Perhaps if organizations would recognize and reward those who strive to nourish, strengthen, and enhance the expressive capacity of relationships, they would unleash their capacity to improvise and innovate.

Implications for non-jazz contexts

Managers often attempt to create the impression that improvisation does not happen in organizations, that tightly designed control systems minimize unnecessary idiosyncratic actions and deviations from formal plans. People in organizations are often jumping into action without clear plans, making up reasons as they proceed, discovering new routes once action is initiated, proposing multiple interpretations, navigating through discrepancies, combining disparate and incomplete materials and then discovering what their original purpose was. To pretend that improvisation is not happening in organizations is to not understand the nature of improvisation.

Many business organizations, under pressure to perform, create cultures that reinforce instrumental, pragmatic, rational, and deliberate action rather than a culture that is expressive, artistic, paradoxical, and spontaneous. In fact, there are locales and durations which seem to rely on routines and predictable outcomes, particularly in functions such as production and manufacturing. Organizations must face a tradeoff between servicing efficiency and stewarding attention as a scarce resource to be focused where needed. In this sense, improvisation is best conceived as an activity that occurs for stretches of human behavior.

Clearly there are certain industries and contexts that require an improvisatory mindset: high velocity, high technology firms; research and development activities; cultures of high urgency and excitement, such as the early days of the Apple Macintosh; interdisciplinary project teams formed to address a specific problem. Certainly popular management literature has created a language that resonates with the jazz idiom: suggesting that organizations need to learn to thrive on chaos; managers are encouraged to create a sense of urgency by "turning things upside down," doing away with job descriptions, and valuing failures as a sign that people are experimenting and learning (Peters 1987).

Are there ways to socialize a mindset that nurtures spontaneity, creativity, experimentation, and dynamic synchronization in organizations? What practices and structures can we implement that might emulate what happens when jazz bands improvise? The jazz band as prototype offers a few suggestions.

1.   Boost the processing of information during and after actions are implemented.
Jazz players act their way into the future, then justify their actions by placing their statements within a context of meaning (chord changes, rhythmic emphasis, etc.). Like jazz soloists who realize how notes, phrases, and chords relate as they look back on what they have created, it is during and after action that people in organizations become aware of the goals and values they implicitly hold and what constraints these values place upon their future actions (Weick 1995). Within the ongoing flow of everyday organizational activity, people retrospectively make sense or construct a story or justification for what they have already done (Staw 1980). These stories can become the seeds for greater discoveries and inventions. Therefore, one implica-

tion is to boost the processing of information and surface multiple interpretations of diverse participants within close proximity to action.

Organizations might consider a strategic orientation that links planning, action, implementation, and environmental scanning. Organizations could benefit from creating virtual strategic planning sessions in which members engage in trial and error thinking, just as jazz musicians do when they solo. Generating multiple, simultaneous alternatives minimizes escalation of commitment to a single option (Staw 1980, Eisenhardt 1989) and allows members to make adjustments and re-orientations as they receive disconfirming feedback regarding any single action scenario. This view would challenge the traditional notion of strategic planning as a form of rational control, or as an abstract exercise divorced from and prior to action. In this spirit, Senge (1990), advocates a view of planning as play or as a "practice field" in which managers practice thinking ahead, predicting, and guessing future moves within various constraints. In virtual planning scenarios managers could try out alternative maps and alter the core assumptions that have remained unquestioned (see Hampden-Turner 1990). This is apparently a practice familiar to managers at Shell Oil (DeGeus 1988) who were asked to respond to multiple (and sometimes contradictory) assumptions regarding their environmental constraints, including entertaining the notion that the price of oil might be slashed in half – something that seemed unthinkable at the time. This became in DeGeus' words, a "license to play." These incremental disruptions also created a larger repertoire of knowledge structures, higher variety of responses, when such an unprecedented event did occur.

2.   Cultivate provocative competence: Create expansive promises and incremental disruptions as occasions for stretching out into unfamiliar territory.

Provocative competence is a leadership skill that involves challenging habits and conventional practices, challenging members to experiment in the margins and to stretch in new directions. Organizational learning theorists (Argyris 1990) write that one of the shortfalls of single loop learning is that managers choose to address only those problems that are familiar, those issues for which a solution is imaginable. Miles Davis surprised his band by disrupting their routines and stretching them beyond comfortable limits: calling unrehearsed songs and familiar songs in foreign keys. Of course there is a potential downside to disruptions. Research suggests that when people confront environmental jolts, they fall back on habitual modes of action (Walsh 1995). Also, there might be a tendency to escalate commitment to a wrong course in the context of a threatening interruption (Staw and Ross 1987).

One way leaders practice provocative competence is by evoking a set of higher values and ideals that inspire passionate engagement. A context in which goals that are beyond the capacity of single individuals to accomplish might enhance the need for improvisation, testing comfortable boundaries, cooperation, and negotiation. Barrett (1995) discusses visionary organizations that make expansive promises that defy "reasonable limits" and stretch members to re-define the boundaries of what they have experienced as constraining. Consider Canon's promise in the 1970s to produce a personal copier that would sell for $1,000 (Prahalad and Hamel 1989). Given the constraints that existed at the time, (the least expensive copier sold for several thousand dollars), such a proposal seemed preposterous. Surprised engineers engaged in different kind of conversations, searching for new approaches, experimenting with substituting a disposable cartridge for the very complex image-transfer mechanism that Xerox and other companies, including Canon, had employed in their copiers. Such tasks demand cooperation, exploration, and improvisation.

3.   *Ensure that everyone has a chance to solo from time to time.*

When self-directed work teams are performing well they are often characterized by distributed, multiple leadership in which people take turns leading various projects as their expertise is needed (Guzzo 1995). In jazz bands, everyone gets a turn to solo. Organizations might consider evolving norms that insist on including diverse voices, giving everyone a regular turn at bat and valuing those who make room for others to shine.

Organizations might experiment with a structured process that provides participants with a chance to solo and offsets those influential members who might control or dominate a group. A simple organizational development tool called the nominal group technique (Delbecq *et al.* 1975) is structured to do just this: every individual in turn "brainstorms" out loud while others listen to his or her ideas. No one is allowed to interrupt or re-direct; people are encouraged to build on others' ideas they have heard. A variation of the structure is that no one speaks twice until every other person in the group speaks at least once. This is an impersonal, nonnegotiable structure that monitors air time, cultivates group creativity and ensures that every individual has voice. This also approximates Habermas's notion of the "ideal speech situation" in which collective learning is enhanced because individuals are free to communicate openly, completely free from compulsion or distortions of power, and the force of the better argument may prevail (Habermas 1970).

4.   *Cultivate comping behaviors.*

Organizations must go beyond merely inviting new voices, but must also create processes that suspend the tendency to criticize, judge, express disbelief that might kill a nascent idea. In order for soloists to have impact, there must be ongoing comping (accompaniment) from supporters. What would be the equivalent of comping in organizations? Perhaps this would suggest supportive behaviors such as mentoring, advocating, encouraging, listening. This means rewarding people who support others to take center stage, including such skills as blending, helping people along the way as they transition and develop ideas at different rates. This might include expanding the stories we tell about creative achievements beyond those that highlight autonomous action, to include the roles of those who assisted, who gave others room, who encouraged fledgling, nascent gestures with subtle nudges much like a jazz pianist comping.

Such deliberate efforts to make room for peers' contributions is close to what jazz musicians do when they comp – agree to suspend judgement, to trust that whatever the soloist is doing right now will lead to something, to blend in to the flow and direction of the idea, rather than to break off in an independent direction. Such democratic structures enhance the likelihood that people not only have the right to be heard, but also have opportunity to influence.

5.   *Create organizational designs that produce redundant information*

From a rational design perspective, organizations should be designed to process information efficiently. However, to maximize flexibility and creativity, one could follow the lessons of jazz bands and create designs that produce a redundancy of information. Following Hutchings (1990) in Weick and Roberts (1993) systems sustain flexible actions and mindful performance when jobs are designed to reproduce overlapping knowledge. Overlapping knowledge creates redundant sets of information that permits people to identify with and take responsibility for whole processes rather than parts of the process. Designing more interdependence into tasks increases members' responsive capacity.

6.   Create organizational climates that value errors as a source for learning.
Good things can happen when people jump in and act even when all plans are not complete and elegant. Rather than over-rely on pre-planned strategies and canonical job descriptions, acknowledge members' capacity for bricolage and pragmatic reasoning, their ability to juxtapose, recombine, and reinterpret past materials to fashion novel response. Organizational learning, then, must be seen as a risky venture, reaching into the unknown with no guarantee of where one's explorations will lead. Since errors are indispensable in the creative process, organizational leaders can create an aesthetic of imperfection and an aesthetic of forgiveness that construes errors as a source of learning that might open new lines of enquiry. Often, however, organizations view errors as a result of individual incompetence rather than systemically determined, leading people to suppress mistakes and deny responsibility (Argyris 1990). This suggests that leaders need to create contexts in which reporting and discussing errors is not risky behavior.

7.   Cultivate serious play: too much control inhibits flow.
Jazz is an activity marked by paradox: musicians must balance structure and freedom, autonomy and interdependence, surrender and control. They grapple with the constrictions of previous patterns and structures: they strive to listen and respond to what is happening; at the same time they try to break out from these patterns to do something new with all the risks that both paths entail. If musicians strive too much to hit a groove, achieve flow (Csikszentmihalyi 1990), or jam (Eisenberg 1990), they obstruct it. Organization theorists have articulated a similar paradox: Quinn (1988) argues that having a conscious purpose with logical, internally consistent abstractions sometimes creates a unidimensional mindset that is blind to emerging cues: "When behaving with conscious purpose, people tend to act upon the environment, not with it" (p. 27). Quinn's discussion of masters of management sounds very much like what master improvisers do:

> The people who come to be masters of management do not see their work environment only in structured, analytic ways. Instead, they also have the capacity to see it as a complex dynamic system that is constantly evolving. In order to interact effectively with it, they employ a variety of different perspectives and frames . . . [b]ecause of these shifts (in contradictory perspectives).
>
> (Quinn 1988, pp. 3–4)

Jazz musicians suggest that one way to manage this paradox is to adopt a disciplined concentration that one adopts when playing a game, the way rock climbers and chess players experience their task (Csikszentmihalyi 1990) or the way that Bill Russell talks about playing basketball (Eisenberg 1990). There is a sense of surrender in play, a willingness to suspend control and giving over of oneself to the flow of the ongoing game. (Perhaps this is what organizations like Southwest Air are hoping to encourage when they declare having fun in the workplace as a core value). This suggests that we re-visit the conventional separation between work and play: legitimate play as a fruitful, meaningful activity, one that enhances the sheer joy of relational activity.

Conclusion and discussion

The mechanistic, bureaucratic model for organizing – in which people do routine, repetitive tasks, in which rules and procedures are devised to handle contingencies, and in which managers are responsible for planning, monitoring and creating command and control systems to guarantee compliance – is no longer adequate. Managers will face more rather than less interactive complexity and uncertainty. This suggests that jazz improvisation is a useful metaphor for understanding organizations interested in learning and innovation. To be innovative, managers – like jazz musicians – must interpret vague cues, face unstructured tasks, process incomplete knowledge, and yet they must take action anyway. Managers, like jazz players, need to engage in dialogue and negotiation, the creation of shared spaces for decision making based on expertise rather than hierarchical position.

Although rich in implications, there are limits to the applicability of the improvisation metaphor. The discussion of jazz bands has held up jazz as an "ideal type." Most of the points discussed so far assume a base level of competence. In reality, not all players are equally competent. This is where the metaphor begins to break down for managerial purposes. No amount of listening, support, or "comping" can enhance a performance if the performer is not up to the task. If an interaction with competent players can enhance individual performance, there might also be an opposite effect: performers of lesser competence can have a debilitating effect on the overall group performance. Also while tolerance of errors is essential to enhance experimentation, there are cases where errors are intolerable: in high reliability organizations, for example. But even beyond high reliability organizations, the consequences of small actions can have large consequences when the structure is loosely coupled (Weick 1991). Consider the collapse of Barings Bank, one of the most prestigious financial institutions in the world, due to the erroneous actions of one man.

By looking at the practices and structures associated with jazz playing, it is possible to see that successful jazz performances are not haphazard or accidental. Musicians prepare themselves to be spontaneous. Jazz improvisation has implications that would suggest ways that managers and executives can prepare organizations to learn while in the process of acting.

Finally, jazz improvisation can be seen as a hopeful activity. It models individual actors as protean agents capable of transforming the direction and flow of events. In that sense, jazz holds an appreciative view (Cooperrider and Srivastva 1987, Barrett 1995) of human potential: it represents the belief in the human capacity to think freshly, to generate novel solutions, to create something new and interesting, reminding us of John Dewey's contention that we are all natural learners. To quote the saxophonist Ornette Coleman, "Jazz is the only music in which the same note can be played night after night but different each time."

Acknowledgments

The author would like to thank Kishore Sengupta, Reuben Harris, Mark Gridley, Ken Peplowski, Karl Weick, and two anonymous reviewers for their helpful comments and suggestions on earlier drafts.

Note

1 Cognitive psychologists distinguish between "automatic" and "controlled" information processing. Automatic modes of processing are effortless, familiar, habitual, outside of conscious awareness. "Controlled" modes of processing are deliberate, effortful, active, strategic, directed, and intentional (Schneider and Shiffrin 1977, Shiffrin and Schneider 1977). Jazz improvising seems to employ a combination of modes of processing. When learning new phrases, or attempting challenging musical ideas, players employ controlled processing. Trumpeter Benny Bailey said, "You just have to keep on doing it (practicing phrases) over and over again until it comes automatically." (Berliner 1994, p. 165). Once learned, these become second nature, or learned habits that one can rely upon. Pianist Bill Evans (1991) explains "You take problems one by one and stay with it ... until the process becomes secondary, or subconscious, then you take on the next problem until it becomes second nature, or subconscious." Pressing (1984, p. 139) describes the switch from controlled to automatic as one in which musicians "completely dispense with conscious monitoring of motor programmes, so that the hands appear to have a life of their own, driven by the musical constraints of the situation."

References

Abdel-Hamid, T., S. Madnick. 1990. The elusive silver lining: How we fail to learn from software development failures. *Sloan Management Review* 32 1 Fall 39–48.
Arendt, H. 1958. *The Human Condition.* Univ. of Chicago Press, Chicago, IL.
Argyris, C. 1990. *Overcoming Organizational Defenses.* Allyn-Bacon, Needham, MA.
Bailey, D. 1992. *Improvisation.* Da Capo Press, New York.
Barrett, F. J. 1995. Creating appreciative learning cultures. *Organization Dynamics* 24 1 Fall 36–49.
——, D. Cooperrider. 1990. Generative metaphor intervention: A new approach to intergroup conflict. *J. Applied Behavioral Science* 26 2 223–244.
Bastien, D., T. Hostagier. 1988. Jazz as a process of organizational innovation. *J. Communication Research* 15 5 October, 582–602.
Bell, D. 1976. *The Coming of the Post-Industrial Society.* Basic Books, New York.
Berliner, P. 1994. *Thinking in Jazz.* Univ. of Chicago Press, Chicago, IL.
Brown, J., P. Duguid. 1991. Organizational learning and communities of practice: Toward a unified view of working, learning, and innovation. *Organization Science* 2 1 40–57.
Carr, D. 1991. *Keith Jarrett.* Da Capo Press, New York.
Cellar, D. F., G. V. Barrett. 1987. Script processing and intrinsic motivation: The cognitive sets underlying cognitive labels. *Organizational Behavior and Human Decision Processes* 40 115–135.
Cohen, M. 1991. Individual learning and organizational routine: Emerging connections. *Organization Science* 2 1 135–139.
Csikszentmihalyi, M. 1990. *Flow: The Psychology of Optimal Experience.* Harper, New York.
DeGeus, A. 1988. Planning as learning. *Harvard Business Review* 66 2 70–74.
Delbecq, A. L., A. H. Van de Ven, D. Gustafson. 1975. *Group Techniques for Program Planning.* Scott-Foresman, Glenview, IL.
Drucker, P. 1989. *The New Realities.* Harper and Row, New York.
Edmonson, A. 1996. Learning from mistakes is easier said than done: Group and organizational influences on the detection and correction of human error. *J. Applied Behavioral Science* 32 1 March 5–28.

Eisenberg, E. 1990. Jamming: Transcendence through organizing. *Communication Research* 17 2 April, 139–164.

Evans, B. 1991. *The Universal Mind of Bill Evans*. Video. Rhapsody Films, New York.

Gioia, T. 1988. *The Imperfect Art*. Oxford Univ. Press, New York.

Gridley, M. 1991. *Jazz Styles*. Prentice-Hall, Englewood Cliffs, N.J.

Guzzo, R., ed. 1995. *Team Effectiveness and Decision Making in Organizations*. Jossey-Bass, San Francisco, CA.

Habermas, J. 1970. Toward a theory of communicative competence. *Inquiry* 13 360–375.

Hampden-Turner, C. 1990. *Charting the Corporate Mind*. Free Press, New York.

Hargreaves, D. J., A. C. Cork, T. Setton. 1991. Cognitive strategies in jazz improvisation: An exploratory study. *Canadian J. Research in Music Education* 33 December 47–54.

Hedberg, B. 1981. How organizations learn and unlearn. N. Nystrom, W. Starbuck, eds, *Handbook of Organizational Design*. Oxford Univ. Press, Oxford, UK.

——, P. Nystrom, W. Starbuck. 1976. Camping on seesaws: Prescriptions for a self-designing organization. *Administrative Science Quarterly* 21 March 41–65.

Herrigel, E. 1989. *Zen in the Art of Archery*. Vintage Books, New York.

Hodgkinson, G. P., G. Johnson. 1994. Exploring the mental models of competitive strategists: The case for a processual approach. *J. Management Studies* 31 525–551.

Lave, J., E. Wenger. 1991. *Situated Learning: Legitimate Peripheral Participation*. Cambridge Univ. Press, Cambridge, UK.

Levi-Strauss, C. 1966. *The Savage Mind*. Univ. of Chicago Press, Chicago, IL.

Levitt, B., J. March. 1988. Organizational learning. *Annual Review of Sociology* 14 319–340.

Louis, M., R. Sutton. 1991. Switching cognitive gears: From habit of mind to active thinking. *Human Relations* 44 1 55–76.

March, J. 1991. Exploration and exploitation in organizational learning. *Organization Science* 2 1 71–87.

Marsalis, Wynton, Frank Stewart. 1995. *Sweet Swing Blues*. Norton and Company, New York.

Nasbitt, J. 1982. *Megatrends*. Warner Books, New York.

Novello, J. 1987. *Contemporary Keyboardist*. Source Productions, Toluea, CA.

Orr, J. 1990. Sharing knowledge, celebrating identity: War stories and community memory in a service culture. D. S. Middleton, D. Edwards, eds, *Collective Remembering: Memory in Society*. Sage, Beverly Hills, CA.

Peplowski, K. 1998. The process of improvisation. *Organization Science* 9 5 560–561.

Pressing, J. 1984. Cognitive processes in improvisation. W. R. Crozier, A. J. Chapman, eds, *Cognitive Processes in the Perception of Art*. Elsevier, Amsterdam, The Netherlands.

Prokesch, S. 1993. Mastering chaos at the high-tech frontier: An interview with Silicon Graphic's Ed McCracken. *Harvard Business Review* November–December.

Purser, R., W. Pasmore. 1992. Organizing for learning. W. Pasmore, R. Woodman, eds, *Research in Organizational Change and Development* 6 37–114.

Quinn, R. E. 1988. *Beyond Rational Management: Mastering the Paradoxes and Competing Demands of High Performance*. Jossey-Bass, San Francisco, CA.

Schneider, W., R. M. Shiffrin. 1977. Controlled and automatic human information processing: I. Detection, search, and attention. *Psychological Review* 84 1–66.

Schuler, G. 1989. *The Swing Era*. Oxford Univ. Press, New York.

Seifert, C., E. Hutchins. 1992. Error as opportunity: Learning in a cooperative task. *Human-Computer Interaction* 7 409–435.

Senge, P. 1990. *The Fifth Discipline*. Doubleday, New York.

Shiffrin, R. M., W. Schneider. 1977. Controlled and automatic human information processing: II. Perceptual learning, automatic attending, and a general theory. *Psychological Review* 84 127–190.

Staw, B. 1980. Rationality and justification in organizational life. B. Staw, L. L. Cummings, eds, *Research in Organizational Behavior* 2 45–80.

——, J. Ross. 1987. Behavior in escalation situations: Antecedents, prototypes and solutions. *Research in Organizational Behavior.* JAI Press, Greenwich, CT.

Takeuchi, H., I. Nonaka. 1986. The new product development game. *Harvard Business Review* January–February 137–146.

Toffler, A. 1981. *The Third Wave.* Bantam Books, New York.

Vygotsky, L. 1987. *The Collected Works of Lev Vygotsky.* Plenum Press, New York.

Walsh, J. 1995. Managerial and organizational cognition: Notes from a trip down memory lane. *Organization Science* 6 3 280–321.

Weick, K. 1990. Managing as improvisation: Lessons from the world of jazz. Aubrey Fisher Memorial Lecture, Univ. of Utah, October 18.

——. 1991a. The nontraditional quality of organizational learning. *Organization Science* 2 1 116–124.

——. 1991b. The vulnerable system: An analysis of the Tenerife air disaster. P. Frost, L. Moore, M. Louis, C. Lundberg, J. Martin, eds, *Reframing Organizational Culture.* Sage Press, Newbury Park, CA. 117–130.

——. 1992. Agenda setting in organizational behavior. *J. Management Inquiry* 1 3 Sept. 171–182.

——. 1993. Organizational redesign as improvisation. G. Huber, W. Glick, eds, *Mastering Organizational Change.* Oxford Press, New York, 346–379.

——. 1995. Creativity and the aesthetics of imperfection. C. Ford, D. Gioia, eds, *Creative Action in Organizations.* Sage Press, Thousand Lakes, CA.

——, K. Roberts. 1993. Collective mind in organizations: Heedful interrelating on flight decks. *Administrative Science Quarterly* 38 357–381.

Zwerin, M. 1983. *Close Enough for Jazz.* Quartet Books, London, UK.

8 The aesthetic of imperfection in orchestras and organizations

Karl E. Weick

The problem I'm concerned with is organizational innovation and renewal, which I think can be understood partly as a problem of how to achieve order within diversity. The way I want to attack this problem is by taking seriously the advice I handed out in the paper titled, *Amendments to Organizational Theory*, namely, if you want to understand organizations, study something else. Part of the rationale for that prescription is that if you understand something, almost anything, in some depth, you will have learned something about order and chaos in the human condition. And once you begin to understand order and chaos, you begin to understand something about large-scale human organizations. The "something else" that I used to illustrate the argument was collective improvisation in jazz orchestras, such as those assembled by Duke Ellington, Woody Herman, and Stan Kenton.

I want to continue extrapolating from orchestras to organizations, but I want to shift the focus of attention to jazz improvisation in general. What I'm trying to do is articulate some ideas that may help us understand why so many organizations, in Tom Peters colorful phrase, cannot innovate their way out of a wet paper bag during a Southeast Asian monsoon. Organizations these days are hard-pressed to come up with single innovations in a timely manner, and continuous innovation is even more uncommon.

Innovation has a macro, structural side, some of which has been documented by Andy Van de Ven's group at Minnesota. The side of innovation that I want to explore is more focused on a micro level of analysis, a concern with process, and with the activity of improvisation as my proxy for innovation.

My aspirations are modest. I want to make the case that a fuller understanding of the process by which jazz is produced and evaluated, is a valuable tool of analysis for organizational theorists who want to understand innovation, the variation process in natural selection, idea generation, and creativity. The key ideas about how jazz is produced that I will explore include, the use of songs as a temporal logic and the use retrospective bricolage as a means to create order within chaos. The key idea about evaluation that I want to develop, is the notion that jazz appreciation involves an aesthetic of imperfection.

Characteristics of jazz

If we examine some basic characteristics of jazz, it immediately becomes clear that several crucial issues in organizational theory are engaged.

For example, jazz is a temporal art form, which means it is more usefully viewed as an activity than as an object. Jazz resembles music, the cinema, and dance, because it cannot be grasped in an instant. While jazz may lack the beauty of the objects of sculpture or architecture, when jazz is judged as an activity, its vitality, intensity and expressive communication between artist and audience become relevant dimensions of variation and appreciation. Jazz is performance art, much like a Jackson Pollack painting, which celebrates the artistic act as much as the artistic work. Pollack's work celebrates the act of painting, just as Sonny Rollins work on tenor saxophone celebrates the act of creating music on the spur of the moment. Jazz, as a temporal, performing art, engages the longstanding interests of organizational theorists in process, development, the temporal logic of the garbage can model, narratives with *beginnings + middles + ends*, routines, and structuration.

All agree that the hallmark of jazz is improvisation, which means that any jazz instrumentalist is "evaluated almost entirely on his ability as a soloist" (Gioia, 1988, p. 51). Improvisation, which Schuller (1986, p. 378) defines as "playing extemporaneously, i.e. without benefit of written music. . . . composing on the spur of the moment," creates much of the controversy and mystery associated with jazz. The controversy turns on the question of how could one possibly consider the imperfect, spur-of-the-moment, "spontaneous prattle" of an improvising musician, anything but a second rate art form. In the words of the composer Elliott Carter, "the musical score serves the essential role of preventing" the performer from playing what he already knows and leads him to explore other new ideas and techniques" (Gioia, 1988, p. 54). As we will see later, some of the best jazz musicians are mindful of the grain of truth in Carter's comment, although by and large, the comment is immensely unsettling, given the hurdles that jazz musicians set for themselves.

From the perspective of the performer, Paul Desmond in this case, the tension in a jazz solo is preventing it from becoming formless, structurally incoherent, tending toward excess. In his words, the improviser must "crawl out on a limb, set one line against another and try to match them, bring them closer together" (Quoted in Gioia, 1988, p. 92). Desmond captures some of the mystery and tension in jazz improvisation, but Alec Wilder has captured it with even more energetic observation, one which puts a very different spin on Carter's observation from the perspective of the composer.

> I wish to God that some neurologists would sit down and figure out how the improviser's brain works, how he selects, out of hundreds of thousands of possibilities, the notes he does at the speed he does – how in God's name, his mind works so damned fast! And why, when the notes come out right, they are right. . . Composing is a slow, arduous, obvious, inch-by-inch process, whereas improvisation is a lightning mystery. In fact, it is the creative mystery of our age.
>
> (Suhor, 1986, p. 134)

It is interesting that, during the relatively brief 70 year history of jazz, the proportion of any musical selection that involves improvisation by a soloist, has steadily expanded from solo breaks inserted into a framework that was largely composed, to the complete discarding of composed music altogether in some avant garde players. The extreme movement away from composition of any kind is exemplified by Keith Jarrett piano concerts, consisting of two hours of melodic accessible music, not a single note of which is composed in advance (Gioia, 1988, p. 59). As the critic Francis Davis (1986, p. 8) notes, "The danger with that practice is that the music can become a progression of cliches. I mean, you go from doing one style you know how to do well to another style you know how to do. I hear him [Jarrett] playing within himself; everything's within his fingers. Composed music faces the same barriers; there's always the problem of getting beyond your limitations, beyond what to you has already become a cliché." So simply discarding a composition altogether, is no guarantee that you won't fall back on overlearned clichés and mannerisms, a point that is potentially crucial for innovation.

Keith Jarrett is not the only example of improvisation run amok. Davis (1986) describes much of modern jazz as a "sham democracy which entitles each band member to solo to his heart's content on every single number (p. 129). The early history of World Saxophone Quartet exemplifies this tendency when members tried to outdo one another in public, leading one critic to describe them as four onanistic virtuosos unable to make the distinction between practice and performance (adapted from Davis, 1986, pp. 245–246).

At the other extreme from that of nothing but solos, is the memorized solo, something that is certain to create unease, if not disgust. The disgust is evident in comments about pianist Ray Bryant.

> How much is improvised? Tonight, Bryant played After Hours in a note-for-note copy of the way he played it on the Dizzy, Rollins, and Stitt album on Verve some fifteen years ago. Was it written then? Or worse. Has he transcribed and memorized his own solo, as if it were an archaeological classic? It was fine blues piano indeed, but it is odd to hear it petrified in this way. Similarly, Bryant concluded each set tonight with a gospelish blues (in C, of course) that was, note-for-note, the same both times. The hall had been cleared at the break, so the few of us that snuck through both sets were faced with the strange fact that some of the freest sounding pieces of the evening were the most mechanical.
>
> (Gioia, 1988, pp. 52–53)

What jazz forces us to consider are what kinds of forms, social and procedural, can prevent solipsism, impose order and a sense of permanence, but not destroy identity, diversity, autonomy, independence? This is an ageless issue in the social sciences, but jazz gives us an excuse to rethink it.

It may be helpful, in trying to grasp improvisation, to imagine what improvisation would look like if other art forms put a premium on it. Here is an example.

> If improvisation is the essential element in jazz, it may also be the most problematic. Perhaps the only way of appreciating its peculiarity is by imagining what twentieth-century art would be like if other art forms placed an equal emphasis on improvisation. Imagine T. S. Eliot giving nightly poetry readings at which, rather than reciting set pieces, he was expected to create impromptu poems – different ones each night, sometimes recited at a fast clip; imagine giving Hitchcock or Fellini a handheld motion picture camera and asking them to film something, anything – at that very moment, without the benefits of script, crew, editing, or scoring; imagine Matisse or Dali giving nightly exhibi-

tions of their skills – exhibitions at which paying audiences would watch them
fill up canvas after canvas with paint, often with only two or three minutes
devoted to each 'masterpiece.'

(Gioia, 1988, p. 52)

It seems to me that, relative to jazz improvisation with its time boundaries, fast
tempos, irreversibility, public exposure, memory of previous improvised lines as
enemy, and acoustical and physical limitations on execution, improvisation in
other kinds of organizations is relatively easy by comparison. People in organizations routinely seem to operate with more time, and fewer constraints within the
moment where composition must occur. But, I think it may be this very freedom
which, like the temptation on Keith Jarrett to trot out the limitations of his vision in
every single concert, may represent the dark side of innovation in organizations.
Either there is too little structure or the wrong kind of structure in organizations,
and this is what makes it hard for them to innovate. This paper won't address
which of those two possibilities is more plausible. For the moment, it is sufficient
to observe that a closer look at jazz suggests the wisdom of re-examining the question of the nature of small structures that seed rather than impede innovation in
organizations.

So far, in my attempt to highlight interesting qualities of jazz, I have focused on
activities, situations, and practices rather than people. Issues of personality and skill
are obviously important. For example, jazz probably attracts more than its share of
people who prefer to make spur of the moment decisions, as Gioia (1988, p. 56) has
argued,

> One can scarcely imagine a Charlie Parker or a Lester Young thriving in an
> environment which demanded the production of elaborate symphonic scores,
> or the ability to survive in the academic milieu of the conservatory or university
> music department. For artists such as these, jazz provides the most suitable
> arena in which they can develop and exercise their talents. Indeed, only a
> particular type of temperament would be attracted to an art form which values
> spur-of-the-moment decisions over carefully considered choices, which prefers
> the haphazard to the premeditated, which views unpredictability as a virtue and
> sees cool-headed calculation as a vice.

If I were to summarize the relevance of jazz as a tool or metaphor or template for
organizational analysis, I would note these things in addition to those I've already
covered:

1   Jazz defies the traditional Western distinction in music between composition
    and performance, and in this defiance, anticipates an analogous tendency in
    organizational theory to separate structure from process, plans from implemen-
    tation, process from product, and prospect from retrospect.
2   Jazz also demonstrates a disdain for any musical division of labor, "the jazz musi-
    cian being both creator and interpreter, soloist and accompanist, artist and
    entertainer" (Gioia, 1988, p. 16).
3   Jazz embodies an aesthetics which is able to recognize beauty in the flawed
    execution of ideas.

4   Jazz musicians are tied together by social forms that coordinate, yet preserve diversity, and that require a minimum of consensus for that coordination to occur.
5   Jazz chronically moves toward the abyss of formlessness, yet usually pulls back just before dropping over the edge, with discoveries of the order that lies closer to entropy, than most of us are willing to risk.

But perhaps the characteristic of jazz that I find most engaging is that it represents a completely different group of people who live by "disciplined imagination." The discipline of the jazz musicians comes from the melodies he or she starts with, the imagination comes in the personalizing of that melody through improvisation. Given my earlier analysis of the work of theory construction as disciplined imagination (Weick, 1989), it seems eminently plausible to me that, in many ways, theorists are jazz musicians, jazz musicians are theorists, and both represent roles that have been neglected, if not discouraged, in organizations.

Sources of form

Jazz is an ideal setting in which to explore more richly, the suggestion that a little structure goes a long way. Jazz improvisation takes place within forms, which seem to facilitate rather than hinder the activity. It is these forms which we need to understand more fully, because they may suggest lessons we would do well to generalize to organizations. While there are social practices such as norms (e.g. each person gets a chance to solo sometime during the evening) and communicative codes (e.g. eye contact can be used to change tempos), as well as local agreements that impose order (see Bastien and Hostager [1988] for an excellent description of those structures), I want to focus on a source of form that seems less obviously represented in organizational innovation, namely, the song.

David Sudnow (1979), starts a stunning essay with the statement that a

> song is a social organizational device par excellence, a format that quite elegantly coordinates the movements of two or more individuals. Its metrical structure, with a beginning and an end and a definite number of grouped pulses, furnishes a planful means for coordinating simultaneous movement and allocating little batches of talk among various players over the course of ongoing play. This one takes a four-measure solo and turns the floor over to another, who knows just where to go and knows when he is likely to get the floor. In various styles of music, little conventional understandings aid this turn-taking. If one starts a solo and decides to play longer than usual, he can speak more intricately. The baroque pianist and the country-and-western bassist can, with little difficulty, do a good job together on Happy Birthday to You. . . . No matter what the musical style and variation in division of voices and functions, everywhere in ensemble song performance everybody is moving through predetermined and scheduled sequences of corporately textured places. The harmony of a song, a marvelous social arrangement, is a temporal and spatial blueprint for concerted action and the paced-placed integration of individual gestures in terms of the song's overall scripted group choreography. Everybody moves toward recurrent

benchmarks, to and through successively unfolding stances of multifaceted places, always having something locationally to say in common, dancing from just this stance to just that one – on time together.

(pp. 105–108)

Interestingly, one of the problems in contemporary music is that many of its younger players do not know many songs. They grew up learning music played on jazz records, but what they learned were chord changes not melodies. Thus they do not know melodies, but perhaps even more crucial, they do not know lyrics, which means, they don't know how to phrase the melody properly (Davis, 1986, p. 87).

Songs seem to be an interesting source of constrained possibilities. They represent a kind of mutual equivalence structure (Wallace, 1961) which allows people to be diverse in equivalent ways, which then allows their actions to be meshed. The song produces cohesion amidst diversity. The song does the coordinating, which leaves people free to focus autonomously on everything else The song IS the interdependence. The structures of a melody impose order continuously, not just at the beginning. This may be their single most crucial property for innovation. Innovation in organizations seems to pay disproportionate attention to beginnings, starts, climate, one-time idea generation. But then, as people develop their ideas at different rates, with different elaboration, and different assumptions, and different transitions, no one knows where anyone else is. Mutual support is impossible, as is blending, or assisting people in intermediate steps.

That's not what happens when improvisation is held together temporally. In jazz, both the soloist and the accompanist know where they are. They have a continuing sense of common place. Notice, that people who try to improvise collectively without temporal coordination, face a problem that is twice as puzzling as the one faced by the jazz musician. The person working in a project team to generate new ideas, is simultaneously trying to find out where everyone is, while at the same time trying to innovate as if he or she had found the common portion of the problem to which everyone's attention was directed.

Songs are continuous minimal constraints that seed the process of innovation and tell everyone else where the improviser is. The song is an automatic shared context that forecloses the often-troubling issue of forging an agreement. The song also frees up people to concentrate on ways to vary, manipulate, augment, diminish, fragment, and regroup the seed pattern of the melody into new variants (Schuller, 1968, p. 58). Within this structure, there is no such thing as a senseless note. There may be wrong notes, sour notes, ugly notes, or dissonant notes, but all of those descriptions are relational statements (e.g. wrong relative to...). The improvised notes remain sensible both to the player and to the listener, and can trigger additional invention.

If organizations have moments when they are loosely coupled and when indeterminacy makes sense making difficult, then the anchor created by a time bound melody that recycles, imposes a tightly coupled structure on that basic indeterminacy. Thus, jazz represents a prototypic situation of simultaneous tight and loose coupling and shows how such an adaptive structure might be constructed and function.

The point of all this for organizational theories of innovation would seem to be that there is some wisdom in trying to unpack the phrase, "singing the organization." To coordinate, with a minimum of consensus and a maximum of diversity, designers need to fashion the equivalent of songs. A song is an organizing device that represents a simple form within which requisite variety can accumulate. The chords within which each note of the melody are embedded create multiple meanings for the melody, and the choice of which of these notes to enact, is an autonomous, creative choice. Yet other people can still make sense of that creative act.

I honestly don't know what structures in organizations serve the same function as does a song for jazz musicians. I do know that something like a song seems crucial for improvisation. It may be that an organizational credo – speed, simplicity, self-confidence in the case of GE – is something like a song, but what it lacks is a temporal character. Maybe, something like a PERT chart is closer, although one does not usually think of it as something that encourages creative departures.

Retrospect as form

Gioia (1988), in his efforts to fathom the nature of form in improvisational music, introduces the contrast between forms developed by the blueprint method and forms developed by the retrospective method. He says of the blueprint method.

> The blueprint method is most clearly represented, as one might gather from its name, in architecture. Here the artist plans in advance every detail of the work of art before beginning any part of its execution. For the architect this plan takes the form of a blueprint; for the painter it is revealed in preliminary sketches; for the novelist it is contained in outlines and rough drafts.
>
> (p. 60)

Gioia then describes an "opposite" approach to art this way:

> One can imagine an opposite approach to art: the artist can start his work with an almost random maneuver – a brush stroke on a canvas, an opening line, a musical motif and then adapt his later moves to this initial gambit. A jazz improviser, for example, might begin his solo with a descending five-note phrase and then see, as he proceeds, that he can use this same five-note phrase in other contexts in the course of his improvisation.
>
> This is, in fact, what happens in Charlie Parker's much analyzed improvisation on Gershwin's Embraceable You. Parker begins with a five-note phrase (melodically similar to "you must remember this" phrase in the song As Time Goes By) which he employs in a variety of ingenious contexts throughout the course of his improvisation. Parker obviously created this solo on the spot (only a few minutes later he recorded a second take with a completely different solo, almost as brilliant as the first), yet this should not lead us to make the foolish claim that his improvisation is formless.
>
> (p. 60)

Gioia (1988, p. 61) notes that improvisation follows the retrospective form and that jazz relies more on the retrospective form than do other arts, including theater and choreography.

Improvisation follows not the blueprint method but this second approach. The improviser may be unable to look ahead at what he is going to play, but he can look behind at what he has just played; thus each new musical phrase can be shaped with relation to what has gone before. He creates his form retrospectively.

Improvisation as a retrospective form is interesting, not just because of its temporal quality of looking back, but also because it suggests the quality of bricolage, and the activity of a bricoleur. A bricoleur is:

> a person who makes things work by ingeniously using whatever is at hand, being unconcerned about the "proper" tools or resources.
>
> (Thayer, 1988, p. 239)

A bricoleur is a pure agent of structure. That person draws organization out of raw material (Thayer, 1988, p. 239). The bricoleur is as much concerned with organization, as the artist is concerned with form. The jazz musician, who creates form retrospectively, builds something that is recognizable from whatever is at hand, contributes to an emerging structure being built by the group in which he or she is playing, and creates possibilities for the other players. This unfolding structuring has in it, elements of loose coupling and commitment.

Since events are improvised and intention is loosely coupled to execution, the musician has no choice but to wade in and see what happens. What will actually happen won't be known until it is too late to do anything directly about it. All the person can do is justify and make sensible, after the fact, whatever is visible in hindsight. Since that residue is irrevocable, and since all of this sensemaking activity occurs in public, and since the person has a continuing choice as to what to do with that residual, this entire scenario seems to contain a microcosm of the committing forces that affect creative coping with the human condition. Within the small space of a single jazz performance, there is indeterminacy, retrospective sensemaking, justification, the improvisation of the bricoleur, limited foresight, imperfection, regrets, opportunities discovered after the fact, a temptation to play remembered lines, and an open-ended future.

If improvisation tends to be shaped either by a blueprint or retrospect, the question arises, is there perhaps a third category consisting of scored improvisation? Can a musician think both compositionally and spur of the moment at the same time? Although rare, this category does seem to exist. Consider this example from the Duke Ellington orchestra.

> He [Ellington] had a way of getting things out of you that you didn't realize you had in you. Let me give you an example. We were doing an album called "A Drum Is a Woman," and Duke came to me and said, "Clark [Terry] I want you to play Buddy Bolden for me on this album."
>
> I said, "Maestro, I don't know who the hell Buddy Bolden is!" Duke said, "Oh sure, you know Buddy Bolden. Buddy Bolden was suave, handsome, and a debonair cat who the ladies loved. Aw, he was so fantastic! He was fabulous! He was always sought after. He had the biggest, fattest trumpet sound in town. He bent notes to the nth degree. He used to tune up in New Orleans and break

glasses in Algiers! He was great with diminisheds. When he played a diminished, he bent those notes, man, like you've never heard them before!"

By this time Duke had me psyched out! He finished by saying, "As a matter of fact, you are Buddy Bolden!" So I thought I was Buddy Bolden.

Duke said, "Play Buddy Bolden for me on this record date."

I played and at the conclusion of the session, Duke came up to me and put his arms around my shoulders and said, "That was Buddy Bolden."

(Crow, 1990, p. 253)

Ellington simultaneously scores Clark Terry's performance by constraining it to the style of Bolden rather than, say the style of Miles Davis or Harry James or Louis Armstrong, yet he encourages improvisation within those constraints. If he had said, "play in these open spaces" it would have been simple improvisation. If Ellington had said, "play Bubber Miley's solo," it would have been composition. But he said neither of those things. Ellington set up for Clark Terry what amounts to an alternative sense of being in the world.

I phrase what Ellington did in that somewhat stilted way because it suggests an unusual quality of leadership that has been singled out by Thayer (1988) in his marvelously original treatment of leadership. Thayer argues that good leaders offer followers alternative relationships with themselves and not just with the leader. Here is the relevant description.

What leadership offers is not so much the relationship with the leader as an alternative relationship with oneself. What leaders create, with the help of their followers, are what George Steiner (1975) refers to as "alternities" – "The world can be other" (than it is). Every instance of leadership is an instance of an alternity, an alternative sense of being in the world which brings leader and follower into a very special relationship in a unique enterprise. Not only do those who "follow" and appreciate Picasso relate to him (his symbolic works, their interpretations of him") in a unique way, but this changed relationship with or within oneself leads one (the follower) to "see" the world and the work of other painters differently from that point on. It is leadership that enables those changes within oneself that change the world (in the sense that one's relationships with certain aspects of the world are altered). Every leader-follower relationship hinges upon a mutually imagined alternity.

(Thayer, 1988, p. 241)

This description of alternities suggests some of what is unique about Ellington's leadership of his various creative jazz ensembles. From the very beginning, Ellington and his musicians had a unique interactive relationship where each created the other. The chords and phrases and voicings Ellington wrote brought out alternative ways of being which the musicians had not previously experienced. Their experimentation with these new voices, in turn, shaped what Ellington wrote for them and for other musicians. These activities are as close to a concrete, explicit, visible examples of mutual influence, structuration, social process creating social forms, as we are likely to find.

Consider this description of the early years of the Ellington orchestra.

Here we find a dramatic example of what has been called the "Ellington effect." It is evident from what has been said above that Miley deserves much credit for this quality, at least in its early manifestations, although it is usually attributed exclusively to Ellington. As in Example 4, such an effect may often have been a joint creation of Duke and his men. There is no doubt that Duke had the opportunity to promote or discourage these stylistic developments. It is a mark of his talent and vision as a leader that in these early days of his band, while he was learning to use the materials he had in hand, he let his musicians lead the way in forming the band's style. It is evident both from the recordings and also from the statements of contemporary musicians that Ellington was very dependent upon his players at this stage, and that they knew it. It is to Duke's credit that he fostered a fierce pride and communal attitude in his band so that it took precedence over the individual contributions and feelings of its members. Through the collaboration of his musicians, Ellington would learn to use the remarkable aggregation of sounds the band contained in a more purely compositional manner.

(Schuller, 1968, pp. 327–328)

As the Ellington orchestra developed, and Ellington became more sure of himself, the scored improvisation changed in what each contributed, but it never disappeared.

Miraculously, the Ellington imagination fed on the particular skills and personalities of his players, while at the same time their musical growth was in turn nurtured by Ellington's maturing compositional craft and vision. This process of cross-fertilization was constant and, given the stability of personnel, self-expanding.

In this complex relationship each constituent was responsible for certain aspects of the total musical/compositional product. For example, it is clear that Ellington's own influence asserted itself most especially in the realms of harmony, instrumental voicing, and form. On the other hand, timbral or sonority aspects were determined largely by the players, simply by virtue of the fact that their unique tone colors automatically added to any given passage a particular timbral imprint. Yet even here the choices were not totally arbitrary, for Ellington was frequently the final arbiter, and through the years he began more and more to color-coordinate, as it were – to blend and mix like a great painter – the individual timbre ingredients of his musicians into combinations which had never been heard before and which, to this day, have not been surpassed. Almost every player – from Johnny Hodges to Harry Camey, from Cootie Williams and Nanton to Lawrence Brown and Tizol, even Sonny Greer, with his discreet drumming and penchant for using a variety of coloristic percussion instruments, and, last but not least, Duke, with his own powerful rich piano sound all these players produced such individual timbres on their "horns" that Ellington had almost as many diverse sonorities at his disposal as a ninety-piece symphony orchestra. He certainly made extraordinary use of his fourteen instruments, in a manner and to a degree that perhaps only a handful of composers like Ravel, Schoenberg, Stravinsky, and Webern could have realized.

(Schuller, 1989, pp. 48–49)

While a great deal could be said about these descriptions, for the moment, I want to preserve the subtle, but important point that, unlike most other composers, Ellington, wrote for people rather than instruments. A composer who writes for instruments creates notes and spaces, a score and an open portion where some anonymous technician is to play ad lib. A composer who writes for people, however, creates notes and a score which anticipate, encourage, and shape the improvisation, and draw it into a complete number. By writing this way, Ellington encouraged the improviser to think compositionally. Because the lead-in sounds so appropriate and so inviting, because the notes fall so naturally on the ear of the person with the unique style, that person simply continues the flow that has already been started. The whole number sounds composed, and yet, on paper, there is a score and there is an unscored section for improvisation.

Interactions in the Ellington orchestra seem to explain the paradox of scored improvisation. They give us a chance to see how the paradox plays out and what it can accomplish. I think some of the problems in organizational innovation occurs because these dynamics are never triggered or they are short-circuited. If innovation is an inherently social process, then innovation gets stalled when this basically social process is collapsed into an individual exercise of brainstorming in which each competes with the other to be cleverer. The improvisation that lies behind significant innovation is more social, more emergent, and more successful at the ongoing management of paradox.

The aesthetics of imperfection

I want to return to the observation that jazz is an imperfect art, in order to initiate some thinking about the beauty that lies within this imperfect art. Jazz is partly about the false starts, failures, and flawed execution that are found so often in organizational life. I don't want to be an apologist for failure, nor do I want to encourage a hasty retreat from excellence and quality. Instead, I want to work toward a mindset, which is more appreciative of the failures that occur when people make a genuine, deep, committed effort to innovate. I am not talking about sloppy failures or lazy failures. I am talking about failures of reach. The goal here is to build toward, what Gioia (1988, p. 55) has called, an "aesthetics of imperfection."

In the second edition of the organizing book (Weick, 1979) I included a Robert Graves poem, *In Broken Images* (p. 224). The poem presented a compact tension in organized life that I had labored earnestly, but somewhat unsuccessfully, to present up to that point in the book.

I used to think the nouns in that poem were the key, reflecting the incompleteness, fragmentation, the bits and pieces we always have to work with. I now think that I paid too little attention to the verb "continues" which crops up over and over. That's where the drama lies. People continue despite the broken images. That's what happens with the jazz musician stuck with a sour note. That's what happens when a novelist rolls another sheet of paper into the typewriter knowing full well that the novel is stuck and not working. That's what happens when one more attempt to design a circuit fails, or when an observer spots yet another hydrogen leak when the temptation must be irresistible to treat the leak as a transient event. These interruptions are commonplace, they often are the prelude to innovation and yet they are seldom recognized as an inherent feature of any process of improvisation. Failure may become normalized as an inevitable property of improvisation, only when we can reframe its aesthetic qualities, and defuse some of the stigma that goes along with failure. Only then will it be possible to encourage people to fail boldly, and mean it, and incur their trust.

As we have seen, jazz is a haphazard art. "Errors will creep in, not only in form but also in execution; the improviser, if he sincerely attempts to be creative, will push himself into areas of expression which his technique may be unable to handle. Too often the finished product will show moments of rare beauty intermixed with technical mistakes and aimless passages" (Gioia, 1988, p. 66).

But if we label jazz as haphazard art, the question remains haphazard relative to what? The answer is, haphazard relative to the planned, methodical, carefully crafted world of products that are symmetrical, balanced, well-formed, perfect. The aesthetic of perfect products, detached from their makers, is not appropriate for spontaneous activities that are inseparable from their producers.

So, we need to articulate a different set of standards which take more account of the raw materials at hand, the context, the situation the person had available to work with when the improvisation unfolded. This is where we find the aesthetics of imperfection.

An aesthetics of imperfection yields judgments like this:

1   given what she started with, this isn't bad;
2   given the opportunities and problems which she set up for herself, this is a clever resolution;
3   given the melody she had to work with, these notes have significantly enlarged that melody;
4   given the temptation towards clichés and busyness that are set up by that melody line, this person consistently avoided those traps.

An aesthetics of imperfection involves judgments made in the context of retrospective blueprints. For example, success is judged against what the person started with, namely, the melody, the chords, the co-workers, and what the person did with those elements.

An aesthetics of imperfection also involves appreciating what people do with imperfections once they occur. For example, given that sour note, was its effect localized, was it blended, was it normalized, was it transformed into a plausible next step?

An aesthetics of imperfection also involves a more refined interpretation of errors themselves. Sample judgments would be, of all of the errors you could have made under these conditions, the ones you actually made were novel, were errors of excessive reach, were untypical for you, were effortful, were original, could not have been made by someone who is lazy or distracted.

David Sudnow has done a marvelous job summarizing the small imperfections that signal true improvisation. He keys on those errors which should appear, unless the performance was worked out earlier and simply memorized.

> Look especially for the [presence] of those little false starts being forever turned into the music as the improvisational hand aligns and realigns itself. Look for [much] in the way of things being said – I mean placed – for things

being placed and then placed again, and then again, before a longer burst of venturing movements. Look for the [appearance] of those clear mistakes that are then turned into parts of the music as the hand cycles back to pick up a sour-sounding note, doing it again for emphasis, making it of the music by elegantly integrating its harshness into a small digression. Watch out for the [appearance] of that special sort of developing tension that resolves with the sense of "Wow, he made it come off." Watch out for many imitations of that tension. And be especially cautious of the intricately fingered melody whose structuring for the hand strongly suggests a lot of prior work just to get that particular one learned.

(Sudnow, 1979, pp. 43–44)

An aesthetics of imperfection creates a different mindset toward error. Errors now become viewed as experiments from which people can learn, as oddities to be incorporated or made normal, as items to be isolated from ongoing processes so their effects will be localized, as an inevitable accompaniment when personal activity rather than an impersonal product is being assessed, as potentially the right notes for some other song, as simply an excuse to say "let it pass," as evidence that intensity, involvement, and testing one's limits is present, as wrong notes only relative to fixed assumptions about what the correct scored passage is, as transient flaws that will work out as events unfold. These interpretations of error are not just excuses, although they may sound that way to some people. Instead, these are judgments that reflect the ways in which processes differ from products, and human activity differs from human intention. An aesthetics of imperfection does not use as its standard, compliance with or deviation from some plan or ideal or blueprint. Instead, it uses as its standard, some estimate of the degree of organization and form that could have been extracted retrospectively from the materials at hand, given that they were generated by a fallible human being acting publicly under time pressure, with fallible tools.

An aesthetic of imperfection treats errors as opportunities rather than threats. This aesthetic contains the implicit recognition that the word "error" is not even particularly meaningful when used to describe brief portions of an activity which itself consists of playing everything BUT the actual notes of the melody itself. Successful improvisation enriches a melody, but what is happening literally is that every one of those improvised notes is an error. Each improvised note is not the same note the composer wrote on a musical staff when the melody was first created. Thus, to talk about errors nested within an activity which is itself a celebration of error, is to suggest the need for a different vocabulary and set of images than those associated with perfection.

An aesthetics of imperfection makes imperfection a personal signature of involvement rather than a public signature of failure. Error is not simply reframed as a virtue, but is seen instead, as a sign of a continuing struggle for virtue glimpsed in spur of the moment improvisation. If an aesthetic of imperfection is diffused, believed, and shared, then people should be more willing to take the risks associated with innovation. It is the aesthetics of perfection, wrongly extrapolated from products isolated from their producers and the conditions of their production, that wreak havoc and inspire fear in those who are told to innovate by bosses blind to the human side of innovation.

Jamming and improvisation

We can begin to pull the pieces of the argument together around the idea that minimalist social structures encourage innovation if there is,

1 temporal coordination by songs
2 structures built retrospectively out of materials at hand
3 valuing of an aesthetics of imperfection
4 frequent "at bats."

Let me say a bit more about "at bats" because that feature of jazz has been implied rather than made explicit. It has been implicit in the sense that almost every time jazz musicians pick up their instruments, they play variations on a theme. Those variations may be mere embellishments. They may be memorized solos. They may be patterns never heard before. Regardless, what is important is that musicians try a lot. In the imagery of Tom Peters, they come to bat many, many times, which is important when the odds of succeeding in any one at bat, are frightfully low. Innovation is a numbers game, but jazz people seem to have learned this more quickly than have most companies who rely on a small number of big projects.

Consider Duke Ellington when he just was starting. He made some 160 recordings between mid-1928 and mid-1931. All of them were interesting although very few were successful artistically. Ellington kept his orchestra together so that he could always hear immediately what he wrote. But, to meet the payroll week after week, the band had to play mostly one-night stands. A band that spends most of its time on the road rather than in the recording studio registers a large number of "at bats." Ellington's band played at least 5 nights a week, often for 5 hours per night, and played anywhere from 35–45 tunes per night (Schuller, 1989, p. 133).

Many of those one-night stands were uninspired and nothing happened. Grover Michell's experience, shortly after he joined the band, is representative.

> I had only been working with him for about a week. The first night or two everybody had gotten on the bandstand and had really roared. But the next two, three, or four nights, maybe there would be five or six of us on the bandstand, and eight or ten guys walking around out in the audience talking to people, or at the bar. One night we were on the bandstand and a waiter came up and told Jimmy Hamilton that his steak was ready. He stepped off the bandstand and started cuttin' into a steak.
>
> Later I says to Duke, "Man, how can you put up with this?" And he told me, "Look, let me tell you something. I live for the nights that this band is great I don't worry about nights like what you're worrying about. If you pay attention to these people, they will drive you crazy. They're not going to drive me crazy.
>
> (Crow, 1990, p. 253)

But even in the off nights, the failures and errors that were made may well have suggested new directions that aided learning.

As I suggested in the beginning, there are several properties of minimal structures that seem to promote improvisation in jazz. Eric Eisenberg's (1990) recent analysis of "jamming," which he exemplifies using a jazz jam session and a basketball pickup game, allows us to sketch some of the larger meaning of jazz improvisation.

One point of entry is the topic of "the management of diversity." Jazz, considered as a social form, is a promising mode of coordination in the face of diversity. Eisenberg (1990) points the way to this conclusion.

> As the world grows smaller, we must deal with diverse, distant peoples. Consequently, we need theories of communication that edify action and humanize without offering openness, disclosure, and shared values as standards by which all social relationships must be judged. Organization is not always facilitated by greater understanding. Revelation of certain kinds of information can be futile or make matters worse. Given the incommensurability of languages and values systems, it is preferable in many cases to seek tolerance of diversity, coordination of activities, and respect for others than it is to work for shared understanding or agreement.
>
> (p. 160)

What we have been examining, through this paper, are instances of fluid behavioral coordination that occurred without detailed knowledge of personality (Eisenberg, 1990, p. 139). And if nothing else, jazz has absorbed and been a home for some very eccentric people. That diversity notwithstanding, these people have worked together. Coordinated actions without disclosure are a form of community that neither curbs diversity nor shrinks adaptability. People coordinate actions by an elementary structure that involves time (tempo, bar lines) and place (be somewhere in this chord at this time). But, why someone is there in that chord, how that person got there, where that person goes from there, how it feels, what that person's goals are, is none of my business and there is no pressing reason for me to make it my business or to agree with that business or to disclose what is my business. I'll have some hunches what you may be feeling as I listen to your notes and watch them play out in your expressions, but a minimum of agreements between us will keep the events moving and coordinated.

Eisenberg makes the same point this way. "(J)amming is a kind of minimalist's view of organizing, of making do with minimal commonalties and elaborating simple structures in complex ways. Relying on the basic rule and role structure, each player sets up interesting possibilities for others and keeps the action going" (p. 154). Because the structure is minimal, jamming encourages simultaneous cooperation and individuation, simultaneous closeness and independence. Little personal information is exchanged, yet important goals can be reached and strong emotions can be shared. As Eisenberg says in summarizing, "Jamming stresses coordination of action over the alignment of cognitions, mutual respect over agreement, trust over empathy, diversity over heterogeneity, loose over tight coupling, and strategic communication over unrestricted candor" (p. 160). There is community within diversity, which unifies the diversity. But the social form built around jazz improvisation, tilts the balance between autonomy and interdependence in the direction of autonomy, which is why the form is well suited for innovation, requisite variety, new ideas, and multiple "at bats." Identity forms and develops within a community, but neither blurs into the other.

Linkages with organizational theory

I suspect that the world of jazz improvisation is much like the world of the entrepreneur. If you examine the list of contrasts that Eisenberg made ["Jamming stresses coordination of action over the alignment of cognitions, mutual respect over agreement, trust over empathy, diversity over heterogeneity, loose over tight coupling, and strategic communication over unrestricted candor" (p. 160)], they sound very much like the descriptive language that people like Gartner and Low (1990) use when they describe entrepreneurial processes. There are other linkages between the less familiar territory of the jazz ensemble and the more familiar territory of other kinds of organizations. For example, people like Rosabeth Kanter and Peter Drucker are notorious for describing managers as similar to conductors. Here's an example from When giants learn to dance (Kanter, 1989):

> Management sage Peter Drucker recently used the image of a symphony orchestra to describe the new model of the leaner, flatter corporation. In the orchestra, performers with different skills concentrate on perfecting their professional competence, while a single conductor coordinates the overall performance; performers with similar specialties form self managed work teams, operating without a bureaucratic hierarchy above them. The image is useful and evocative as far as it goes. But for corporate players to make beautiful music together they must achieve a balance between concentrating on their own areas of skill and responsibility and working together with others. They need to do their own jobs well while keeping one eye on what might be useful for someone else. They need to understand enough about the company's other areas to identify possibilities for joint action and mutual enhancement. They need to simultaneously focus and collaborate. They must function in many roles: as soloist, ensemble players, and member of the orchestra.
>
> (p. 116)

Conductors are most effective, not when they control and regulate, but when they give information that allows self-control and self-management by players. This subtle, but crucial nuance of leadership is nicely captured in Sudnow's (1979) description of effective conductors.

> His efficacy as a leader partially depends upon his visual presence to the others, aside from preparatory rehearsals. This presence is sustained out of the corner of every eye in the orchestra. Although the score serves as a chief basis for everyone's individual movements, its instructions being designed for a desired coincidence of places in accordance with a pulse running similarly through each part, the conductor serves to mirror the composite effort. An embodied reflection of the piece as a whole, his undulating movements bear ongoing witness to the relations of the various voices to one another.
>
> Created in the experience of the composer's single body, the piece is now reincarnated in this spokesman's movements. Through the sights of the music present in the conductors gestures, each player has one means for imaginarily projecting himself beyond the confines of his sounding location in the crowd. The conductor aids musicians as a visual amplification of the sounding

movements of others some distance away, the perceived volume of faraway voices actually increasing in the looks of the conductor's orchestral body.

(pp. 112–113)

And conductors have their own eccentricities that make things work. Consider Duke Ellington's aversion to firing anyone (Schuller, 1989, pp. 69–70).

> Duke had in recent years felt some dissatisfaction with Wellman Braud, his bass player since 1927, who at age forty-four was now the oldest member of the band. As Ellington's music became more sophisticated harmonically and rhythmically, and particularly as the new 4/4 swing feeling crept into the band's style, Braud's inadequacies became uncomfortably apparent. But Ellington's genteel nature and basic loyalty to his men, then as later, prohibited him from firing any player. Duke took the expedient alternative of hiring a second bass player, Billy Taylor, also a McKinney alumnus. (When Braud eventually left the band, Duke liked the musical possibilities with two basses so much that he replaced Braud with Hayes Alvis, and for some three years Ellington orchestra boasted a bass section of two.)

My point is simply that the majestic simplifications implicit in the metaphor of manager as maestro, simply won't do. The best maestros are more interactive, more like followers, and better sensing media than are the managers who take from maestros the lesson that their presence should be commanding, directive, and controlling, in short, the embodiment of one way communication.

A jazz ensemble illustrates what it means to be a system that is simultaneously tight (players must be at the same place in the same tune at the same time) and loose (players can associate different notes with that common place as well as different time accents, and they can remain silent if they want to).

Peter Vaill (1984), who delights in describing management as a performing art, would find many jazz ensembles to be high performing systems. One need simply recall Vaill's criterion of a good performance: energy is held in place, from beginning to end, in the face of obstacles. That is jazz when it works.

A jazz ensemble is a system that produces interpretations by translating a melody into categories and phrases that are meaningful within the group. If we treat jazz as an interpretation system (Daft and Weick, 1984), then this suggests that jazz is not a homogeneous activity, and that groups can be allocated to the 4 cells involving assumptions about the environment (analyzable/unanalyzable) and style with which the environment is engaged (active/passive). Organizations with different strategic styles in the Miles and Snow framework, might want to model different examples of jazz improvisation in order to increase their opportunities for continuous innovation.

I also think jazz is an ideal setting to explore in more detail, what it means to renew an organization. Jazz involves new treatments of old tunes, which is the essence of the renewal process. What is interesting to me are the many ways in which jazz uses old material in new ways.

Conclusion

I think we can learn a lot about improvisation in organizations and in daily life, if we discipline our imaginations with the images of the risks and thrills inherent in jazz as a performance art. We all are in the innovation business, whether we like it or not. Consider this description which Tom Peters pulled out of Ann Beattie's novel *Picturing Will.*

> Do everything right, all the time, and the child will prosper. It's as simple as that, except for fate, luck, heredity, chance, the astrological sign under which the child was born, his order of birth, his first encounter with evil, the girl who jilts him in spite of his excellent qualities, the war that is being fought when he is a young man, the drugs he may try once or too many times, the friends he makes, how he scores on tests, how well he endures kidding about his shortcomings, how ambitious he becomes, how far he falls behind, circumstancial evidence, ironic perspective, danger when it is least expected, difficulty in triumphing over circumstance, people with hidden agendas, and animals with rabies.
>
> (From Mel's Journal in Picturing Will, a novel by Ann Beattie, cited in Peters [unpublished manuscript], "Get innovative or get dead;")

But we should give a jazz musician the last word. Paul Desmond, who was born Paul Emil Breitenteld on November 15, 1924, changed his name to Desmond while paging thru a phone book (Gioia, 1988, p. 87). Desmond, more than most people, was a spontaneous, spur of the moment decision-maker who let the philosophy of improvisation govern much of his life outside music. Desmond, who played alto saxophone with the Dave Brubeck quartet, swears that the question he was asked most often by airline stewardesses was, "How many of you are there in a quartet?" He planned to use this question as the title of the autobiography he never wrote.

When asked about his goals, Desmond said, "The things I'm after musically are clarity, emotional communication on a not-too-obvious level, form in a chorus that doesn't hit you over the head but is there if you look for it, humor, and construction that sounds logical in an unexpected way. That and a good dependable high F-sharp and I'll be happy" (Gioia, 1988, p. 89).

I cannot imagine a better model!

References

Bastien, D. and Hostager, T. (1988). Jazz as a process of organizational innovation. *Communication Research*, *15* (5), 582–602.

Crow, B. (1990). *Jazz anecdotes.* New York: Oxford.

Daft, R. L. and Weick, K. E. (1984). Toward a model of organizations as interpretation systems. *Academy of Management Review*, *9*, 284–295.

Davis, F. (1986). *In the moment.* New York: Oxford.

Eisenberg, E. (1990). Jamming: Transcendence through organizing. *Communication Research*, *17* (2), 139–164.

Gartner, W. B. and Low, M. B. (1990). Trust as an organizing trope. Presented to entrepreneurship division. *Academy of Management.* August 1990.

Gioia, T. (1988). *The imperfect art.* New York: Oxford.

Kanter, R. M. (1989). *When giants learn to dance.* New York: Simon & Schuster.

Schuler, G. (1968). *Early jazz.* New York: Oxford.

Schuler, G. (1989). *The swing era.* New York: Oxford.

Sudnow, D. (1979). *Talk's body.* New York: Knopf.

Suhor, C. (1986). Jazz improvisation and language performance: Parallel competencies. *ETC,* *43* (4), 133–140.

Thayer, L. (1988). Leadership/Communication: A critical review and a modest proposal. In G. M. Goldhaber and G. A. Barnett (Eds), *Handbook of organizational communication* (pp. 231–264). Norwood, NJ: Ablex.

Vaill, P. B. (1984). The purposing of high-performing systems. In T. J. Sergiovanni and J. E. Corbally (Eds), *Leadership and organization culture* (pp. 85–104). Urbana: University of Illinois.

Wallace, A. F. C. (1961). *Culture and personality.* New York: Random.

Weick, K. E. (1979). *The social psychology of organizing* (2nd ed.). Reading, MA: Addison-Wesley.

Weick, K. E. (1989). Theory construction as disciplined imagination. *Academy of Management Review, 14* (4), 516–531.

9 Improvising organizational transformation over time

A situated change perspective

Wanda J. Orlikowski

Organizational transformation – substantially changing an organization's structure and practices – has always been of interest to researchers and practitioners. For decades, however, questions of transformation remained largely backstage as organizational thinking and practice engaged in a discourse dominated by questions of stability. Oriented around the organizing principles of mass production and bureaucracy, such a discourse emphasized routinization, standardization, control, and automation. Today however, many organizations face an altered economic, political, and technological world, a world in which flexibility, customization, and learning are the watchwords, and visions of agile manufacturing, virtual corporations, and self-organizing teams are prominent. In such a world, stability is out, change is in.

As the backstage becomes increasingly center stage, it seems appropriate to examine the kinds of models that currently inform our understandings of organizational transformation, and to consider their adequacy in the light of this new organizational stage. A range of perspectives on organizational transformation have developed over the past few decades (see Pettigrew (1985) and Wilson (1992) for extensive reviews). However, many of these perspectives – grounded as they are in the prior discourse of stability – are often poorly suited to a world where change is no longer a background activity but a way of organizational life. These perspectives embody assumptions about agency, context, technology, and change which may be inappropriate given the different social, technological, and economic conditions emerging today. To illustrate, consider three perspectives that have influenced studies of technology-based organizational transformation – planned change, technological imperative, and punctuated equilibrium.

Planned change models presume that managers are the primary source of organizational change, and that these actors deliberately initiate and implement changes in response to perceived opportunities to improve organizational performance or "fit" with the environment. Such models have dominated the organizational change and development literatures, and include force field analysis (Lewin, 1951), contingency frameworks (Burns and Stalker, 1961; Dunphy and Stace, 1988; Galbraith, 1973; Miles and Snow, 1984), innovation theories (Hage and Aiken, 1970; Meyer and Goes, 1983; Zaltman *et al.*, 1973), and practitioner-oriented prescriptions for organizational effectiveness (Deming, 1986; Hammer and Champy, 1993; Peters and Waterman, 1982). This perspective has been criticized for treating change as a discrete event to be managed separately from the ongoing processes of organizing, and for placing undue weight on the rationality of managers directing the change (Pettigrew, 1985). From the vantage point of the new organizing discourse with its presumption of frequent change, learning, and self-organizing, such disembedding of change from the ongoing stream of organizational action, and heavy reliance on foresightful managerial action, are problematic.

In opposition to the voluntarism of planned change models, the technological imperative perspective affords little discretion to managers or any other organizational actors. Technology is seen as a primary and relatively autonomous driver of organizational change, so that the adoption of new technology creates predictable changes in organizations' structures, work routines, information flows, and performance (Blau *et al.*, 1976; Carter, 1984; Huber, 1990). These organizational notions of a "technological imperative" echo a broader strain of technological determinism evident in socio-historical studies (Winner, 1986), economic analyses (Heilbroner, 1967), and contemporary culture (Smith and Marx, 1994) where the seduction of a "technological fix" is largely taken for granted. The absence of any significant role for agency in this perspective undermines possibilities for proactive organizational change, which is problematic for the new organizing discourse where assumptions of agility and flexibility require actors to explore, learn, and innovate new alternatives for working and organizing over time and in different circumstances. In addition, the deterministic logic of the technological imperative is incompatible with the open-ended nature of many new technologies which assume considerable user customization (Malone, 1995), and thus user construction of capabilities and effects.

Punctuated equilibrium models arose in opposition to gradualist models which posit that organizational change is slow, incremental, and cumulative (Meyer *et al.*, 1993). In contrast, punctuated equilibrium models assume change to be rapid, episodic, and radical. Gersick (1991: 12) writes that: "relatively long periods of stability (equilibrium) [are] punctuated by compact periods of qualitative, metamorphic change (revolution)." Punctuated discontinuities are typically triggered by modifications in environmental or internal conditions, for example, new technology, process redesign, or industry deregulation. Such punctuated models have informed macro studies of long-term shifts in various industries (Abernathy and Clark, 1985; Romanelli and Tushman, 1994; Tushman and Romanelli, 1985), while elaborations of this perspective have proposed a hybrid of the punctuated equilibrium and gradualist logics (Miller and Friesen, 1984; Mintzberg, 1987; Pettigrew *et al.*, 1992; Tushman and Anderson, 1986). Both the punctuated equilibrium perspective and its hybrids raise difficulties for the new organizing discourse because they are premised on the primacy of organizational stability. Whether improving an existing status quo or shifting to a new one, the assumption underlying these models is that the preferred condition for organizations is some sort of steady state or "equilibrium" (Mintzberg, 1987). This presumption of stability (which is also shared, although more implicitly, by the planned change and technological imperative perspectives) begs questioning in a context of organizations experimenting with essentially non-stable organizational forms, processes, and technologies (e.g. self-organizing, flexible, customizable).

All three of the perspectives reviewed above also neglect what – following Mintzberg's (1979, 1987) distinction between deliberate and emergent strategies –

may be termed "emergent change." Where deliberate change is the realization of a new pattern of organizing precisely as originally intended, emergent change is the realization of a new pattern of organizing in the absence of explicit, a priori intentions. Such emergent change is only realized in action and cannot be anticipated or planned (Mintzberg and Waters, 1985). Because they are abstracted from the ongoing and grounded activities of organizational actors, the three perspectives on technology-based organizational transformation do not easily account for emergent change. Yet, the notion of emergence is particularly relevant today as unprecedented environmental, technological, and organizational developments facilitate patterns of organizing which cannot be explained or prescribed by appealing to a priori plans and intentions. The variety of economic and social activity that has appeared on the World Wide Web in the past two years is just one recent and powerful example of such emergence.

The current discourse on technology-based organizational transformation thus embodies assumptions which are problematic in the light of an organizing discourse emphasizing emergence, flexibility, and self-organization. A perspective that posits change rather than stability as a way of organizational life may offer a more appropriate conceptual lens with which to think about change in contemporary organizations. I outline such an additional perspective in this chapter, suggesting that it affords a particularly powerful analytical strategy for examining and explaining technology-based organizational transformation.

A situated change perspective

The new perspective proposed here is premised on the primacy of organizing practices in organizational change. While earlier practice-based research challenged the conventional wisdom that incremental changes always occur gradually (Tyre and Orlikowski, 1994), the research discussed here questions the beliefs that organizational change must be planned, that technology is the primary cause of technology-based organizational transformation, and that radical changes always occur rapidly and discontinuously. While recognizing that organizational transformation can be and often is performed as a deliberate, orchestrated main event with key players, substantial technological and other resources, and considerable observable and experiential commotion, I want to explore another kind of organizational transformation here, one that is enacted more subtly, more slowly, and more smoothly, but no less significantly. Such organizational transformation is grounded in the ongoing practices of organizational actors, and emerges out of their (tacit and not so tacit) accommodations to and experiments with the everyday contingencies, breakdowns, exceptions, opportunities, and unintended consequences that they encounter. March (1981: 564) notes:

> Because of the magnitude of some changes in organizations, we are inclined to look for comparably dramatic explanations for change, but the search for drama may often be a mistake ... Change takes place because most of the time most people in an organization do about what they are supposed to do; that is, they are intelligently attentive to their environments and their jobs.

Barley (1988: 51), similarly writes:

because forms of action and interaction are always negotiated and confirmed as actors with different interests and interpretations encounter shifting events [...], slippage between institutional templates and the actualities of daily life is probable. In such slippage resides the possibility of social innovation.

In this perspective, organizational transformation is not portrayed as a drama staged by deliberate directors with predefined scripts and choreographed moves, or the inevitable outcome of a technological logic, or a sudden discontinuity that fundamentally invalidates the status quo. Rather, organizational transformation is seen here to be an ongoing improvisation enacted by organizational actors trying to make sense of and act coherently in the world.

Invoking the notion of improvisation to understand organizational transformation owes much to Weick's (1993) claim that our ideas about organization design are based on an inappropriate architectural metaphor which portrays it as "as a bounded activity that occurs at a fixed point in time," focusing on "structures rather than processes ... [where] structures are assumed to be stable solutions to a set of current problems" (1993: 347). Instead, Weick 1993: 348–351 proposes the metaphor of theatrical improvisation, where organization design

> tends to be emergent and visible only after the fact. Thus, the design is a piece of history, not a piece of architecture.... Design, viewed from the perspective of improvisation, is more emergent, more continuous, more filled with surprise, more difficult to control, more tied to the content of action, and more affected by what people pay attention to than are the designs implied by architecture.

The notion of change as ongoing improvisation resonates with the focus on situated action taken by practice researchers (Hutchins, 1991; Lave, 1992; Suchman, 1989). In contrast to the classical view of change as a process of managerial planning, design, and intervention, Hutchins, for example, argues that "several important aspects of a new organization are achieved not by conscious reflection but by local adaptations" (1991: 14). In research on information technology, Rice and Rogers' (1980) concept of "reinvention" and Ciborra and Lanzara's (1991) notion of "designing-in-action," similarly echo some of the situated and improvisational ideas invoked here.

The kind of change process I intend with the notion of situated change is well illustrated by Escher's *Metamorphose* series (see Figure 9.1) where, as the artist explains, through the passage of time, "a dynamic character is obtained by a succession of figures in which changes of form appear gradually" (Escher, 1986: 120). Each variation of a given form is not an abrupt or discrete event, neither is it, by

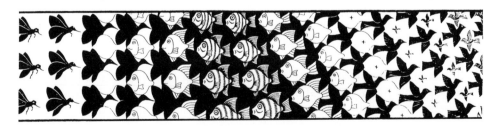

Figure 9.1 Metamorphosis II.

itself, discontinuous. Rather, through a series of ongoing and situated accommodations, adaptations, and alterations (that draw on previous variations and mediate future ones), sufficient modifications may be enacted over time that fundamental changes are achieved. There is no deliberate orchestration of change here,[1] no technological inevitability, no dramatic discontinuity, just recurrent and reciprocal variations in practice over time. Each shift in practice creates the conditions for further breakdowns, unanticipated outcomes, and innovations, which in their turn are responded to with more variations. And such variations are ongoing; there is no beginning or end point in this change process.

A view of organizational transformation as situated change is grounded in assumptions of action, not stability. Organizations are enacted. They are constituted by the ongoing agency of organizational members, and have no existence apart from such action (Giddens, 1984). Every action taken by organization members either reproduces existing organizational properties or it alters them. Through sustained adjustments in organizing practices – however unintentional and unacknowledged – social changes can be enacted. Change is thus inherent in everyday human action. This basic premise of the situated change perspective echoes March's observation that "in its fundamental structure a theory of organizational change should not be remarkably different from a theory of ordinary action" (1981: 564). Informed by Giddens' (1984) notions of structuring, Weick's (1993) improvisational metaphor, and the insights of practice research, this chapter outlines a perspective on change as inherent in everyday practice and as inseparable from the ongoing and situated actions of organizational members. Such a perspective emerged as central to my analysis of an organization implementing and using new information technology.

In the research study described below, I examine how subtle shifts in action by organizational actors transformed – over a two-year period – aspects of their work practices, organizing structures, and coordination mechanisms, and I explore the implications of such shifts for the organization. My analysis laid the groundwork for a practice-based perspective which offers a conceptual lens with which to focus on types of transformations not discernible to the perspectives of planned change, technological imperative, and punctuated equilibrium. The situated change perspective is offered as a complement to, not a substitute for, the existing change perspectives. In most organizations, transformations will occur through a variety of logics. Indeed, the study discussed below reveals elements of planned and punctuated change triggered by managerial action around the implementation of new technology. More significantly, however, the study reveals the critical role of situated change enacted by organizational members using the technology over time. Such a practice logic has been largely overlooked in studies of organizational transformation, and appears to be particularly relevant to contemporary concerns of organizing; hence, it is the focus of my attention here.

Research setting and methodology

Site

Zeta Corporation[2] is a software company headquartered in the Midwest, with sales and client service field offices throughout the US and the world. Zeta is one of the

Top 50 software companies in the US, with $100 million in revenues and about 1000 employees. The company produces and sells a range of powerful software products, which run on a variety of computing platforms. These products provide capabilities of decision support and executive information analysis, and are used by thousands of corporations around the world.

The focus of my study was the Customer Support Department (CSD) which is part of the Technical Services Division headed by a senior vice-president. The CSD is a fifty-three-person department run by a director and two managers, which has traditionally had a very cooperative culture, reflecting a collegial management style and a shared interest in solving customer problems. The mission of the CSD is to provide technical support via telephone to all users of Zeta's products, including clients, consultants, Zeta field service representatives, and other Zeta employees. This technical support is provided by Customer Support Specialists (hereafter referred to as specialists), all of whom have been extensively trained in Zeta's products and in techniques of technical support. The department has grown from ten specialists in 1990 to its current high of fifty specialists. All the specialists have college degrees, mostly in computer science, engineering, and business information technology. Many of the specialists view their current position as an entry point into the high-tech industry, and few intend to make technical support a career. Although turnover of specialists in CSD is high (as in other companies), the rate has declined over the past two years. When specialists leave the CSD many stay within Zeta, moving laterally into departments such as product management and field service.

Customer support at Zeta, as is often the case in technical support (Pentland, 1992), is a complex activity. Customer calls are rarely resolved with a brief answer. They typically require several hours of research and include searches of reference material, review of program code, and attempts to replicate the problem. Some incidents will require interaction with members of other departments such as development and quality assurance. Problems identified by specialists as bugs are sent on to product development where they will be assessed for criticality and, if appropriate, scheduled for correction. The volume of calls to the CSD has increased significantly in recent years due to new product introductions and the growing range of operating platforms supported. Currently, the department receives an average of 100 calls a day, although volumes fluctuate by time of month, season, and maturity of product. Specialists, working in four-hour shifts, rotate their time "on the phones," so that in any one day about twenty specialists will take calls from customers.

In January 1992, an initial purchase of the Notes technology (from Lotus Development Corporation) was made to explore the feasibility of using Notes as a technological platform for tracking customer calls. At the time, the CSD was using a home-grown system (Inform), but significant problems with its use made replacement a priority. On the acquisition of Notes, an implementation team including a developer newly assigned to the Technical Services Division, one of the CSD managers, and several specialists designed and tested a trial call-tracking system within Notes. By mid-1992, the Incident Tracking Support System (ITSS) had been developed, and evaluations of its use in practice began. Two phases of this evaluation were conducted: an experimental pilot from July to September 1992, and an expanded pilot from September to December 1992. By the end of 1992, the decision was made to commit to the use of Notes as the platform for tracking all customer calls, and additional licenses for Notes were bought. This set the stage for a full roll-out of ITSS to all members of the CSD, and the enactment of the organizational changes which are the focus of this discussion.

Data collection and analysis

Data collection at Zeta was conducted in two phases. Phase I (see Gallivan *et al.* 1993) took place at the time of the two pilots (August–December 1992), while Phase II occurred two years later (July–December 1994). Both phases involved the use of unstructured and semi-structured interviewing, observation, and document review. Fifty-one interviews of sixty to ninety minutes in length were conducted across the two phases. All interviews were recorded and transcribed. Participants spanned vertical levels and functional groupings, and included specialists from the CSD, both CSD managers, the CSD director, the Technical Services senior vice-president, the technologists responsible for the new technology, and members of the product development, product management, and quality assurance departments (Table 9.1 shows a breakdown by function, level, and phase). Observation took the form of sitting with specialists when they were on and off the phones, and taking notes on their work practices, particularly their use of the Inform and ITSS technologies. Specialists were encouraged to talk aloud about what they were doing, and these descriptions were supplemented with questions probing particular issues. Materials reviewed included the set of user manuals for Notes and ITSS (which provided detailed information on the design and functionality of the technology), the report documenting the feasibility of acquiring a new incident tracking system (which revealed the intentions underlying the implementation of ITSS), management reports generated in ITSS (which showed the kinds of resource and output tracking conducted by the CSD managers), and samples of the ITSS database records (which allowed an examination of the types of documentation being generated by specialists).

I used qualitative techniques to analyze the data (Eisenhardt, 1989; Miles and Huberman, 1984; Pettigrew, 1990; Strauss and Corbin, 1990), informed by the overall focus on practices, change, and structuring and a more detailed attention to grounded concepts. I first read all the interview transcripts, observation notes, and documentation to identify issues and topics that related to work practices and change. After analyzing and aggregating these to arrive at a set of common or recurring themes, I then re-examined the data in terms of the new set of common themes, paying particular attention to the enactment of change, the role of technology, and the passage of time. The feasibility report completed in 1991 and the Phase I data collected during 1992 allowed me to distinguish between deliberate and emergent organizational changes, and to determine the timing of deliberate changes. The timing and order of emergent changes were more difficult to establish but were assessed from participants' interviews and the schedule of technology updates. I shared my preliminary findings with the specialists and managers of the CSD, and they provided helpful comments which confirmed and elaborated the identified issues and themes.

The focus of analysis in this study was the everyday practices of the specialists and their managers, and while work practices were observed during on-site data collection, the ongoing changes enacted over the two years were not observed first hand.

Table 9.1 Number and type of interviews in Zeta in Phases I and II.

	Phase I	*Phase II*	*Total*
Senior Management (division and department)	2	3	5
Group Management	4	4	8
Specialists	7	20	27
Technologists	1	6	7
Other members (developers, QA, etc)	–	4	4
Total	14	37	51

Ideally, a study of such changes would involve the sorts of extensive and intensive participant observation enabled by techniques of organizational ethnography (Van Maanen, 1979, 1988). This was not possible in the current study, but the data collected proved adequate to distinguish five different situated changes.

Results

My analysis suggests that the organizing practices and structures of Zeta's CSD changed considerably over the two years following implementation of the ITSS technology. The transformation, while enabled by the technology, was not caused by it. Rather, it occurred through the ongoing, gradual, and reciprocal adjustments, accommodations, and improvisations enacted by the CSD members. As will be detailed below, their action subtly and significantly altered the organizing practices and structures of the CSD workplace over time, transforming the texture of work, nature of knowledge, patterns of interaction, distribution of work, forms of accountability and control, and mechanisms of coordination. Five metamorphoses may be distinguished during the two year period, and while this analytical division provides a convenient way of anchoring a discussion of CSD's transformation, it is conceptually imprecise because the organizational changes were (and continue to be) fluid and ongoing, so that any sharp partitioning of change is misleading. The process of gradual transformation in the CSD was practically enacted in a much less discrete and organized fashion than can be suggested textually. Depiction of the overlapping and ongoing nature of this transformation is attempted in Figure 9.2 which shows the situated changes as enacted through a structuring process over time.

The structuring process underlies the ongoing production and change of social practices. It posits a recursive relationship between the everyday actions of human agents and the social structures which are both medium and outcome of those actions. Figure 9.2 depicts the social structures focused on here, the organizational properties of Zeta and the CSD. These included authority relations, division of labor, strategies, incentive systems, evaluation criteria, policies, work culture, etc., which represented the institutionalized aspects of the Zeta and CSD social systems. These constrained and enabled the production of ongoing practices by members of the CSD, while also being changed over time by those practices, as suggested by the variation in shading of Figure 9.2. Technology is not specifically depicted in Figure 9.2, but it played a critical role in mediating the changes in practices and structures. The conceptualization of technology drawn on here is informed by structurational analyses of technology in organizations (DeSanctis and Poole, 1994; Orlikowski, 1992), and posits technology not as physical entity or social construction, but as a set of constraints and enablements realized in practice by the appropriation of technological features (Orlikowski, 1995). Information technology in the CSD plays a role similar to that of organizational properties – shaping the production of situated practices, and being shaped by those practices in turn.

Each of the CSD's five metamorphoses can be characterized by: (i) an analysis of the practices which enacted the changes, including the organizational properties which influenced and which were influenced by those changes; (ii) the specific technological features which were appropriated in use; and (iii) the unanticipated outcomes which resulted from the changes and which influenced further changes. The following metamorphoses are discussed below:

- *Metamorphosis I:* the organizational changes associated with the shift to electronic capture, documentation, and searching of call records in the ITSS database;
- *Metamorphosis II:* the organizational changes associated with the redistribution of work from individual to shared responsibility;
- *Metamorphosis III:* the organizational changes associated with the emergence of a proactive form of collaboration among the specialists;
- *Metamorphosis IV:* the organizational changes associated with expanding into a global support practice, and with creating inter-departmental and cross-functional linkages;
- *Metamorphosis V:* the organizational changes associated with controlling access to and distributing extracts of the knowledge contained within the ITSS database.

A brief overview of the work practices within the CSD before the arrival of the new technology is useful background for the subsequent discussion of metamorphic changes.

Work in the CSD before implementation of the new technology

The acquisition of the Notes technology and the creation of an incident tracking system within it marked a significant technological and ultimately organizational change for the CSD. There was no division of labor within the department. Specialists who had been in the CSD for at least a year were informally regarded as "senior specialists," and recognized as being more knowledgeable and experienced. All specialists took calls, scribbling problem descriptions on slips of paper and then working on the problems individually until they were resolved. The process of work was not documented or reviewed in any way. Problem-solving was the central activity of customer support. While specialists were expected to record their call resolutions in the Inform database, entry was haphazard at best. The records actually entered typically exhibited limited detail and questionable accuracy, and as a result searching in this database was often unproductive. Figure 9.3 displays a sample record from the Inform database.

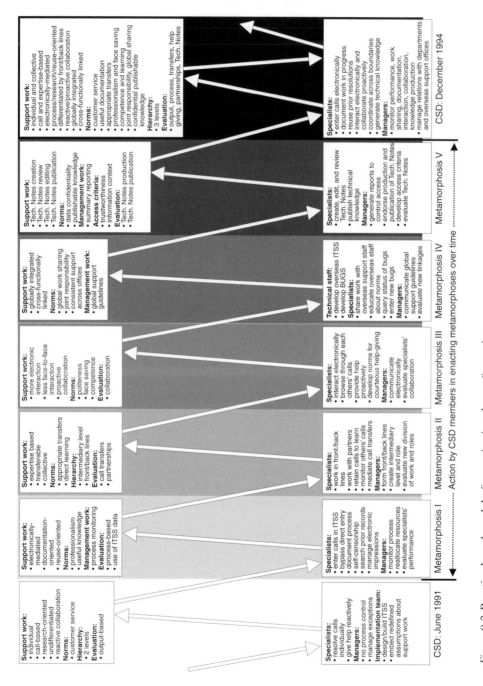

Figure 9.2 Practice-based model of organizational transformation.

PROBLEM REPORT
_____

Problem Number: 9871457   User Problem Number:
Bug/Enhancement Number:
_____

Name: JENNY   Date: 10/31/90   Time: 11:00AM
Others: Duane King
_____

Client Name: John Doe   PHONE: 999-000-1234
Company: Acme Co.   STATUS:
Time Spent: 30-45 min.   Answered Date: 10/31/90   Time: 11:30AM
Product: Omni   Version No: 3.0   Operating System:
_____

Description: READ DIF FILE INTO WORKSHEET UNRAVEL INTO VARIABLE UPDATE
             REORGANIZE RECEIVED: SYSTEM ERROR ARGET01 PROBLEM HAS
             OCCURRED. EXPORT/IMPORT DATABASE
Solution: TOLD HIM THIS WAS NOT GOOD! SHOULD EITHER 1) RESTORE FROM
           BACKUP AND CHECK DB OR 2) EXPORT/IMPORT DB.

Problem Category:
_____

Figure 9.3 Sample record from the Inform Database.

Managers performed no monitoring of the specialists' work process, evaluating them essentially on output. They were frustrated by their inability to track calls, analyze the status of particular calls, assess the department's workload, balance its resources, and identify issues and problems before they became crises. Managers' motivation in acquiring a new incident tracking system was influenced by these frustrations. As one manager recalled:

> We were totally unable to produce any type of weekly reporting or any statistics about who called us and why. We weren't quickly able to categorize any of our problems. We had a system, but you questioned the data that was in there because it was cumbersome to get the data in there.... [Also] if a month had gone by, I had no clue what had gone on. So I would have to go and find the specialist who had worked on the problem and ask them to either remember what had happened or try and find some piece of paper that might have been written down.

ITSS design and implementation

In contrast to Inform, ITSS was designed so that specialists would create an incident record in the ITSS database as each call was received, and then regularly update the incident record with the progress being made on the incident. They were to enter not just the problem description and its resolution, but also all the steps taken in the process of resolving the incident. Because ITSS was implemented in Notes, which allows databases stored on a server to be accessed from distributed, networked personal computers, the incident records in the ITSS call database were designed to be accessible by all members of the CSD. The design of ITSS was accompanied by procedural redefinitions of customer support work, and these modifications were introduced to the specialists through a series of training sessions that included hands-on use of ITSS during which specialists directly entered calls into the ITSS database and updated ITSS records by documenting their process of resolving customers' problems.

Once trained, specialists began to use ITSS to do their support work, and as they responded to the modifications in their work and appropriated the technological features of ITSS, they enacted some of the changes intended by the implementation team. Other changes emerged as specialists and their managers accommodated issues and breakdowns in the use of ITSS, and improvised techniques and norms to effectively utilize the new technology in their changing work practices.

Metamorphosis I

Figure 9.4 depicts the first set of metamorphic changes enacted with ITSS in the CSD. As indicated in the figure, these changes were both deliberate and emergent, involved specialists' and managers' work practices, were associated with some unanticipated outcomes, and involved particular features of the ITSS technology. The changes involved those specifically intended by the implementation team: electronic recording of all customer calls taken by the CSD; electronic documentation of work done on those calls; electronic reuse of prior call resolutions to avoid duplication of effort; and electronic monitoring of process and performance to facilitate process tracing and resource management.

Electronic entry of calls

One of the premises underlying the design of ITSS was that specialists should enter incidents directly into the ITSS database while on the phone with customers. The ITSS technology, designed to operate as an on-line, real-time database system, facilitated such direct entry with its "Compose New Incident" feature which provided a structured data entry screen for recording the new call. Specialists were trained to invoke this feature on receiving a new call and enter the customer's data in the structured and free-form fields when talking to them on the phone. While this feature enabled direct entry, some aspects of its design were also constraining, sufficiently so that most of the specialists continued to use paper to record their phone interactions with customers, entering these calls into ITSS at a later time. This practice of bypassing direct entry persisted despite ongoing urging by managers, and despite a recognition by specialists of the advantages of direct entry (e.g. being able to give customers an incident number as reference, being able to get an early indication of the day's workload, being able to record the time calls are received, and avoiding the risk of misplacing calls by misplacing the paper on which they were noted).

The specialists had a number of reasons for choosing to retain their original work practice of recording calls on paper. For some, limited typing proficiency inhibited direct entry of calls:

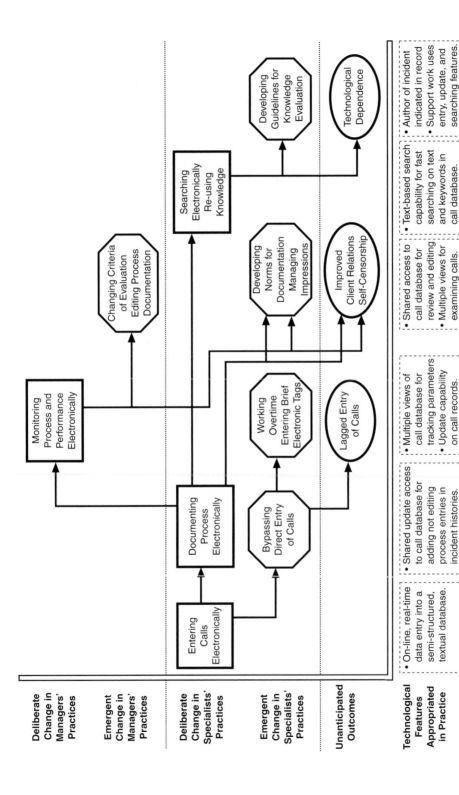

Deliberate Change in Managers' Practices

Emergent Change in Managers' Practices

Deliberate Change in Specialists' Practices

Emergent Change in Specialists' Practices

Unanticipated Outcomes

Technological Features Appropriated in Practice

- On-line, real-time data entry into a semi-structured, textual database.

- Shared update access to call database for adding not editing process entries in incident histories.

- Multiple views of call database for tracking parameters
- Update capability on call records.

- Shared access to call database for review and editing
- Multiple views for examining calls.

- Text-based search capability for fast searching on text and keywords in call database.

- Author of incident indicated in record
- Support work uses entry, update, and searching features.

Monitoring Process and Performance Electronically

Changing Criteria of Evaluation Editing Process Documentation

Searching Electronically Re-using Knowledge

Developing Guidelines for Knowledge Evaluation

Technological Dependence

Developing Norms for Documentation Managing Impressions

Improved Client Relations Self-Censorship

Documenting Process Electronically

Bypassing Direct Entry of Calls

Working Overtime Entering Brief Electronic Tags

Lagged Entry of Calls

Entering Calls Electronically

Figure 9.4 Metamorphosis I – changes in support work and management enacted with use of ITSS over time.

> If you're not confident in your typing skills, there's just no way you're going to put a call in on-line. Because you're going to have typing mistakes, you'll be trying to fix them, and then you can't read what you've typed.
>
> When calls come in, I just jot them down first. I mean I tried both ways, by killing two birds with one stone by entering and listening, but my typing skills, I guess, aren't fast enough so I can't obtain all the information if I type.

Specialists further noted that the navigation of ITSS' structured data entry screen was incompatible with how information was provided by customers. Consequently, specialists found the mechanics of manipulating the ITSS data entry screen distracting when they were trying to understand customers' often complex problems:

> I'm not comfortable typing in the incident as they're telling it. I find it's more of a distraction. I'm trying to figure out what piece of the form to fill in and they're talking rapidly about a problem. So my concentration is split and I find myself not being able to ask the right questions or forgetting some piece of information.
>
> When I get a call I personally write it down first. I think that is because I'm trying to pay attention more to what the client's talking about and trying to understand the problem. And I think that if I were actually trying to type in that information into ITSS I would lose something. . . . It's not like, "I've heard this before, I know what this is." I really need to understand what they're doing, because in order for me to either try and recreate it or try and fix it, I really need to make sure I fully understand exactly what they're doing. It's different every time.

In addition, specialists were aware that the ITSS technology and underlying network might fail occasionally. As a result, many of them utilized paper as an improvised (manual) backup system:

> When I take a call I always write it out. . . . [so that] if the network goes down, I've got their phone number on a piece of paper.

This improvisation allowed specialists to continue working on their calls even when the technology became unavailable.

Specialists' continued manual recording of calls (and avoidance of direct entry into ITSS) sometimes created problems when they received many calls in a day, and their subsequent electronic entry lagged behind. Most specialists improvised ways of dealing with backlogged data entry, for example, working after hours to get caught up, or entering brief information initially to tag the call and enter it into ITSS, and then elaborating the description when they had more time.

Specialists' practice in working around the direct electronic entry of calls suggests, to invoke Heidegger, that the ITSS technology is not as "ready at hand" as pen and paper. Both the structured nature of the technology's data entry screen and the act of typing interjected an interface into the activities of listening, interacting, comprehending, and articulating the problem. Specialists ended up focusing on the interface and on manipulating it accurately, an explicit concentration which does not arise when writing free-form with pen on paper. For the specialists (as for most of us), writing with pen and paper in an unstructured manner is familiar since grade school, and hence simply part of the background, taken for granted. In contrast, use of the ITSS technology required typing and screen-manipulation skills which diverted concentration from customers and their problems. The occasional unpredictability of the technology at the time of a call (whether slow or inaccessible) further raised barriers to the feasibility of direct electronic entry. All of these elements served to increase the "unreadiness-to-hand" of the ITSS technology, so that to specialists it appeared as a distinct object and interface that had to be attended to consciously. To avoid such cognitive diversion and concentrate on interacting intelligently with customers while on the phones, specialists had improvised various practices to bypass direct entry and compensate for the time lag when they fell behind.

Electronic process documentation

ITSS was deliberately designed to enable users to record, chronologically, the work being done on each incident, as it was being done. Figure 9.5 shows a sample record from the ITSS database. The top half shows the structured fields in which specialists had to enter specific information (aided by the provision of "pick lists" where the system offers a menu of acceptable values), and the lower section contains the unstructured "Incident History" field in which narrative descriptions of work in progress could be entered to create a chronological trace of the work process over time.

Specialists were now required to record the progress being made on each call in the "Incident History" field of that call's ITSS record. This change in specialists' job requirements was enabled by the edit feature in ITSS which allowed specialists to update incident records previously entered. When specialists completed some activity on a customer's incident, they updated that incident's record in the ITSS database by noting the kind of work done and the steps to be followed next. ITSS was designed to allow this process documentation to be open-ended. The Incident History field in which specialists made their progress updates was unstructured, allowing entry of free-form text. ITSS automatically appended information identifying the time, date, and person making the update, and arranged the updates in reverse chronological order. The ITSS edit feature, however, was restricted in that specialists could only add new entries to the Incident History field, they could not edit any previous entries made. Once an item had been added to the Incident History field, it remained there permanently. This history could not be rewritten, and as we shall see, the permanent nature of this recording led to some self-censorship on the part of the specialists.

An interesting unanticipated outcome of electronic process documentation within ITSS was that it altered the CSD's relationship with its customers:

> It has dramatically changed communications with customers. We are no longer guilty until we can prove we're innocent. We have all the facts at hand. So when customers call up and say "I called two weeks ago and nobody ever called me back," either a specialist or a manager can just immediately say "Well, let me look at the database. I see that you called last Tuesday at 4:13pm and we called you back at 5:06pm and closed your call." We get countless calls like that,

Incident Form

Incident: **XX-1-0999**
Owner: Gillian Smith   Opened: 11/28/94   09:45 AM

Company:	**Acme Co.**		
Caller:	**John Doe**	Title:	
Location:	444 Science Park	Rel:	
	Vista City, MA 02139		
Phone:	999-000-1234	Fax:	999-000-9999
Call Back:		Phone:	

Product:	DSX 4.13 {4.1700}		
Platform:	PC STANDALONE - 486	Environment:	DOS 5.0
Module:	N/A	Workstation:	N/A

Incident Description

Title: In DSX 4.x, how do you populate insample for each mrentry?
Description: Insample is dimensioned by geog, time, and mrentry. Doe wants to populate insample differently for different mrentries, but doesn't know how. He wants to know how.
Res. Type: General Question
Resolution:

Incident Management

Assignee:	Tom Brown		
Status:	Work in Progress	Close Date:	
Time Now:	10	Time Total:	50 minutes
Bug Number:		Severity:	4
Interoffice #:		T/O Assignee:	
Other #s:		Transfer Date:	
Reviewed:	Not Reviewed		
Review Date:		Reviewer:	

Incident History

***** 12/06/94 09:27:25 AM Jenny Jones (US) {Total Time = 50} (Work in Progress) (S4)
      [Tom Brown = Assignee] [Gillian Smith, Tom Brown = MailTo]
"INSAMPLE is a keyword in the control file; you can set it as follows:

ControlfileKeyword	ControlFileValue
INSAMPLE	INSAMPLE 01011
INSAMPLE	INSAMPLE 01013

Can be set with however many measures you want.
I've tried to reach Doe at the above #, but unable to. If he calls back we can give him this info. "
***** 12/02/94 12:41:43 PM Tom Brown (US) {Total Time = 40} (Work in Progress) (S4)
      [Tom Brown = Assignee] [Gillian Smith = MailTo]
"Not sure if this is possible. Will consult with Jenny and see .... might have to wait for Arthur ? We'll see. Searched GROUCHO for some details. Nothing like this found for 4.13 - only references to the DOS DataServer."
***** 12/02/94 11:59:21 AM   Martha Robinson (US) {Total Time = 20} (Work in Progress) (S4)
      [Tom Brown = Assignee] [Tom Brown, Gillian Smith = MailTo]
"Tom, can you please take a look at this call? Apparently Doe called back and would like an answer soon. If you can't take it please let me know. Thanks, Martha."
***** 11/29/94 10:11:06 AM Gillian Smith (US) {Total Time = 10} (Open) (S4)
"Talked to Arthur. He has worked with this issue before, and explained that it's complicated. He will refresh his memory and get back to me."

Figure 9.5 Sample record from the ITSS database.

people ranting and raving without any specifics, and the minute we can get specific and tell them what we did or didn't do for them, they immediately retract their statements and start being nice.... It's a great shield for the support people, their butts are covered. That's not something we anticipated.

Process documentation, electronic or other, had not previously been part of specialists' work practices. The definitions of support work had been changed to reflect the requirement to document process electronically, and evaluation criteria adjusted accordingly. These new organizational conditions (communicated via intensive training on the use of ITSS) changed specialists' understanding of their jobs, and once ITSS was fully deployed, all proceeded to appropriate ITSS to document their work process. In this action, the specialists enacted the deliberate change intended by the implementation team, thereby generating the audit trail deemed necessary to make specialists and their managers more accountable for the work of the CSD. Through such ongoing enactment, specialists reinforced and eventually institutionalized a new set of work practices, substantially mediated by information technology and expanded to include documentation. In the process, specialists had also become accountable, institutionally, not just for their output but also for their work in progress.

Electronic monitoring

With specialists producing electronic process documentation of their work in progress, managers were able to use the ITSS technology for dynamic monitoring of call load, work process, and individual performance. In this, they were strongly influenced by the institutionalized properties of Zeta, which required them to provide various statistics on departmental workload to justify their headcount, to show that they were utilizing their resources and new technology effectively, and which held them accountable for providing quality technical support to customers. To conduct their monitoring, the three CSD managers appropriated various features of ITSS, particularly the View feature which facilitated the presentation of ITSS data in multiple ways. The ITSS technology was also constraining in that there was not a strong statistical capability, so that only straightforward counts and categorized reports could be obtained. Anything more complex required the data to be extracted into another system and manipulated there.

In monitoring specialists' process documentation through ITSS, managers changed their work practices to reflect the window they now had on specialists' ongoing performance, a view that had not been possible before. This deliberate change in managers' practices occasioned an emergent change in how they evaluated specialists. They now assessed technical competence and problem-solving strategies (at least, as these were documented):

> We evaluate their technical skills. Notes is part of the way we do that: looking at the calls they close and how well they resolve them. Where did they go to look for help? Do they get in and get their hands dirty?... I also look at problem-solving skills ... reviewing their calls and seeing what history and thought process they've gone through.

In addition, managers began to evaluate the process documentation itself, not merely using it as an indicator of actions and strategies. In this way, they reinforced the new definition of the customer support job as comprising both problem-solving and documentation. Indeed, keeping process documentations up to date was presented as just as critical, or even more important than problem solving, as one manager observed:

> I explain to [the specialists] that it's more important that they document the call than solve it quickly. And I give the example of the executive vice-president of development walking into my office and asking me what's wrong at a particular site. And I can double-click, and I've got the information right there. And if that's up to date, we're golden, and we look good. And if it's not, and I have to go chase somebody down to get the most recent information, we don't look good, and that database all of a sudden isn't valid. He'll never trust it again.

In their on-line and ongoing examination of the ITSS database, managers occasionally entered comments or edits to improve the quality of the documentation or to communicate with specialists. For example, a specialist I was observing received electronic mail notification that one of his incidents had been updated. On accessing the record, he found that one of the managers had made the following entry in the record's Incident History field:

> Milt, is this one closed out? Please update, thanks, Isobel.

Specialists responded to this electronic monitoring by developing norms about what and how to document, and managing impressions of themselves through their electronic text.

Norms for process documentation

While the requirement of process documentation had been well established, the precise nature and representation of this documentation was left largely unspecified. As noted above, the technology imposed few restrictions in the Incident History field, allowing the entry of free-form text of unspecified length. The implementation team indicated that they had also not provided any documentation guidelines, preferring "to keep things voluntary and democratic." This technological "freedom" was both enabling (allowing a variety of expressions and formats) and constraining (allowing inconsistency and ambiguity). As a result, documentation during the early period of ITSS use was characterized by considerable variability in quality and detail as the specialists experimented with different styles and details in their descriptions of process. Over time, however, a number of informal norms about effective process documentation emerged, influenced by the occasional comments or edits made by managers in the ITSS records, and by the experience of specialists who realized in practice the value of documenting well and consistently. A vivid illustration of the latter was the story, recounted many times, of the specialist who was working on one of her calls, searched in ITSS and located an incident which exactly matched the error message she was researching. Delighted, she accessed the Incident History field only to find that "it was, like, totally nothing. I mean, it was useless." Frustrated and angry at the creator of the incident, she looked at the field indicating authorship, only to discover it was herself. This story, as another specialist commented:

> makes you realize that it's really going to benefit people if, you know, if even your thought process and everything can get into the incidents.

The norms that emerged from specialists' use of ITSS reflected their recognition that the database was a shared resource and that value lay in making the content of incident records reusable, whether by other specialists in the group, or by themselves at a future time:

> In my incidents I try to be very specific, even though I find sometimes it's boring to do that. . . . I mean I'm really tired of typing [all the details] in, but I figure some poor sap in another year is going to be trying to solve this problem he's never seen before, so I still need to write all that down.
>
> You need to be a little more thoughtful about how you present information so that it's useful for other people. . . . You have to have the description in there in such a way that you've made sure you've used key words that other people might search on. . . . There's a lot more thought involved rather than just kind of a scratch pad situation.

These norms, once shared and practiced within the CSD for some time, became reinforced and established as important cultural norms about the representation of work process within electronic documentation. Norms also emerged about the representation of self within this electronic text.

Impression management

Specialists were very aware that as they worked with the ITSS technology, their use reflected, very visibly and immediately, on their work practices and on themselves as support specialists. The boundary between private work and public space had shifted significantly as specialists used ITSS to produce an ongoing electronic text of their work process, which was available for future use and served as the basis on which managers had begun to evaluate them. Before their use of ITSS, specialists had tended to do much of their research work in private, making public only their questions to colleagues and their problem resolutions to customers. With ITSS, specialists now made public most aspects of their research work through their own documentation of their ongoing work in progress. They participated in making their work (and thereby, themselves) electronically visible and accountable. While specialists retained some discretion over what, how, and when to make their work visible, they had changed the nature of their work from being largely off-line (done privately in one's own space and never recorded) to being largely on-line (done privately but recorded publicly in a shared space). The transparency of the electronic text ensured that specialists' work life was now more "on display" or at least potentially so, through the medium of ITSS.

Many specialists were acutely aware of their new visibility – some of them referred to it as "Big Brother" – and responded by improvising some informal guidelines about what they would and would not articulate within the electronic text. In so doing, they began to appropriate the features of ITSS to manufacture a virtual or "electronic persona" of themselves by consciously engaging in impression management (Goffman, 1959). Goffman's distinction of front and back regions is useful here to explain specialists' use of such impression management. The "front region" is where the performance takes place and where individuals strive to maintain and embody certain standards of politeness and decorum (1959: 107), while the "back region" is where the impression managed by a performance is openly constructed, rehearsed, and contradicted (1959: 112). The ITSS records represented the (electronic) front region of the specialists' back region work. It was here that they expressed the activities they had performed backstage in terms that were compatible with the norms of front stage behavior. In this public recounting of private work, there occurred an accounting of effort in a manner designed (whether deliberately or not) to create a particular professional representation of self:

I am definitely more careful about how I say things now. If I want to say some guy was a real jerk to me, I might phrase that a little differently and say that he was not very nice. . . . We have to be more careful about entering information. We have to be more diplomatic.

There is like a general rule that you've got to be courteous and use the right language. You have to use the correct and politically correct language. You don't want to use any slang. You just want to be professional about it.

In representing their work publicly, specialists were conforming to the standards of the front region by their impression management, the unanticipated result of which was self-censorship, limiting what was documented within the ITSS database. For example:

The accessibility of the database is something that I'm always aware of and I think I'm very guarded in what I put into the database. I am always concerned about being politically correct, professional, diplomatic.

It's kind of like – if you don't want anyone to read this, don't write it, you know. What I may do is vent by just typing something and then erasing it.

What was interesting about this electronic impression management was that it was not actual electronic scrutiny within the front region that compelled "political correctness," but the possibility of such scrutiny – inherent in the notion of a front region – that focused specialists' attention on what impression of themselves was being conveyed in electronic text:

It's not obvious if they're watching the numbers. There is an undercurrent of scrutiny, Big Brother is there but it's below the surface.

Such self-regulation is a form of "participatory surveillance" (Poster, 1990), and an interesting electronic example of Foucault's panoptic discipline (Orlikowski, 1991; Zuboff, 1988). As Foucault (1979: 202–203) notes: "He who is subjected to a field of visibility, and who knows it, assumes responsibility for the constraints of power; . . . he becomes the principle of his own subjection."

While some specialists felt the electronic exposure provided by their and their managers' use of ITSS as vulnerability, others saw some advantages:

> I know that it's kind of like Big Brother watching over you, but it really doesn't bother me in that way. It's good because . . . you get so many calls that you forget what's going on . . . and that you should have alerted these people. And by having the managers look at our database and say, "Oh, this is this client and we need to alert this, that or the other," it helps. I think it's more of a team approach than having singular people entering in.
>
> It's a record of what we're doing, and . . . it's a number that we can point to show how we are working, and how well we are working.

In particular, those specialists who felt they were "high performers" welcomed the electronic scrutiny as it made their accomplishments more visible:

> [ITSS] is a working database of what I'm doing. . . . It's my brag record. I have more calls in there than anybody else.
>
> For a while I had taken an incredible number of calls. And [ITSS] sort of validated the fact that I am very busy, I am taking a lot of calls, I am really contributing to the group effort.

Thus, for some specialists, the use of ITSS created a forum in which to showcase their efforts, occasions to manage impressions of themselves as highly productive. Indeed, the electronic text provided opportunities for individuals to "make-work" (Goffman, 1959) by fabricating or embellishing work in their documentation of work in progress. Specialists continually engaging with and contributing to such a transparent electronic text changed how they represented themselves to others, engaging in the construction of professional electronic personae. Such constitution of self was facilitated by the cognitive and normative awareness of how different their work practices were when they were mediated by the technology:

> There's more of a record. It's more of an online mentality . . . It's a different mental attitude. . . . It's a mindset of everything being online and everything being accessible to everybody, and recording everything in the computer, as opposed to, you know, presenting a report to your boss at the end of the month. The ongoing thing. The idea that anybody can read your words if you want them to, or if they have the right access, and that some people can get in there and read your notes even if you haven't given them access.

With the expansion of support work to include process documentation and the adjustment of evaluation criteria to reinforce that change, the boundaries of public and private work space have shifted. Both managers and specialists have become much more attentive to the process of customer support. However, this change masks another more subtle shift in the texture of work within CSD – a focus less on process per se, than a focus on the process as documented in incident records within ITSS. This is a technologically-mediated process orientation, where the interest is less in the execution of work than in the symbolic artifacts that describe the execution of work and which are immediately and continually available through the technology. The text has become central. Poster (1995: 85), drawing on Foucault's analysis of discourse, suggests that "databases are discourse," because they "effect a constitution of the subject." Such a constitution of specialists is present in the creation, examination, and monitoring of the ITSS electronic text, where the incident records serve as symbolic surrogates for the specialists, traces of and testaments to their work. To retain some discretion in this discourse, specialists developed norms for the construction and manipulation of the text, strategies for managing impressions and expressions within it, and an awareness of some of the political and personal consequences – intended and other – of its use.

Electronic searching

The ITSS database of calls with its documentation of process and resolutions soon contained enough prior incidents to make searching the database a useful step in researching problems. Specialists expanded their appropriation of ITSS features by beginning to use the powerful search engine available to quickly scan the ITSS database on specified keywords or text. By including such searching as part of their problem-solving activities, specialists enacted a deliberate change in their work practices intended in the original design of ITSS. Searching the ITSS database became increasingly valuable over time, as the number of incident records grew, from some 4,000 in December 1992 to 35,000 in December 1994. Searching ITSS located possibly reusable problem resolutions that often saved time and effort, and offered insight into approaches and strategies for resolving various problems. Specialists reported resolving up to 50 percent of their problems through electronic searching, an accomplishment that had not been possible without the mediation of support work by the ITSS technology.

As specialists depended increasingly on searching to do their problem solving, the reliability of the knowledge in ITSS became a central concern. The ITSS technology itself offered no indicators or guarantees of the reliability or relevance of the data contained within it. Such a concern led specialists to develop some social heuristics for assessing the quality of knowledge in the ITSS records. The ITSS technology was designed to automatically assign a unique number to each incident entered into the database. This number included a code which identified the particular specialist who had documented the incident. Specialists learned each other's identifying codes, and enacted an emergent change in their work practices when they began relying on this identifier to gauge the likely quality of potentially reusable incidents:

> You tend to evaluate information differently from different people. So if you see 40 items from a search you go to the incidents of those folks you've gotten good information from in the past.
>
> I know certain people in the department, and I know that Arthur has a reputation for writing short novels as resolutions. I mean, he's a wonderful source of information and when he has an incident, he really spends the time to put a lot of detail in it. And it's extremely helpful. So when I get an incident from him, I'm very comfortable with that information. Whereas, some of the other people

in the department ... For example, Beavis has a reputation that he doesn't do much research.

Thus, specialists in the CSD improvised techniques for judging the quality of the electronic texts they chose to use in their own work.

The change in specialists' work practices to include electronic searching led, over time, to the unanticipated outcome of technological dependence, which seems almost an inevitable result of mediating work practices through technology. Technological dependence within the CSD has both a physical and a psychological referent. Dependence resulted from the ever-increasing use of the ITSS technology. Thus, when the system broke down, the specialists lost their ability to execute much of their ongoing work.

> We had a power outage last week because of the thunderstorm, and there was virtually nothing I could do. Almost everything I needed to do was on the networks. So we were pretty much paralyzed.
>
> You must have heard, we lost part of our searching capability for, like, two days. Monday, Groucho died. [author's note: Groucho is the name of one of the file servers used to store the ITSS database. The others are Chico, Moe, and Curley.] ... I mean, we came in Monday morning and – it's dead. And we didn't have it for two days. ... It was really actually very crippling. It was very hard to do your job, because so much depends on it. You know, you get a call and your first resource is to search in ITSS, and it was like "My resources aren't here!"

Some specialists were less dependent than others and managed to devise ways of working around technological breakdowns:

> I would say we're very dependent on ITSS as a whole. ... And we sort of work around it when it's down. We pull out a sheet of paper and just start writing ... The other side of that is the searching tool. Certainly when it's down you become a little crippled, because the information that you could pull up in a matter of seconds now might take a little longer because you have to find the right person.

Not all specialists, however, were able to fall back on other forms of working when the technology was not available. In particular, junior specialists who had learned support work in the context of ITSS, had no cognitive and behavioral resources for working without the technology:

> We're extremely dependent on these databases. Without them I feel underconfident. I feel I can't do this. I would be much more stressed out without them ... because I would feel like more calls are coming in that I can't answer than I can. So, psychologically, it would be difficult.

Such dependence was also reflected in junior specialists' behavior. While I was observing a junior specialist at work, he kept issuing searches within ITSS to try to find an incident that resembled a problem he was researching. His remarks while doing so reflected the expectation that "all the answers" are in the database: "Hmm

– why can't I find anything here? There's got to be something in here. I'll keep trying." And he did, for quite a while, until eventually abandoning his search and moving on to another incident.

Metamorphosis II

The second set of metamorphic changes enacted with ITSS in the CSD is displayed in Figure 9.6, which shows the emergent changes in work practices that evolved from the previous deliberate changes in electronic entry of calls and process documentation. These changes comprised a redistribution of work and responsibility within the CSD from being primarily individual and undifferentiated to being more collective and involving new roles and hierarchical levels.

Sharing work via partners

After about a year of using ITSS, the managers and senior specialists initiated an emergent change in how work was distributed within the CSD. This change had not been planned prior to the implementation of ITSS, but the growing reliance on ITSS and the communication capabilities of the Notes technology created an opportunity for the CSD to redistribute call loads. In particular, the informal distinction between "junior" and "senior" specialists was formalized in the structural division of "front line" and "back line" support levels. Junior specialists were designated as on the front line, where they were expected to take all calls, resolve as many as they could by searching the ITSS database, and then electronically transfer those calls they felt they could not manage to the senior specialists assigned to the back line. A manager noted:

> We call it "Partners," and the way it works is that newer members of the group spend an average of 40 to 50 percent of their time taking incoming calls. And they're partnered with a more senior member of the group during their shift.... The partner gets assigned problems that the junior member doesn't need to worry about.

The new distribution of work shifted responsibility for a call from being the sole purview of the individual who initially took it to being the shared responsibility of the individual and his/her partner. When enacted by the specialists, this shift changed the organizing structure and work practices of the CSD. A new role, the partner, had been introduced and the department had become hierarchically differentiated by expertise, experience, and status. The change in organizing structure had not been intended prior to the implementation of ITSS, but ongoing experience with ITSS created an awareness among managers and specialists of its feasibility and advantages. The key features of the technology that enabled the structural change were the capability for all specialists to share access to the ITSS database, the capability within ITSS for calls to be reassigned to other specialists (via a simple "Assign To" button on the ITSS Edit screen), and the capability for the system to automatically issue electronic mail messages to specialists notifying them that they have been assigned calls. Use of the ITSS technology over time and

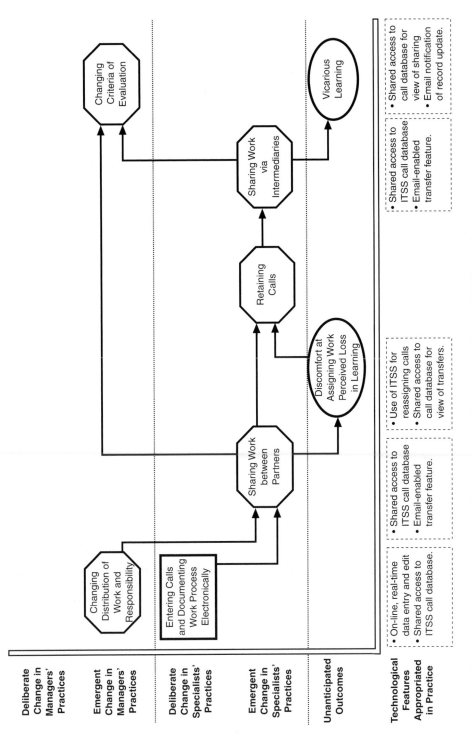

Deliberate
Change in
Managers'
Practices

Emergent
Change in
Managers'
Practices

Deliberate
Change in
Specialists'
Practices

Emergent
Change in
Specialists'
Practices

Unanticipated
Outcomes

Technological
Features
Appropriated
in Practice

Changing
Criteria of
Evaluation

Vicarious
Learning

Sharing Work
via
Intermediaries

Retaining
Calls

Discomfort at
Assigning Work
Perceived Loss
in Learning

Sharing Work
between
Partners

Changing
Distribution
of Work and
Responsibility

Entering Calls
and Documenting
Work Process
Electronically

• On-line, real-time
  data entry and edit
• Shared access to
  ITSS call database.

• Shared access to
  ITSS call database
• Email-enabled
  transfer feature.

• Use of ITSS for
  reassigning calls
• Shared access to
  call database for
  view of transfers.

• Shared access to
  ITSS call database
• Email-enabled
  transfer feature.

• Shared access to
  call database for
  view of sharing
• Email notification
  of record update.

Figure 9.6 Metamorphosis II – changes in distribution of work enacted with use of ITSS over time.

increased knowledge of its capabilities had thus enabled the CSD to institute a new division of labor.

As specialists began to enact their new organizing structure by changing their work practices, realization of the new division of labor ran into difficulties. Many specialists refrained from assigning calls to their designated partners as instructed, retaining their old practice of handling all the calls they took themselves. Two reasons cited by specialists seem to account for such action. One, they were uncomfortable assigning work to senior colleagues:

> You can just assign a call to a partner, but I don't. I only assign the call if he offers to take it. That way you're not really dumping on the other person.
>
>   My rule of thumb is if I really don't know anything about the product or the issue and I know it's definitely not my area of expertise, then I would send email and ask [my partner], "What do I do? Do you have any suggestions?" But I keep ownership of the incident, because it takes the pressure off of that person.

Two, some junior specialists preferred to solve their own problems, seeing such action as both a sign of competence and as a learning opportunity. For example:

> I don't like passing off calls,. . . it's kind of like a cop-out for me because I want to learn more about things and it would be kind of a way of not learning. It wouldn't be a learning process.

Sharing work via intermediaries

Managers reacted to this unanticipated reluctance to transfer calls by creating a new role – that of an intermediary – to facilitate the distribution and transfer of work between the front and back lines. Two senior specialists were designated as intermediaries and their work practices changed significantly. From taking calls and solving problems, they now electronically monitored the incidents entered into ITSS by junior specialists and ensured that assignments to senior specialists, where they felt appropriate, took place. One intermediary described her role:

> I monitor the incoming calls to make sure that the people that are taking incoming calls can either handle the call or else refer the call to someone else. Because we have support set up with front and back lines, we have people that take incoming calls, and if they can't answer them in an amount of time then we transfer the call to someone who is more experienced, maybe more expert in that type of problem.

While junior specialists did lose direct experience with solving certain problems, they did not give up all opportunities for learning. The technology included a feature that enabled them to be notified whenever any action was taken on a record. Thus, a junior specialist, having assigned a call to a partner, could request that the system send electronic mail each time the partner updated the record. This way, junior specialists could follow the progress of calls and learn vicariously, at least.

The sample ITSS record shown in Figure 9.5 illustrates some of the shared responsibility for work that the specialists had enacted with ITSS and the creation of partner and intermediary roles. The call was originally taken by Gillian Smith, a front-line specialist, who entered the call into the ITSS database on 11/28/94. The next day, she updated the incident's history (see bottom entry of history field), indicating that she had talked to Arthur, a senior specialist and the local expert on the DSX product, and was waiting for his recommendation. No further documented work took place on this call until 12/2/94, when an intermediary, Martha Robinson, stepped in and reassigned the call to Tom Brown, a senior specialist and Gillian's designated partner. This reassignment was indicated under the Incident Management section of the record and was prompted by the fact that a number of days had passed without activity and that the customer had called back requesting a response. The email-enabled feature of the technology is visible under the entry on 12/2/94, where both Tom Brown and Gillian Smith are designated as "MailTo" which means they were sent electronic mail notifying them of any subsequent update to this record. Tom responded to the newly assigned call within the hour, indicated that he had unsuccessfully searched the ITSS database for clues, and that he would consult with Jenny, another senior specialist knowledgeable about DSX. On 12/6/94, Jenny Jones, the senior specialist consulted by Tom, updated the record with a possible solution.

In response to the new distribution of work, managers adjusted their evaluation criteria to reflect the changed responsibilities and roles within the CSD. This involved browsing the ITSS database to determine how senior specialists helped their junior partners resolve their calls, and the extent to which the intermediaries stepped in to reassign calls when necessary. This emergent change in managers' practices further reinforced the structural change by distinguishing the roles of partner and intermediary, and differentiating the evaluation of front and back line specialists.

Metamorphosis III

The third set of metamorphic changes enacted with ITSS in the CSD is presented in Figure 9.7. Again, the changes were mainly emergent, being occasioned by specialists' responses to the first two metamorphic changes: the deliberate changes in electronic entry, process documentation, and on-line searching, as well as the emergent changes in work sharing and call reassignment. Here, the situated changes involved a shift towards more electronic interaction among the specialists, and the development of a new, technology-enabled form of collaboration which was proactive rather than reactive, and which offered unexpected benefits in problem-solving activities.

Electronic interaction

The increased use of ITSS to accomplish much of support work led specialists to spend considerably more time interacting electronically, an emergent change in their work practices. Specialists began to use the ITSS technology not only to enter, document, research, and reassign calls, but also to communicate with each other via the electronic mail facility available in the underlying Notes system. They sent

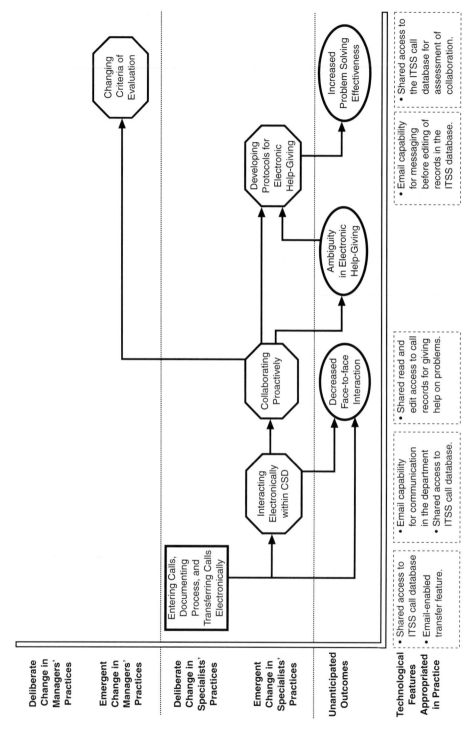

Deliberate
Change in
Managers'
Practices

Emergent
Change in
Managers'
Practices

Deliberate
Change in
Specialists'
Practices

Emergent
Change in
Specialists'
Practices

Unanticipated
Outcomes

Technological
Features
Appropriated
in Practice

Changing
Criteria of
Evaluation

Developing
Protocols for
Electronic
Help-Giving

Increased
Problem Solving
Effectiveness

Ambiguity
in Electronic
Help-Giving

Collaborating
Proactively

Decreased
Face-to-face
Interaction

Interacting
Electronically
within CSD

Entering Calls,
Documenting
Process, and
Transferring Calls
Electronically

• Shared access to
  ITSS call database.
• Email-enabled
  transfer feature.

• Email capability
  for communication
  in the department
• Shared access to
  ITSS call database.

• Shared read and
  edit access to call
  records for giving
  help on problems.

• Email capability
  for messaging
  before editing of
  records in the
  ITSS database.

• Shared access to
  the ITSS call
  database for
  assessment of
  collaboration.

Figure 9.7 Metamorphosis III – changes in interaction and collaboration enacted with use of ITSS over time.

messages seeking technical advice, distributing departmental announcements, and sharing humor. This increased use of ITSS as a medium of interaction had the unanticipated consequence of decreasing specialists' face-to-face interaction, shifting the CSD's strongly oral culture towards one that was more written and electronic.

> I've noticed stretches of two to three days where I'm at my desk trying to resolve my calls as quickly as possible, and I haven't talked to anyone.... It's like, if Lotus Notes has the answers why should I go talk to anyone?

Some specialists compensated for this shift in interaction medium by creating occasions for getting together with colleagues, either at lunch or informal meetings:

> If I thought something important enough came up that everybody in the XSS group – and there's only four of us – I would say, all right, let's get together and discuss this, even if it was for a half an hour. We'd just kind of sit down and go back and forth.

The increased use of electronic interaction also set the stage for an interesting emergent change in specialists' collaboration.

Proactive collaboration

With specialists interacting more through ITSS, and sharing access to all calls in the ITSS database, an electronic form of collaboration emerged in their work practices. Shared commitment to customer service had been a strong norm in the department since its inception, and it had recently been reinforced by the structural shift to partners and intermediaries. Nevertheless, before ITSS, collaboration was essentially reactive. Because all calls were held individually, specialists could only provide help on each others' problems when asked to do so. The technology of ITSS provided all specialists with access to everybody's problems, essentially a window on the problems currently being worked on within the department. Specialists discovered that with this virtual window into the work load of their peers they could browse through each others' calls to locate those they could provide help on. Then, using the technology to send electronic mail or enter comments in a record's Incident History, specialists could provide suggestions or solutions to each other. In this way, they improvised a form of proactive help-giving where they actively sought problems in the electronic database that they had solutions for, rather than waiting to be asked if they had a solution to a particular problem. This emergent change in collaboration implicitly acknowledged specialists' awareness of their shared responsibility for calls received by the CSD.

Specialists – both junior and senior – changed their work practices so that they routinely engaged in electronic help giving, whether solicited or not:

> We all help each other out, you know. Like if I see Martha's gotten 15 calls and I've only gotten 3, I'm going to go in and I'm going to help her, whether she feels she needs it or not. I'm going to do some research for her. She does the same for me. And it's because, you know that one day you'll get killed, the next

day you don't get killed. So, you're going to help whoever's getting hit the hardest that day.

Sometimes, if I see something that's open on somebody's calls which I've seen before, I may put a note in the incident and say "Hey, I think I've seen this before, this might be this and this." . . . I find a couple of times that's really been helpful for me.

Proactive electronic help-giving, however, was not simply a straightforward matter of providing knowledge or suggestions. It also involved a social interaction with particular issues of "courtesy." The appropriate etiquette for giving or receiving unsolicited help was, at least initially, quite ambiguous. Specialists were concerned about being rude or intrusive, and so they evolved a set of social protocols over time:

Sometimes if I don't have a lot open, I may check around and see if anybody else has something that they need done, to, you know, help around. I would go in and see who looked overwhelmed, and I'd say, "Boy, you looked like you had quite a day yesterday, do you need some help?" I would do that in person. It would be very rude to go in and resolve their call.

A lot of times I'll see something that's similar to what I may have already worked on. And I might be able to save them some time from even having to search by telling them what call I resolved this in. I'll send them Notes mail with my resolution. I won't close the call for them, but I'll give them what resolution I've used.

They also qualified their comments and descriptions so as not to mislead colleagues:

[When] I put a note in Duane's call, I said "I'm not sure, but it looks like it might be this and this." And I was very careful to say, you know, "I don't want to lead you astray here, but . . ."

Specialists also had norms for acknowledging the help received from colleagues, for example:

We all welcome whatever help we can get . . . [and] we always send back a note, "Thanks, you just saved me some time. I appreciate your help."

I observed one specialist writing in the Incident History of her own call: "This could be a nightmare" which, she explained, was intended "to warn anyone who might be interested in helping out," so that they knew what they were getting into before they began working on it.

Specialists also attempted to maintain a sense of collegiality in their electronic collaboration. See for example, some of the comments entered in the ITSS record displayed in Figure 9.5. During my observation I noticed one senior specialist entering comments in junior specialists' call records by addressing them by name and signing her own name. She explained:

I'm mucking around in their calls, so I do [use first names], otherwise it's so impersonal. It takes the formality out of it. It takes the edge out of it. So if I'm being somewhat critical it doesn't come across negatively.

An unanticipated consequence of the emergence of proactive collaboration was an increase in the effectiveness with which problems were solved. Managers responded by changing their evaluation criteria of specialists to take such unsolicited and courteous help-giving into account:

When I'm looking at incidents, I'll see what help other people have offered, and that does give me another indication of how well they're working as a team.

The use of ITSS facilitated proactive help-giving by specialists which included but also transcended the formal division of labor into front and back lines. This unexpected innovation in work practices and the emergence of norms around the courteous and diplomatic giving of unsolicited help both reflected the cooperative culture of the CSD and its shared focus on solving customer problems.

Metamorphosis IV

Figure 9.8 shows the fourth set of metamorphic changes enacted with ITSS in the CSD. Here, both emergent and deliberate changes were enacted by specialists and managers to facilitate a global support practice and an inter-departmental coordination mechanism.

Electronic linkages with overseas support offices

During 1993 and early 1994, the senior vice-president of the Technical Services Division authorized the implementation of the ITSS technology in the three main overseas offices that had customer support departments – the UK, Europe, and Australia. In addition, the technology was configured so that the four support departments shared copies of each other's ITSS databases, which were replicated every two to three hours. This meant that all four of the support offices had access to each other's databases, increasing the sources of knowledge that specialists could draw on in their research. This linkage of the four ITSS databases facilitated a global distribution of work, with overseas support specialists using the ITSS technology to transfer calls they could not solve to the US support office, which was larger and had more expertise. Previously, overseas support staff would have transferred incidents to the US via faxes and phone calls, but such exchanges were often ambiguous, necessitating lengthy clarification dialogues, and complicated by time zone differences, which made synchronous telephone conversations difficult to schedule. Use of ITSS as a transfer medium overcame the synchronicity constraint and ensured that more information about each incident were included.

Integrating the various support offices into a global support practice, however, did not just require a technological linkage. Social norms and expectations about call responsibility and work load were also necessary to facilitate cooperation across the remote offices. Initially, different customs and expectations generated ambiguity and created breakdowns in communication among the support staff

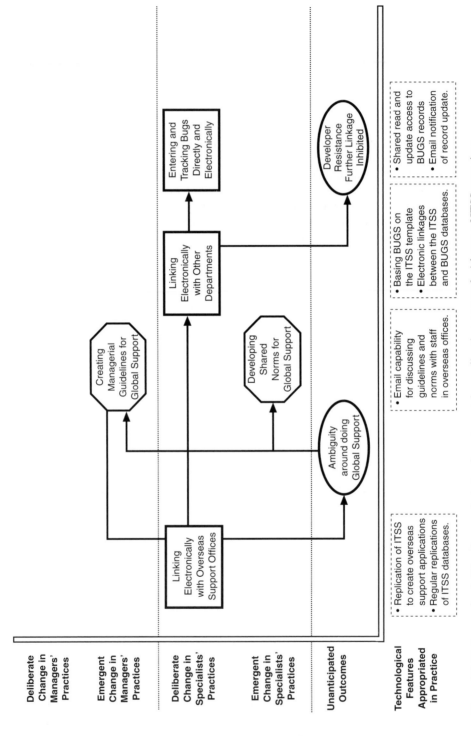

Figure 9.8 Metamorphosis IV – changes in inter-departmental coordination enacted with use of ITSS over time.

across the various offices. The US specialists, for example, resented what they saw as the tendency by overseas specialists to "just throw things over the wall," a sense exacerbated by the asynchronicity and impersonality of the ITSS-based electronic transfers. Such apparently non-collaborative behavior violated the CSD specialists' norms about support, which they had come to regard as a collective and shared activity:

> A lot of times, it's almost as though we're getting the problem without any analysis or testing on the part of the other office.... If we ask for details on a certain piece of it or ask them to clarify a certain point, it may be days, sometimes it's weeks before a response will come through,... and then they say we talk down to them.
>
> I would say there is a fair amount of [calls] that if they bothered to search in the database they would have found the answer and it wouldn't have generated the transfer to us. It's just very frustrating because here you are, working with somebody, you work for the same company, you're on the same team, and you get attitudes back and forth.

Research has pointed to the importance of developing shared assumptions and expectations about use of a new technology (Orlikowski and Gash, 1994), and the US specialists' frustrations suggest that the overseas specialists have a different understanding of the division of responsibility among support offices. Used to the collaborative problem-solving norms that have developed within the CSD, the US specialists expected a similar relationship with their overseas colleagues. Overseas specialists, in contrast, had just started using the ITSS technology and had not had time to develop norms of collaborative problem-solving around incidents. They may have understood the relationship with the US office as one of assigning responsibility for incidents. Responding to these breakdowns, the CSD managers contacted their overseas counterparts by phone and electronic mail, and together they generated a set of guidelines that explicitly articulated the procedures and expectations associated with a global support practice. Similarly, specialists began to send electronic mail to their overseas counterparts to clarify their expectations around joint responsibility for calls, and offered specific suggestions for how their collaboration could be facilitated.

Electronic linkages with other departments

Based on the success of the ITSS expansion into overseas offices, the senior vice-president of the Technical Services Division authorized the development of a number of Notes-based bug tracking systems (one for each Zeta product) for installation within Zeta's product development, product management, and quality assurance departments. These bug systems (BUGS), modeled on the ITSS system and linked directly to it, were motivated by CSD's interest in being able to report and track bugs more efficiently, and hence were initiated, developed, and paid for by the Technical Services Division.

The bug tracking systems were built to allow a direct linkage from the ITSS database to the BUGS database. For example, if a specialist working on an incident discovered that the problem was due to a bug she could directly access the appropriate

BUGS database to report the bug. The reference number assigned to that bug would appear in the original incident record (see the field "Bug Number" under Incident Management in Figure 9.5). Later, if she were curious about the status of that bug, she could open the original incident in ITSS, click on the bug field, and be directly connected to the appropriate BUGS record for determining the progress to date on that bug. Thus, specialists changed their work practices of reporting and querying bugs. They now electronically transferred bugs that they had found directly into the appropriate bug tracking system, and they electronically queried the status of various bugs simply by calling up those records directly. This eased the task of reporting bugs to product development (previously a manual process) and gave specialists up-to-date information on the status of bugs when they needed it. By using the email-enabled notification feature they could have the system notify them whenever someone updated a particular record in one of the bug databases. Specialists found these inter-departmental electronic linkages useful:

> The bug system provides a way to keep track of the work between the QA department finding the bug, the development fixing the bugs, and the status of the fix. But what's great is that we've actually hooked it into our incident system so that when a call comes into support and it turns out that it's a bug, we just click on a field and boom, it merges into the bug system, and so now we can keep track of it. Before that was really frustrating, we really went into a black hole.
>
>   Whenever someone goes in and makes a modification to that bug from development, we're notified immediately. So, we're not hanging around, you know, having to go in and check every couple of days or every couple of months to see when our bugs get fixed. . . . We're notified every time they do something.

An unanticipated consequence of this inter-departmental expansion of ITSS use was the resistance it evoked from the Zeta product developers. They were reluctant to change their work practices to use BUGS, in part because they saw use of these systems as unimportant given that bug fixing represented only a small aspect of their work responsibilities:

> It's probably a sense that [bug tracking] isn't the real work. This is a little bit outside. We're trying to produce a product. [BUGS] is only a tool that helps us maintain a product, but it's not really part of the product itself.

In contrast, use of ITSS by the CSD specialists was central to most of their work practices. Developers also worked under significant time constraints to get the next release of their product out, and hence were reluctant to take the time to learn to use a new system to facilitate their fixing of the old product. Their attention and interest were clearly focused elsewhere. The unanticipated outcome of developer resistance to use the Notes technology in their work or to change their work practices consequently inhibited future attempts by the CSD to more closely integrate the activities of the support and development departments.

Metamorphosis V

Figure 9.9 depicts the fifth set of metamorphic changes realized in the CSD with use of ITSS. It shows the deliberate and emergent changes that specialists and managers enacted in response to an increasing demand for access to the knowledge generated and archived within ITSS.

Electronic access control

With the ITSS database emerging as an increasingly valuable knowledge archive through the work practices of the specialists, others in Zeta began to demand access to this database, either to assess trends in customer problems, or to directly obtain resolutions to specific problems. Because of the level of detail in the ITSS database, CSD managers and specialists were concerned about who had access to the ITSS database, and how the accessed information would be used. For example, they feared information would be used against the department or individual specialists:

> There are people in the company who say, "Well, I just want a copy of this entire database so that I can use it to research problems for my customers and I won't have to call you." But sure as shooting, they'll look at it and say, "Well, I don't agree with that answer, and why did it take two days to get that answer? [...: [Our] fear is that finger-pointing is an outcropping of access. It's not everybody's motivation going in, but it happens.
>
> Since we use this database all day long and pretty much everything we do is in here, you're under the microscope. And there's a lot of people in the company who could essentially look at this database and start criticizing.

They also feared that the ITSS information would be taken out of context and used inappropriately:

> [ITSS] isn't really a knowledge base, it's a history of all the problems we take in. And just because one incident might tell you to do something one way, doesn't necessarily mean that it's going to solve [every] problem.... Somebody in the sales group is not going to understand that ... they will read it and take it as gospel, and it's not.
>
> All we attempt to do in support is answer the question to the best of our abilities. There's no guarantees that it's right.... I don't think we want a situation where somebody passes something onto a client, and it ends up being a big problem for the client, and then everybody turns around to us and says, "Well, we got it from your database, so what's going on?"

Over time, the CSD managers developed various mechanisms for dealing with this unanticipated demand; at the same time, norms around electronic access control gradually emerged, being improvised through a process of learning and experience in use. As a manager observed:

> Initially, I knew why I didn't want them to have it, and that was that it could be used against me. But at that point, I wasn't secure in being able to articulate

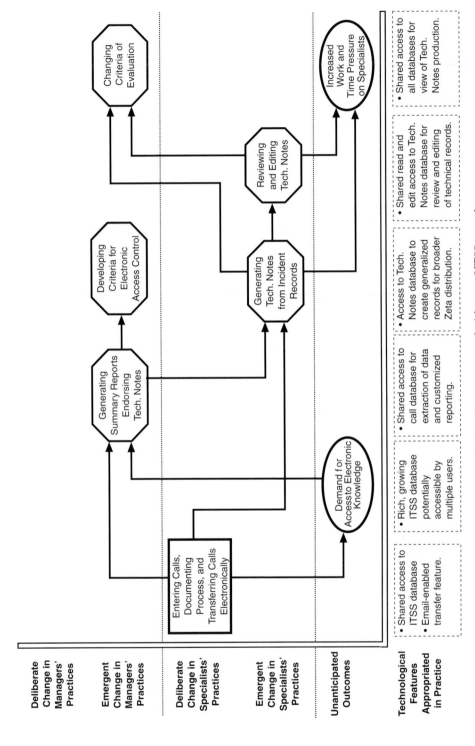

Deliberate Change in Managers' Practices

Emergent Change in Managers' Practices

Deliberate Change in Specialists' Practices

Emergent Change in Specialists' Practices

Unanticipated Outcomes

Technological Features Appropriated in Practice

Changing Criteria of Evaluation

Developing Criteria for Electronic Access Control

Reviewing and Editing Tech. Notes

Generating Tech. Notes from Incident Records

Generating Summary Reports Endorsing Tech. Notes

Increased Work and Time Pressure on Specialists

Demand for Access to Electronic Knowledge

Entering Calls, Documenting Process, and Transferring Calls Electronically

- Shared access to ITSS database
- Email-enabled transfer feature.

- Rich, growing ITSS database potentially accessible by multiple users.

- Shared access to call database for extraction of data and customized reporting.

- Access to Tech. Notes database to create generalized records for broader Zeta distribution.

- Shared read and edit access to Tech. Notes database for review and editing of technical records.

- Shared access to all databases for view of Tech. Notes production.

Figure 9.9 Metamorphosis V – changes in knowledge distribution enacted with use of ITSS over time.

that, maybe because I didn't have enough knowledge. I couldn't have looked the [President of Zeta] in the face and told him that that data could be used against me, and felt strongly enough about it. I guess I had to experience – I had to go through a couple of years with that system knowing, experiencing different situations, and say to myself, "Gee, if they had access to my data I'd be dead right now." . . . And now, I just have a much better perspective, and I'll go up against anybody when it comes to access of this data.

At first, managers established a strong position of refusing ITSS access to anyone outside of the CSD. For individuals seeking information on customer trends, they offered as an alternative, customized, summary reports. A manager described a specific example:

> The western region heard about this great database that we had. And they were particularly interested in finding out what their clients call us about. . . . So, as a way to pacify them I got a copy of a client list from them, and I would on a weekly basis go in and just highlight the week's activity in a view of those clients, . . . and fax it to them.

For individuals seeking technical information, managers referred them to a mechanism improvised by the specialists and known as "Tech. Notes," which disseminated sanitized extracts of ITSS data throughout Zeta (see below). Only after some time did managers relax their strong position on "no access to ITSS," although still only allowing access to selected individuals:

> We have given access to a few product management type people, on the basis of whether we felt we could trust them with the information. If other people were to move into [those positions] we'd take the access away.

The CSD also communicated its position on ITSS access in the on-line ITSS users' guide:

> ITSS is, for the most part, the backbone of Technical Support. It has become so valuable that other groups are requesting access to it for everything from account management to Client addresses. Reasonable requests for access to ITSS information will be considered, but let the users beware!!! ITSS is intended as a call tracking application, not a technical notes database or a Client tracking database. The information in ITSS is provided "as is", with no guarantees. It represents the best efforts of Technical Support Specialists working in a very complex support environment under serious time constraints. [highlighted in red] **Any use of ITSS that negatively impacts Support will not be allowed, and all offenders will have their access revoked immediately.**

Electronic knowledge dissemination

After many months of using ITSS and realizing the benefit of the ITSS knowledge base, the specialists began to generate sanitized summaries of information about particularly common or difficult problems. They shared these summaries among themselves and disseminated them to other Zeta departments. This practice, which had started informally among the specialists, received a big boost when the CSD managers used it to justify denying requests for direct access to ITSS. Zeta had in place a number of company-wide electronic bulletin boards known as Source Zeta (implemented in the cc:Mail software package). Different departments (e.g. customer support, product management) used these bulletin boards to announce information or distribute knowledge about various products. Specialists proposed the idea of taking common or important customer problems from ITSS, documenting them with clear descriptions and appropriate solutions, and then disseminating them via Source Zeta to the rest of Zeta (including the many field service representatives who represented up to 30 percent of the CSD's callers).

The transfer of knowledge from the ITSS database to Source Zeta took a few steps. First, individual specialists voluntarily wrote up sanitized and generalized "position papers" as Tech. Notes on specific technical issues. These Tech. Notes were entered into the Tech. Notes Review database (within the Notes technology) where they were reviewed by a (volunteer) committee of specialists whose comments triggered corrections and elaborations by the original author. This review cycle was facilitated by the shared access to databases provided by the technology. After iterating a few times through the review cycle, a Tech. Note would be published on the Source Zeta bulletin board, and thus disseminated throughout the firm. The initiative for producing Tech. Notes lay with the specialists. While not a mandatory part of their job, many specialists included this activity in their work practices, motivated by an interest in reducing calls from field service representatives, and a desire to increase their personal visibility within Zeta:

> The incentive is more or less trying to save somebody else time. You document something that you spent a lot of time on so that somebody else doesn't have to spend the time later on.
>
> It is a very visible note of productivity.... The primary author's name is associated with it, and it's distributed in a way that indicates it came from support. So I suppose it has both personal and group recognition.

The practice of generating and reviewing Tech. Notes was applauded by the managers, who modified their evaluation criteria to include such activity in their assessment of individuals' performance. An unanticipated outcome, however, of the use of Tech. Notes as access control was that it increased specialists' work load. Converting the electronic knowledge in ITSS from its situated, specific form to a more generic, abstract, and accurate form more suitable for broader dissemination was time-consuming, and at the time of my final interviews, specialists were finding that this voluntary activity had begun to add to their sense of time pressure. Presumably, further metamorphoses will occur as responses to these pressures.

Implications

Almost fifteen years ago now, March called for theoretical developments that explain "how substantial changes occur as the routine consequence of standard procedures or as the unintended consequence of ordinary adaptation" (1981: 575).

The practice-based perspective outlined in this chapter attempts to take this call seriously. By focusing on change as situated, it provides a way of seeing that change may not always be as planned, inevitable, or discontinuous as we imagine. Rather, it is often realized through the ongoing variations which emerge frequently, even imperceptibly, in the slippages and improvisations of everyday activity. Those variations that are repeated, shared, amplified, and sustained can, over time, produce perceptible and striking organizational changes.

Such situated changes were associated with the implementation and use of new technology in the customer support department of Zeta Corporation. The appropriation of this technology by members of the CSD, and the adaptations and adjustments they enacted over time facilitated the slow, sometimes subtle, but surprisingly significant transformation of the organizing practices and structures of the CSD. In particular, we saw changes in the following areas: the nature and texture of work (from tacit, private, and unstructured to articulated, public, and more structured); patterns of interaction (from face-to-face and reactive to electronic and proactive); distribution of work (from call-based to expertise-based); evaluation of performance (from output-focused to a focus on process and output as documented); forms of accountability (from manual and imprecise to electronic and detailed); nature of knowledge (from tacit, experiential, and local to formulated, procedural, and distributed); and mechanisms of coordination (from manual, functional, local, and sporadic to electronic, cross-functional, global, and continuous).

Figure 9.2 depicts these transformational changes in the CSD as emerging out of the ongoing practices of organizational actors. The theoretical premise is that these practices are generated through a structuring process, where the everyday actions of organizational members produce, reproduce, and change their organizing structures. Changes in the CSD's organizing practices (and hence its structures) were initially triggered by the design and installation of a new information technology to mediate support work. In contrast to the technological imperative perspective however, this new technology did not cause particular predetermined organizational changes. Rather it was designed and constructed by the CSD implementation team to provide a set of features which both constrained and enabled the ITSS users in ways anticipated and unanticipated by the implementation team. The ITSS technology enabled specialists and managers of the CSD to allow the representation and storage of structured and free-form data about each call entered into the database, provide shared access to networked users, support fast searching of records in the database, facilitate communication and call transfers, allow replication of distributed databases, and afford direct links to related databases. But the ITSS technology also constrained the practice of support work by formalizing and encoding particular procedures for conducting support work, providing only particular structured views of the data in the form of fixed entry and edit screens (manipulation of which required careful attention), restricting structured fields to only certain values, thus legitimating only certain meanings, presenting a strictly chronological trace of work in progress that endorses documentation not action, preventing the alteration of incident histories, making work process visible and measurable, providing few cues or clues about communication and collaboration norms, offering little statistical capability, and mediating work so that when the technology breaks down or exhibits errors, breakdowns arise in user routines.

As members of the CSD attempted to make sense of and appropriate the new technology and its embedded constraints and enablements, they enacted – through the structuring process – a series of metamorphic changes in their organizing practices and structures. These changes were grounded in members' daily actions and interactions as they responded to the expected and unexpected outcomes, breakdowns, and opportunities that their technological sensemaking and appropriation afforded. While some of the changes were deliberate and intended, others were emergent and unanticipated. In contrast to the planned change perspective, thus, many of the changes realized by the CSD were not planned a priori, and neither were they discrete events. Rather, they revealed a pattern of contextualized innovations in practice enacted by all members of the CSD and proceeding over time with no predetermined endpoint. A comparison of CSD practices and structures in June 1991 and December 1994 (see Figure 9.2) reveals significant changes in work, norms, structure, coordination mechanisms, evaluation criteria, and technology use. These changes were not all implemented with the initial deployment of the technology (Metamorphosis I), but emerged and evolved through moments of situated practice over time. These findings suggest – contrary to the punctuated equilibrium prediction that organizations do not experience transformations gradually – that local variations in practice can, over time, shade into a set of substantial organizational metamorphoses.

The five metamorphoses in Zeta's CSD provide one instance of situated organizational change. Considerable further empirical research is necessary. As indicated earlier, the current research is limited by the retrospective nature of much of the data. Studies that allow long-term observation of ongoing practices would clearly deepen and extend the analysis, begun here, of organizational change as situated in moments of practice. Further empirical research is also needed to determine the extent to which a practice-based perspective on transformative change is useful in other contexts, and how different organizational and technological conditions influence the improvisations attempted and implemented. While the changes in the CSD were relatively effective, one may imagine, for example, that in a more hierarchically organized or more rigidly controlled workplace, the sorts of workarounds, adjustments, and innovations enacted by Zeta actors may not have been tolerated or successful. Organizational inertia and resistance to change – often seen in organizations and predicted by a number of change theories – were not apparent within the CSD. Members of the CSD appeared to be open to exploring alternative ways of working, of learning from and changing with the new technology. The CSD managers initiated and encouraged such experimentation and learning, thus providing a legitimating context for ongoing improvisation. Indeed, these ongoing changes continue within the CSD, and as the research study ended, there was no sense of a transformation completed. Metamorphosis continues, as one manager observed:

> We've had ITSS for two years. I'm surprised that the enthusiasm hasn't gone away.... I think it's because it's been changed on a regular basis. And there's always some new feature, or we think about . . . other things that we can do with it. Knowing that they're going to get implemented keeps you wanting to think about it, and keep going.

Similarly, more research is needed to investigate how the nature of the technology used influences the change process and shapes the possibilities for ongoing organizational change. Had a more rigid, more fixed-function technology been used, the pattern of use and change realized within the CSD would have been different. The specific ITSS technology was built within a general technological platform (the Notes groupware system) which is more open-ended, generic, and user-customizable than traditional transaction processing or single-user computer systems. Such technological capabilities represent a new class of organizational computing, which Malone *et al.* (1992) aptly refer to as *radically-tailorable tools*. The distinguishing capability of such tools is that they enable users to construct or customize specific versions and local adaptations of the underlying techno-logical features. This capability has two important implications for practice. One, it allows for easy ongoing changes to the technology in use, in contrast to more rigid, fixed-function technologies which are difficult and costly, if not impossible, to change during use. Two, because customization is required for effective use, ongoing learning in use and consequent technological and organi-zational changes are encouraged. As Orlikowski *et al.* (1995) suggest, because new customizable technologies are so general, local adaptations and ongoing accom-modations of such technologies and their use are necessary to make them relevant (and keep them relevant) to particular contexts and situated work practices. Such adaptations and accommodations cannot be known upfront and typically have to be enacted *in situ*. The practice-based logic of change followed by the CSD would appear to be a particularly useful process for implementing and using such new technologies.

The particular kinds of metamorphoses identified in Zeta's CSD – increased doc-umentation, accountability, visibility, and differentiation, shared responsibility, proactive collaboration, distributed and cross-functional coordination, and know-ledge dissemination – are clearly specific to one unit (CSD) within one organization (Zeta). This is appropriate in a perspective of situated change, which by definition, assumes context specificity. However, the *process* of change outlined here – ongoing local improvisations in response to deliberate and emergent variations in practice – is potentially generalizable and is offered as a stimulus for further research. Of particular interest is the general usefulness of this perspective in those organizations embracing calls for flexibility, experimenting with ongoing learning, or investing in open-ended, tailorable technologies.

The dominant models of technology-based organizational transformation – planned change, technological imperative, and punctuated equilibrium – each make a number of assumptions about the nature of agency, context, technology, and change which are appropriate to an organizing practice premised on stability. Contemporary demands for organizations to be flexible, responsive, and capable of learning require organizing practices to deal with ongoing change. I have proposed an additional perspective on organizational transformation that avoids the strong assumptions that have character-ized prior change perspectives because it focuses on the situated micro-level changes that actors enact over time as they make sense of and act in the world. In its presump-tion of ongoing action, a practice lens allows for the possibility of ongoing change. It conceives of change as situated and endemic to the practice of organizing. It affords an analysis of technology-based organizational transformations that is ongoing, improvisa-tional, and grounded in everyday, knowledgeable agency. As such, it may offer a unique and especially appropriate strategy of interpretation for the new organizing dis-course becoming increasingly common today.

Acknowledgments

I would like to thank the members of Zeta Corporation who participated in this research, as well as Michael Gallivan, Cheng Goh, Lorin Hitt, and George Wyner who collected data during the first research phase. Comments of the issue editors and anonymous reviewers on an earlier draft of this chapter were very helpful. This research was supported by the Center for Coordination Science at the Massachusetts Institute of Technology.

Notes

1   While Escher, as artist, clearly orchestrated the metamorphoses exhibited, he has depicted the transformation process as driven by a situated momentum.
2   Names of the organization, its departments, products, and technology applications have all been disguised.

References

Abernathy, W.J. and Clark, K.B. 1985. "Innovation: Mapping the Winds of Creative Destruction," *Research Policy*, 14: 3–22.

Barley, S.R. 1988. "Technology, Power, and the Social Organization of Work," in Tomaso, N. (ed.), *Research in the Sociology of Organizations*, Greenwich, CT: JAI Press, 6: 33–80.

Blau, P., McHugh-Falbe, C., McKinley, W. and Phelps, T. 1976. "Technology and Organization in Manufacturing," *Administrative Science Quarterly*, 21: 20–40.

Burns, T. and Stalker, G.M. 1961. *The Management of Innovation*, London: Tavistock.

Cameron, K.S., Freeman, S.J. and Mishra, A.K. 1993. "Downsizing and Redesigning Organizations," in Huber, G.P. and Glick, W.H. (eds) *Organizational Change and Redesign*, New York, NY: Oxford University Press: 19–65.

Carter, N.M. 1984. "Computerization as a Predominate Technology: Its Influence on the Structure of Newspaper Organizations," *Academy of Management Journal*, 27: 247–70.

Child, J. and Smith, C. 1987. "The Context and Process of Organizational Transformation: Cadbury Ltd. in its sector," *Journal of Management Studies*, 24: 565–94.

Ciborra, C.U. and Lanzara, G.F. 1991. "Designing Networks in Action: Formative Contexts and Post-Modern Systems Development," in Clarke, R. and Cameron, J. (eds) *Managing Information Technology's Organisational Impact*, Amsterdam, Holland: Elsevier Science Publishers: 265–79.

Deming, W.E. 1986. *Out of the Crisis*, Cambridge, MA: MIT Press.

DeSanctis, G. and Poole, M.S. 1994. "Capturing the Complexity in Advanced Technology Use: Adaptive Structuration Theory," *Organization Science*, 5, 2: 121–47.

Dunphy, D.C. and Stace, D.A. 1988. "Transformational and Coercive Strategies for Planned Organizational Change," *Organizational Studies*, 9, 3: 317–34.

Eisenhardt, K.M. 1989. "Building Theories from Case Study Research," *Academy of Management Review*, 14, 4: 532–50.

Escher, M.C. 1986. *Escher on Escher: Exploring the Infinite*, New York, NY: Harry N. Abrams Inc.

Foucault, M. 1979. *Discipline and Punish*, New York, NY: Vintage Books.

Galbraith, J.R. 1973. *Designing Complex Organizations*, Reading, MA: Addison-Wesley.

Gersick, C.J.G. 1991. "Revolutionary Change Theories: A Multilevel Exploration of the Punctuated Equilibrium Paradigm," *Academy of Management Review*, 16, 1: 10–36.

Gallivan, M., Goh, C.H., Hitt, L.M. and Wyner, G. 1993. "Incident Tracking at InfoCorp: Case Study of a Pilot Notes implementation," Working Paper # 3590–93, Center for Coordination Science, MIT Sloan School: Cambridge, MA.

Giddens, A. 1984. *The Constitution of Society: Outline of the Theory of Structure*, Berkeley, CA: University of California Press.

Goffman, E. 1959. *The Presentation of Self in Everyday Life*, New York, NY: Doubleday Anchor.

Hage, J. and Aiken, M. 1970. *Social Change in Complex Organizations*, New York, NY: Random House.

Hammer, M. and Champy, J. 1993. *Reengineering the Corporation*, New York, NY: HarperCollins.

Heidegger, M. 1977. *The Question Concerning Technology* (translated by W. Lovitt), New York, NY: Harper & Row.

Heilbroner, R.L. 1967. "Do Machines Make History?" *Technology and Culture*, 8: 335–45.

Huber, G.P. 1990. "A theory of the effects of advanced information technologies on oganizational design, intelligence, and decision making," *Academy of Management Review*, 15, 1: 47–71.

Hutchins, E. 1991. "Organizing Work by Adaptation," *Organization Science*, 2, 1: 14–39.

Johnson, B.M. and Rice, R.E. 1987. *Managing Organizational Innovation: The Evolution from Word Processing to Office Information Systems*, New York, NY: Columbia University Press.

Kimberly, J.R. and Miles, R.H. (eds) 1980. *The Organizational Life-Cycle: Issues in the Creation, Transformation, and Decline of Organizations*, San Francisco, CA: Jossey Bass.

Lave, J. 1988. *Cognition in Practice*, Cambridge, UK: Cambridge University Press.

Lewin, K. 1951. *Field Theory in Social Science*, New York, NY: Harper & Row.

Malone, T.W. 1995. "Commentary on Suchman Article and Winograd Response," *CSCW Journal*, 3, 1: 36–8.

Malone, T.W., Lai, K.Y. and Fry, C. 1992. "Experiments with OVAL: A Radically Tailorable Tool for Cooperative Work," *Proceedings of the Conference on Computer Supported Cooperative Work*, Toronto, Canada: ACM/SIGCHI & SIGOIS: 289–97.

March, J.G. 1981. "Footnotes to Organizational Change," *Administrative Science Quarterly*, 26: 563–77.

Meyer, A.D. and Goes, J.D. 1988. "Organizational Assimilation of Innovations: A Multilevel Contextual Analysis," *Academy of Management Journal*, 31, 4: 897–923.

Meyer, A.D., Goes, J.D. and Brooks, G.R. 1993. "Organizations Reacting to Hyperturbulence," in Huber, G.P. and Glick, W.H. (eds) *Organizational Change and Redesign*, New York: Oxford University Press: 66–111.

Miles, M.B. and Huberman, A.M. 1984. *Qualitative Data Analysis: A Sourcebook of New Methods*, Newbury Park, CA: Sage Publications.

Miles, R.E. and Snow, C.C. 1984. "Fit, Failure, and the Hall of Fame," *California Management Review*, 26, 3: 10–28.

Miller, D. 1982. "Evolution and Revolution: A Quantum View of Structural Change in Organizations," *Journal of Management Studies*, 19: 131–51.

Miller, D. and Friesen, P.H. 1984. *Organizations: A Quantum View*, New York, NY: Prentice-Hall.

Mintzberg, H. 1979. "An Emerging Strategy of 'Direct' Research," *Administrative Science Quarterly*, 24: 582–9.

Mintzberg, H. 1987. "Crafting Strategy," *Harvard Business Review*, July–August: 66–75.

Mintzberg, H. and Waters, J.A. 1985. "Of Strategies: Deliberate and Emergent," *Strategic Management Journal*, 6: 257–72.

Orlikowski, W.J. 1991. "Integrated Information Environment or Matrix of Control?: The Contradictory Implications of Information Technology," *Accounting, Management, and Information Technologies*, 1, 1: 9–42.

Orlikowski, W.J. 1995. "Action and Artifact: The Structuring of Technologies-in-Use," Sloan School Working Paper, Cambridge, MA: MIT.

Orlikowski, W.J. and Gash, D.C. 1994. "Technological Frames: Making Sense of Information Technology in Organizations," *ACM Transactions on Information Systems*, 12: 174–207.

Orlikowski, W.J., Yates, J. Okamura, K. and Fujimoto, M. 1995. "Shaping Electronic Communication: The Metastructuring of Technology in Use," *Organization Science*, 6, 4: 423–44.

Pentland, B.T. 1992. "Organizing Moves in Software Support Hot Lines," *Administrative Science Quarterly,* 37: 527–48.

Peters, T.J. and Waterman, R.H. 1982. *In Search of Excellence: Lessons from America's Best-Run Companies,* New York, NY: Harper & Row.

Pettigrew, A.M. 1985. *The Awakening Giant.* Oxford, UK: Blackwell Publishers.

Pettigrew, A.M. 1990. "Longitudinal Field Research on Change: Theory and Practice," *Organization Science,* 1, 3: 267–92.

Pettigrew, A.M., Ferlie, E. and McKee, L. 1992. *Shaping Strategic Change: Managing Change in Large Organizations,* Newbury Park, CA: Sage Publications.

Poster, M. 1990. *The Mode of Information: Poststructuralism and Social Context,* Chicago, IL: University of Chicago Press.

Poster, M. 1995. *The Second Media Age,* Cambridge, UK: Polity Press.

Rice, R.E. and Rogers, E.M. 1980. "Reinvention in the Innovation Process," *Knowledge,* 1, 4: 499–514.

Romanelli, E. and Tushman, M.L. 1994. "Organizational Transformation as Punctuated Equilibrium: An Empirical Test," *Academy of Management Journal,* 37, 5: 1141–66.

Smith, M.R. and Marx, L. (eds) 1984. *Does Technology Drive History? The Dilemma of Technological Determinism,* Cambridge, MA: MIT Press.

Strauss, A. and Corbin, J. 1990. *Basics of Qualitative Research: Grounded Theory, Procedures, and Techniques,* Newbury Park, CA: Sage Publications.

Suchman, L. 1987. *Plans and Situated Action,* Cambridge, UK: Cambridge University Press.

Tushman, M.L. and Anderson, P. 1986. "Technological Discontinuities and Organizational Environments," *Administrative Science Quarterly,* 31: 439–65.

Tushman, M.L. and Romanelli, E. 1985. "Organizational Evolution: A Metamorphosis Model of Convergence and Reorientation," *Research in Organizational Behavior,* 7: 171–222.

Tyre, M.J. and Orlikowski, W.J. 1994. "Windows of Opportunity: Temporal Patterns of Technological Adaptation in Organizations," *Organization Science,* 5, 1: 98–118.

Van Maanen, J. 1979. "The Fact of Fiction in Organizational Ethnography," *Administrative Science Quarterly,* 24: 539–50.

Van Maanen, J. 1988. *Tales from the Field,* Chicago, IL: University of Chicago Press.

Weick, K.E. 1993. "Organizational Redesign as Improvisation," in Huber, G.P. and Glick, W.H. (eds) *Organizational Change and Redesign,* New York, NY: Oxford University Press: 346–79.

Wilson, D.C. 1992. *A Strategy of Change: Concepts and Controversies in the Management of Change,* London, UK: Routledge.

Winner, L. 1986. *The Whale and the Reactor: A Search for Limits in an Age of High Technology,* Chicago, IL: University of Chicago Press.

Zaltman, G., Duncan, R. and Holbek, J. 1973. *Innovations and Organizations,* New York, NY: Wiley.

Zuboff, S. 1988. *In the Age of the Smart Machine,* New York, NY: Basic Books.

10 The art of continuous change

Linking complexity theory and time-paced evolution in relentlessly shifting organizations

Shona L. Brown and Kathleen M. Eisenhardt

In contrast to the punctuated equilibrium model of change, this inductive study of multiple-product innovation in six firms in the computer industry examines how organizations engage in continuous change. Comparisons of successful and less-successful firms show, first, that successful multiple-product innovation blends limited structure around responsibilities and priorities with extensive communication and design freedom to create improvisation within current projects. This combination is neither so structured that change cannot occur nor so unstructured that chaos ensues. Second, successful firms rely on a wide variety of low-cost probes into the future, including experimental products, futurists, and strategic alliances. Neither planning nor reacting is as effective. Third, successful firms link the present and future together through rhythmic, time-paced transition processes. We develop the ideas of "semistructures," "links in time," and "sequenced steps" to crystallize the key properties of these continuously changing organizations and to extend thinking about complexity theory, time-paced evolution, and the nature of core capabilities.

The punctuated equilibrium model of change assumes that long periods of small, incremental change are interrupted by brief periods of discontinuous, radical change (Abernathy and Utterback, 1978; Tushman and Anderson, 1986; Rosenkopf and Tushman, 1995). Fundamental breakthroughs such as DNA cloning, the automobile, jet aircraft, and xerography are examples of radical change. The central argument of the punctuated equilibrium model is that change oscillates between long periods of stability and short bursts of radical change that fundamentally alter an industry (Gersick, 1991). Although incremental change is assumed to occur, radical change is the focus of interest in the punctuated equilibrium model (e.g. Tushman and Anderson, 1986; Romanelli and Tushman, 1994; Utterback, 1994).

While the punctuated equilibrium model is in the foreground of academic interest, it is in the background of the experience of many firms. Many firms compete by changing continuously. For example, Sears' president, Arthur Martinez, recently claimed, "If you look at the best retailers out there, they are constantly reinventing themselves" (Greenwald, 1996: 54). For firms such as Intel, Wal-Mart, 3M, Hewlett-Packard, and Gillette, the ability to change rapidly and continuously, especially by developing new products, is not only a core competence, it is also at the heart of their cultures. For these firms, change is not the rare, episodic phenomenon described by the punctuated equilibrium model but, rather, it is endemic to the way these organizations compete. Moreover, in high-velocity industries with short product cycles and rapidly competitive landscapes, the ability to engage in rapid and relentless continuous change is a crucial capability for survival (Eisenhardt, 1989b; D'Aveni, 1994).

Several authors have begun to explore the implications of continuous change, notably in pricing and routes within the airline industry (Miller and Chen, 1994), in charter shifts to capture constantly shifting market opportunities in the electronics industry (Galunic and Eisenhardt, 1996), and in market moves and countermoves (D'Aveni, 1994; Eisenhardt and Tabrizi, 1995). In these industries, the ability to change continuously is a critical factor in the success of firms. In addition, what is also becoming apparent is that this continuous change is often played out through product innovation as firms change and ultimately even transform through continuously altering their products (Burgelman, 1991; Chakravarthy, 1997). A classic case is Hewlett-Packard, which changed from an instruments company to a computer firm through rapid, continuous product innovation, rather than through an abrupt, punctuated change. In firms undergoing continuous change, innovation is intimately related to broader organization change. Yet research to date has revealed very little about the underlying structures and processes by which firms actually achieve continuous innovation and, ultimately, change.

The purpose of this paper is to explore how organizations continuously change and thereby to extend thinking beyond the traditional punctuated equilibrium view, in which change is primarily seen as rare, risky, and episodic, to one in which change is frequent, relentless, and even endemic to the firm. In particular, we explore continuous change in the context of multiple-product innovation.

The setting is the high-velocity computer industry. This industry is an attractive one for this study because of its extraordinary rate of change. During the 1993–1995 period of this study, there was a growing convergence with telecommunications and consumer electronics, a rise in multimedia applications, assaults on standards, and the emergence of the Internet, all of which put a premium on the ability to change continuously, especially through multiple-product innovation. Moreover, this pace of change has gone on for many years within the industry, and coping with this change is a key to competitive success (e.g. Bourgeois and Eisenhardt, 1988). As Michael Dell, founder of a major computer firm, explained, "The only constant thing about our business is that everything is changing. We have to take advantage of change... We have to be ahead of the game" (Narayandas and Rangan, 1996: 1).

The underlying logic of the research presented here is grounded theory building, which involves inducting insights from field-based, case data. We chose grounded theory building because of our interest in looking at a rarely explored phenomenon for which extant theory did not appear to be useful. In such situations, a grounded theory-building approach is more likely to generate novel and accurate insights into the phenomenon under study than reliance on either past research or office-bound thought experiments (Glaser and Strauss, 1967).

The major results from the study were theoretical insights concerning the organizational structures and processes that characterize successful multiple-product innovation and, more broadly, continuously changing organizations. First, we found that, rather than just communicate, successful managers combine limited structure (e.g. priorities, responsibilities) with extensive interaction and freedom to improvise current products. This combination is neither so rigid as to control the process nor so chaotic that the process falls apart. Second, successful managers explore the future by experimenting with a wide variety of low-cost probes. They neither rely on a single plan for the future nor are they completely reactive. Third, rather than ignoring change or never changing, they link products together over time through rhythmic transition processes from present projects to future ones, creating a relentless pace of change. All of these insights are empirically grounded.

A primary contribution of the paper is a sketch of an emerging organizational paradigm that combines field insights with complexity theory and time-paced evolution to describe organizations in which change is frequent, rapid, and even endemic to the firm. This perspective contrasts with many paradigms in organizational and strategic thinking, such as transaction cost economics, agency theory, and organization ecology, in which organizations are assumed to be static or nearly so. These theories were developed in the 1970s when speed and flexibility were less relevant to organizational success than they are for contemporary firms. So while these theories accurately describe organizations in slow-moving or very powerful environments, they are not well suited to describing successful organizations in the highly competitive, high-velocity oligopolies in which many contemporary firms compete. In these environments, the ability to change continuously is a core capability of successful firms.

As is typical of inductive research, we begin by discussing theory-building through the multiple case method. We then describe the data and the insights drawn from them and conclude by tying these insights to the broader agenda of exploring continuously changing organizations, which seem to have three key properties: (1) "semistructures" that balance between order and disorder, (2) "links in time" that direct attention simultaneously to different time frames and the ties between them, and (3) "sequenced steps," which are the recipe by which these organizations are created over time. Overall, this work extends complexity theory from mathematical simulations to real organizational practices and suggests insights into the nature of core capabilities, time-paced evolution, and punctuated equilibrium.

Methods

Research design

The research design is multiple-case, which permits a "replication" logic (Yin, 1984), in which the cases are treated as a series of independent experiments that confirm or disconfirm emerging conceptual insights. We gathered information on the perspectives of two and often three levels of the management hierarchy. We also incorporated into the analysis the impact of company- and industry-level forces. In addition, this study includes both real-time observations and retrospective data.

This research is part of a study of nine strategic business units (SBUs) across nine firms in the computer industry. The dataset includes six US, two European, and one Asian site. All firms are publicly held, multibusiness computer firms. The SBUs studied are a mixture of four hardware and five software SBUs, all of which compete in markets that are extremely competitive and have high rates of technological change. Thus, this dataset is ideal for studying rapid, frequent change. The SBU was selected as the unit of analysis because of its centrality in the product innovation process. Typically, the management team of an SBU makes important strategic decisions and yet is also directly involved in daily management.

Table 10.1 Description of case data.

	Strategic profile	Total interviews	High-level interviews	Low-level interviews	Projects in SBU
Titan	Mainframe to client/server	12	4	8	10
Midas	Technology pioneer	7	3	4	5
Cruising	Component integrator	8	3	5	6
NewWave	Technology pioneer	7	5	3	6
Saturn	Mainframe to client/server	12	5	7	8
Wanderer	Component integrator	9	3	6	6

Table 10.1 describes the six cases used in this paper. We selected three SBUs that had successful multiple-product-development portfolios and three that did not. We defined successful portfolios as our informants did, in terms of positive project characteristics (e.g. on schedule) and negative ones (e.g. stop-gap, stuttering). For this paper, we eliminated the larger study's "middle" three cases so that we could more clearly distinguish the key processes and describe them in a limited space. Fortuitously, these six cases include three pairs of strategically similar firms in which one firm had a successful product portfolio and one did not. There is a pair of firms pursuing pioneering technical strategies, a pair of moderately innovative, component-integrator firms in extraordinarily competitive markets, and a pair of mature companies switching from mainframe to client/server technology.

Data collection

We collected data through interviews, questionnaires, observations, and secondary sources. The primary source was semistructured interviews with individual respondents. At each site we interviewed two types of respondents: those responsible in some capacity for a single project (low-level interview) and those responsible for multiple projects (high-level interview). High-level respondents were a mixture of general managers and vice presidents, with responsibility for the entire SBU, and those who reported directly to them, who were responsible for some portion of the SBU. At both the high and low levels, there was a mix of marketing and engineering informants.

We conducted interviews during several-day site visits to the SBU. The 81 interviews we conducted were taped and transcribed. Interviews typically lasted 90 minutes, although a few ran as long as three hours. During the site visit, we kept a daily record of impressions and recorded informal observations we made as we participated in activities such as lunches, coffee breaks, and product demonstrations. In addition, whenever possible, one of us attended meetings as a passive note taker. These observations provided real-time data.

We used two interview guides to conduct the two levels of semistructured interviews. In both bases, we asked respondents open-ended questions that let them relate their stories of how particular product development projects had evolved. We asked probing questions to establish details (e.g. when a particular event occurred). The high-level interview guide had four sections. It began with the background of the respondent and the competitive sector. The second part of the interview focused on strategic issues, and the third part concentrated on structure, human resource management, and generally on the process of managing multiple projects.

The final part of the interview was a structured questionnaire that asked respondents to give numerically scaled responses to identify characteristics (e.g. communication levels) of the current set of projects.

The low-level interview guide had three sections. It began with the personal background of the respondent and a detailed chronology of the particular project. In the second part of the interview, the questions focused on strategic issues for the project. The third part concentrated on group processes within the team and the team's relationship with other projects. In both the second and third sections of this interview, some questions asked respondents to give numerically scaled responses to characterize their projects.

In addition, a finance-staff member completed a financial questionnaire. We also gathered secondary data on-site and from the media about the SBU and its parent to build an understanding of the forces the industry and parent firm exerted on the SBU.

Data analysis

As is typical in inductive research, we analyzed the data by first building individual case studies and then comparing across cases to construct a conceptual framework (Eisenhardt, 1989a). As first step, we entered all transcribed responses into a database indexed by case, interview number, interview type, and question number. Next, we constructed a single version of both the high- and low-level interviews for each case by collecting all responses to the same question together as a single response.

Using these interviews and secondary sources, we wrote a case study for each site. This was an iterative process in which we revisited the data as important features of multiple-product innovation within each case emerged. Although we noted similarities and differences with other cases, we left further analysis until we had completed all case write-ups to maintain the independence of the replication logic. As a check on the emerging case stories, a second researcher read through the original interviews and formed an independent view of each case. We then used this view to cross-check the emerging story. The case-writing process took about six months to complete.

Once the individual case studies were complete, we used a cross-case analysis, relying on methods suggested by Miles and Huberman (1984) and Eisenhardt (1989a), to develop the conceptual insights. We had no a priori hypotheses. Initially, we compared the cases to identify common dilemmas and refine the unique aspects of each particular case. We created tables and graphs to facilitate further comparisons and compared successive pairs of cases for similarities and differences to develop the emerging constructs and theoretical logic. With each iteration, we used new permutations of case pairs to refine the conceptual insights. We took several breaks during the analysis process to refresh our thinking. The rough outline of the insights in this paper emerged after about three months. We then worked in two more three-month blocks, separated by several week-long breaks, to refine the analysis. As the analysis evolved, we raised the level of abstraction. Each time that we completed a pass at building the insights, we then went back through the cases to confirm and adjust our ideas as needed. We also went back to the original interviews to ensure that our ideas continued to be consistent with the data.

During the editorial process, the editor and anonymous reviewers pushed us further to develop our analysis of the less successful product portfolios. This lengthy, iterative process led to the insights that follow.

Organizing multiple-product innovation

What emerged from our data were insights that linked successful product development portfolios with a set of organizational structures and processes that are related to continuous change. We defined successful product portfolios as our informants did, in terms of both the presence of positive portfolio characteristics (i.e. on schedule, on time to market, on target to market projects) and the absence of negative ones (e.g. make-work, competing, stop-gap, stripped, endless, stuttering projects).

We assessed the positive characteristics in several ways, First, we asked informants to determine whether each project in the present portfolio was currently on time to market and on schedule. We supplemented these data with a questionnaire in which informants were asked to rate the overall on-target-to-market and on-schedule performance of each project using a 10-point Likert scale. We then averaged these scores across projects. We also gathered qualitative assessments from the interviews. Table 10.2 shows this combination of qualitative and quantitative data, which creates a more robust assessment than either data type alone.

We assessed the negative characteristics using a two-step process. We began by developing a list of project characteristics that were identified by our informants as problems in their portfolios that would hamper product development efforts and/or the commercial success of products. These characteristics fell into categories that included stripped, competing, stuttering (stopping and starting), make-work, and stop-gap projects. We then computed the percentage of projects with problems, problems per project, and firm rankings. As before, we complemented these data with qualitative assessments.

As indicated in Table 10.2, there were substantial differences in product portfolios across firms. Three firms (Cruising, Titan, Midas) had successful product portfolios. On average, over 90 percent of their projects were on time to market and on schedule, while less than 10 per cent had problems. Their average on-target performance was rated 9 out of 10, and informants reported few problems. For example, Cruising had a virtually problem-free product portfolio.

In contrast, three other firms (NewWave, Wanderer, Saturn) had less successful portfolios. Their on-time-to-market, on-target, and on-schedule performances were, on average, much lower than those of the first three firms, and they reported numerous problems. For example, Wanderer had three of five projects that were behind schedule, none that were on time to market, and an average of 2.8 problems per project.

In attempting to understand these differences, we found that managers with successful product portfolios combined limited structure, in the form of clear responsibilities, priorities, and formal meetings, with extensive communication to manage current projects. Second, they looked to the future using a variety of low-cost probes. Finally, these managers linked present projects to future ones through rhythmic transitions from one project to the next. This framework is colorfully captured by an informant's analogy. Successful managers are like "Tarzan," they swing

Table 10.2 Summary of data on product portfolio performance.

Case	On time to market	On target to market[1]	On schedule[2]	Problems	Rank[3]	Examples
Titan	Yes 100% 10 of 10 on time. Anticipate markets and release many products ahead of competitors. "Our reaction time (for new products) is very short."	Yes Average = 9 Products meet needs of current customers "We work very closely together with customers, so we avoid having a product which is not accepted in the market."	Yes 100% 10 of 10 projects on schedule. Average = 8 "I think that this was one of the great things we have solved within the last 3 years – to be really better in not just planning the functionality (of projects), but in being on time."	No 0% with problems Problem-free portfolio of complementary products.	1	"This company is so successful because we deliver new functions rapidly."
Midas	Yes 100% 5 of 5 on time. By regularly releasing products, they have built a technology lead over competitors. Whenever they get a new product out, customers are waiting. "We serve our lunatic fringe customer base. They either want to do things faster than anyone can do them or they want to do things that no one else can do."	Yes Average = 8 Products meet most needs of customers. "We will have customers' engineers in before the product is released. We will do everything in our power to see that their applications run on day one."	Yes 80% 4 of 5 projects on schedule. Average = 9 New products released like clockwork every two years. Core products have not slipped schedule in 8 years. "I (GM) can definitely produce products on time. That's why they hired me."	No 20% with problems Almost problem free portfolio of core and experimental products – 1 experimental product behind schedule.	2	"Once we set a date, we don't miss it."
Cruising	Yes 85% 5 of 6 on time. Focus is hitting market windows with latest technologies that consumers want. "We've got market windows and so we try to be very aggressive, but realistic about technologies."	Yes Average = 10 Products have the right set of tradeoffs. "Quite frankly, we've developed a good feel for this marketplace. We've got a lot of horse sense when it comes to what's needed and what isn't."	Yes 85% 5 of 6 projects on schedule. Average = 8 "We are able to take a group of folks and put a product together in a very short time frame."	No 15% with problems Almost problem free portfolio of low-end, high-end and experimental products: 1 behind schedule, 1 late to market.	3	"We've been told – we've had a lot of consultants in here in the last couple of years – that we are the best implementors in the industry. We can take technologies and make the right set of tradeoffs."
NewWave	No 0% 0 of 6 on time.	Mixed Average = 8	No 0% 0 of 6 projects on schedule. Average = 5	Yes 100% with problems.	4	"In some cases we are creating more 'features' than we need."

continued

Table 10.2 continued.

Case	On time to market	On target to market[1]	On schedule[2]	Problems	Rank[3]	Examples
NewWave *continued*	Products already late for market windows. Rushing so will not miss windows altogether. "Now we're scrambling to catch up and to develop technology that we really needed a year for, but only have 6 months to do it."	Products are roughly on target, but there are problems with specific features. "The group is bright and creative but they don't understand how to create the specific products needed by this industry."	Schedules are not being met. "It is kind of random. I guess if I don't meet (schedule) milestones I might hear about it."	Problematic portfolio. An average of 2.3 problems per project: 6 behind schedule, 6 late to market, 2 stripped of resources.		"We have brought headcount off (stripped) projects shipping in the second round to help this first round. It means things aren't going well."
Saturn	No 25% 2 of 8 on time. Many products released after market windows have closed. Even their most cutting edge product is late to market. "There are competitors in this area. I'd say they were earlier into the market."	No Average = 6 Most products developed with little understanding of how they fulfill market needs. "We just continued on with the development. I think we have only sold 2 or 3 copies and we were hoping to sell about 20."	Mixed 50% 4 of 8 projects on schedule. Average = 7.	Yes 100% with problems Problematic portfolio. An average of 2.5 problems/ project: 4 behind schedule, 6 late to market, 4 stop gap, 2 make work, 1 stuttering, 2 endless, 2 competing.	5	"What you tend to find is projects have a life of their own and when the project begins to wane it looks for other products to justify its existence." "We end up with competition between rival products within the company . . . it confuses the customer."
Wanderer	No 0% 0 of 5 on time, 1 too early to tell. Products often late, sometimes miss windows completely. "I had people investigating (Product X) for 9 months . . . it is very similar to the machine that a competitor just announced . . . and now we don't have one!"	No Average = 7 Products often miss market needs. "We miss a lot of opportunities in the market by not completely understanding the markets we are in. We misfire the gun a few times because we don't understand the markets."	No 40% 2 of 5 projects on schedule. Average = 5. Some projects on time, others slowed down because time is wasted negotiating about resources. "Dave (senior executive) thinks we are late on everything."	Yes 100% with problems Problematic portfolio. An average of 2.8 problems/ projects: 3 behind schedule, 4 late to market, 1 stop gap, 1 stopped, 2 stuttering, 1 make work, 2 competing.	6	"We would not be doing it (stop gap) if we could do (the late product) quicker." "They began it (stuttering) in December. Team members were dispersed when the project was stopped in late March. Later they tried to bring them back in mid-May when the project was restarted, but some had been assigned to other projects."

1 The averages in this column are the average ratings by firm informants of how well current projects match market needs, on a 0–10 point scale.
2 The averages in this column are the average ratings by firm informants of how well current projects perform in meeting schedules, on a 0–10 point scale.
3 Average rank based on first 4 columns

on the current vine, look ahead for the next, and make the switch between the two. In the next sections, we elaborate on these insights and describe their grounding in the data.

Improvising in the present

Why do some firms have successful product portfolios while others do not? Previous research (e.g. Burns and Stalker, 1961) suggests that organic structures may be the answer. Firms with fluid job descriptions, loose organization charts, high communication, and few rules may be conducive to innovation because they free developers from constraints, allowing them to change flexibly and create novel ideas (March, 1981; Peters, 1994). Typical of an organic structure is the organization referred to in one executive's comment (Burns and Stalker, 1961: 93), "Of course, nobody knows his job here."

The evidence from this study, summarized in Table 10.3, suggests an alternate view. While communication was associated with successful product portfolios, purely organic structures were not. In fact, neither organic nor mechanistic structure was the answer. Rather, the managers of these firms balanced between mechanistic and organic by combining clear responsibilities and priorities with extensive communication. One illustration is Cruising. Here, there were well-defined managerial responsibilities and clear project priorities. Marketing managers were explicitly responsible for product definition and the financial performance of projects, while engineering managers drove project schedules. Their job was to ensure that the actions related to these responsibilities happened. This was in stark contrast to earlier days at Cruising. As a marketing manager described, "In past organizational structures, it was really pretty hard to hold anybody responsible ... now this is more of a holistic (entire project) approach, more their own little businesses."

Similarly, there were sharply defined project priorities. Cruising managers used their assessment of market potential to determine project priorities, with products having the largest potential markets gaining highest priority. The priority-setting process was wrenching. As a senior manager described, "We go through a pretty excruciating process. We prioritize everything that we're doing. We draw a cut line and take a good hard look at it and take a big swallow... If that one below the line is really a priority then you better be willing to kick something off the list. That's the gut check, it's tough." The result was crystal-clear priorities. As a marketing manager observed, "We're well aware of where we sit in the priorities and we have a very specific priorities list. You know your number, you know where you sit on that list." Although Cruising managers claimed that "we're always looking for a better way to set priorities," they also observed, that without priorities, "you never get focused on the core business." These priorities were then tightly tied to resource allocations.

Cruising managers complemented these structures with extensive communication. As one manager explained, "There's a tremendous grapevine inside this company and of course, we've got a great e-mail system." Some of the communication was internal to projects. As shown in Table 10.3, there was extensive within-project communication. One manager described it, "Team members may go out to lunch or go into the lab to look at displays and others' things, think about tradeoffs, and do models, form focus groups together, a lot of close work."

Table 10.3 Improvising in the present.

	Communication		
Case	Within-project[1]	Cross-project[2]	External[3]
Titan	High Average = 8 Extensive communication among team members. "Communication is very good."	High Average = 8 Special cross-department teams exist for projects that cross boundaries. "The normal way we work is to communicate across projects. Most of the time we are talking with each other across different projects."	High Average = 8 Developers have frequent contact with customers, both off site and on customer service hot lines. "All the developers join customer groups. They have to."
Midas	High Average = 7 Collaboration between team members is frequent, open. "I would characterize it as friendly, open exchange."	Moderate Average = 6 Communication across projects is frequent and informal. "Informally, everyone has dinner together every night at the cafeteria, on the GM. A tremendous amount of engineering happens at dinner." "Everyone pretty much knows what the others are up to."	High Average = 8 Frequent visits to customers and vice versa. ". . . the way the GM runs the organization is that he wants the engineers to know the market, as opposed to relying on marketing to tell them what the market is."
Cruising	High Average = 7 Communication is now part of the culture. "We meet a lot. It's the way the company's built. You hammer it out."	High Average = 7 Cross-project communication high and increasing. "Now everybody is borrowing everybody's stuff, the cycle is short, the pressure is so intense."	High Average = 7 Marketing does extensive user prototyping and works in pairs with engineering. "We do a lot of customer research, so we test a lot of concepts."
NewWave	High Average = 7 Open communication. "It's not cool to withhold information."	Low Average = 4 Cross project communication is not seen as critical. "We are very compartmentalized because we are all so focused on our own tasks."	Moderate Average = 6 The management team has modest exposure to customers. "We kind of forget our audience."
Saturn	High Average = 7 Fairly extensive communication. "It's quite high."	Low Average = 3 Very little communication across projects. "Communication is a funny thing. People complain when it's not there but it's very difficult to get them interested in it."	Low/Moderate Average = 5 Modest contact with customers. "I don't think we're well-informed by our customers."
Wanderer	Moderate Average = 6 Most communication. "It (within team communication) could be better."	Low Average = 3 Very little communication across projects. "One of the issues when I (GM) first came here was the lack of vertical and horizontal communication. It still needs work."	Low/moderate Average = 5 Modest contact with customers. "We have tended to deal with customer feedback as more of an afterthought . . ."

Table 10.3 Continued.

	Structure	
Responsibilities	*Priorities*	*Formal cross-project meetings*
Yes *Profitability:* Department head. *Product definition:* Project manager. *Schedule:* Project manager.	Yes *Clarity:* High. There is an explicit priority list. "There is a priority list which is part of internal development, that has to be referred to and discussed . . ." *Basis:* Market opportunities as decided by key managers.	Yes Monthly meetings. Written status reports are prepared for this meeting. "In the monthly meeting, we have a summary of all the products."
Yes *Profitability:* GM. *Product definition:* Director or project manager. *Schedule:* Director or project manager, depending on project scale.	Yes *Clarity:* High. There is an explicit priority cycle. Core product is first, except during transitions. "You always want to make your highest priority project succeed." *Basis:* Products giving greatest revenue in shortest time. "Biggest bang for the buck . . . we do things that are fundamental first."	Yes Weekly meetings. "We have elbow to elbow discussions."
Yes *Profitability:* Marketing manager. *Product definition:* Marketing manager. *Schedule:* Engineering manager.	Yes *Clarity:* High. There is an explicit priority list. "We are all aware of where we sit in the priorities and we have a very specific priorities list." *Basis:* Market opportunities as assessed by key SBU executives. "We have a prioritization process based on market opportunity."	Yes Weekly meetings. "On Thursdays, a quick update on today's products. We have an intense tracking system."
No *Profitability:* Nobody. *Product definition:* Ambiguous. "To own a project (you) need to know everything that is going on. No such person exists in the structure right now." *Schedule:* Program managers, but lack authority. "We don't have a schedule and we don't know what we're doing."	Mixed *Clarity:* Low. Formal priorities differ from informal. "It's one of those breaking the rules things." *Basis:* Planned release date.	No Weekly meetings. These meetings are not very effective. "One of the first things I noticed when I came here was the lack of organization of meetings. Never any agenda, never know when the meeting is going to be."
No *Profitability:* Nobody. *Product definition:* Nobody. *Schedule:* Nobody.	No *Clarity:* No consensus. "The engineers don't know where their priorities should be." *Basis:* None. "It's ill-defined."	No "The degree to which things get reviewed at the group level is not a very detailed review of things."
No *Profitability:* Nobody. *Product definition:* Nobody. *Schedule:* Engineering manager.	No *Clarity:* No consensus. "The projects are being treated as though they all have equal priority." *Basis:* None.	No Weekly staff meetings are general in nature, not managers reviewing projects' status.

1 The averages in this column are the average levels of communication within project teams, on a 0–10-point scale.

2 The averages in this column are the average levels of communication between project teams, on a 0–10-point scale.

3 The averages in this column are the average levels of project team communication with customers, on a 0–10-point scale.

More striking, however, was the cross-project communication, because Cruising managers had transformed the firm from one in which there was little cross-project communication to one that emphasized the necessity for it. As one manager explained, "It used to be that it was a badge of honor not to use anybody else's ideas or to improve upon them . . . now everybody's borrowing everybody's stuff, the cycle is just so short and the pressure is so intense." Another manager described, "We encourage a lot of spreading the word back and forth across projects." A third summarized cross-project communication as "dramatic, a tremendous amount."

Much of this communication occurred in formal meetings. There was a weekly, cross-project engineering meeting and a Thursday product-planning meeting that was a cross-project review. These meetings provided opportunities to trade insights across projects. As one manager described, "It's typical for someone to say 'oh you're doing that for this latest do da' or 'maybe I should do that same technology'. Even if it's not your own project everybody comes to the meeting because they discover what other people are doing."

Finally, equally important was what was *not* structured. While responsibilities, priorities, and some communication were, there was no evidence that the actual design process was tightly structured. In fact, Cruising had previously actually dismantled a very structured design approach. Developers were now free to create designs iteratively and flexibly. As one claimed, "We fiddle right up until the very end." So, while limited structures such as priorities and some responsibilities were set, most of the design process was not.

At Titan, as at Cruising, there were well-defined responsibilities and clear project priorities, but other aspects of the design process were not well-specified. Managerial roles were defined such that "ownership" of project schedules, profitability, and product definitions were clearly defined. The project manager was responsible for the definition of the product and the schedule. The head of the department was responsible for product profitability. In addition, there were also clearly defined priorities, which although they were regularly reexamined, were fixed at any point in time.

Titan managers complemented these structures with extensive communication. As at Cruising, much of it was cross-project. They held frequent status meetings, including a monthly product meeting that all development managers attended. These meetings kept managers well informed about the status of each other's activities. In preparation for this meeting, all project managers prepared a written status report of their projects that provided "a summary of all the products." These status reports were also circulated throughout the company to keep all developers well informed about projects across the SBU. In addition, approximately 30 percent of all projects were cross-department projects involving multiple development groups. These projects provided a vehicle for sharing information about the current status of development throughout the firm. More informally, there was extensive communication among Titan's product developers. Coffee bars were scattered throughout the development area explicitly to encourage informal connections and problem solving during breaks. One manager described the high communication at Titan: "The normal way we work is to communicate across projects . . . most of the time the developers are talking with each other across different projects."

In contrast, firms with less-successful portfolios (NewWave, Saturn, Wanderer) lacked well-defined responsibilities and priorities. Managers either did not have or did not agree on project priorities. Responsibilities for product profitability, definition, and schedules were often unclear. Although there was often communication within projects, communication across projects was particularly low. The way that these executives managed current products was in contrast to the limited structuring that the successful firms used.

The approach at Saturn and Wanderer was a very structured development process. Managers had created processes in which projects were planned out with work broken down into small tasks and then passed through a structured sequence of steps from concept specification to pre-prototype and so on. The objective was efficiency. One manager called it "a process-bound environment." As each step was completed, the project passed to the next step. The whole process was governed by specifications, procedures, and checkpoints. Once started, a project proceeded through a sequence of lock-steps in which developers completed their own tasks and then passed the project to the next developers. Ironically, despite all this structure, no one was actually responsible for overall tasks such as product definition, schedule, or financial performance. As one manager described it, "Most people only look at their part – they say I have this spec. If it fits the specs, meets the spec, then it's good." Another told us, "The work of everyone else doesn't really affect my work." In contrast, at the more-successful firms, although shaped by priorities and responsibilities, the work itself was more *ad hoc* and iterative.

Some managers regarded these highly structured processes as effective. Several Wanderer managers called project management one of "our competences." Another said, "I think the distinctive thing about here is discipline and the extent to which we do this." While sometimes projects did finish quickly, it was difficult for managers at Saturn and Wanderer to adjust in mid-project to changing markets and technologies. For example, Saturn developed a product that sold only a tenth of what was expected. The product was originally well conceived but was never adjusted to changing market conditions during its development. One manager summarized: "I think where we went wrong is we did not stop and check 'what is the business case for taking this through to development', and we just sort of continued on with the development and release process." Many of Saturn's other projects missed market windows. Similarly, managers at Wanderer had difficulty adjusting projects to changing conditions. Once started, the process took over. It was hard to backtrack or reshape product specifications as circumstances changed. As one manager lamented, 'By the time we figure out that there is a problem, it's already too late." Rather, Wanderer managers relied on extreme adjustments such as stopping projects.

At NewWave, the approach was different. Here there was a very unstructured process. Managers described their culture as "rule breaking." It was acceptable and even encouraged to minimize structure and violate rules. One manager related, "It's part of the culture not to write things down." Meetings existed, but they were free-form. As one project manager noted, "One of the first things I noticed when I came here was the lack of organization of meetings as a form of communication. Never any agenda, never knowing when the meeting is going to be." Responsibilities were unclear. No one was accountable for the financial performance of specific products under development. Responsibility for product definition was ambiguous because two groups, graphics and software, considered themselves in charge. Program management, a third group, was responsible for schedules. Although these managers were supposed to combine software and graphics schedules into a coherent master schedule, managers told us that they did not actually do this because of the mire between software and graphics. Also, these program managers were non-technical people, overburdened with too many projects. As one manager described the situation: "Program managers have very little real authority. Mostly what they have been is facilitators." Structure was further obscured because senior executives often skipped over these managers to tell developers directly what to do. As one manager described, "The conceptualization of the products keeps changing. . . . What happens is the VP will walk down the hall and say, 'You should add this' to the developers."

Confusion reigned at NewWave. While some managers saw this as Silicon-Valley organic management and reveled in the excitement of panicked product development, others agreed that the "rule-breaking culture" and chaotic structures and processes were "a problem." They created "enormous time wasting." All NewWave products were behind schedule.

One reason why clear responsibilities and priorities coupled with extensive communication were associated with successful product portfolios is that they may be highly motivating. Extensive communication with colleagues and the external environment is likely to create feedback on performance, while clear responsibilities and priorities provide autonomy and accountability for significant aspects of the task. These, in turn, create intrinsically motivating jobs and, ultimately, high performance (Hackman and Oldham, 1975).

Another reason may be that these limited structures help people to make sense of a fast-changing environment. In such environments, it is easy to become confused, make mistakes, and fall behind. Previous research indicates that structure helps people to make sense of change. For example, Weick's (1993) discussion of smokejumpers in a firestorm indicates that loss of structure hampered sense-making and was central to the tragedy. Similarly, Eisenhardt (1989b) found that fast decision makers used structures to create an understanding of their surroundings and build the confidence to act.

A third reason may be that the combination of clear responsibilities and priorities coupled with extensive communication lets developers improvise. Improvisation is an organizing strategy of "making it up as you go along" (Miner and Moorman, 1995: 1) or more formally "activities in which composition and execution of action approach convergence with each other in time" (Moorman and Miner, 1996: 2). In the context of jazz improvisation, this means creating music while adjusting to the changing musical interpretations of others. In the context of product innovation, it means creating a product while simultaneously adapting to changing markets and technologies. Although improvisation is popularly thought of as "winging it," true improvisation relies on two key properties that mirror our data. It involves (1) performers intensively communicating in real time with one another, yet (2) doing so within a structure of a few, very specific rules (e.g. order of soloing, valid chord sequences) (Bastien and Hostager, 1988; Hatch, 1997). The limited structure provides the overarching framework without which there are too many degrees of freedom. The communication allows the players to coordinate and mutually adjust within that framework. Together, people can adaptively accomplish tasks even as the context is changing.

Finally, these ideas relate to product development research. As expected (e.g. Allen, 1977; Von Hippel, 1988; Ancona and Caldwell, 1990; Dougherty, 1992; Henderson, 1994), internal and external communication were related to successful products. What was unexpected was the importance of limited structure – e.g. clear priorities and responsibilities – to successful product portfolios. Managers of successful portfolios relied on structures that were neither too extensive (Wanderer, Saturn) nor chaotic (NewWave). Further, this suggests a metaphor shift from product development as "disciplined problem solving" (Clark and Fujimoto, 1991; Brown and Eisenhardt, 1995) to "improvisation" (Miner *et al.*, 1996), in which projects are adapted to changing circumstances even as they are being developed. This latter metaphor better captures the flexibility and dynamism of rapid, continuous innovation that occurs in many high-velocity industries.

Probing into the future

Building on the resource-based view of the firm, past research has emphasized lever-aging firm competences to create successful products. The idea is to capitalize on what the firm does well. For example, Iansiti and Clark (1994) found that building on past knowledge for current projects was related to successful product genera-tions in the mainframe computer and auto industries. So perhaps building on the past is key to successful multiple-product innovation.

Yet, while building on the past may be advisable, we found that looking to the future was critical. The managers with successful product portfolios (Cruising, Midas, Titan) seemed to have a good sense of the future and a vision for their organizations within that future. For example, at Cruising, we were frequently told about the vision of the firm as "*the* portable computing company of the '90s." At Midas, people shared a vision of themselves as the creators of the "fastest software on earth." At all three successful firms, managers claimed not only to react to the future but also sometimes to anticipate and even create it.

The managers at the other firms (NewWave, Wanderer, Saturn) were quite dif-ferent. They had little sense of the future. As one said, "We don't know strategically what the hell we're doing." Another complained, "We miss a lot of opportunities." As they struggled to meet the future, their portfolios were plagued with problems. These firms were constantly playing catch-up.

How did the managers of the successful portfolios look to the future? The data revealed that these managers did not extensively plan or invest in any one version of the future. Yet they were not reactive either. Rather, they balanced between the rigidity of planning and the chaos of reacting by frequently probing the future using a variety of low-cost lenses. Table 10.4 describes the four specific tactics that emerged from the data: experimental products, futurists, strategic partnerships, and frequent meetings.

Midas provides a good example of how managers probe the future. Midas man-agers routinely created experimental products to probe new markets. These product probes were typically product options that were potentially useful in new markets. If successful, these experiments were incorporated into future generations of the core product. As the engineering director described, "we are creating a more specialized system out of the more generalized system to meet the unique require-ments of a variety of markets." These experimental projects were relatively low-cost investments involving between five and ten developers, compared with teams of 40 developers for core projects.

Strategic alliances were also used to probe the future. Managers at Midas allied with major, leading-edge customers – their "lunatic fringe" – and with potential customers to understand both future needs in existing markets and potential customers in new markets. As one developer described it: "The way Midas works is that we will go after a market area. We find out if there are people who want to use the product in that area. We justify how big that market is and see if we want to tailor our system."

Midas also had two futurists. One had a marketing orientation, while the other

Table 10.4 Probing the future.

Case	Experimental products	Strategic alliances	Futurists	Meetings
Titan	Yes Explore new growth markets by stripping down existing products. "Within the next 7 or 8 months we will have a low end product. We will strip back (an existing product) and sell it in a PC shop. It is a new market. We can play this game very easily and at nearly no cost."	Yes Partner complementary technologies and key customers. "We have established a partnership with (leading PC SW company). They help us in developing user interfaces."	Yes Each development group is represented by a board member who is focused on the long term and is an expert on both the technology and the markets of that group.	Yes Monthly strategy meetings. "The real strategic decisions within the company are not made by one person. They are made for development in these monthly meetings."
Midas	Yes Explore new growth markets with options on existing products. "We deliver a (experimental) product and we drive it into what we think are our key markets. Then we try to get feedback as quickly as possible."	Yes Partner current and potential customers in existing and new markets. "The way Midas works is that we will go after a market area and we find out if there are people (current and potential customers) who want to use the product in that area. We justify how big that market is and see if we want to tailor our system . . . in order to grab more of that market."	Yes Senior technical and marketing gurus. "There is a lot of creativity in determining, given the hardware that we have, what new set of features we can do. Brian and George are the sort of people who make those kind of decisions."	Yes Informal regular discussions between GM and VPs, and between GM and technical gurus.
Cruising	Yes Explore new growth markets with new consumer products and with experimental options on current products. "For (these new products) we are not focusing on the corporate market. We are focusing on consumers (new market). Our approach to the technology is different. We are not just looking at traditional technology. We are looking at other types."	Yes Partner key component vendors in new complementary technologies. "We were one of the earlier adopters of this technology which gives a very brilliant color . . . (a partner) said 'We've got this technology, why don't you guys find a product to take it into?' "	Yes Long-range planner. "Our long-range planner said 'Gee, we are missing the whole low end of the marketplace' . . . We hadn't realized that before. We were sitting there running on 50/60% real profit margin, just fat, dumb, and happy, while our market share was going away."	Yes Weekly strategy meetings, plus occasional brainstorming sessions. "We have Wednesday morning strategy meetings. Right now we are trying to look at 1997 and figure out where we are going to be then."

Table 10.4 continued.

Case	Experimental products	Strategic alliances	Futurists	Meetings
NewWave	No	No	No Many knowledgeable people, but no one has the futurist role. "Forget the future and worry about it later."	No "People are busy and the priority is on the projects. It's a luxury to think about the future."
Saturn	No	No Two backward-looking relationships to extend life of old products.	No No one within the SBU focuses on the future. "We don't know strategically what the hell we're doing."	No No discussion of strategy within SBU. The GM is involved in strategy discussions but doesn't communicate them down. "I wish (the GM) would give us more guidance and be more clear about what the company's direction is."
Wanderer	No	No	No No one within the SBU focuses on the future. "We are so focused on today's tactics that sometimes we can't see the forest for the trees. We are really thinking only one program ahead. We really need to be thinking multiple programs ahead."	No No discussion of strategy within SBU. "Reactive" decision making from above. "How does (strategy) get decided other than Dave (boss) has a 'dream'! Dave looks at the product plan, decides he doesn't like it and comes up with a new plan."

was a technology "guru." Both met frequently with the management team to create possible visions of the future. One manager summarized the multiprobe approach to the future: "We drive into what we think are our key markets trying to get feedback as quickly as we can. We try to align with partners in growth areas. At the same time, we look at technology and try to see where it will be in 2.5 years."

Titan managers, too, relied on quickly developed, experimental products. For example, they created a quick product probe to learn about low-end markets. Although the product was attractive to users, it was actually a "quick and dirty" design. After gaining a look at this new market, Titan managers then revamped the product. As one manager said, "It's a new market... We can play this game (i.e. experimental product probes) very easily and at nearly no cost."

Titan managers also used alliances to anticipate the future. They described one with a leading accounting firm that helped Titan managers correctly predict European tax law changes. These laws substantially affected Titan's software, and their accurate prediction gave them an advantage over the competition. As a manager recounted, "The European taxes were changed at the beginning of last year and there was a different approach in all 16 European countries that we had to handle. So we asked our partner what the changes would mean, before the law had even passed. Our reaction time was very short."

Titan also had several senior executives with PhDs who were charged with thinking about the future. They were both experts on specific technologies and well acquainted with particular customer markets. Titan executives also met monthly explicitly to ponder the future.

In contrast, managers at the firms with less-successful product portfolios (NewWave, Wanderer, Saturn) did not use these or other tactics to probe the future. There were no organized meetings about the future and no experimental products. Although many people were knowledgeable at these firms, no one played the futurist role. Only Saturn had strategic alliances; ironically, these were backward-looking relationships to extend old products.

Rather than probing the future, managers at Saturn and NewWave planned the future. Managers at each firm described spending several months prior to this study building a comprehensive strategy and then creating a follow-on product development plan. In effect, they created a single view of the future and then bet their product development portfolio on that view, a tactic that was ineffective. For example, at Saturn, managers misjudged the timing of the future. As one manager related, "They thought everything was going to the new technology and they responded too soon really. There is a large customer base out there for the old technology ... we got disconnected from our customers for a year in the process, which was silly." Saturn managers tried to recover by extending old products and creating new, stop-gap projects. But, as it turned out, they did not know much about the future that did arrive. As one manager claimed, "The company is drifting."

At NewWave, the strategy relied on a vision of the future that was never refreshed in light of changing competition. At the time of our study, the strategy appeared promising. But, as NewWave managers learned some months later, the strategy was outdated. As one told us, "Unfortunately the critical assumption about technology turned out to be different from what we expected it to be ... a lot of these people's skills were wasted." Ironically, NewWave managers had become so caught up in managing current products that they never reassessed the future. One executive said, "People are busy and the priority is the projects... It is a luxury to think about the future." NewWave managers ended up stripping resources at the last minute from one set of projects to give to another to meet the future that did arrive.

At Wanderer, the approach was different. Here managers reacted to the future. In a process known cynically as "Rick has a dream," a senior executive periodically imposed a fresh strategic vision on Wanderer. Rick's "dreams" were often not connected from one time to the next. Rather, they were simply the reactions of this busy executive to unanticipated industry events. As one manager put it: "We're followers. I would like the industry to be following us." This practice was problematic in several ways. Because of the emphasis on reaction, products were typically late in getting launched and were behind the competition. In one case, Wanderer was so far behind competitors in a critical high-end product that managers rushed in a stop-gap product that extended old technology. But it was a poorly designed product that was embarrassingly described by its developers as a "big head on a little body." Reaction also created several "stuttering" (i.e. start, stop, restart) projects. As one manager recalled, "They began Project A in December. Team members were pulled in and then dispersed when the project was stopped in late March. Later, they tried to bring them back in mid-May when the project was picked up again, but some had been assigned to other projects. As a result, new people had to be brought on and there was a big learning curve." More insidiously, this practice sapped the interest of Wanderer's managers in developing their own future awareness. They were left to focus on the day-to-day management of projects. As one manager complained, "We are so focused on today's tactics that sometimes we cannot see the forest for the trees. We're really thinking only one program ahead. We really need to be thinking multiple programs ahead. We're not doing a good job of that."

One reason that probing the future is associated with successful product portfolios may be that probes give managers options for the future. In high-velocity industries, new futures arrive quickly, making it particularly challenging to predict which of the possible futures will arrive and when. Given this uncertainty, options give managers more possible responses. When the future does arrive, managers are more likely to have something readily available to do and can more quickly adjust. Further, since the probes that we observed are relatively low cost, managers can afford to create more of them, thereby increasing the probability that they will have viable options available.

A wide variety of probes (i.e. alliances, experimental products, futurists, meetings) is also effective because it lowers the probability of being surprised by an unanticipated future. Relying on one type of probe leaves a firm vulnerable to changes in other areas. For example, focusing on the future needs of existing customers can leave firms vulnerable to new entrants with emerging technologies (Christensen and Bower, 1994). Variety in who (e.g. customers, alliance partners, top management team) assesses the outcome of the probe is also valuable. Variety not only in number and types of variations but also in selection mechanisms (i.e. how the outcome of a probe is assessed) creates particularly effective change (Adner and Levinthal, 1995).

A wide variety of low-cost probes also enhances learning about possible futures. Learning is critical because, while the future is uncertain, it is usually possible to learn something about it, making it easier for managers to anticipate and potentially even create the future. The probes that emerged from our data were effective learning devices for several reasons. Direct, hands-on experience through experimental products and strategic alliances creates "learning by doing," which is a particularly good way to learn, especially compared with vicarious or second-hand learning (Brown, Collins, and Duguid, 1989). "Small losses" through experimental products that fail or futurists' predictions that do not come true are among the most powerful learning devices (Sitkin, 1992). Such losses are particularly effective because they capture attention but do not raise defense mechanisms that inhibit learning. A variety of probes creates a mix of direct, hands-on (experimental products and strategic alliances) and indirect (meetings and futurists) experiences. This mix enhances learning because of the interplay among reinforcing sources of knowledge (Lave and Wenger, 1991). Such a triangulation of learning media helps people to learn more effectively. Overall, these tactics combine to enhance learning about the future, allowing managers to be more proactive. In contrast, planning (NewWave, Saturn) is risky, because the future is so hard to predict, while reacting (Wanderer) forces managers constantly to play catch-up.

Evolving from present to future

The third and most surprising distinction among the cases is the link between current and future projects. The data revealed that the managers of successful product portfolios (Cruising, Midas, Titan) carefully managed the transition between the present and the future. Much like the pitstop in a car race or the baton pass in track, this transition appeared critical for successful product portfolios. In contrast, at the other firms (NewWave, Wanderer, Saturn), managing the link between past and future projects was usually an afterthought. This haphazard approach created problems such as delays and make-work projects as managers struggled to organize between projects.

How did successful managers move from one project to the next? Instead of leaving transitions to chance or rigidly avoiding transitioning at all, the data revealed that the managers of successful product portfolios created an almost seamless switch from one project to the next. Table 10.5 describes the two tactics for achieving this switch that emerged from the data: predictable time intervals between successive projects and choreographed transition procedures.

At Midas, a transition was made to a new generation of the core product every 24 months. As the engineering director noted, "We know we are going to do a new project just about every two years." Transition procedures were well choreographed. Transitions were led by technical gurus, who were charged with developing the overall product concept. Their work began while the previous core product was being passed to manufacturing. During the six-month period while the gurus completed the concept development, the remaining engineers worked on small, state-of-the-art projects. At the end of six months, these engineers then transitioned back, according to technical speciality, onto the next generation of the core product.

At Cruising, a transition from one product to the next occurred, like clockwork, every 12 months within a product line. A major platform transition occurred every 24 months. As the VP of marketing explained, "I have a goal in mind of keeping a product in the market for 8 quarters. . . . That is pretty much the same across product lines." In addition to making timing predictable, a transition procedure made switching from one project to the next a familiar routine at Cruising. Marketing managers led the project transitions. They began work on the definitions of the next products for each line while the engineers were still completing the current product and shifting it into manufacturing. Just prior to the launch of the current product, engineers began interacting informally with marketers at a concept level. As one marketing manager described, "What we will do is grab an engineering manager who is really working on something else and we will say, 'Well what do you think about these kinds of ideas?' " Simultaneously, a small core team was also formed that carried the project through product concept. These teams consisted of an engineering manager for the hardware design, a marketing manager, and a manufacturing manager. When the current product entered volume manufacturing, the new project was formally begun at the engineering "kick off" meeting. At this point, the rest of the team from the old project joined the new project.

At Titan, transitions were timed for every 18 months. While old projects were being wound down, project coordinators led the transitions to the new projects. The new teams always consisted of a combination of old and new team members. In this way, current employees who understood old versions of the product shared that

Table 10.5 Evolving from present to future.

Case	Predictable intervals	Transition procedure
Titan	Yes 18 months. Regular 18-month synchronization points pace development. "Projects are synchronized through release dates. You have to be ready with the project on the release date."	Yes Project coordinator leads project transitions. As a version of an existing product is finished, team members transition to working on new projects. New teams are always a mix of old and new team members. A kernel team starts cross-department projects and pulls others onto the team as needed.
Midas	Yes 24 months. A core product is released every two years, like clockwork. "We know we are going to do a new project just about every 2 years."	Yes Technical gurus lead transitions with concept development. During concept development for next core product, other developers focus on small, state-of-the-art projects. Once core product concept development is complete, they transition onto the core project, by technical speciality.
Cruising	Yes 12 to 24 months. 4 and 8 quarter rules of thumb for product replacement. "I have a goal in mind of keeping a platform in the market for 8 quarters and any particular product is about 4 quarters. We're always upgrading about $\frac{1}{2}$ way through the cycle. That's pretty much the same across lines."	Yes Marketing managers lead transitions to new projects by beginning with product definitions, while engineers are still working on completing current products and shifting them to manufacturing. Just prior to launch, engineers/marketers work together informally and a small core team forms. Others transition onto the new project at "kick off" when the current product goes into volume production.
NewWave	No Intervals vary.	None No particular routine. A mad dash, so transitions are not organized. They occur as resources free up. "We threw all the projects up on the board and people kind of said 'I want this and I want that,' and I sat back and said 'OK I'll take what's left'." "We will move the mass of people as they free up and play catch-up on the next products."
Saturn	No Intervals vary, some projects never transition.	None There is no routine for transitions. "It's very unstructured, ill-defined. It's all a bit messy, a bit of a shambles." Some projects do not finish . . . two have been going on for 15 years. You have to have a reason for moving people (off a project)."
Wanderer	No Intervals vary.	None There is no routine for transitions. When new projects arise, often without warning, then managers negotiate with each other to try to figure out how to staff the project. There is a lull while resources are sorted out and then the project begins. "People are anxious to get started. Right now things are a little slow. We are waiting for people to get off other projects, we are having meetings. We know the end point, but people haven't been able to get going yet."

knowledge with new team members. At the same time, new members linked existing project teams to fresh ideas.

Although there were transition routines in the three successful firms, the transitions were not completely rigid. Rather, managers frequently reassessed their transitions, fine-tuning their processes. Cruising managers were considering shortening their project intervals to nine months to pick up the pace against competitors. Titan managers had recently elaborated their transition procedures to match their increasingly broad product line.

Finally, what was particularly striking among these three firms was what happened in the few instances in which predictable time intervals and transition routines were not followed. Midas managers described how they had once interrupted their normal 24-month interval to release an extra product. The rationale was to insert an extra product to meet a competitive threat, but because this extra product tied up substantial resources, the critical core product was delayed. Moreover, developers and salespeople became confused about product distinctions. Ultimately, core product sales suffered. As one manager described it, "In the development of the previous core product we did an interim product. In the end there was a lot of fragmentation of understanding on how that core product worked. It was difficult to sell." Managers vowed never again to disrupt regular product intervals.

In contrast, the less-successful product portfolios (NewWave, Wanderer, Saturn) had neither predictable intervals nor choreographed transition procedures. Projects lasted for varying times and ended unexpectedly. The transition procedures were also not defined as they were at the firms with successful product portfolios. For the most part, the transitions at these firms were managed haphazardly. As old projects wound down, developers attempted to land new project assignments on their own. One manager described this process as "going out into the parking lot for three months to find a new job." When new projects arose, managers negotiated with each other to figure out how to staff the project. Whoever happened to be free when a project came up received an assignment. One engineer described such an assignment. He recalled, "I was assigned to be working on another project, but it got canceled, so I was free. . . . Since I was available, the management position was offered to me."

The data indicate that these haphazard transition procedures were problematic. The unexpected endings sometimes caught managers with too few people, which delayed projects. An engineering manager at Wanderer described such a project: "I have absolutely no way to staff it, and I have to figure out how to staff it and it is about 10 people worth of work. It is my responsibility . . . to put together the whole project plan – the headcount, the dollars, and everything else." This project was eventually late.

At other times, too many staff members were available, and managers took on make-work projects. A manager described one of these projects: "This project does not strategically fit. . . . I would rather put those resources on doing something for our business." Ironically, this manager eventually needed some of the people who were assigned to the make-work project for an important new one, but she had to wait until these people were free.

In contrast to these haphazard transitions, two Saturn projects never had transitions. Although there were occasional product releases, these projects were never reconsidered, restaffed, or reprioritized. Managers claimed that there was no formal way to stop them, and developers became rigidly locked into these seemingly endless projects. As one manager complained, "Some projects do not finish . . . two have been going on for 15 years."

One reason why the transition between present and future products relates to successful product portfolios is that it is easy for the present and the future to become decoupled. While some managers are busy focusing on developing current products and others are creating a sense of the future, the two time perspectives often drift apart. Transition procedures put the two together in an efficient way that coordinates a complex task involving many people and resources. Just as a routinized pitstop in car racing quickly brings competitors back to the race so, too, may a choreographed transition procedure get developers back to creating products quickly and maintaining their flow through time.

A second reason may be that, when specific behaviors are combined with predictable time intervals, a rhythm is created. Rhythm, which depends on a consistent ritual of uniformly recurring behaviors, enables people to pace their work, synchronize their energies with one another, and ultimately get into a "flow." They become focused, efficient, and even confident about the task at hand. Like a tennis player in the rhythm of a match or a skier in the rhythm of a mogul field, transitions at predictable times are likely to create a focusing flow of attention that enhances performance. In addition, predictable transitions create a relentless sense of urgency that keeps people driven to maintain the pace.

A third reason may be that the rhythm created by the transition processes may become entrained to the rhythm of the environment. Entrainment (Ancona and Chong, 1994), a biological concept, refers to the linking of the periodicity of two related rhythmic processes. That is, related rhythmic processes tend to synchronize with one another over time. For example, human body rhythms synchronize with night and day cycles. Similarly, rhythmic product innovation may become entrained with market cycles, allowing managers to get in step with the market, hit market windows on target again and again, and perhaps even create the competitive tempo for the rest of the industry.

Finally, our work on transitions relates to Gersick's compelling research (Gersick, 1988, 1989, 1994). Her focus is on single projects and the midpoint transition that occurs between launch and deadline. Our focus is on multiple-product innovation and the continuous change that it creates. The common theme is time-paced evolution, in which change is keyed to the passage of time, not the occurrence of particular events. Time-paced evolution is powerful in fast-changing settings because it creates a regular, explicit opportunity to reassess actions. This is vital in uncertain settings because it limits excessive commitment to obsolete courses of action (Gersick, 1994; Okhuysen and Eisenhardt, 1997). Further, the rhythmic transitions that we observed reveal how time-paced change may entrain organizations to their environment and, more strikingly, permit them proactively to set the tempo of their industries. In contrast, event-paced change, which is the dominant perspective in traditional thinking (Tyre *et al.*, 1996), emphasizes reactive change in response to failure. Taken together, Gersick's work and our own offer a more proactive view of change than the event-paced one and suggest that time-paced transitions may be central to understanding how organizations continuously change.

Discussion

This paper explores organizations that can continuously change. In particular, the focus is on multiple-product innovation as firms regularly shift in competitive, high-velocity settings. As noted at the outset, this kind of change is increasingly crucial for firms (see also Miller and Chen, 1994; D'Aveni, 1994; Galunic and Eisenhardt, 1996) but is rarely discussed in the literature.

There are three key findings. Managers with successful multiple-product innovation improvise current projects by combining clear responsibilities and priorities with extensive communication and freedom. They probe into the future with a variety of low-cost experiments. Finally, they link current products to future ones using predictable product intervals and choreographed transition procedures. Table 10.6 summarizes the supporting data.

Table 10.6 Summary of data analysis.

Case	Strategic profile	Product portfolio	SBU Study[1]	SBU Post-study[2]	Current	Future	Transition
			Performance			*Organization*	
Titan	Mainframe to client/server	High	*Rising Star* Moderately successful, regional firm. Ranking: 1 of 4 Rating: 8	*Market Leader* Worldwide market leader, successfully entering new markets. Revenue growth 50%, up from 30%. Profits rising faster than sales. "They're giving us hell." (*competitor*) 'Titan is on top." (*major publication*)	Improvisa-tional	Probing	Choreo-graphed
Midas	Technology pioneer	High	*Market Leader* Perennial market leader. Ranking: 1 of 5 Rating: 8	*Market Leader* Perennial market leader. Revenue growth over 15%. Profitability steady, highest in the industry. "They set the standard." (*competitor*)	Improvisa-tional	Probing	Choreo-graphed
Cruising	Component integrator	High	*Turnaround* Also-ran firm in the midst of a turnaround. Ranking: 2 of 6 Rating: 8	*Market Leader* Market leader in high-competition segment. Revenue growth up 20%. Profitability steady despite price cutting in the segment. "Such a rapid and dramatic turnaround was not an easy task. Cruising has been the big winner. (*major publication*)	Improvisa-tional	Probing	Choreo-graphed
NewWave	Technology pioneer	Low	*Rising Star* High growth firm. Ranking: 2 of 6 Rating: 9	*Disappointment* Revenue growth well below expectations. Profitability down 50%, lost money. "They're behind their best dreams of how they would take off." (*analyst*)	Unstructured	Planned	Haphazard
Saturn	Mainframe to client/server	Low	*Mediocre* Mid-pack firm. Ranking: 3 of 5 Rating: 5.5	*Mediocre* Mid-pack firm, struggling to enter new markets. Revenue growth flat. Profitability flat. "We're an 8 or 9 in the old products, but much worse in the new." (*self*)	Structured	Planned	Haphazard

Table 10.6 Continued.

Case	Strategic profile	Product portfolio	SBU Study[1]	SBU Post-study[2]	Current	Future	Transition
			Performance			*Organization*	
Wanderer	Component integrator	Low	*Mediocre* Mid-pack firm. Rank: 3 of 5 Rating: 7	*Mediocre* Sacrificed profits for growth, but could not catch leaders. Revenue growth up 7%. Profits down 6%. "We have been reasonably successful. But then looking at (*competitors*) which are even more successful than we are . . . should that be the place where we put all our investments?" (*self*)	Structured	Reactive	Mostly haphazard, but several never transition

1 Rankings in this column are the average rankings by firm informants of SBU performance in its segment; the ratings
   are the average ratings by firm informants of SBU performance on a 0–10-point scale.
2 Post-study data from secondary and firm sources.

We also measured the pre- and post-study performance of the firms. Although firm performance is affected by many factors and confidentiality agreements limit what we can reveal, the data do indicate a positive link between successful product portfolios and post-study firm performance. For example, prior to our study, Midas dominated its market for a decade. Since our study, this firm has continued its domination and become a widely cited managerial exemplar. Titan was a long-established, regional firm that was taking off as our study began. Post-study, Titan has become the worldwide leader in its industry segment. Cruising was a flagging performer with falling market share and profits in the two years before our study. Post-study, Cruising rebounded to become the leader in a hotly contested industry segment. In contrast, Saturn and Wanderer were mediocre performers, while NewWave has not lived up to expectations. Overall, these results suggest that these multiple-product innovation practices form a core capability that is central to organizational success.[1]

Nature of continuous innovation and change

Our work ties in closely to strategy and organization theory. In these domains, change is traditionally modeled as a punctuated equilibrium process in which long periods of incremental movement are interrupted by brief periods of cataclysmic adjustment (Miller and Friesen, 1984; Tushman and Romanelli, 1985). In innovation, this has meant that invention has often been categorized as radical or incremental (e.g. Tushman and Anderson, 1986; Tripsas, 1997). In organizational change more broadly, this has meant a focus on change as rare, disruptive, and often ill-advised reorientation (Hannan and Freeman, 1984; Romanelli and Tushman, 1994). Radical processes have been the focus of interest.

This research began as an exploration of the less-studied incremental processes. The setting was the 1993–1995 computer industry, in which there were numerous innovations surrounding the Pentium processor, multimedia, Internet, and convergence with telephony and consumer electronics. The rate and scale of innovation within the industry and among our firms was such that the term "incremental" seemed, in retrospect, stretched. Yet it was not radical innovation such as DNA cloning, either. As one manager observed, "I don't know if I'd call this innovation a breakthrough, but it's probably somewhere between that and next generation." Similarly, managers described "constantly reinventing" themselves. This too seemed more than incremental (i.e. unlike replacing a top manager here and there) but also not the massive, rare, and risky change of the organizational and strategy literatures. And so we realized that we were probably looking at a third kind of process that is neither incremental nor radical and that does not fit the punctuated equilibrium model and its critical "deep structure" assumption (Gersick, 1991).

Two fundamental organizational characteristics emerge from this research that appear to be particularly related to this continuous change. One is what we term 'semistructures." By semistructures we mean organizations in which some features are prescribed or determined (e.g. responsibilities, project priorities, time intervals between projects), but other aspects are not. Semistructures exhibit partial order, and they lie between the extremes of very rigid and highly chaotic organization.

For the organizations with successful product portfolios, we found that semistructures emerged in each time frame. For example, the effective management of current projects lay between very structured, mechanistic organization, in which bureaucratic procedures were tightly determined, and very unstructured, organic organization, in which there were few, if any, rules, responsibilities, or procedures. For the successful portfolios, some responsibilities, meetings, and priorities were set, but the actual design process was almost completely unfettered. For the future, the managers of these more successful portfolios probed using tactics such as futurists, experimental products, and strategic alliances. They neither rigidly planned nor chaotically reacted. And they executed choreographed transitions from current projects to future ones that were neither haphazard nor rigid connections between present and future. The managers with successful product portfolios thus balanced on the edge between the extreme structures used by managers with less-successful portfolios.

Several managers offered unsolicited descriptions of semistructures to us. They emphasized the challenge of staying poised on this edge between extreme structures. Managers at Midas described how they operated at the edge of too little structure. One related, "We do things on the fly. . . . I've done some things at IBM and other companies where there is a very structured environment – these companies are failing and we are leading the way. I'm not comfortable with the lack of structure, but I hesitate to mess with what is working. . . . We've gotten away with it so far." At Cruising, managers related their tendency to slip into too much structure. One told us, "It is real easy for the division to sort of just put its head down in blinders and just go run forward and implement . . . we've got to force ourselves to step back."

Others have also begun to note this same semistructure phenomenon. Uzzi (1997) described how firms that are only partially embedded in alliance networks within the New York garment industry are more adaptive than firms that are either more or less embedded. Moorman and Miner (1996), in their theoretical work on improvisation, observed the relationship between semistructures and change in a wide variety of contexts, including the arts, the military, and manufacturing. At the industry level of analysis, Garud and Jain (1996) tied partial industry standards to high rates of innovation. Perhaps closest to our research is work on complexity theory (Gell-Mann, 1994; Kauffman, 1995). Like organizations, complex systems have large numbers of independent yet interacting actors. Rather than ever reaching a stable equilibrium, the most adaptive of these complex systems (e.g. intertidal zones) keep changing continuously by remaining at the poetically termed "edge of chaos" that exists between order and disorder. By staying in this intermediate zone, these systems never quite settle into a stable equilibrium but never quite fall apart. Rather, these systems, which stay constantly poised between order and disorder, exhibit the most prolific, complex, and continuous change (Waldrop, 1992; Kelly, 1994; Kauffman, 1995).

Although speculative, our underlying argument is that change readily occurs because semistructures are sufficiently rigid so that change can be organized to happen, but not so rigid that it cannot occur. Too little structure makes it difficult to coordinate change. Too much structure makes it hard to move. Finally, sustaining this semistructured state is challenging because it is a dissipative equilibrium and so requires constant managerial vigilance to avoid slipping into pure chaos or pure structure. If future research validates these observations, the existence of semistructures could be an essential insight into frequently changing organizations.

The second characteristic of organizations that can continuously change is what we term "links in time": the explicit organizational practices that address past, present, and future time horizons and the transitions between them. What we observed was that managers with successful portfolios created such links in time. They explicitly focused their attention on managing current projects. At the same time, they also developed a sense of where to go next through future probes. And they organized how to get from the present to the future through choreographed transitions. Related was their proactive view of change. They saw themselves as "aggressive," "opportunistic," and "striking first." Theirs was a time-paced, not an event-paced, approach to change.

In contrast, the managers of less-successful portfolios lacked links in time. Without an up-to-date view of the future, they could not effectively anticipate it. This left them behind the competition. Without stitching current projects to future ones, they fell further behind. Rather than creating links in time, these managers operated in the present, struggling to finish current projects with little sense of the future or how to get there. Transitions were chaotic and the future was a surprise. Change became labored and reactive. Managers saw themselves as "following," "reacting," and "drifting."

A few others have also begun to identify time as essential to change processes. Eisenhardt (1989b) found that the CEOs making fast decisions retained a simultaneous awareness of the present and the future. Arie Lewin has observed that Toyota has innovated more continuously than other Japanese auto firms by simultaneously attending to the present and future.[2] Moorman and Miner (1996) noted the importance of the past for change in the form of declarative and procedural memories. Closely related, Gersick (1994) described how a new venture remained adaptive through time-spaced change. The CEO created a longitudinal path of successive milestones spaced through time. As described earlier, these milestones served as triggers to check current progress, reassess the future, and readjust the path as needed. Weick (1995) sketched how songs create longitudinal threads that carry musical performance through time.

Our argument is that organizational change readily occurs because links in time create the direction, continuity, and tempo of change. Attention to the present and future gives direction to change. Without a grasp of the present, it is difficult to have a base from which to change. Without a sense of the future, change becomes inefficient, aimless, and even random (Holland, 1975). Transitions provide the continuity and tempo of change. Transitions keep organizations relentlessly and sometimes even rhythmically moving from the past to the present and forward into the future. If subsequent research supports these ideas, the existence of links in time may offer a second insight into how organizations continuously change.

Origins of core capabilities

Our work also ties closely to strategy research on core capabilities. Although our data and confidentiality agreements do not permit us to provide detailed histories of why some managers created continuous change while others did not, we can offer some insights. In particular, two firms fortuitously provide a window into how some managers are able to achieve this core capability, while others failed.

Prior to the study, both Cruising and Saturn had substantial problems with multiple-product innovation, which their managers were attempting to overcome. Cruising succeeded. Managers described to us, in some detail, how they altered their processes for developing products. They began by focusing on current projects and getting rid of their lock-step and bureaucratic process, increasing communication, and adding project-level responsibilities. With that accomplished, they concentrated on developing their sense of the future through tactics such as futurists and alliances with leading-edge technology providers. Lastly, they turned to the transition between current and future projects, ultimately settling on a 4/8 quarter rhythm and a marketing-led transition. Ultimately, Cruising became the market leader. In contrast, Saturn managers faced with the same problem began with the future. They described developing a future strategy and then attempting to execute it. But, as their managers told us, they kept getting bogged down with problems in their current projects and were ultimately unable to revisit or implement their vision of the future.

Although speculative, this comparison between Cruising and Saturn suggests three further insights about continuously changing organizations and the properties of core capabilities. One is that such organizations must be grown, not assembled at a single point in time. For example, Cruising managers did not instantly create their organization but, rather, "grew" it over a period of several years. They developed and stabilized some pieces of the process, and then moved on to the next. Second, Cruising managers relied on particular "sequenced steps" of implementation. That is, they started with the current time frame, then tackled the future, and finished with the linkages across time. In contrast, Saturn managers began with the future but were consistently waylaid by problems with developing current products and maintaining current revenues. They never really got to the future. To use a sports analogy, Cruising managers perfected their moves and then developed a game plan, while Saturn managers attempted a game plan before they had the moves.[3] Third, sequencing and growth contribute to the inimitability of this important capability (see also Peteraf, 1993). In particular, sequencing and growth help to explain why the managers with weak portfolios could not easily imitate the "best practices" of others. Imitating these practices requires not only knowing what the critical processes are (a difficult task from outside of the organization) but also the sequence in which they need to be adopted. So would-be imitators need both a "snapshot" of the organizational practices at a single point in time and the "recipe" of sequenced steps to build a continuously changing organization. This suggests that inimitability is determined not only by tacitness of the capability (Peteraf, 1993) but also by a complex, time-sequenced implementation process such as we have here.

"Bad management" and links to contingency thinking

Finally, were the poor product portfolios at Saturn, Wanderer, and NewWave simply the result of "bad management"? While we certainly observed a number of practices that many would call bad management, we think that this explanation is too simplistic. These managers were often engaging in managerial practices that would have been reasonable and possibly even effective in other settings. For example, at Wanderer, the lock-step procedures for managing current products have been described as exemplar by other authors and were quite successful in Wanderer's sister SBUs, where the marketplace evolves more incrementally. Unfortunately, they emerged as ill-suited to the fast-moving industry in which Wanderer competes. The strategic planning at Saturn was done well, but the contemporary computer industry is a poor setting for extensive planning. At NewWave, managers created a very unstructured organization that might have been successful for radical invention in settings without competitive pressure. Indeed, one NewWave manager poignantly told us, "the group is a giant petri dish that we have all been thrown into with an agenda to grow some stuff . . . unfortunately we also have to produce results." So, rather than attributing lack of success to bad management (although there probably was some), a more useful observation is that these managers were engaging in practices that fit closely with the punctuated equilibrium perspective, but did *not* mesh with the demands of their very competitive, high-velocity settings.

Conclusion

This paper explores continuously changing organizations in the context of multiple-product innovation. The rationale is that organization and strategy research have become locked into the punctuated equilibrium view that emphasizes radical change at the expense of understanding the kind of rapid, continuous change that is in the foreground of many managers' experience. Gersick (1994: 11) captured our spirit in suggesting that research should focus "on when and how organizations steer successfully through changing environments."

Successful multiple-product innovation involves improvisation of current projects through limited structures and real-time communication, experimentation into the future with a wide variety of low-cost probes, and rhythmically choreographed transitions from present to future. These practices form a core capability for creating frequent, relentless, and endemic change that is associated with the success of firms in high-velocity, competitive settings.

At a more fundamental level, the paper suggests a paradigm that combines field insights with complexity theory and time-paced evolution to describe organizations that are much more dynamic than they are assumed to be in traditional organization and strategy theories. Continuously changing organizations are likely to be complex adaptive systems with semistructures that poise the organization on the edge of order and chaos and links in time that force simultaneous attention and linkage among past, present, and future. These organizations seem to grow over time through a series of sequenced steps, and they are associated with success in highly competitive, high-velocity environments. If these inductive insights survive empirical test, then they will extend our theories beyond a static conception of organizations and the punctuated equilibrium view of change to a paradigm that emphasizes dynamic organizations and continuous change and that is a more realistic description of how many firms actually compete.

Acknowledgement

This research was very generously supported by the Alfred P. Sloan Foundation via the Stanford Computer Industry Project. We very much appreciate the on-going guidance of Marshall Meyer. We also appreciate the expert assistance of Linda Lakats and the very helpful comments of James March, Robert Sutton, our reviewers, and seminar participants at UCLA, Harvard University, University of Pennsylvania, University of Texas at Austin, Stanford University, University of Washington, Duke University, University of British Columbia, University of Oregon, UC Berkeley, and University of Michigan.

Notes

1 The three "middle" performing cases provide further empirical support. Current projects were organized using the same tactics as the most successful firms, the future was only weakly probed, and transitions were not choreographed at all.
2 Arie Lewin, personal communication, 1996.
3 The three "middle" performing cases provide further empirical support for sequenced steps as well (see Note 1).

References

Abernathy, William J., and James M. Utterback 1978 "Patterns of industrial innovation." Technology Review, 80: 40–47.

Adner, Ron, and Daniel Levinthal 1995 "Organizational renewal: Variated feedback and technological change." Working paper, Wharton School, University of Pennsylvania.

Allen, Thomas J. 1977 Managing the Flow of Technology. Cambridge, MA: MIT Press.

Ancona, Deborah G., and David Caldwell 1990 "Beyond boundary spanning: Managing external dependence in product development teams." Journal of High Technology Management Research, 1: 119–135.

Ancona, Deborah G., and C. L. Chong 1994 "Entertainment: Cycles and synergy in organizational behavior." Working paper, Sloan School, Massachusetts Institute of Technology.

Bastien, David T., and Todd J. Hostager 1988 "Jazz as a process of organizational innovation." Communication Research, 15: 582–602.

Bourgeois, L. J., III, and Kathleen M. Eisenhardt 1988 "Strategic decision processes in high velocity environments: Four cases in the microcomputer industry." Management Science, 34: 816–835.

Brown, John Seely, Allan Collins, and Paul Duguid 1989 "Situated cognition and the culture of learning." Educational Researcher, 18: 32–42.

Brown, Shona L., and Kathleen M. Eisenhardt 1995 "Product development: Past research, present findings, and future directions." Academy of Management Review, 20: 343–378.

Burgelman, Robert A. 1991 "Intraorganizational ecology of strategy making and organizational adaptation: Theory and field research." Organization Science, 2: 239–262.

Burns, Tom, and G. M. Stalker 1961 The Management of Innovation. London: Tavistock.

Chakravarthy, Bala 1997 "A new strategy framework for coping with turbulence." Sloan Management Review, Winter: 69–82.

Christensen, Clay M., and Joseph L. Bower 1994 "Customer power, technology investment, and the failure of leading firms." Working paper, Harvard Business School, Harvard University.

Clark, Kim B., and Takahiro Fujimoto 1991 Product Development Performance in the World Auto Industry. Boston: Harvard Business School Press.

D'Aveni, Richard A. 1994 Hypercompetition: Managing the Dynamics of Strategic Maneuvring. New York: Free Press.

Dougherty, Deborah 1992 "Interpretive barriers to successful product innovation in large firms." Organization Science, 3: 179–202.

Eisenhardt, Kathleen M. 1989a "Building theories from case study research." Academy of Management Review, 14: 488–511.

Eisenhardt, Kathleen M. 1989b "Making fast strategic decisions in high-velocity environments." Academy of Management Journal, 32: 543–576.

Eisenhardt, Kathleen M., and Behnam N. Tabrizi 1995 "Accelerating adaptive processes: Product innovation in the global computer industry." Administrative Science Quarterly, 40: 84–110.

Galunic, D. Charles, and Kathleen M. Eisenhardt 1996 "The evolution of intracorporate domains: Changing divisional charters in high-technology, multidivisional corporations." Organization Science, 7: 255–282.

Garud, Raghu, and Sanjay Jain 1996 "The embeddedness of technological systems." In J. Baum and J. Dutton (eds), Advances in Strategic Management, 13: 389–408. Greenwich, CT: JAI Press.

Gell-Mann, Murray 1994 The Quark and the Jaguar: Adventures in the Simple and the Complex. New York: W. H. Freeman.

Gersick, Connie J. G. 1988 "Time and transition in work teams: Toward a new model of group development." Academy of Management Journal, 31: 9–41.

1989 "Making time: Predictable transitions in task groups." Academy of Management Journal, 32: 274–309.

1991 "Revolutionary change theories: A multilevel exploration of the punctuated equilibrium paradigm." Academy of Management Review, 32: 274–309.

1994 "Pacing strategic change: The case of a new venture." Academy of Management Journal, 37: 9–45.

Glaser, Barney G., and Anselm L. Strauss 1967 The Discovery of Grounded Theory: Strategies for Qualitative Research. London: Weidenfeld and Nicholson.

Greenwald, John 1996 "Reinventing Sears." Time, Dec. 23: 53–55.

Hackman, J. Richard, and Greg Oldham 1975 "Development of the job diagnostic survey." Journal of Applied Psychology, 60: 159–170.

Hannan, Michael T., and John H. Freeman 1984 "Structural inertia and organizational change." American Sociological Review, 49: 149–164.

Hatch, Mary Jo 1997 "Exploring the empty spaces of organizing: How jazz can help us understand organizational structure." Working paper, Cranfield School of Management.

Henderson, Rebecca M. 1994 "The evolution of integrative capability: Innovation in cardiovascular drug discovery." Industrial and Corporate Change, 3: 607–630.

Holland, John 1975 Adaptation in Natural and Artificial Systems. Ann Arbor, MI: University of Michigan Press.

Iansiti, Marco, and Kim B. Clark 1994 "Integration and dynamic capability: Evidence from product development in automobiles and mainframe computers." Industrial and Corporate Change, 3: 557–605.

Kauffman, Stuart 1995 At Home in the Universe. New York: Oxford University Press.

Kelly, Kevin 1994 Out of Control: The Rise of Neo-biological Civilization. Reading, MA: Addison-Wesley.

Lave, Jean, and Etienne Wenger 1991 Situated Learning. Cambridge: Cambridge University Press.

March, James G. 1981 "Footnotes to organizational change." Administrative Science Quarterly, 26: 563–577.

Miles, Matthew B., and A. Michael Huberman 1984 Qualitative Data Analysis. Beverley Hills, CA: Sage.

Miller, Danny, and Ming-Jer Chen 1994 "Sources and consequences of competitive inertia: A study of the U.S. airline industry." Administrative Science Quarterly, 39: 1–23.

Miller, Danny, and Peter Friesen 1984 Organizations: A Quantum View. Englewood Cliffs, NJ: Prentice-Hall.

Miner, Anne S., and Christine Moorman 1995 "Organizational improvisation and long-term learning: The case of how firms 'make it up as they go along'." Working paper, School of Management, University of Wisconsin.

Miner, Anne S., Christine Moorman, and Paula Bassoff 1996 "Organizational improvisation and new product development." Working paper, School of Management, University of Wisconsin.

Moorman, Christine, and Anne S. Miner 1996 "Organizational improvisation and organizational memory." Working paper, Marketing Science Institute.

Narayandas, Das, and V. Kasturi Rangan 1996 Dell Computer Corporation. Boston: Harvard Business School Publishing.

Okhuysen, Gerardo A., and Kathleen M. Eisenhardt 1997 "Creating opportunities for change: How formal problem solving interventions work." Working paper, Department of Industrial Engineering and Engineering Management, Stanford University.

Peteraf, Margaret 1993 "The cornerstones of competitive advantage: A resource-based biew." Strategic Management Journal, 14: 179–191.

Peters, Tom 1994 The Tom Peters Seminar: Crazy Times Call for Crazy Organizations. New York: Vintage Books.

Romanelli, Elaine, and Michael L. Tushman 1994 "Organizational transformation as punctuated equilibrium: An empirical test." Academy of Management Journal, 5: 1141–1166.

Rosenkopf, Lori, and Michael L. Tushman 1995 "Network evolution over the technology cycle: Lessons from the flight simulation community." Working paper, Department of Management, University of Pennsylvania.

Sitkin, Sim B. 1992 "A strategy of learning through failure: The strategy of small losses." In B. M. Staw and L. Cummings (eds), Research in Organizational Behavior, 14: 231–266. Greenwich, CT: JAI Press.

Tripsas, Mary 1997 "Surviving radical technological change through dynamic capability: Evidence from the typesetter industry." Industrial and Corporate Change, Vol. 6 (in press).

Tushman, Michael L., and Philip Anderson 1986 "Technological discontinuities and organizational environments." Administrative Science Quarterly, 31: 439–465.

Tushman, Michael L., and Elaine Romanelli 1985 "Organizational evolution: A metamorphosis model of convergence and reorientation." In L. L. Cummings and B. M. Staw (eds), Research in Organizational Behavior, 7: 171–222. Greenwich, CT: JAI Press.

Tyre, Marcie, Leslie Perlow, Nancy Staudenmayer, and Christina Wasson 1996 "Time as a trigger for organizational change." Working paper, Sloan School, Massachusetts Institute of Technology.

Utterback, James M. 1994 Mastering the Dynamics of Innovation: How Companies Can Seize Opportunities in the Face of Technological Change. Boston: Harvard Business School Press.

Uzzi, Brian 1997 "Social structure and competition in interfirm networks: The paradox of embeddedness." Administrative Science Quarterly, 42: 35–67.

Von Hippel, Eric 1988 The Sources of Innovation. New York: Oxford University Press.

Waldrop, W. Mitchell 1992 Complexity: The Emerging Science at the Edge of Order and Chaos. New York: Touchstone.

Weick, Karl E. 1995 "Song." Working paper, Graduate School of Business, University of Michigan.

Weick, Karl E. 1993 "The collapse of sensemaking in organizations: The Mann Gulch disaster.' Administrative Science Quarterly, 38: 628–652.

Yin, Robert K. 1984 Case Study Research: Design and Methods. Beverley Hills, CA: Sage.

11 The convergence of planning and execution

Improvisation in new product development

Christine Moorman and Anne S. Miner

The fields of marketing strategy in general and new product development in particular appear to assume that marketing strategy should occur by first composing a plan on the basis of a careful review of environmental and firm information and then executing that plan. In this article, we question this assumption by suggesting that there are cases when the composition and execution of an action converge in time so that, in the limit, they occur simultaneously. We define such a convergence of composition and execution as *improvisation* and suggest that the narrower the time gap between composing and performing (or planning and implementation), the more that act is improvisational.

Marketing literature, similar to many businesses fields, has paid relatively little attention to extemporaneous behavior and has taken a rather strong stand in favor of marketing planning, especially of a formal type (e.g. Armstrong 1982; Sinha 1990). Although there have been important exceptions in marketing and related literature (Holbrook 1995; Hutt *et al.*, 1988; March and Simon 1958; Mintzberg 1994), a rational planning norm has become deeply entrenched. Table 11.1 overviews a sample of marketing and product strategy textbooks that indicates a fairly uniform acceptance of the belief that marketing strategies should, in general, first be formulated and then implemented.

Table 11.1 Overview of how marketing strategy textbooks view the timing of planning and implementation.

Aaker (1988)	Figure 2.1 provides an overview of the strategic market management process. This figure shows external and self-analysis occurring first, followed by strategy identification and selection, which includes, in order: mission specification, strategic alternative identification, strategy selection, implementation, and evaluation (p. 22).
Boyd and Walker (1990)	The authors define strategy as "a fundamental pattern of present and planned objectives, resource deployments, and interactions of an organization with markets, competitors, and other environmental factors" (p. 43). This definition emphasizes planning, or the setting of objectives, as an integral part of strategy formulation.
Boyd, Walker and Larréché (1998)	Exhibit 1–7 depicts the marketing management process as moving from analysis to the formulation of strategic marketing programs, and finally to the implementation and control of such programs (p. 16).
Cravens and Lamb (1993)	"Strategic planning is a continuing cycle of making plans, launching them, tracking performance, identifying performance gaps, and then initiating problem-solving actions" (p. 688). The authors provide eight comprehensive steps in preparing and implementing the strategic marketing plan (Exhibit 1, p. 688).

Table 11.1 Continued.

Dalrymple and Parsons (1990)	"Once marketing plans have been prepared, they are used to guide field marketing activities for the planning period." Marketing performance should be monitored to compare results with the goals of the marketing plan (p. 822).
Day (1990)	Although Day incorporates both bottom-up and top-down approaches to decision making, the implicit strategy model in his book is that strategic planning precedes implementation and execution of the plan. This is evidenced in Figure 2.1 and because implementation is not an important part of the text; instead, the emphasis is on strategy development.
Dickson (1997)	Defines improvisation as "impromptu action" and notes (p. 37), "An organization's survival depends on its ability to learn and adapt quickly; in practice, this means that plans often must be altered at the very time they are being implemented." He sums up his position on improvisation when he notes (p. 399), "In summary, the ying and the yang of product development is the planning discipline of up-front continuous environmental analysis, targeting/positioning, product specification, judicious stage-gate reviews of the emerging product's fit, feasibility, and estimated profitability combined with the creative improvisation from a team's many iterations of prototype design and testing."
Jain (1997)	Exhibit 2.4 depicts the process of strategic marketing, which involves a clear separation of strategy development and strategy implementation (p. 33).
Kerin and Peterson (1995)	"The selection of a course of action must be followed by development of a plan for its implementation. Simply deciding what to do will not make it happen. The execution phase is critical, and planning for it forces [you] to consider source allocation and timing questions" (pp. 35–36).
Kotler (1994)	Figure 3.1 (p. 63) shows a linear process moving from planning to implementing to controlling. The process has feedback loops from controlling back to implementation and planning.
Lehmann and Winer (1994)	"In general, the planning process works as shown in Figure 2.4. Whereas the collection and analysis of data and the development of product strategies takes place in a limited time frame, there is no beginning or ending to the planning process as a whole. The formal part of the process is followed by implementation, during which programs such as distribution, promotion, advertising, and the like are executed. Monitoring and evaluating both the performance of the plan and changes in competition and customers in the external environment are also continuous tasks. This information feeds back to the formal planning part of the process" (p. 31).
Peter and Donnelly (1998)	"[T]he organization gathers information about the changing elements of its environment. . . . This information is useful in aiding the organization to adapt better to these changes through the process of strategic planning. The strategic plan(s) and supporting plan are then implemented in the environment" (p. 10).
Quelch, Dolan, and Kosnik (1993)	"The marketing process can be divided in several different ways. (Our) conceptualization of marketing tasks is: (1) marketing research, (2) marketing strategic formulation, (3) marketing planning, programming, and budgeting, and (4) marketing organization and implementation" (p. 9).

Much of the research literature in marketing shares this view. For example, a review of published articles cited in a recent special issue of the *Journal of Marketing Research* on innovation and new products reveals a tendency to view planning as the accepted norm while acknowledging that business environments are becoming increasingly dynamic (Wind and Mahajan 1997). Studies there and elsewhere suggest that product development cycle times are faster (Griffin 1997), failure rates lower (Cooper and Kleinschmidt 1986; Montoya-Weiss and Calatone 1994), financial returns greater (Ittner and Larcker 1997; Song and Parry 1997), and innovation levels higher (Olson *et al.*, 1995) when companies take certain advanced planning steps.

Our purpose in this article is not to detract from the value of planning. We believe that planning is an important aspect of effective marketing management and decision making. However, prior theory also points to several reasons why improvisation sometimes can be a valuable and effective approach to marketing action. First, improvisation can be an effective choice when a firm faces environmental turbulence that requires action in a time frame that is shorter than a regular planning cycle. For example, Egge (1986) describes how a salesperson might improvise when immediate action is required in the face of changing client demands; Dickson (1997) suggests that fast learning and adaption without much advance planning are important to firm survival; Moorman and Miner (1995) describe how a team improvised a new product formula in response to a surprise introduction of a competitive product; and Eisenhardt and Tabrizi (1995) find that an experiential strategy involving improvisation works better in the computer industry when product development must operate within the high level of uncertainty created by quickly changing markets and technologies.

Second, improvisation might be prompted when planning has not provided all the details or tactics of implementation. Quinn's (1980, 1986) investigation of ten large organizations finds that these organizations refined their general strategic course incrementally as new information emerged from the environment. Likewise, researchers have reported that many tactical marketing decisions are not included in marketing plans (Cossé and Swan 1983; Sutton 1990).

These reasons for improvisation are consistent with a more behaviourally based view of strategy development, which asserts that organizational[1] action often occurs without much advance planning (Cohen *et al.*, 1972; Cyert and March 1992; Pfeffer 1982; Weick 1979). This research tradition therefore tends to focus on the behavioral dynamics that produce effective action as opposed to documenting whether organizations adhere to normative models of action (Burgelman 1983; Miner 1987, 1990; Mintzberg and McHugh 1985).

Several marketing scholars have followed in this tradition and suggest that there is a gap between normative and descriptive accounts of marketing strategy (Anderson 1982; Day and Wensley 1983; Wind and Robertson 1983). For example, Hutt *et al.*, (1988) find that unplanned, innovate new product activities, or autonomous strategic behavior (Burgelman 1983), occur in organizations and that marketing plays a key role in such activities by virtue of its boundary-spanning and product-championing behavior.

Therefore, there is a precedent both in and outside marketing literature for examining the topic of unplanned, innovative behavior. However, there are few cases of systematic empirical investigations of improvisation specifically. Outside marketing, research has tended to focus on depth analysis of single improvisations by persons, groups, or organizations (e.g. Hutchins 1991; Preston 1991; Weick 1993a). In marketing, research has been qualitative (Moorman and Miner 1995) or focused more broadly on innovation (Hutt *et al.*, 1988).

We build on these important observations by developing and systematically testing a framework that studies the incidence of improvisation in new product activities. Because improvisation is a type of innovative behavior that often involves fast learning (Eisenhardt and Tabrizi 1995), we draw on existing literature on innovation and learning to make our case for why certain environmental and organizational factors are important to improvisation. However, we are also careful to show that improvisation is distinct from innovation and that these factors provide special insight into improvisation, given its extemporaneous nature.

In addition to examining the incidence of improvisation, we also seek to understand the conditions in which improvisation is effective. As we have reviewed previously, one research tradition is based on the belief that a lack of advance planning reduces the chances of a firm's success (e.g. Cooper and Kleinschmit 1986, 1987). Other research, however, has found success stories when organizations have improvised. For example, Mintzberg and McHugh (1985) detail the effective improvisations of the National Film Board of Canada; Preston (1991) describes a group of managers that improvise an effective solution to a manufacturing plant strike; Eisenhardt and Tabrizi (1995) show that an experiential approach involving improvisation accelerates product development in the computer industry; Weick (1993a) describes the effective improvisations several firefighters used to escape the firestorm at Mann Gulch; and Pascale's (1984) portrait of Honda's successful introduction of its 50cc bikes into the US market involves improvisation.

It is not our goal to suggest that improvisation inherently is either helpful or harmful for organizations. Instead, we study the literature on improvisation to uncover the systematic influence of various factors that affect whether improvisation hurts or helps organizations. We seek to supplement current knowledge regarding the types of environmental conditions and organizational competencies that might determine the effectiveness of improvisation. Therefore, our objectives are twofold: (1) to investigate the conditions in which improvisation is likely to occur and (2) to examine the conditions in which improvisation is likely to be effective.

Improvisation

Definition and discrimination from related constructs

Our review of prior research suggests that an assessment of whether improvisation occurs requires looking not just at what happens, but also at the temporal order in which it happens (see also Moorman and Miner 1998). Observers typically assume that composition or planning occurs first and is followed at a later time by implementation or execution. In improvisation, the time gap between these events narrows so that, in the limit, composition converges with execution (Weick 1993a). Therefore, the more proximate the design and implementation of an activity in time, the more that activity is improvisational.[2]

This definition is consistent with core conceptualizations of improvisation in several bodies of literature. For example, improvisation is referred to as "thinking in the midst of action" in education (Irby 1992, p. 630), occurring when "acts of composing and performing are inseparable" in communication (Bastien and Hostager 1992, p. 95), "reading and reacting in parallel" in sports psychology (Bjurwill 1993, p. 1383), "real-time composition" (Pressing 1984, p. 142; Pressing 1988) and "making decisions affecting the composition of music during its performance" (Solomon 1986, p. 226) in music, and representing "no split between design and production" in organizational studies (Weick 1993a, p. 6). By focusing on the simultaneity of events, this research also follows in the tradition of organizational theories of temporal order (Cohen *et al.* 1972; Van de Ven 1986, 1993).

Improvisation also can be distinguished from other, related concepts in literature (Moorman and Miner 1998). Most important, we argue that improvisation is a special case of intraorganizational *innovation*, which is defined as deviation from existing practices or knowledge (Rogers 1983; Zaltman *et al.* 1973). All improvisation, by definition, involves some degree of innovation because improvisation involves the creation of action outside current plans and routines. There are many other kinds of innovation beyond improvisation, however. For example, if an organization innovates a new way to distribute a product by analyzing customer needs, gathering facts, and planning a new channel, the organization has innovated but not improvised. In addition, though all improvisation has some degree of innovation, the degree of innovativeness can vary enormously. For example, some improvisations are very innovative and deviate far from existing routines, such as in the case of "free jazz" (Berliner 1994) or of NASA teams improvising to rescue Apollo XIII by making radical use of objects outside prior routines or structures (Lovell and Kluger 1995). Other improvisations only involve minor deviations from current routines, such as when musicians add embellishments to existing melodies (Bailey 1980) or product development teams add features to existing products (Miner *et al.* 1997).

Improvisation is also distinct from other constructs important to strategic firm behavior, such as adaptation, learning, and opportunism. First, improvisation is distinct from *adaptation*, which involves the adjustment of a system to external conditions (Campbell 1989). We argue that adaptation does not necessarily invoke improvisational action by organizations. Instead, adaptation can be achieved in a variety of ways, including both preplanning and improvisation. Second, if *learning* is a process that requires the discovery, retention, and exploitation of stored knowledge, including information or behavioral routines (Huber 1991; Levitt and March 1988), then not all learning is improvisation. For example, learning might involve a carefully preplanned experiment whose results are recorded and interpreted and that requires no improvisation whatsoever. Third, when organizations are described as *opportunistic*, they are likely to seize attractive, unexpected developments or opportunities proactively (Aaker 1988; Miner 1987; Mintzberg and McHugh 1985; Quinn 1980, 1986).[3] As with the other discrimination variables, opportunism can be achieved through means other than improvisation, such as developing a plan. In addition, improvisation sometimes arises in disastrous situations and involves overcoming obstacles more than it does taking advantage of unexpected opportunities.

Organizational improvisation

Many observers have described improvisation by individuals. For example, people have described ways in which individual actors, athletes, therapists, musicians, or teachers improvise in different settings. Weick (1993a) describes in detail the improvisational and other actions of individual firefighters in a disastrous firetrap, though he also explores team aspects of the situation.

In addition to individual improvisation, observers have emphasized that collective improvisation also occurs (Crossan and Sorrenti 1997; Preston 1991; Weick

1993a, b, c). One detailed report (Hutchins 1991) describes actions taken by the crew of a ship whose navigational system had broken to make their way into a harbor. To avoid danger, the crew members called out estimates of coordinates, calculated subparts of the data needed to make navigational choices, and communicated partial information to one another repeatedly. Although a transcript of their interactions indicates that no one crew member understood the complete system they had improvised or exactly why they were succeeding, the crew developed a set of routines that worked to get the ship into the harbor.

We follow this approach by focusing on *organizational improvisation*, which includes improvisation by groups, departments, or whole organizations. Many observers assume that such entities generate and execute plans. Therefore, we attempt to study them as carrying out these activities either in sequence or nearly simultaneously, and thus improvising or not. Although the nature of collective or organizational features remains contentious (Argyris and Schön 1978; Walsh 1995), we follow other work describing organizational features, such as culture (Deshpandé *et al.* 1993; Deshpandé and Webster 1989), organizational information routines (Jaworski and Kohli 1993; Kohli and Jaworski 1990; Moorman 1995), and memory (Cohen 1991; Huber 1991; Moorman and Miner 1997; Walsh 1995; Walsh and Ungson 1991). To highlight the nature of organizational improvisation, Appendix A provides examples of firms varying in the degree of improvisation in their new product activities.

Prior research suggests that interactions among persons who are improvising frequently produces collective improvisation. In an improvisational theatrical group, for example, one actor might make a comment, to which a second will respond with an association between the comment and another topic, and then a third actor might link these issues to a third, inclusive topic (Crossan and Sorrenti 1997; Mangham 1986; Spolin 1963). The theatrical group did not plan the scene in advance and the pattern that arises is not a simple sum of independent improvisational actions. Instead, it represents a collective system of interaction that creates and enacts the scene simultaneously.

The idea that a system of interaction can produce collective improvisation also is supported by Hutchins's (1991) case study of the crew improvising a solution to their ship's failed navigation system and by Barley's (1986) observation that hospital technicians and radiologists jointly improvised routines in response to new technology. In a powerful set of case studies displaying improvisation, Dougherty (1992) describes new product development teams interacting in ways that do not follow established organizational routines and notes, "Successful developers violated ... routines and created a new social order for their collaborative efforts. They developed mutually adaptive interactions in which knowledge of the work was developed as the work unfolded" (p. 192). In one example, Dougherty (1992) cites the case of SALECO's development team, which broke routines by using products assembled from off-the-shelf parts purchased externally rather than those manufactured in-house. This team also opted to introduce a software product with some bugs in it instead of holding to the routine of perfect quality control, because they realized that users cared more about the number of applications than they did about perfect operation.

These examples and others suggest that collective improvisation often builds on and incorporates individual improvisation. However, individual improvisation alone is not sufficient for collective improvisation. Instead, the joint activities of individual people create a collective system of improvisional action. In addition, there are occasions in which a person's behavior, planned or improvisational, sparks collective activities that are improvisational in nature (Burgelman 1983; Hutt *et al.*, 1988). For example, in the case of planned or deliberate individual behavior creating organizational improvisation, Eisenhardt and Tabrizi (1995) find that leaders' deliberate behaviors played an important role in speeding the development of highly iterative and experiential new product development (see also Miner 1987; Quinn 1986). Other times, collective improvisation results from individual behavior that is itself highly extemporaneous (Mintzberg and McHugh 1985). In either case, the individual improvisation must move to the organizational level for collective improvisation to occur. In short, there must be an element of collective design and execution.

Conceptual framework

Having established the nature of improvisation and its potential importance to contemporary organizations, we develop arguments about the incidence and effectiveness of improvisation in organizations.

Factors influencing the incidence of improvisation

Theory and prior research suggest many factors that might enhance the chances that improvisation will occur in organizational activity. First, improvisation might occur because of a lack of organizational discipline, so that an organization makes up new plans as it goes along simply because it lacks the rigor to follow prior plans (Cooper and Kleinschmidt 1986; Etzioni 1964). Second, an organization deliberately might encourage spontaneous activities that are inconsistent with prior plans or activities, suggesting that it has "learned to improvise" (Burgelman 1983; Hutt *et al.*, 1988; March 1976; Moorman and Miner 1998). Third, improvisation might occur within what we call the *logic of responsiveness.* This stream of thinking suggests that organizations sometimes face unexpected jolts or surprises that make prior plans irrelevant or incomplete in important ways. Such jolts often are coupled with a context in which it is difficult to refrain from taking action or complete a new planning cycle before taking action. Weick's (1993a) work on improvisation by firefighters, Preston's (1991) example of improvised decision making during a strike, and Eisenhardt and Tabrizi's (1995) findings about improvisational styles in product development all focus on settings in which unexpected stimuli create the need for organizational action but also weaken the effectiveness of prior planning. The central premise of this line of thinking is that improvisation might have special value in these circumstances (Miner 1987). We formalize the logic of this stream of thought in the next three hypotheses, which are shown in Figure 11.1.

The impact of environmental turbulence. When the environment in which an organization operates experiences a lot of change, the organization has several choices. It can ignore external demands or shocks that suggest the need to change plans and continue with previously planned activities; it can attempt to speed up its planning and execution cycles so that they remain distinct but happen more quickly (Eisen-

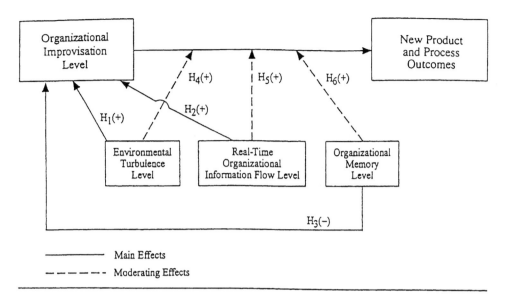

Figure 11.1 Factors influencing the incidence and effectiveness of organizational improvisation.

hardt and Tabrizi 1995); or it can move toward an improvisational approach that
merges planning and execution processes.

In some cases, fast-changing environments can destroy the value of existing competencies (Tushman and Anderson 1986). In such circumstances, organizations
might find it necessary to improvise or compose new behaviors while executing
them. As Weick (1979, p. 102) states, "If there exists a truly novel situation, one in
which there is no analogous experience in the past, then the only thing the person
can do is act." In other words, strategy implementation actually can be "made up as
firms go along" (Weick 1993c, p. 2). Consistent with this view, organizational scholars have argued that the increased pace of competition might require organizations
to develop an improvisational competency to prosper (Brown and Eisenhardt 1995;
Eisenhardt and Tabrizi 1995; Mintzberg and McHugh 1985). The basic logic here is
that exogenous shocks or demands come along more rapidly than an organization
can anticipate, and organizations often respond to such situations by improvising
rather than not responding. We hypothesize that:

> H_1: The greater the level of environmental turbulence, the greater the inci-
> dence of organizational improvisation in new product actions.

The impact of real-time organizational information flows. The logic of responsiveness
implies that awareness of external or internal surprises can trigger organizational
improvisation. Therefore, the more an organization maintains access to information flows, the more likely it is to become aware of either external shocks or unexpected internal surprises.

Some literature points to a particular type of information flow – that which flows
in real-time interactions among group members – as an important stimulus to

group improvisation. Bastien and Hostager (1988), for example, document the nonverbal cues band members give one another in jazz improvisations. Likewise, Spolin (1963) points to the criticality of real-time cues flowing among improvisational theater players as their scenes unfold. In addition, real-time information flows between the actors and the audience not only inform but also stimulate specific improvisational activities. For example, a troupe might extend an improvisational skit, spurred by real-time audience reactions.

We define *real-time information flows* as those that occur during or immediately prior to an action (Eisenhardt 1989). These flows contrast to information processes that occur well in advance of an action or that are used after an action to evaluate its impact. Real-time information flows are likely to occur in face-to-face interactions and electronic communications, in which there are few time delays and great opportunities for feedback (Eisenhardt 1989; Sproull and Keisler 1991). Therefore, team meetings in which decisions and interpretations are made and behaviors are carried out are often sources of real-time information flows (Dickson 1997).

Using our logic of responsiveness, we predict that heavier real-time information flows will create more possibilities for organizations to be exposed to unexpected information that invites improvised action. We make this prediction for three reasons. First, real-time information is, by definition, timely. Therefore, unlike information that may get to a decision maker too late for action to be taken, real-time information is inherently more actionable. Second, because it occurs during or immediately prior to an action, real-time information has an urgency to it that is likely to evoke immediate responses, which probably cannot be planned. Third, real-time information flows are more novel because they evolve in a more random manner than non-real-time information. For example, real-time information flows during a meeting would be more likely to involve unexpected information than those emanating from a series of written memos. These qualities provide greater potential for improvisational activity. We predict that:

> H₂: The greater the level of real-time organizational information flows, the greater the incidence of organizational improvisation in new product actions.

The impact of organizational memory. We have suggested that real-time information about internal or external surprises might enhance the chances that improvisation will occur. In contrast, prior work suggests that stored information, in the form of organizational memory, will reduce these chances. As with organizational improvisation, there is some disagreement regarding whether organizations store information in memory as people do. However, there is a growing sense across disciplines that organizations have frames of reference, routines, and structures that reflect the presence of stored knowledge (for a review of this literature, see Cohen 1991; Cohen and Bacdayan 1994; Cohen and Levinthal 1990; Walsh 1995; Walsh and Ungson 1991; Winter 1987). We adopt that perspective in this article but focus on the level of knowledge contained in an organization's *memory*, which we previously have defined as collectively held beliefs, behaviors, or physical artifacts (Moorman and Miner 1997, p. 93). Therefore, a high level of organizational memory would be present when a project or action phase represents familiar territory, a new product requires only a modest change in an old project, the technological or customer basis for the new product is part of the firm's longstanding repertoire, there are well-established team routines because the duration of the team members' service is high, or a particular action phase (e.g. prototype development) is an established firm-level competency (Moorman and Miner 1997).

By definition, organizational memory represents learned ways of thinking and behaving. As such, memory often is activated automatically in certain situations. For example, firms tend to develop line extensions of existing products rather than create completely new ones (Andrew and Smith 1996). Firms also tend to use well-developed routines and processes for developing and introducing new products (Day 1994; Leonard-Barton 1992; March 1991; Moorman 1995; Moorman and Miner 1997) and therefore learn fewer new routines (Sinkula 1994).

Preston (1991, p. 89) discusses the negative effect that prior memory is likely to have on the incidence of improvisation, noting: "In the case of these familiar situations ... the scope for improvisation is more constrained." Likewise, jazz musicians have commented on the paradox of needing to learn great artists' works to improvise well but then finding themselves trapped by this learning (Weick 1993c). As Berliner (1994, p. 206) notes, 'In one of the greatest ironies associated with improvisation, as soon as artists complete the rigorous practice required to place a vocabulary pattern into their larger store, they must guard against its habituated and uninspired use."

The tendency for existing knowledge to restrict the range of options is a common challenge for innovation of all types but is an especially strong impediment to improvisational action. In improvisation, the time between composing and executing is small and/or nonexistent. We suggest that the pressure of fast action enhances the possibility that an organization will rely on existing routines, regardless of whether a learned response is warranted. Therefore, we hypothesize that:

> H_3: The greater the organizational memory, the lower the incidence of organizational improvisation in new product actions.

Factors influencing the effectiveness of improvisation

In the prior section, we highlighted three factors that we predict will influence the incidence of improvisation. The value or effectiveness of that improvisation, once engaged in by a firm, is another matter. There has been a tendency to think of improvisation as either helpful or hurtful to organizations, as we noted previously. We address these equivocal perspectives by identifying selected factors that moderate the impact of improvisation and determine whether improvisation benefits or hurts organizations. We begin our discussion of these factors by identifying the new product development outcomes we believe might be potentially associated with improvisation. We then consider how the same important informational factors that influence the *incidence* of improvisation also might moderate its *impact* on these outcomes. This dual role creates several potential trade-offs for organizations to manage.

Focal new product development outcomes. There are several outcomes typically associated with improvisation (Brown and Eisenhardt 1995; Eisenhardt and Tabrizi 1995; Preston 1991; Weick 1993a, c, 1996). For example, when improvisation works well, it can produce aesthetically pleasing outcomes in a theatrical or musical setting (Hatch 1997). Likewise, it can provide instrumental value for organizations or groups by solving problems or capitalizing on unique opportunities (Weick 1993b, 1996).

Here, we investigate several types of outcomes that focus on *organizational effectiveness*, which we define as the degree to which an action achieves instrumental outcomes of value for a firm (Walker and Ruekert 1987). We focus on two types of effectiveness outcomes: product and process.

For product outcomes, we investigate *design effectiveness*, defined as the degree to which new product features are high quality and high performance, and *market effectiveness*, defined as the degree to which the new product meets the demands of target customers. An organizational example of these outcomes might be a product development team's improvisation of a new casing unit for a previously unprotected part on a commercial research instrument. Effective improvisation of the unit would require that the materials and size of the casing match each other and reflect a quality level (design effectiveness), and that the unit fit the customer's needs so that the product works in the settings for which it was designed (market effectiveness).

Improvisation not only influences the effectiveness of a new product, but, we reasoned, it also could affect the effectiveness of the new product development process. Two indicators of term process effectiveness seemed particularly important: *team functioning*, which refers to the team's commitment level to the project, and *team learning*, the level of knowledge the team gains in performing a new product action. Finally, the effectiveness of new product development processes is also, to some degree, revealed in the *cost efficiency* (financial investment level) and *time efficiency* (time investment level).[4] The next three sections relate improvisation to these product and process outcomes.

The moderating impact of environmental turbulence. We predict that the rate of environmental turbulence will moderate the improvisation–effectiveness relationship, because it shifts the advantages of formal planning versus improvisation. If, for example, an organization's environment is stable and continuous, planning in advance of action offers that organization many possible advantages (e.g. Armstrong 1982; Miller and Cardinal 1994). The organization can take the time to do complete planning, knowing that the assumptions and facts guiding the plans probably will still hold at the end of the planning cycle. Thus, the organization can harvest the tremendous coordination and control benefits of good planning, including avoiding inconsistent and wasteful action, coordinating activities of multiple actors who may not communicate easily with one another, and assuring that most actions are focused on a single goal. Improvisation offers no particular advantage in this setting. Therefore, in the presence of low environmental change, improvisation will be more disruptive than helpful.

In contrast, rapid environmental turbulence increases the odds that improvisation will provide value. Extensive formal plans in such conditions can have negative consequences because they consume time and resources and provide counterproductive guides to action when the context changes faster than the planning cycle (Eisenhardt and Tabrizi 1995). These circumstances, therefore, actually improve the chances that improvisation will be effective. We propose the following:

> H₄: The greater the level of environmental turbulence, the greater the likelihood that improvisation will generate effective (a) products and (b) processes in new product development.

The moderating impact of real-time organizational information flows. Real-time information flows also can facilitate a positive effect for improvisation by playing a powerful coordinating role. One of the crucial functions of plans is to coordinate the action of multiple actors (Galbraith 1973). In the absence of plans, coordination must occur through other mechanisms. Immediate information about the context in which the action is occurring and the actions of other participants enables such coordination (Bastien and Hostager 1988, 1992; Menzel 1981). In theatrical improvisation, for example, actors continually attend to and process instant information on audience reaction to guide their subsequent actions (Spolin 1963). This feedback replaces the coordinating function of a plan because the actors respond to the same audience cues (Huber and McDaniel 1986).

In a product development context, Robins (1991) describes a thriving company that introduces new products at least once a month but has no formal strategic planning. He claims that coordination was achieved because teams have "an insatiable appetite for market intelligence," and each team member "continuously gathers and disseminates anecdotal data from the marketplace" (p. 336). Imai, Nonaka, and Takeuchi (1985, p. 358) also describe product development projects marked by a high degree of experimentation as effective when team members are encouraged "to extract as much information from the marketplace and ... to bounce [ideas] off other members." Following this research, we suggest that real-time information flows can not only bring the "news" that prompts improvisation (H_2), but also replace the coordinating role of a plan when actors improvise to the same incoming information.

In addition to providing coordination, real-time information flows enable actors to learn the consequences of their actions as they improvise. This immediate information, in turn, enhances the chance that improvisation will be effective because it creates learning about relevant ongoing events (Gioia 1988; Granovetter 1973, 1985). Consistent with this line of reasoning, Eisenhardt and Tabrizi (1995) find that repeated iterations in the product development cycle – which, they argue, provide real-time feedback – are important to the success of the new product outcomes. We predict that

> H_5: The greater the level of organizational real-time information flows, the greater the likelihood that improvisation will generate effective (a) products and (b) processes in new product development.

The moderating impact of organizational memory. Although H_3 predicts that organizational memory will reduce the *incidence* of improvisation, there is considerable prior research supporting the idea that a strong organizational memory will enhance the *effectiveness* of improvisational action. First, much improvisation appears to arise from the recombination of previously successful subroutines of knowledge and action (Borko and Livingston 1989; Levi-Strauss 1967; Nonaka 1990). For example, a firm with well-developed marketing research competencies and significant consumer insight could recombine existing knowledge and skills to improvise new strategies to respond to unanticipated changes in consumer behavior. In support of this idea, Weick's (1993a) analysis of the Mann Gulch disaster emphasizes that the ability of key members of the fire team to use their existing skills in a novel way was crucial to effective improvisation. Music observers note that musicians with strong preexisting repertoires of melodies, chords, and rhythms and familiarity with other players produce the most powerful improvisations (Berliner

1994). Weick's (1993b, p. 353) characterization of organization design as involving improvisation reflects the importance of memory. He states, "If we think of designers as people who improvise, then the materials they have available to work with are the residue of their past experience and the past experience of people in their design group, the meanings attached to this past experience, observational skills, and their own willingness to rely on imaginative recombination of these materials."

The now-famous account of Honda's introduction of the US Supercub in the United States provides a final example of the importance of organizational memory. Honda's planned introduction of large motorcycles experienced technical difficulties while nontraditional motorcycle customers tried to buy the small Supercubs being ridden by Honda's representatives. The Honda team responded to this demand by improvising a new strategy to sell Supercubs through sports stores, in contrast to following their original plan to focus on large motorcycles. Clearly, the effectiveness of this improvisation depended on the Honda team having a rich repertoire of marketing, sales, financial management, and technical routines that could be recombined into an internally consistent strategy that linked successfully to the changing environment (Mintzberg 1996; Mintzberg et al. 1996; Pascale 1996).

Although this argument applies to many forms of innovation, we believe it carries special strength with respect to improvisation. In planned innovation, organizations can gather in advance the tools needed to implement change. They can acquire physical resources, such as machines, as well as advice and ideas from sources outside the organization. The extemporaneous nature of improvisation, however, dictates that there is little or no space between conceiving of and executing an innovation. Thus, the improvisation–effectiveness relationship will be even more dependent on existing organizational memory. We predict the following:

H_6: The greater the organizational memory, the greater the likelihood that improvisation will generate effective (a) products and (b) processes in new product development.

Method

Setting

Data were collected from two midsized firms: FastTrack, a developer of electronic instruments, and SeeFoods, a manufacturer of food products. These companies offer several advantages for testing our hypotheses. First, both companies are well established and have formalized structures but vary in size ($2.4 million and $2.6 billion in annual sales, respectively). In addition, both companies have formalized product development processes. Each has detailed steps through which the development process must go and various hurdles to meet before its products move from step to step. For example, SeeFoods has developed its product planning process to the degree that it considers the process a distinct competency and treats it as a trade secret. FastTrack successfully has achieved ISO9000 certification of its product development processes, which indicates some degree of formalization. These properties make the firms good settings for examining improvisation. The firms also provide rich settings for testing our hypotheses because each company takes product development seriously and links it to overall organizational success. They therefore engage in various product development activities, which provided us with many opportunities to observe the development process.

The two firms do contrast on two dimensions, therefore providing some variation in our study conditions. First, one is a consumer packaged-goods firm, and the other a technology-oriented industrial firm. Second, in one firm we studied, the project was in the concept and prototype development stages, whereas in the other firm, the project was in the market development and product introduction stages of the new product development process. Both aspects of differentiation improve the generalizability of our results. In both firms, employees understood we were conducting a study of product development, but no mention was made of improvisation to avoid demand effects about its incidence or impact. In each firm, we focused on one development project, which was selected because it was representative of other projects in each firm. The teams working on these projects both were cross-functional, with ten active members at SeeFoods and seven at FastTrack.

Data collection procedures

Investigators attended, recorded, and transcribed the meetings of the product development teams during a nine-month period. Meetings generally were held once a week. However, holidays, vacations, and schedule conflicts meant some meetings were missed, which resulted in approximately 25–30 meetings attended in each of the firms. To generate fine-grained but systematic data at the level of specific team actions, we identified action events from these meetings and asked key informants to evaluate them in terms of a wide variety of variables, including activities that occurred prior to or at the same time as the event and outcomes associated with the action event.

Determining the scope and nature of these action events was, therefore, an important part of the research effort. New product development projects are composed of a series of ongoing activities that are, in some sense, seamless. Therefore, to understand and evaluate improvisation, we had to both appreciate this larger unfolding of activities and decide how to divide it into a series of events that could be evaluated and judged independently.

Action events are defined as discrete activities undertaken by a new product development unit. Following from our conceptualization, we restricted our sample to *organizational-level* actions, defined as those undertaken by the new product team. Therefore, actions taken outside of the group or without the group's approval were not considered organizational for our purposes. An action event could involve a team engaging in any of the following activities: making changes to a new product, calling a supplier to change the size of a part, making a decision to use a new distributor, releasing test procedures, finding product problems, preparing documents for regulation filing, doing a store walk, creating concept boards, making targeting decisions, generating brand names, deciding to delay a project, engaging in a focus group briefing, or participating in a focus group or a creativity session. One additional condition was placed on the action identification process: The action had to have some possibility (even remote) of influencing new product outcomes. This condition did not bias our sample toward actions that were likely to influence outcomes. Instead, it eliminated minor activities of the team, such as decisions about when and where to meet and other conversation that was related to social activities among team members and not the product.

To ensure that our identification of the actions was complete and unbiased, we used several safeguards. First, four transcripts were selected randomly from each site, and action events were coded independently by two investigators familiar with the site. This approach yielded high interjudge reliability (92% agreement). Second, product development team meetings evolved as primary data sources from which we derived action events because they represented a consistent vehicle that brought all the project members together and because the meetings were the primary means by which members exchanged information about actions that influenced the project. To reduce the possible bias in team meetings, project teams were asked on three different occasions to list all the things they had done on behalf of a project during the preceding week. These lists were compared with meeting transcripts, and coverage was adequate (90% coverage).

Each of the team meetings we observed could potentially produce dozens of actions, making their evaluation by respondents difficult and burdensome. Therefore, to reduce the set of actions that would constitute our sample, we randomly selected 2 organizational actions from those coded in a given meeting.[5] This resulted in the selection of 107 action events for our sample. When an action event was selected for informant evaluation, we set in motion a series of data collection events. To begin, informants completed an action assessment form, within a week of the action occurring, that asked them to rate the action and various environmental and organizational activities that occurred prior to and during the time the action was unfolding. This included an informant rating of organizational improvisation, memory, and real-time information flows and an assessment of the level of environmental turbulence associated with the action event. After approximately four weeks, the same informants evaluated the short-term impact of each action event in terms of product and process outcomes. The key informants completing both forms were the team leaders who were in attendance at every meeting, were aware of team actions, and had a broad view of the project.

Measures

In this section, we report the properties of our measures, approximately half of which were multi-item and half single-item measures. Multi-item measures were a mix of formative and reflective indicators. This mix was adopted to safeguard against the hazards of key informant burnout. Each of our key informants completed approximately 100 questionnaires: 50 action assessments immediately following the action and 50 short-term impact forms four weeks after the action. Therefore, they completed two questionnaires each week for the study. Given this workload, we tried to make each questionnaire no more than a page long. This meant sacrificing some depth on individual measures. We focused our efforts on developing multi-item measures for those constructs that were considered a priori difficult to measure, such as improvisation.

Because the composition of formative measures is driven by conceptual criteria – which is coverage of the construct domain – and not by predictions of correlation between items in that space, formative measures were not subject to reliability or factor analytic approaches (Bagozzi 1994). The remaining reflective measures were examined for unidimensionality and reliability. In Table 11.2, we present an overview of the psychometrics associated with each measure.

Table 11.2 Measurement information.

	Mean	Standard deviation	(1)	(2)	(3)	(4)	(5)	(6)	(7)	(8)	(9)	(10)
(1) Organizational improvisation	4.25	1.98	.83									
(2) Environmental turbulence	2.12	1.22	.18	−[a]								
(3) Organizational real-time information flows	5.86	1.85	.03	−.14	−[b]							
(4) Organizational memory	4.36	1.78	−.60	−.07	.04	.84						
(5) Design effectiveness	5.03	1.06	−.08	−.23	.30	.07	−[a]					
(6) Market effectiveness	4.87	.81	−.22	−.12	.30	.29	.65	.70				
(7) Cost efficiency	4.05	.76	−.08	−.20	.06	.08	.19	.11	−[b]			
(8) Time efficiency	4.08	.89	.01	−.14	.20	.03	.05	.03	.35	.89		
(9) Team functioning	4.61	.80	−.34	−.12	.20	.17	.43	.60	.11	.16	.86	
(10) Team learning	5.12	.93	−.30	−.24	.29	.25	.53	.64	.17	.13	.60	.73

[a] Formative scale, therefore alpha is not reported.
[b] Single-item measure, therefore no alpha or correlation is reported.

Notes: The coefficient alpha for each measure is on the diagonal and the intercorrelations among the measures are on the off-diagonal. Correlation coefficients greater than .20 are significant, $p < .05$.

Appendix B contains a complete listing of all the measures used in this study. The organizational improvisation level of each action event was evaluated on the action assessment form and was measured on three semantic differential seven-point scales with the following anchors: (1) figured out action as we went along/action followed a strict plan as it was taken, (2) improvised in carrying out this action/strictly followed our plan in carrying out this action, and (3) ad-libbed action/not an ad-libbed action. The mean improvisation level is $M = 4.252$ (s.d. = 1.985) and the coefficient alpha exceeded acceptable standards ($\alpha = .79$).[6]

Because of the centrality of improvisation to our work, two additional safeguards were taken to measure it. First, it was rated by two investigators involved in the site, and there was 70% agreement regarding whether improvisation was low (1), moderate (4), or high (7). The mean investigator rating ($M = 4.014$, s.d. = 1.539) compared well with the mean informant rating. Second, because we claim that improvisation is distinct from innovation, we examined the discriminant validity of the level of improvisation and the level of innovation of the focal action. Informants rated innovation and improvisation on the same form. Innovativeness was measured by asking key informants to rate the level of innovation on a two-item semantic differential scale with (1) innovative action-ordinary action and (2) novel action/standard action as the anchors. The two innovativeness items correlated well ($p = .70$).

The test of discriminant validity between innovation and improvisation required constraining and freeing the phi coefficient between the two measures using LISREL 8. The model with the free coefficient was found to be superior to the fixed coefficient ($\Delta\chi^2_{(1)} = 5.31$), exceeding the standard necessary to show discriminant validity ($\Delta\chi^2_{(1)} = 3.84$). Therefore, innovation and improvisation are empirically distinct.[7]

The three explanatory variables were measured on seven-point Likert scales in which the anchors depended on the variable. The degree of environmental turbulence occurring around the action event was measured using a three-item, formative measure, where 1 was "none" and 7 was "a lot" for the following items: When the action was taken, how would you rate the level of change [defined as any deviation from the status quo] within (1) your team, (2) your firm, and (3) external sources [customers, suppliers, distributors]. The mean level of external change was 2.136 (s.d. = 1.243). Because the measure is a formative indicator, rather than reflective, we do not report a reliability coefficient.

Informants also evaluated the level of real-time organizational information flows that occurred using a single-item measure that asked for a rating of the level of face-to-face, telephone, or e-mail information transferred among team members just before the focal action ($M = 4.078$, s.d. = 1.058), using the same anchors.

Organizational memory level was measured by asking informants to evaluate the memory level regarding an action using a four-item scale adapted from our previous (1997) study. Informants were asked to rate the extent of their agreement with the following items: For this action, my team has (1) well-defined procedures, (2) a standard approach, (3) a great deal of knowledge, and (4) strong skills. The measure had a mean of 4.392 (s.d. = 1.784) and adequate reliability ($\alpha = .79$).[6]

Of all the independent variables, organizational improvisation and memory are the only measures that are multi-item and reflective in nature. Therefore, we examined the discriminant validity of organizational memory and improvisation. As previously, the test of discriminant validity involved constraining and freeing the phi coefficient between the two measures using LISREL 8. The model with the free coefficient again was found to be far superior to the fixed coefficient ($\Delta\chi^2_{(1)} = 52.00$), which indicated discriminant validity between organizational memory and improvisation.

Dependent variables. These variables were assessed by our informants four weeks after the action event occurred. Informants were given a one-page survey with the action event described in detail at the top of the page. In addition, because of the time lag, a portion of the transcript relevant to the action was attached to the page to jar the informant's memory of the event. Informants did not have access to their original evaluations of the event or their ratings of the informational actions occurring around it. All dependent variables were evaluated on a seven-point scale, where 7 was a positive and 1 was a negative effect of the action on the particular outcome. Informants were asked to rate how, "on balance," the action event has or is likely to have influenced each dependent variable. They appeared to have no problems in making such assessments.

Following our conceptualization, two product-effectiveness dependent measures were used in this research. Design effectiveness was measured with a two-item formative scale that assessed the impact of the action on the performance and design of the product. The two items have an acceptable correlation ($p = .48$). Influenced by Griffin and Page's (1993, 1996) work, we measured market effectiveness with a three-item scale that described the impact of the action on the sales, customer acceptance, and success of the new product. The items have an alpha of .70.

Four process effectiveness dependent variables also were evaluated. Cost efficiency was measured by a single-item measure of the estimated cost structure of the new product (Griffin and Page 1993, 1996). Time efficiency was measured by a three-item measure that asked respondents to rate the (1) length of the product development process, (2) speed of the product development process, and (3) project timeliness. These items are reliable ($\alpha = .89$).

Team functioning refers to the impact of the action event on the degree to which the team works well together. This was evaluated using a three-item measure that asked informants to assess the impact of the action on (1) team commitment level, (2) team functioning, and (3) team enthusiasm. These items are reliable ($\alpha = .86$). Finally, team learning was measured by asking informants to assess the impact of the action on (1) the way the team thinks about the project, (2) the team's certainty level, (3) the team's understanding level, and (4) how much the team learned. These four items are reliable ($\alpha = .73$).

Three of the process effectiveness outcomes (time efficiency, team functioning, and team learning) are multi-item and reflective in nature. Therefore, measure development required examining their discriminant validity. As we did previously, we established a base model that did not reflect the correlation between measures. Then we examined how model fit changed when we constrained the phi coefficient between different pairs of the three measures to equal one. Results indicate that the model with the free phi coefficient was a better fit in all three cases, which indicated discriminant validity in time efficiency and team learning ($\Delta\chi^2_{(1)} = 16.53$), time efficiency and team functioning ($\Delta\chi^2_{(1)} = 28.17$), and team learning and team functioning ($\Delta\chi^2_{(1)} = 8.78$).

Model-testing approaches

We used three distinct model testing approaches to examine the proposed hypotheses. First, we used simple descriptive statistics to examine the existence of improvisation in the new product actions we sampled. Second, we used a multivariate linear regression model to examine the impact of environmental turbulence, organizational real-time information flows, and organizational memory on the incidence of improvisation in new product actions. Third, we performed a split group analysis (Arnold 1982; Cohen and Cohen 1983) to examine the impact of the three moderators – environmental turbulence, organizational real-time information flows, and organizational memory – on the organizational improvisation–effectiveness relationships. This approach involved creating high and low levels of each moderator variable by performing a median split. We then examined the relationship between improvisation and the various outcomes in the high and low moderator variable conditions and compared the regression results from these two conditions using a t-test, to determine if the regression coefficients were different across the two moderator conditions (Pedhazur 1982). If the t-test of differences in the beta coefficients was significant, we had found evidence of moderation and inspected the direction of moderation. We chose this approach over moderator regression analysis (MRA) because MRA demands that all main and interaction effects associated with the proposed moderating influences be entered into the model (Pedhazur 1982).[8] In this study, MRA would have involved seven predictors (i.e. improvisation, memory, real-time information, environmental turbulence, improvisation $\times$ memory, improvisation $\times$ real-time information, and improvisation $\times$ environmental turbulence). Using MRA with the number of variables and the sample size of this study likely would have resulted in underpowered tests of the hypotheses.

Results

The incidence of improvisation

Simple descriptive statistics suggest that organizational improvisation occurred in our sample of new product actions. The mean level of improvisation, as rated by informants, was 4.252 on a seven-point Likert scale (s.d. = 1.985), where 7 represents greater improvisation. The scale exhibited considerable range, running from 1 to 7 with a mode of 5 and a median of 4.667. The distribution is fairly even across all levels of improvisation but is skewed slightly toward higher levels of improvisation. For example, if we defined as "primarily improvisational" those actions that were rated higher than five, 47.5% of the actions would qualify; if we used a cutoff of higher than six, 24.1% would qualify. The central tendency then was toward improvisation. However, with a standard deviation of 1.98, there was also quite a bit of variance in improvised behavior. In Table 11.3, Part A, we depict the frequency distribution of improvisation in our sample.

Factors influencing the incidence of improvisation

Considering the factors that could influence the incidence of improvisation, we tested the first three hypotheses in a single multivariate regression model. The

Table 11.3 Tests of hypothesized relationships.

A. The incidence of organizational improvisation

Mean: 4.25
Standard Deviation: 1.98
Mode: 5.00
Median: 4.67

	Frequency	Percentage
1.00	14	13.1%
1.01–1.99	4	3.8
2.00–2.99	7	6.5
3.00–3.99	18	16.8
4.00–4.99	13	12.1
5.00–5.99	25	23.4
6.00–6.99	9	8.2
7.00	17	15.9
	107	100%

B. Factors influencing the incidence of organizational improvisation

Overall model, $F_{(3.88)} = 20.97$, $p < .001$, Adjusted $R^2 = .39$

	Independent variables					
	Environmental turbulence level		Real-time information flow level		Organizational memory level	
Dependent variable	b	t-value	b	t-value	b	t-value
Improvisation	.252	(1.88**)	.100	(1.14)	−.687	(−7.52*)

C. Factors influencing the effectiveness of organizational improvisation

	Moderating variables								
	Environmental turbulence level (n = 86)			Real-time information flow level (n = 95)			Organizational memory level (n = 94)		
Dependent variables	Low[a]	High	t-value	Low	High	t-value	Low	High	t-value
Product effectiveness									
Design effectiveness	−.17	.17	2.83*	−.57	−.01	6.21*	−.13	.08	1.65**
Market effectiveness	−.27	−.16	1.21	−.54	−.18	4.76*	−.13	−.06	.64
Process effectiveness									
Cost efficiency	.02	−.22	−2.91*	−.14	.09	.66	−.18	.09	2.83*
Time efficiency	.07	.09	.16	.09	.02	−.46	−.18	.17	3.15*
Team functioning	−.36	−.20	1.98*	−.40	−.39	.10	−.41	−.23	1.98*
Team learning	−.35	.00	3.42*	−.59	−.28	3.81*	−.32	−.11	1.98*

[a] Numbers in the low and high columns represent the standardized beta coefficient (b) for the impact of improvisation on each dependent variable under low and high moderating conditions.
*$p < .05$.
**$p < .10$.

results, which appear in Table 11.3, Part B, suggest that the overall model is significant (Adjusted $R^2 = .39$, $F_{(3.88)} = 20.97$, $p < .001$). Results also indicate that environmental turbulence is a marginally significant, positive predictor of the level of improvisation in new product actions (b = .252, t = 1.88, $p < .10$, two-tailed test), in support of H_1. Organizational real-time information flows do not have a significant impact on the incidence of organizational improvisation (b = .100, t = 1.14, $p > .10$), thus failing to support H_2. Finally, organizational memory has a negative effect on the level of improvisation (b = $-.687$, t = -7.520, $p < .001$), in support of H_3.

Factors influencing the effectiveness of improvisation

The split group analyses results appear in Table 11.3, Part C. We note there that high levels of environmental turbulence have a positive influence on improvisation's impact on design effectiveness ($t_{(86)} = 2.83$, $p < .05$). We find that when environmental turbulence is low, improvisation has a negative effect on design effectiveness, but in the presence of high environmental turbulence, improvisation improves design effectiveness. Environmental turbulence does not have, however, a statistically significant moderating impact on market effectiveness ($t_{(86)} = 1.21$, $p > .10$). These results thereby support H_{4a} with respect to technical design and quality outcomes but not in terms of the product's effectiveness using market indicators.

Environmental turbulence has equally mixed effects on the improvisation–process outcome relationships. Turbulence improves the extent to which the team reports it learned ($t_{(86)} = 3.42$, $p < .05$) and functioned smoothly ($t_{(86)} = 1.98$, $p < .05$) while taking improvisational actions, in support of H_{4b}. However, the improvisation–cost efficiency relationship becomes weaker and more negative when turbulence is high, and the improvisation–time efficiency relationship is not influenced at all, thus failing to support H_{4b}. These results suggest important trade-offs for the use of improvisation in conditions of environmental turbulence.

Organizational real-time information flows have a more uniform positive influence on the extent to which improvised new product actions influence design ($t_{(94)} = 6.21$, $p < .05$) and market ($t_{(94)} = 4.76$, $p < .05$) effectiveness, in support of H_{5a}. However, real-time information flows do not have the same positive influence on process outcomes, thus failing to support H_{5b}. Improvised new product actions do not have a greater impact on cost efficiency ($t_{(94)} = .66$, $p > .10$), time efficiency ($t_{(94)} = -1.46$, $p > .10$), or team functioning ($t_{(94)} = .10$, $p > .10$) when real-time information flows are high rather than low (see Table 11.3, Part C). Only the impact of improvisation on team learning improves when real-time information flows are high ($t_{(94)} = 3.81$, $p < .05$).

Finally, H_6 predicts that high levels of organizational memory will increase the likelihood that improvisation will generate effective products and processes in new product development. The results indicate that organizational memory uniformly improves the impact of improvisation on various process outcomes, including cost efficiency ($t_{(94)} = 2.83$, $p < .05$), time efficiency ($t_{(94)} = 1.98$, $p < .05$), team functioning ($t_{(94)} = 3.15$, $p < .05$), and team learning ($t_{(94)} = 1.98$, $p < .05$). These results support H_{6b}. Likewise, organizational memory marginally improves the extent to which improvised new product actions result in design effectiveness ($t_{(94)} = 1.65$, $p < .10$).

However, memory does not improve the likelihood that improvised new product actions will result in market effectiveness ($t_{(94)} = .64$, $p > .10$), thus providing mixed support for H_{6a}.

Discussion and implications

Our conceptual work builds on prior interdisciplinary research and suggests that improvisation can play a role in new product development. An investigation of marketing literature provides few positive empirical accounts of extemporaneous action in managerial action, suggesting instead that more fruitful action is planned and then executed. In an attempt to address this gap in the literature, we have documented the incidence of improvisation and the factors that influence that incidence. Drawing on equivocalities in literature, we further suggest that improvisation is understood best as perhaps having both positive and negative outcomes for firms. This mixed assessment draws us to try to understand the conditions in which improvisation might be deployed effectively by organizations. We propose and test several such conditions.

In this section, we address the theoretical and practical potential of our view of improvisation in several ways. First, we discuss the limitations of our work. Second, we review the pattern of our results in more detail and with an eye toward understanding the conditions in which the moderators (1) change improvisation's effect from negative to positive or (2) reduce the negative impact of improvisation. Third, we discuss several trade-offs in managing the incidence and effectiveness of improvisation in organizations and highlight the implications of these trade-offs.

Limitations

Our research has several limitations. First, despite the longitudinal approach we adopted, the use of two firms limits the generalizability of our results. Similar to Hutt *et al.* (1988), we initially sought to control for many of the firm factors that might influence either the rate of improvisation or its impact by limiting ourselves to two firms. Furthermore, the challenges of longitudinal access to organizations, especially to proprietary activities such as new product development processes, made our method choice more reasonable. This is particularly true given that we selected actions from among those that occurred during weekly product development meetings, all of which were attended, recorded, and transcribed. Other approaches that may be more externally valid might have created other problems in generating an unbiased sample of actions. Therefore, our approach offers solid, internally-valid evidence of improvisation that further research might examine in more firms using a less sensitive methodology.

Second, our hypotheses focus on three information factors that have been discussed in prior literature on improvisation and that deserve empirical attention. Although still limited, these factors include the effect of different information sources (internal and external) and types (stocks and flows) on improvisation. Further research could involve considering a more comprehensive study of improvisation that extends the connections between information and improvisation presented here. This approach could develop a more general framework of the antecedents and consequences of improvisation in new product development, using relevant industry, firm, product, environmental, and individual team factors. Many of the factors examined by Hutt *et al.* (1988) would be fruitful avenues for such a framework. For example, the role of culture, structure, boundary spanners, and product champions as catalysts for and facilitators of improvisation would be appropriate factors. Additional research also could involve examining the role of individual improvisation in organizational improvisation, a factor we did not investigate.

Third, though this research involved examining the impact of improvisation on short-term new product effectiveness, it also would be valuable to examine the impact of improvisation on long-term organizational outcomes. Our research also was limited to new product development actions. However, many other marketing contexts are also relevant contexts for the study of improvisation. Advertising and personal selling stand out as areas in which we would expect improvisation to occur at even higher levels. Additional research could examine the incidence of improvisation and attempt to demonstrate the generalizability of our findings across multiple contexts.

Finally, further research could address the possibility of common methods variance influencing our results, because the same informants rated aspects of both actions and outcomes. However, because observers independently identified the action, the ratings of actions and outcomes were accomplished at significantly different times, and informants had no record of prior ratings when performing their outcome ratings, the chance of informant preconceptions producing the results here is reduced. Further research could use multiple measures of actions and outcomes to ensure even further the lack of common methods or informant bias.

Pattern of improvisation results

Considerable research on organizations suggests that formalized organizations with well-developed product development procedures are relatively unlikely to engage in improvisation (Scott 1987). Contrary to that research, our first basic finding is that, even in two well-established organizations with formal structures, roles, and procedures, improvisation occurs with substantial regularity in the product development process.

Prior research also has tended to highlight either the dangers of improvisation or its potential for helping firms adapt. Our pattern of results supports a more contingent view of improvisation. For example, we provide some support for the traditional concern regarding the risks of improvisation because, in five of the specific outcome variables we observed, our moderating variables had a positive effect but worked by reducing the negative effect of improvisation. Thus, though the moderating conditions enhanced the value of improvisation, as we had expected, the conditions were not strong enough to make the net effect of improvisation positive.

In other cases, however, the moderating conditions reversed the negative impact of improvisation. For example, in conditions with low organizational memory, improvisation had a negative effect on design effectiveness, cost efficiency, and time efficiency. However, in the presence of high organizational memory, improvisation had a positive effect on these outcomes. These findings support the general argument that emergent processes might have value in uncertain or ambiguous conditions (Burgelman 1983; Miner 1987). They also support the more recent arguments of scholars who claim that improvisation represents an important competency that can produce value for organizations in certain conditions (Eisenhardt and Tabrizi 1995; Moorman and Miner 1998; Weick 1987).

Trade-offs in improvisation

A common theme that runs through our conceptual framework and results is that improvisation, similar to most strategic actions, involves trade-offs and potential synergies for organizations. This theme is evidenced in several ways.

Recall that our findings show that memory reduces the likelihood of improvisation, but it also increases the effectiveness of improvisation when improvisation does occur. Therefore, the same organizational feature that makes improvisation effective is likely to reduce the chances of its occurrence. Too powerful a memory, then, can remove improvisation from the organization's repertoire, whereas too little memory can render the improvisation that occurs ineffective. This result suggests that there is a threshold of memory level at which improvisation is a valuable organizational activity, with levels below or above this threshold reducing the chances of such an impact. This trade-off implies that organizations must minimize the fixating aspects of memory when improvisation is needed and evoke memory as improvisation is unfolding if it is to be effective. This delicate balance of restraining and infusing memory at certain times requires a greater understanding of memory, its forms, and the degree to which these forms restrict extemporaneous actions in organizations. For example, in a forthcoming article (1998), we distinguish between the effects of declarative organizational memory (facts and theories) on the novelty of organizational outcomes versus the effects of procedural organizational memory (skills and routines) on the timeliness of organizational outcomes.

Another trade-off associated with memory that is evident in our results is that organizational memory facilitates the impact of improvisation on all new product and process outcomes, except those associated with external market effectiveness. Although this is consistent with research that suggests an internal firm focus should reduce market success (Day and Nedungadi 1994; Deshpandé, Farley, and Webster 1993), none of our memory measures involve skills and knowledge regarding how a new product activity fits with customer needs and wants. Therefore, the value of memory appears to be linked tightly to its measured content.

Real-time information flows moving through organizations present a different set of trade-offs for firms. Real-time flows were found to increase the extent to which improvisation produces effective new products but to reduce the positive effect of improvisation on process outcomes (excluding learning). Improvisations were less cost and time efficient, and groups engaging in them appeared to function less effectively when the level of real-time information transfer was high. Despite the inefficiencies associated with real-time information flows, improvisation continued to promote design and market effectiveness when real-time flows were high. Therefore, similar to our prior discussion of memory, our results appear to recommend a restricted zone of real-time information flow in which sufficient amounts of real-time information are needed to promote a positive relationship between improvisation and product effectiveness. However, flows cannot be so high as to create negative improvisation–process effectiveness relationships, which, over time, might undermine product effectiveness levels.

Finally, as with the other informational moderators, the influx of information about environmental change brings with it certain trade-offs. In particular, our results suggest that high levels of information about environmental changes during improvisation result in increased product design effectiveness. Across all of the informational moderators, product design effectiveness has the most to gain from highly improvisational actions when levels of information are high. However, consistent with the other results, firms have to accept that the influx of the high levels of environmental change information might have corresponding risks, particularly higher costs. Such trade-offs also appear in other research on new products (Griffin and Page 1993; Moorman 1995).

In summary, these results suggest that improvisation is a strategy of emergent learning (Mintzberg 1996) that can be employed as a substitute for planning (Weick 1987). However, our results clearly suggest that improvisation is not necessarily a free good, nor is it one that translates into effective outcomes in all conditions. On the contrary, our results consistently emphasize that improvisation must be directed explicitly, its trade-offs and tensions acknowledged and managed, and the conditions in which it is effective understood and nurtured by organizations.

Future research issues

There are many issues that our initial inquiry into improvisation did not consider. We discuss several here as a way of establishing a strategy for additional research on this topic. Regarding improvisation generally, we recommend that further research consider whether improvisation is driven by firm mismanagement, environmental change, or the decision to use improvisation purposively as part of firm strategy. In the domain of product development, we encourage investigation of improvisation's occurrence and impact in different (1) project phases, (2) product categories, and (3) industries. Whether a product development project represents an incremental or a radical change from a prior product is an especially important contingent worthy of further research. The risks for improvisation intuitively seem higher in radical product development projects because of the probable lack of relevant organizational memory to inform the product development process. At the same time, improvisation may be more likely to occur in radical product development projects that lack memory. Teasing out these and other possibilities is an important next step.

Another topic we did not address is the nature of the group or individual factors that spawn improvisation during the new product development process. The research tradition on product championing includes projects that are initiated outside the formal new product development process (Burgelman 1983; Hutt, Reingen, and Ronchetto 1988). It would be interesting to consider what motivates these informal improvisation efforts. What form does improvisation take when the focus is on a major strategic decision that involves multiple stakeholders across business units? The focus of the present study is restricted to improvisation in the narrow confines of a structured development process.

Our focus was the impact of improvisional activities on the project in which they occurred. However, it is possible that improvisations have long-term impacts as well. Team members sometimes observed that a particular improvisational action not only worked in the current project but also could be used in other setting or future projects. Our quantitative results support such an impact and suggest that improvisation positively affected team learning outcomes in high information conditions. Additional research could fruitfully investigate whether improvisation serves as a systematic form of unplanned experimentation in organizations. If this function is confirmed, the potential "second-order" impact creates an additional factor in the calculus of improvisation's value to organizations. Each improvisation might have, on average, a low expected value as a possible new routine for the organization. But on rare occasions, an improvisational act (or "local experiment") might represent a real improvement over prior practices and thus be a very useful experiment (Miner *et al.* 1997).

Finally, our qualitative observations lead us to suspect that, in addition to building a baseline model of factors that can move improvisation from a hindrance to a potential advantage, contemporary researchers should entertain the possibility that the boundary conditions for organizational improvisation might be changing. Corporate intranets, computer-aided design, and manufacturing and point-of-sale data can change the temporal links between actions in ways that previously were not possible. In many ways, this change enhances the potential for accurate planning; however, it also might enhance the possibility of fusing planning and acting. Therefore, it appears that improvisation's boundary conditions are changing even as we begin to examine the phenomenon in a systematic way.

Conclusion

This article examines the incidence and effectiveness of improvisation during the new product development process. Hypotheses were developed examining the impact of various types and sources of information on the level and effectiveness of improvisation. We find that improvisation is prevalent and occurs when organizational memory is low but environmental turbulence is high. Our results support traditional concerns that improvisation can reduce new product effectiveness but also indicate that informational factors emanating from the environment and organization can reduce these negative effects or even create a positive effect of improvisation on new product outcomes.

These results suggest that there are conditions in which improvisation might be not only what organizations *do* practice but also what they *should* practice to flourish. We suggest that these conditions involve the careful deployment and management of other organizational resources, such as memory, real-time information flows, and the influx of information about environmental turbulence, so as to promote effective new product development outcomes when improvisation occurs. The management of such resources requires attention to the trade-offs and synergies between improvisation, organizational factors, and the environmental context.

Appendix A

An example of organizational improvisation

To make concrete the distinction between improvisational and nonimprovisational activities, consider the contrast between two product development processes in a single organization. For Product A, the organization follows its typical product development procedure. The marketing department analyzes market potential, pricing questions, and details of customer demand for a new instrument that is based on an emerging technology. The engineering department analyzes technical problems with prior products, the feasibility of meeting quality specifications at certain price levels, the availability of key components at particular prices, and the time needed to produce the new product. On the basis of these analyses, the senior officers approve a plan, budget, and timeline for this product's development, manufacturing, and launch. A product team is appointed to implement detailed design and prototyping activities. After being checked, final manufacturing specifications and procedures are approved and trigger implementation of the manufacturing process and product introduction.

Product B follows a different path. A customer of one of the firm's current scientific testing instruments complains to members of the original design-and-support team that he needs an instrument to assess certain features of selected opaque liquids, instead of those of the clear liquids for which the instrument was designed. Team members meet and think of a recent scientific advance that may make it possible to investigate necessary materials. Using time between other projects to which they officially were assigned, two team members pull together a new product in three months that uses parts from old products and a few new parts they had ordered. They build the new machine themselves as they progress. At the end of the processes, they sell the custom-designed machine to the customer.

In Product A, planning formally preceded implementation in both design and manufacturing activities. Details of both product features (price, performance specifications, components, and potential sources for them) and the product development process (team members, responsibilities, checkpoints, and intermediate target dates) were specified before they were implemented. Manufacturing plans specified in advance, detailed aspects of production outcomes and procedures. Clearly, Product B represented a more improvisational activity. A broad goal, but little product or manufacturing planning, preceded development. Final technical performance levels, exact components, size, shape, and actual assembly all unfolded as the team progressed. Although small improvisations to solve unexpected design problems arose during development of Product A, a dramatically greater proportion of both the product and manufacturing design occurred directly during their implementation for Product B, indicating improvisation.

Appendix B

Measures

Organizational improvisation   New measure
Seven-point semantic differential scale.
Rate the action:
- Figured out action as we went along/Action followed a strict plan as it was taken.
- Improvised in carrying out this action/Strictly followed our plan in carrying out this action.
- Ad-libbed action/Not an ad-libbed action.

Environmental turbulence   **New measure**
Seven-point Likert scale, where 1 is none and 7 is a lot.
When the action was taken, how would you rate the level of change in the following areas?
(change is defined as any deviation from the status quo):
- Within your team.
- Within your firm.
- Within external sources (customers, suppliers, distributors).

Organizational real-time flows   **New measure**
Seven-point Likert scale, where 1 is none and 7 is a lot.
Of information received from this source, how much was face-to-face, phone, or e-mail:
- Team members.

Organizational memory   **Adapted from Moorman and Miner (1997)**
Seven-point Likert scale, where 1 is disagree and 7 is agree.
For this action, my team has:
- well-defined procedures.
- a standard approach.
- a great deal of knowledge.
- strong skills.

Product effectiveness outcomes
Seven-point Likert scale, where 1 is a negative effect and 7 is a positive effect.
This action has or is likely to have the following effect on:
a. Design effectiveness.   **New measure**
  - Product design
  - Product performance
b. Market Effectiveness.   **Driven, in part, by Griffin and Page (1993, 1996)**
  - Product sales
  - Customer acceptance
  - General success of the product

Process effectiveness outcomes
Seven-point Likert scale, where 1 is a negative effect and 7 is a positive effect.
This action has or is likely to have the following effect on:
a. Cost efficiency.   **Driven, in part, by Griffin and Page (1993, 1996)**
  - Product costs
b. Time efficiency.   **Moorman (1995)**
  - Length of project development process
  - Speed of product development process
  - Project timeliness
c. Team functioning.   **New measure**
  - Team commitment level
  - Team functioning
  - Team enthusiasm
d. Team learning.   **New measure**
  - The way we think about the project
  - Our certainty level
  - Our understanding level
  - How much we have learned

Notes

1 Although we use the term *organizational* throughout this article, we do not mean to suggest that the focal action is necessarily at the overall organizational level. In general, measurement of organizational phenomena occurs within a strategic business unit (Eisenhardt and Tabrizi 1995).

2 A field study completed after this publication led us to propose a refined definition: "Improvisation is the deliberate and substantive fusion of the design and execution of a novel production" (Miner, Bassoff and Moorman, 2001, "Organizational Improvisation and Learning: A Field Study," *Administrative Science Quarterly,* June, 2001, in press). Repeated review of field data pointed to the critical importance of substantive convergence. Specifically, the execution process informs the design process and vice versa as they unfold together in real time. Such substantive convergence implies temporal convergence. Temporal convergence, however, does not guarantee substantive convergence.

3 This view of opportunism as benign (Miner 1987, p. 334) runs counter to the definition of opportunism as "self-seeking with guile" that Williamson (1975) proposes.

4 Although it is more typical to separate efficiency and effectiveness, product development efficiency can influence overall organizational effectiveness. Therefore, to maintain a common, unifying focus on new product effectiveness, we place efficiency under the rubric of effectiveness in our mix of dependent variables.

5 Our initial goal was to sample systematically high and low improvisation actions to ensure that our sample would contain variance. However, after attempting to do this for several weeks, we abandoned the approach for two reasons. First, from our observations of team meetings and interviews with key informants, it seemed that much of what occurred during meetings was, at least in part, an improvisation. Therefore, variance was easier than we had expected to capture. Second, we determined it was more appropriate for our informants to assess the degree to which they improvised than for us to make such judgments without a clear understanding, a priori, of how much or how little planning had preceded an action. This realization shifted our design, and we allowed informants to rate the degree of improvisation in an action following its enactment.

6 After publication, we realized there was a discrepancy between the alpha reported here and the alpha reported in Table 11.2. The table is correct.

7 We ideally would have performed discriminant validity checks between all the variables from which we previously conceptually distinguished improvisation (including adaptation, learning, and opportunism). However, because of the severe constraints imposed on our informants, we chose to focus our empirical efforts on innovation. We believe it is closest conceptually to improvisation and, therefore, perhaps the competing variable most crucial to our perspective.

8 Despite differences at the multivariate level, a univariate MRA test is identical in structure to the split-group analysis used here (for related proofs, see Arnold 1982; Cohen and Cohen 1983).

References

Aaker, David A. (1988), *Strategic Market Management*, 2nd ed. New York: John Wiley & Sons.
Anderson, Paul F. (1982), "Marketing, Strategic Planning, and the Theory of the Firm," *Journal of Marketing*, 46 (Spring), 15–26.
Andrews, Jonlee and Daniel C. Smith (1996), "In Search of the Marketing Imagination: Factors Affecting the Creativity of Marketing Programs for Mature Products," *Journal of Marketing Research*, 33 (May), 174–87.
Argyris, Chris and Donald Schön, (1978), *Organizational Learning: A Theory of Action Perspective*. Reading, MA: Addison-Wesley.
Armstrong, J. Scott (1982), "The Value of Formal Planning for Strategic Decisions: Review of Empirical Research," *Strategic Management Journal*, 3 (July/September), 197–211.
Arnold, Hugh H. (1982), "Moderator Variables: A Clarification of Conceptual, Analytic,

and Psychometric Issues," *Organizational Behavior and Human Performance*, 29 (April), 43–175.

Bagozzi, Richard P. (1994), "Structural Equation Models in Marketing Research: Basic Principles," in *Principles of Marketing Research*, Richard P. Bagozzi, ed. Cambridge, MA: Blackwell, 317–84.

Bailey, Derek (1980), *Improvisation: Its Nature and Practice in Music*. Ashbourne, Derbyshire, Great Britain: Moorlan Publishing Co. Ltd.

Barley, Stephen R. (1986), "Technology as an Occasion for Structuring: Evidence from Observations of CT Scanners and the Social Order of Radiology Departments," *Administrative Science Quarterly*, 31 (March), 78–108.

Bastien, David T. and Todd J. Hostager (1988), "Jazz as a Process of Organizational Innovation," *Communication Research*, 15 (5), 582–602.

—— and —— (1992), "Cooperation as Communicative Accomplishment: A Symbolic Interaction Analysis of an Improvised Jazz Concert," *Communication Studies*, 43 (Summer), 92–104.

Berliner, Paul F. (1994), *Thinking in Jazz: The Infinite Art of Improvisation*. Chicago: University of Chicago Press.

Bjurwill, Christer (1993), "Read and React: The Football Formula," *Perceptual and Motor Skills*, 76 (June), 1383–86.

Borko, Hilda and Carol Livingston (1989), "Cognition and Improvisation: Differences in Mathematics Instruction by Expert and Novice Teachers," *American Educational Research Journal*, 26 (Winter), 473–98.

Boyd, Harper W., Jr. and Orville C. Walker Jr. (1990), *Marketing Management: A Strategic Approach*. Homewood, IL: Richard D. Irwin Inc.

——, ——, and Jean-Claude Larréché (1998), *Marketing Management: A Strategic Approach with a Global Orientation*, 3rd ed. Boston: Irwin/McGraw-Hill.

Brown, Shona L. and Kathleen M. Eisenhardt (1995), "Product Development: Past Research, Present Findings, and Future Directions," *Academy of Management Review*, 20 (April), 343–78.

Burgelman, Robert A. (1983), "A Process Model of Internal Corporate Venturing in the Diversified Major Firm," *Administrative Science Quarterly*, 28 (June), 223–44.

—— (1994), "Fading Memories: A Process Theory of Strategic Business Exit in Dynamic Environments," *Administrative Science Quarterly*, 39 (March), 24–56.

Campbell, David (1989), "An Introduction to Nonlinear Dynamics," in *Lectures in the Sciences of Complexity: XIII–XXII*, Daniel L. Stein, ed. Redwood, CA: Addison-Wesley.

Cohen, Jacob and Patricia Cohen (1983), *Applied Multiple Regression/Correlation Analysis for Behavioral Sciences*. Hillsdale, NJ: Lawrence Erlbaum Associates.

Cohen, Michael D. (1991), "Individual Learning and Organizational Routine: Emerging Connections," *Organization Science*, 2 (February), 135–39.

—— and Paul Bacdayan (1994), "Organizational Routines Are Stored as Procedural Memory: Evidence from a Laboratory Study," *Organization Science*, 4 (November), 554–68.

——, James G. March, and Johan Olson (1972), "A Garbage Can Model of Organizational Choice," *Administrative Science Quarterly*, 17 (March), 1–25.

Cohen, Wesley M. and Daniel A. Levinthal (1990), "Absorptive Capacity: A New Perspective on Learning and Innovation," *Administrative Science Quarterly*, 35 (March), 128–52.

Cooper, Robert G. and Elko J. Kleinschmidt (1986), "An Investigation into the New Product Process: Steps, Deficiencies, and Impact," *Journal of Product Innovation Management*, 3 (June), 71–85.

—— and —— (1987), "New Products: What Separates Winners from Losers," *Journal of Product Innovation Management*, 4 (3), 169–84.

Cossé, Thomas J. and John E. Swan (1983), "Strategic Marketing Planning by Product Managers – Room for Improvement," *Journal of Marketing*, 47 (Summer), 92–102.

Cravens, David W. and Charles W. Lamb Jr. (1993), *Strategic Marketing Management Cases*, 4th edn. Homewood, IL: Richard D. Irwin Inc.

Crossan, Mary and Marc Sorrenti (1997), "Making Sense of Improvisation," in *Advances in Strategic Management*, Vol. 14, James P. Walsh and Ann Huff, eds. Greenwich, CT: JAI Press, 155–80.

Cyert, Richard M. and James G. March ([1963] 1992), *A Behavioral Theory of the Firm*, 2d edn. Oxford: Blackwell.

Dalrymple, Douglas J. and Leonard J. Parsons (1990), *Marketing Management: Strategy and Cases*, 5th edn. New York: John Wiley & Sons.

Day, George (1990), *Market-Driven Strategy*. New York: The Free Press.

—— (1994), "The Capabilities of Market-Driven Organizations," *Journal of Marketing*, 58 (October), 37–52.

—— and Prakash Nedungadi (1994), "Managerial Representations of Competitive Advantage," *Journal of Marketing*, 58 (April), 31–44.

—— and Robin Wensley (1983), "Marketing Theory with a Strategic Orientation," *Journal of Marketing*, 47 (Fall), 79–89.

Deshpandé, Rohit, John U. Farley, and Frederick E. Webster Jr. (1993), "Corporate Culture, Customer Orientation, and Innovativeness in Japanese Firms: A Quadrad Analysis," *Journal of Marketing*, 52 (January), 23–36.

—— and Frederick E. Webster Jr. (1989), "Organizational Culture and Marketing: Defining the Research Agenda," *Journal of Marketing*, 53 (January), 3–15.

Dickson, Peter R. (1997), *Marketing Management*, 2d ed. New York: The Dryden Press.

Dougherty, Deborah (1992), "Interpretive Barriers to Successful Product Innovation in Large Firms," *Organization Science*, 3 (May), 179–202.

Egge, Eric (1986), "Motivating Buyer Actions," *American Salesman*, 31 (August), 24–27.

Eisenhardt, Kathleen M. (1989), "Making Fast Strategic Decisions in High-Velocity Environments," *Academy of Management Journal*, 32 (September), 543–76.

—— and Behnam N. Tabrizi (1995), "Accelerating Adaptive Processes: Product Innovation in the Global Computer Industry," *Administrative Science Quarterly*, 40 (March), 84–110.

Etzioni, Amitai (1964), *Modern Organizations*. Englewood Cliffs, NJ: Prentice Hall.

Galbraith, Jay (1973), *Designing Complex Organizations*. Reading, MA: Addison-Wesley.

Gioia, Theodore (1988), *The Imperfect Art*. New York: Oxford University Press.

Granovetter, Mark (1973), "The Strength of Weak Ties," *American Journal of Sociology*, 78 (May), 1360–80.

—— (1985), "Economic Action and Social Structure: The Problem of Embeddedness," *American Journal of Sociology*, 91 (November), 481–510.

Griffin, Abbie (1997), "The Effect of Project and Process Characteristics on Product Development Cycle Time," *Journal of Marketing Research*, 34 (February), 24–35.

—— and Albert L. Page (1993), "An Interim Report on Measuring Product Development Success and Failure," *Journal of Product Innovation Management*, 10 (September), 291–308.

—— and —— (1996), "PDMA Success Measurement Project: Recommended Measures for Product Development Success and Failure," *Journal of Product Innovation Management*, 13 (November), 478–96.

Hatch, Mary Jo (1997), "Jazzing Up the Theory of Organizational Improvisation," *Advances in Strategic Management*, Vol. 14, James P. Walsh and Ann Huff, eds. Greenwich, CT: JAI Press, 181–91.

Holbrook, Morris B. (1995), *Consumer Research: Introspective Essays on the Study of Consumption*. Thousand Oaks, CA: Sage Publications.

Huber, George P. (1991), "Organizational Learning: The Contributing Processes and the Literatures," *Organizational Science*, 2 (February), 88–115.

—— and Reuben R. McDaniel (1986), "Decision-Making Paradigm of Organizational Design," *Management Science*, 32 (May), 572–89.

Hutchins, Edwin (1991), "Organizing Work by Adaptation," *Organization Science*, 2 (February), 14–39.

Hutt, Michael D., Peter H. Reingen, and John R. Ronchetto Jr. (1988), "Tracing Emergent Processes in Marketing Strategy Formation," *Journal of Marketing*, 52 (January), 4–19.

Imai, Ken-ichi, Ikujiro Nonaka, and Hirotaka Takeuchi (1985), "Managing the New Product Development Process: How Japanese Companies Learn and Unlearn," in *The Uneasy Alliance*, K.B. Clark, R.H. Hayes, and C. Lorenz, eds. Cambridge, MA: Harvard University Press, 337–81.

Irby, David M. (1992), "How Attending Physicians Make Instructional Decisions when Conducting Teaching Rounds," *Academic Medicine*, 67 (10), 630–38.

Ittner, Christopher and David F. Larcker (1997), "Product Development Cycle Time and Organizational Performance," *Journal of Marketing Research*, 34 (February), 13–33.

Jain, Subhash C. (1997), *Marketing Planning and Strategy*, 5th ed. Cincinnati: South-Western College Publishing.

Jaworski, Bernard J. and Ajay K. Kohli (1993), "Market Orientation: Antecedents and Consequences," *Journal of Marketing*, 57 (July), 53–71.

Kerin, Roger A. and Robert A. Peterson (1995), *Strategic Marketing Problems: Cases and Comments*, 7th ed. Englewood Cliffs, NJ: Prentice Hall.

Kohli, Ajay K. and Bernard J. Jaworski (1990), "Market Orientation: The Construct, Research Propositions, and Managerial Implications," *Journal of Marketing*, 54 (April), 1–18.

Kotler, Philip (1994), *Marketing Management: Analysis, Planning, Implementation, and Control*, 8th ed. Englewood Cliffs, NJ: Prentice Hall.

Lehmann, Donald R. and Russell S. Winer (1994), *Product Management*. Boston: Richard D. Irwin Inc.

Leonard-Baron, Dorothy (1992), "Core Capabilities and Core Rigidities: A Paradox in Managing New Product Development," *Strategic Management Journal*, 13 (Summer), 111–25.

Levi-Strauss, Claude (1967), *The Savage Mind*. Chicago: University of Chicago Press.

Levitt, Barbara and James G. March (1988), "Organizational Learning," *Annual Review of Sociology*, 14, 319–40.

Lovell, Jim and Jeffrey Kluger (1995), *Apollo XIII*. New York: Simon and Schuster Inc.

Mangham, Iain L. (1986), *Power and Performance in Organizations: An Exploration of Executive Process*. Oxford: Basil Blackwell.

March, James G. (1976), "The Technology of Foolishness," in *Ambiguity and Choice in Organizations*, James G. March and Johan P. Olsen, eds. Norway: Universitetsfarlgt. 69–81.

—— (1991), "Exploration and Exploitation in Organizational Learning," *Organisation Science*, 2 (February), 71–78.

—— and Herbert A. Simon (1958), *Organizations*. New York: John Wiley & Sons.

Menzel, M. (1981), "Interpersonal and Unplanned Communications: Indispensable or Obsolete?" in *Biomedical Innovation*, E.B. Roberts et al., eds. Cambridge, MA: MIT Press, 155–63.

Miller, Chet C. and Laura B. Cardinal (1994), "Strategic Planning and Firm Performance: A Synthesis of More than Two Decades of Research," *Academy of Management Journal*, 37 (6), 1649–65.

Miner, Anne S. (1987), "Idiosyncratic Jobs in Formalized Organizations," *Administrative Science Quarterly*, 32 (September), 327–51.

—— (1990), "Structural Evolution Through Idiosyncratic Jobs: The Potential for Unplanned Learning," *Organization Science*, 1 (2), 195–210.

——, Christine Moorman, and Paula Bassoff (1997), "Organization Improvisation in New Product Development," *Market Science Institute Report No. 97–110*. Cambridge, MA: Marketing Science Institute.

Mintzberg, Henry (1994), *The Rise and Fall of Strategic Planning*. New York: The Free Press.

—— (1996), "Learning 1, Planning 0," *California Management Review*, 38 (Summer), 92–93.

—— and Alexandra McHugh (1985), "Strategic Formation in an Adhocracy," *Administrative Science Quarterly*, 30 (June), 160–97.

——, Richard T. Pascale, Michael Goold, and Richard P. Rumelt (1996), "The 'Honda Effect' Revisited," *California Management Review*, 38 (Summer), 78–117.

Montoya-Weiss, Mitzi M. and Roger Calantone (1994), "Determinants of New Product Performance: A Review and Meta-Analysis," *Journal of Product Innovation Management*, 11 (November), 397–417.

Moorman, Christine (1995), "Organizational Market Information Processes: Cultural Antecedents and New Product Outcomes," *Journal of Marketing Research*, 32 (August), 318–35.

—— and Anne S. Miner (1995), "Walking the Tightrope: Improvisation and Information Use in New Product Development," *Marketing Science Institute Report No. 95–101*. Cambridge, MA: Marketing Science Institute.

—— and —— (1997), "The Impact of Organizational Memory on New Product Performance and Creativity," *Journal of Marketing Research*, 34 (February), 91–107.

—— and —— (1998), "Organizational Improvisation and Organizational Memory," *Academy of Management Review*, forthcoming.

Nonaka, Ikujiro (1990), "Redundant, Overlapping Organization: A Japanese Approach to Managing the Innovation Process," *California Management Review*, 32 (Spring), 27–38.

Olson, Eric M., Orville C. Walker, and Robert W. Rukert (1995), "Organizing for Effective New Product Development: The Moderating Role of Product Innovativeness," *Journal of Marketing*, 59 (January), 48–62.

Pascale, Richard T. (1984), "The Honda Effect," excerpted from "Perspectives on Strategy: The Real Story Behind Honda's Success," *California Management Review*, 26 (Spring), 47–72.

—— (1996), "Reflections on Honda," *California Management Review*, 38 (Summer), 112–17.

Pedhazur, Elazar J. (1982), *Multiple Regression in Behavioral Research: Explanation and Prediction*. New York: Holt, Rinehart, and Winston Inc.

Peter, J. Paul and James H. Donnelly Jr. (1998), *Marketing Management: Knowledge and Skills*, 5th ed. Boston: Irwin/McGraw-Hill.

Pfeffer, Jeffrey (1982), *Organizations and Organization Theory*. New York: Putnam.

Pressing, Jeff (1984), "Cognitive Processes in Improvisation," in *Cognitive Processes in the Perception of Art*, W.R. Crozier and A.J. Chapman, eds. Amsterdam: North-Holland, 345–63.

—— (1988), "Improvisation: Methods and Models," in *Generative Processes in Music: The Psychology of Performance, Improvisation, and Composition*, John A. Sloboda, ed. Oxford: Oxford University Press, 129–78.

Preston, Alistair (1991), "Improvising Order," in *Organization Analysis and Development*, I.L. Mangham, ed. New York: John Wiley & Sons.

Quelch, John A., Robert J. Dolan, and Thomas J. Kosnik (1993), *Marketing Management: Test and Cases*. Homewood, IL: Richard D. Irwin Inc.

Quinn, James B. (1980), *Strategies for Change: Logical Incrementalism*. Homewood, IL: Richard D. Irwin Inc.

—— (1986), "Innovation and Corporate Strategy: Managed Chaos," in *Technology in the Modern Corporation: A Strategic Perspective*, Mel Horwich, ed. New York: Pergamon Press, 167–83.

Robins, Fred (1991), "Marketing Planning in the Large Family Business," *Journal of Marketing Management*, 7 (October), 325–41.

Rogers, Everett (1983), *The Diffusion of Innovations*. New York: The Free Press.

Scott, Richard W. (1987), *Organizations: Rational, Natural, and Open Systems*, 2d ed. Englewood Cliffs, NJ: Prentice Hall.

Sinha, Deepak K. (1990), "The Contribution of Formal Planning to Decisions," *Strategic Management Journal*, 11 (6), 479–92.

Sinkula, James M. (1994), "Market Information Processing and Organizational Learning," *Journal of Marketing*, 58 (January), 35–45.

Solomon, Larry (1986), "Improvisation II," *Perspectives of New Music*, 24 (2), 225–35.

Song, Z. Michael and Mark E. Parry (1997), "The Determinants of Japanese New Product Successes." *Journal of Marketing Research*, 34 (February), 64–76.

Spolin, Viola (1963), *Improvisation for the Theater: A Handbook of Teaching and Directing Techniques*. Evanston, IL: Northwestern University Press.

Sproull, Lee and Sara Keisler (1991), *Connections: New Ways of Working in the Networked Organization*. Cambridge, MA: MIT Press.

Sutton, Howard (1990), *Marketing Planning*. New York: The Conference Board.

Tushman, Michael and Phillip Anderson (1986), "Technological Discontinuities and Organizational Environments," *Administrative Science Quarterly*, 31 (September), 439–65.

Van de Ven, Andrew H. (1986), "Central Problems in the Management of Innovation," *Management Science*, 32 (May), 590–607.

—— (1993), "Managing the Process of Organizational Innovation," in *Organizational Change and Redesign*, George P. Huber and William H. Glick, eds. Cary, NC: Oxford University Press, 269–94.

Walker, Orville C., Jr. and Robert W. Ruekert (1987), "Marketing's Role in the Implementation of Business Strategies," *Journal of Marketing*, 51 (July), 15–33.

Walsh, James P. (1995), "Managerial and Organizational Cognition: Notes from a Trip Down Memory Lane," *Organization Science*, 6 (May–June), 280–321.

—— and Gerardo Rivera Ungson (1991), "Organizational Memory," *Academy of Management Review*, 16 (January), 57–91.

Weick, Karl E. (1979), *The Social Psychology of Organizing*, 2d ed. Reading, MA: Addison-Wesley.

—— (1987), "Substitutes for Strategy," in *The Competitive Challenge: Strategies for Industrial Innovation and Renewal*, David J. Teece, ed. New York: Harper and Row, 221–33.

—— (1993a), "The Collapse of Sensemaking in Organizations: The Mann Gulch Disaster," *Administrative Science Quarterly*, 38 (December), 628–52.

—— (1993b), "Organizational Redesign as Improvisation," in *Organizational Change and Redesign*, George P. Huber and William H. Glick, eds. Cary, NC: Oxford University Press, 346–79.

—— (1993c), "Managing as Improvisation: Lessons from the World of Jazz," working paper, University of Michigan Graduate School of Business Administration.

—— (1996), "Drop Your Tools: An Allegory for Organizational Studies," *Administrative Science Quarterly*, 41 (June), 301–13.

Williamson, Oliver E. (1975), *Markets and Hierarchies: Analysis and Antitrust Implications*. New York: The Free Press.

Wind, Jerry and Vijay Mahajan (1997), "Issues and Opportunities in New Product Development: An Introduction to the Special Issue," *Journal of Marketing Research*, 34 (February), 1–11.

—— and Thomas S. Robertson (1983), "Marketing Strategic: New Directions for Theory and Research," *Journal of Marketing*, 47 (Spring), 12–25.

Winter, Sidney G. (1987), "Knowledge and Competence as Strategic Assets," in *The Competitive Challenge: Strategies for Industrial Innovation and Renewal*, David J. Teece, ed. New York: Harper and Row, 159–85.

Zaltman, Gerald, Robert Duncan, and Jonny Holbek (1973), *Innovations and Organizations*. New York: John Wiley & Sons.

12 Once again: what, when, how and why

A prospectus for research in organizational improvisation

João Vieira da Cunha, Ken N. Kamoche and Miguel Pina e Cunha

Introduction

What makes an organization adaptive? Many answers have been provided to this classical question. They include learning capabilities, core competences, the willingness to change, market orientation, good leadership, and so forth. Rarely, however, is organizational improvisation alluded to. To a certain extent, this is not surprising, since most of us were taught that good management is about planning. Or, as Mintzberg (1973) taught us, good-impression-management is about planning. Due to this deeply ingrained assumption about the functioning of organizations, improvisation has been, until recently, an almost ignored theme. Changes in the world of work and the concomitant inadequacy of traditional models to explain these changes have, however, altered the picture. The seemingly erratic, opportunity-grabbing behaviour of new economy organizations (Eisenhardt and Sull, 2001), the success of serendipitous discoveries (Nayak and Ketteringham, 1997), the pressure to solve problems instantaneously (Perry, 1991), are examples of how useful improvisation might be to organizations. Despite such potential usefulness, discussions of organizational adaptiveness still tend to revolve around such topics as strategic resources (Martens *et al.*, 1997), scenario planning (Goodwin and Wright, 2001), strategic flexibility (Sanchez, 1997) and other mainly planned courses of action. Despite the importance of these approaches, there is certainly space to balance interest for the preparation of the future (Hamel and Prahalad, 1994; Heene and Vermeylen, 1997) by devoting more attention to the present.

In this final chapter we will present a research prospectus for organizational improvisation. Before turning to the future, however, we will discuss the present, in order to uncover why improvisation now seems to be blooming as a 'proper' research topic. To do so, we will briefly contrast a traditional, inherited view on management and organization from where improvisation is almost absent, with an emergent view, where improvisation can be considered as a relevant property of adaptive organizations.

As shown in Table 12.1, the last several years have witnessed an increased attention to the analysis of organizational change as a continuous process instead of a sequence of discrete events. These continuous changes may take place very rapidly, which forces organizations not only to define what vision of the future they intend to realize, but also the capacity to nurture organizational flexibility. All these chal-

Table 12.1 Organizational characteristics under the discrete versus continuous change views.

	Discrete change	*Continuous change*
Business landscape	Incrementally-evolving	Fast moving
Strategy as	Anticipatory	Anticipatory and reactive
Structure as	Source of stability	Source of flexibility
Learning	Guided, methodical	Exploratory, emergent
Action	Routine, efficiency-oriented	Innovation, speed-oriented
Sources of advantage	Exploring stable market positions	Discovering new opportunities
Sustainability	Potential	Unpredictable

lenges led to a significant interest in the concept of organizational learning, under-stood not only as composed of guided and methodical learning but also as explo-ration and serendipity. Significant changes can also be found in the perception of the sources of organizational advantage and their sustainability. Due to rapid changes in business landscapes, advantage may be a consequence, at least in some cases (Eisenhardt and Martin, 2000), of the capacity to discover new opportunities, more than of the ability to exploit stable and well protected market positions.

The salience of high-speed environments and the untenability of routine-oriented structures to an increasing number of organizations made the concept of improvisation more visible. Organizations may improvise not because they are incompetent planners but because they are fast learners. They improvise not to sub-stitute strategy or vision but to complement it. And improvisation takes place because of structure and not in spite of it. Before turning to the discussion of a research prospectus for organizational improvisation, we will briefly summarize, in a schematic way, what improvisation is and what it is not.

Improvisation is:

1   the conception of action as it unfolds, drawing on available resources;
2   a paradoxical process, involving structure and ad-hockery, intention and emer-gence, planning and invention (see Figure 12.1);
3   thinking in action, i.e. a desired course of action, whose contours are defined while action takes place;
4   a demanding task, that captures the essence of the concept of a 'reflective prac-titioner';
5   a departure from stored procedural memory, which may be difficult given the essence of organizing as forgetting and variety reducing (Weick and Westley, 1996);
6   a process aiming to increase the chances of organizational adaptation;
7   a pervasive organizational process.

Improvisation is not:

1   a new quick-fix for twenty-first-century organizations;
2   merely a substitute for planning;
3   a syndrome of the lack of anticipatory capacity;
4   a dysfunctional organizational behaviour;
5   a one-size-fits-all prescription;
6   a recent discovery of vanguardist organizations;
7   a nice new metaphor.

Improvisation: a research prospectus

To conclude this volume, a research prospectus for organizational improvisation is proposed. This should not be taken as a definitive effort, but as an invitation for the study of improvisation. As such, many other topics are certainly available (for an ad-hoc sample of research questions, see Appendix 12.1). With this in mind, we should start by considering that organizational improvisation is still an embryonic research topic. We believe that research effort in the field is now leaving an initial stage of development, to a large extent metaphor-based, and entering a second stage, where the first empirical efforts go hand-in-hand with theoretical attempts aiming to give a more organizational flavour to a formerly jazz-based theory of this phenomenon. While there is nothing wrong with metaphor-based theory building, empirical efforts are necessary to submit jazz-inspired assumptions to organizational reality checks. This possibly will, in a third moment, stimulate the refinement of empirically-based theory. In the following sections we present some of the issues that we expect will help define the contours of organizational improvisation research in the forthcoming years. The discussion is organized around the 'what', 'how', 'why' and 'when' of improvisation research. This chapter may then be understood as elaborating our review in Chapter 6 with an eye on the future.

What: the core constructs

An important step for the purpose of theory building in organizational improvisation is the specification of the 'nomological net' of its core constructs (Whetten, 1997). In the case of improvisation, as shown in Figure 12.1, this cluster of constructs refers to the way the organization deals with its environment, or more precisely, how its actions and interactions with the environment lead to an interplay between planning and action, resulting in improvisation. This cluster includes the core constructs of planning, improvisation and change, and delineates the relevant set of variables for studying the essence and conditions of organizational improvisation. Considering our definition of improvisation as intentional but not planned change efforts, our nomological net (see Figure 12.1) includes all the relevant variables.

Table 12.2 Three stages in the evolution of improvisation research.

Stage 1	Jazz-based theory building	• Fuelling interest • Translating jazz elements to the organizational context
Stage 2	Organizational theorizing and empirical progression	• Entering the organizational field • Critical analysis of the jazz metaphor.
Stage 3	Empirical progression and theory development	• Empirical test of models of organizational improvisation • Contingency analysis of improvisation in organizations • Generating alternative metaphors.

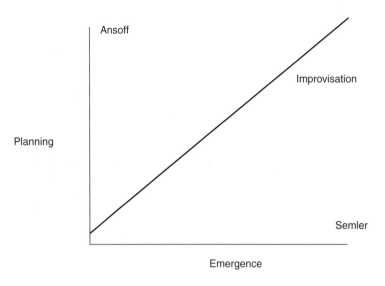

Figure 12.1

In our view, organizations improvise when their planning efforts are inadequate or insufficient to deal with environmental changes. Confronted with the limitations of planning, organizations need to seek for adequate variations of their current repertoire. Improvisations can thus be understood as intentional variations aiming to improve fit. Some of these variations will work better than others, leading to a change that repairs a desired relationship with the environment. These may be retained and incorporated in the planned organizational functioning. Others will simply be forgotten.

This nomological net, although familiar to organizational researchers (given, for example, its resemblance with the cybernetic view of organizational control and adaptation, e.g. Hofstede, 1978), has not been empirically tested. It suggests several research questions, including:

Q1: What does improvisation mean to managers (e.g. failure of planning, Real-time decision making)?
Q2: What are the elements of organizational improvisation?
Q3: What constitutes improvisational skills?
Q4: What distinguishes improvisation from related constructs (e.g. learning, adaptation)?
Q5: What does improvisation mean at different organizational levels?

These and other related questions will certainly help to define the construct of improvisation. Currently, there seems to be general agreement about the essence of improvisation (real-time action), but not about its elements, which may include, for example, minimal structures (Kamoche and Cunha, 2001), bricolage (Weick, 1993) and intentionality (Moorman and Miner, this volume). It is the combination of these referents that will define the core features of improvisation and (dis)confirm its dialectical nature (Kamoche and Cunha, 2001), voluntary character and relation to other change theories. The clarification of the concept will, in turn, help researchers in their efforts of operationalization and measurement.

How: relationships between constructs

This section is organized around two themes: research questions and research approaches. The first of these refers to the conceptual relationships between the constructs. The discussion is structured on the basis of the three pairs or relationships considered in our nomological net: planning and improvisation, improvisation and change, and change and planning. The second section discusses how these relationships may be approached. Two dimensions will be contrasted: the quantity versus quality dimension, and the discrete versus processual dimension.

How: research questions

It is important to explicitly define the concept of improvisation. Such an endeavour will be facilitated by the analysis of the relationships between key variables in the nomological net specified above. The relationships between planning, improvisation and change can be analysed according to an evolutionary framework (Weick, 1979; Aldrich, 1999). As discussed, improvisation may introduce the variation necessary to cope with unexpected changes. Some of these variations, presumably the most effective, will be selected and retained, while others will be rejected and kept away from organizational memory. Research on the improvisational process should then involve the specification of variables and processes associated with the relationships between the concepts of the nomological net, i.e.: (1) planning and improvisation, (2) improvisation and change, (3) change and planning.

   Questions arising from these relationships could include (but are not limited to) the following.

Planning and improvisation

Q1: How does an organization notice the failure (or limitations) of plans?
Q2: How do organizational conditions shift an organization's focus from strategic intention to situational attention?
Q3: How can planning processes promote improvisational moves?
Q4: How, in what conditions and with what results, can improvisations complement detailed plans?

These research questions basically consider the need to understand the way organizations combine attempts of anticipation with efforts of reaction. The contradiction involved in the combination of plans and action via improvisation may be a fruitful avenue for research, in the sense that, instead of 'condemning' the planning process, it tries to stretch it, by analyzing its properties on the basis of non-conventional angles.

Improvisation and change

Q5: How do improvisational behaviours contribute to change the organization's strategy, structure and/or processes?

Q6: How do organizational structures facilitate change in an improvisational mode?
Q7: Why do some types of environments (e.g. hypercompetitive, high-speed environments) stimulate more improvisation-led changes than others?

These research questions consider the need to study change not only in planned or emergent ways, but also change as improvisation and improvisation as intentional change. Research on high-speed environments (e.g. Brown and Eisenhardt, this volume, Chapter 10) demonstrated that improvisational change may actually be sought intentionally. In other words, some organizations seem to have incorporated improvisation as normal practice. Apparently, in some cases at least (Brown and Eisenhardt, this volume, Chapter 10), this improved the organization's capacity to adapt to fast-changing environments. Future research should address the improvisational practices of organizations in more traditional environments as well as the conditions, both internal and external, that facilitate or hinder improvisational effectiveness under different circumstances.

Change and planning

Q8: How do successful improvisations get retained in the organization's memory?
Q9: How can organizations appropriate the tacit knowledge developed in an improvisational way?
Q10: How do yesterday's improvisations become a template for tomorrow's plans?

This last set of 'How' questions refers to aspects related to the retention and appropriation of improvisations. Successful improvisations can probably be retained by means of organizational learning, but the assimilation and appropriation mechanisms remain unexplored (see also Kamoche and Mueller, 1998).

How: research approaches

Another way of addressing the how of organizational improvisation is by considering possible research approaches. In this case, we will consider the possibilities resulting from the combination of two dimensions for the analysis of improvisation: the quantity versus quality of improvisation, and improvisations as discrete events or as unfolding processes.

The four combinations displayed in Table 12.3 may be helpful for developing a theory of organizational improvisation. By taking improvisation as a qualitative and discrete event (Cell I research in the table), one may access the characteristics/qualities of improvisation in a particular moment. The analysis of improvisational 'flashes' will allow an in-depth understanding of particular episodes and their contextual determinants.

Cell II research (qualitative and processual) refers to the changing nature of improvisations over time (how do improvisations change?). This type of research is necessary in order to analyse how improvisations combine with or relate to the existing organizational context, namely with plans, expectations and political activity.

Cell III research, focuses on the quantitative aspects of improvisations taken as discrete events. It will be adequate, for example, to compare rates of improvisation

Table 12.3 How: Research approaches.

I. Qualitative and discrete	II. Qualitative and processual
Research problem: The quality of organizational improvisation in a certain moment *Examples*: What are the influencing factors of improvisational behaviour? Are improvised behaviours effective?	*Research problem*: The qualities of improvisations over time *Examples*: How do improvisational practices evolve over time? Are there periods more favourable to improvising? How is improvisational knowledge appropriated? Are successful improvisations formalized?
III. Quantitative and discrete	IV. Quantitative and processual
Research problem: The quantity of improvisation on Time 1 *Examples*: Are there interorganizational differences in the number of improvisations? Are there differences between industries? Do different industries stimulate different types of improvisation?	*Research problem*: The quantity of improvisations over time *Examples*: Do young organizations improvise more than mature organizations? Does the number and type of improvisations change along with cultural changes?

(and of successful improvisations) within an industry or between industries. The comparison of traditional sectors with sectors of the new economy may be helpful to uncover how pervasive is organizational improvisation in different organizational fields. Quantitative comparisons may also focus on the relationship between the degree of professionalism and the number and type of improvisations. Assuming that more organizations with higher degrees of professionalism allow more discretion to their employees, it will be interesting to analyse how more discretion impacts on improvisation.

Finally, organizational improvisation may be approached as a quantitative and processual phenomenon. As illustrated in Cell IV, interest is focused on the quantity of improvisations over time. It seems relevant, for example, to analyse if organizations in different phases of their life cycles exhibit significantly different rates of improvisation. The improvisational impacts of changes in organizational size, type of leadership and environmental conditions are other examples of potential causes of change in the number of improvisations over time in one organization or population of organizations.

Why: underlying assumptions

One important condition for advancing knowledge on organizational improvisation relates to the need to clarify the assumptions underpinning the improvisational theory of organizing. To relate improvisation with prevalent theories of organizing, we may position improvisation in a three-dimensional space that tries to capture the importance of voluntarism for organizations (see Figure 12.2).

Figure 12.1 is structured around two axis. The first is the axis of organizing as planning. The planning perspective has a long history in management theory: with good planning, managers would be able to transform an organization from its present position to some desirable future (e.g. Ansoff, 1965). In this sense, managers are planners, not improvisers. They are expected to forecast, to predetermine, to quantify, to detach themselves from organizational details (Mintzberg, 1994). In

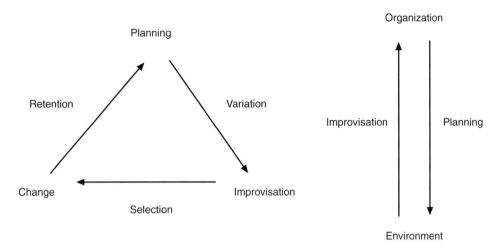

Figure 12.2

sum, they are expected to anticipate, not to react; to lead, not to be led; to be in charge, not to remedy. These assumptions are in stark contrast with those of the second axis, the axis of emergence. The idea of emergence, although familiar to organizational researchers (e.g. Trist, 1997), gained a new impulse with recent advances in the science of complexity (Anderson, 1999). Complexity theory exposed the intrinsic unpredictability of complex systems. If systems are unpredictable, and if the interactions by means of which they build their contexts are not predetermined, then the future can not be anticipated, because there is nothing but trends, to be anticipated. Some organizations seemed to have taken this assumption seriously.

One of the well-known examples of managing in an emergent mode is Semco, a famous if controversial Brazilian firm led by Ricardo Semler, author of the best-selling book *Maverick* (1993) and of a series of *Harvard Business Review* articles (Semler, 1989, 1994, 2000). Semco is an excellent example of managing by emergence, or of how self-organization, or natural management as Semler prefers to call it, may apply to contemporary business firms. In his most recent *HBR* article, for example, Semler discusses how Semco went digital without a strategy. Therefore, this axis represents the negation of the previous one. One may wonder, of course, how generalizable is the experience of one single case. The Semco model, however, seems to be gaining some acceptance elsewhere. The new economy firms studied by Eisenhardt and Sull (2001), for example, apparently share the notion of 'strategizing-by-doing' with Semco.

A third model of organizing, whose importance grows with the turbulence of organizational environments consists in understanding management as improvisation. Considering the paradoxical nature of improvisation, where both high levels of planning/control and freedom are present (Brown and Eisenhardt, this volume, Chapter 10; Kamoche and Cunha, 2001), improvisation may constitute an appealing alternative to both the traditional model (thesis) and its modern alternative (antithesis). In our model of organizing, improvisation should thus be considered as a space where the old meets the new, where control meets freedom, where the future is built upon the present (and not detached from it). This does not mean eliminating the two opposite poles of a paradox through a synthesis, but instead finding a synthesis in their relationship (see also Tatikonda and Rosenthal, 2000).

By drawing on the concept of organizational improvisation, it seems possible to contribute towards developing skills to respond to events as they unfold, in real time. In this instance, plans are not abandoned but reconceptualized: they are now to organizations what musical scores are to jazz musicians (Kamoche and Cunha, 1999): roadmaps or minimally structured courses of action that coordinate members' activities and give them the freedom to conceive their actions while these are taking place. Long range planning (not long range plans) can be used, to paraphrase Wack (1985), to foster the organization's self-confidence, which is of much greater importance than its confidence in its plans, because it is the core characteristic that allows it to thrive even in the face of the most turbulent of environments.

These are the assumptions underlying our study of improvisation. By making them explicit, we invite scholars to discuss them, to test them and to identify alternatives that may better explain organizing and improvisation.

When/where/who: limiting parameters

One important challenge to the community of scholars investigating improvisation will be the discovery of the limits of improvisation. So little is known about the topic, that it is difficult to answer such central questions as the impact of improvisation on speed, the safe contexts for organizational improvisation, the triggers of improvisational behaviours and so forth. Additionally, it will be necessary to study the impacts of successful improvisations on existing plans: do they reinforce plans or expose their limitations? Some of the chapters in this volume have gone some way towards addressing these and related issues, but much work remains to be done.

The study of the 'when', 'where' and 'who' of improvisation is necessary to avoid taking it as a new universal recipe for organizational success. As expressed in our underlying assumptions, we believe there is sufficient scope in the field of organization studies to seriously consider this emergent paradigm. This is not to say that improvisation is necessarily or always a good thing. Researchers will need to investigate the circumstances in which improvisations are desirable and for whom they are desirable; when not to improvise; what 'degrees' of improvisation are required; how to look out for solipsism; how to create improvisational skills in individuals/teams; who are the 'champions' of improvisational discovery, and so forth.

Answers to these questions suggest a contingency theory of improvisation. To arrive at such a theory it would appear necessary to study improvisation in all of the four quadrants presented in Table 12.3. Such a diversity of approaches will shed light on how young and mature organizations differ in terms of improvisational proficiency and use, on the relationship between the level of formalization and the quantity/quality of improvisations, on the propensity of organizations to improvise action given their configuration of existing resources (including human resources), on the impact of environmental turbulence over organizational willingness to improvise, and so forth.

The exploration of the boundaries of organizational improvisation should be as central an objective as the discovery of its core dimensions and processes. This exploration/investigation should proceed both theoretically and empirically:

- Theoretically, looking beyond the jazz metaphor may prove an invaluable effort, in the sense that one way of seeing is one way of not seeing (Morgan, 1986). Thus, different metaphors should make the limits of current theorizing more explicit. Additional theoretical efforts may address, for example, to what extent planning and improvisation are mirror activities or qualitatively different processes. Or the contribution of improvisation to the process of learning by doing
- At the empirical level, the features of improvisation in different organizational activities should be subject to investigation. Analyses of the improvisational elements involved in negotiation (Valley and Keros, 2000) or organizational change (Orlikowsi, 1996), should be extended to other domains, like leadership (e.g. how do leaders decide to institutionalize a once-improvised solution?) or decision making (e.g. what cognitive factors undermine the quality of on-the-spot decisions?).

So what: implications and consequences

While discussing the consequences (both theoretical and empirical) of an emergent field like improvisation, some authors (e.g. Whetten, 1997) argue that critics of the existing theory have the obligation to propose something better. In the case of improvisation, to propose something new or better does not mean to negate previous theory. On the contrary, the build-up of research on planned organizational change provided much useful knowledge both for understanding the processes of organizational change as well as to help change agents in their practical efforts.

Until recently, most research efforts referred to the planning side of organization and management. Notable exceptions are those studies devoted to how organizations change in an emergent fashion, meaning how they sometimes end up changing in unexpected ways (Mintzberg and Waters, 1982). Research on improvised action within the context of organizational change is much less common, but no less important. To make the concept more meaningful, we now need to combine conceptual and abstract approaches with grounded and applied ones. It is imperative, in other words, to secure both scientific credibility and empirical support. This requires both good research practice and an eye on the practitioner's interest. In improvisation, like in most other topical areas of organization studies, it will be necessary to discover how best to strike a balance between description and prescription, explanation and prediction, particularism and generalism. The affirmation of improvisation as a critical area of organization studies will largely depend upon the ability of our community of scholars to combine academic interest with practical utility, achieving both rigour and relevance, especially in moving beyond Stage I in our three-stage model of research (see Table 12.2).

Closing thought

Until fairly recently, many people thought of improvisation as an outcome of the lack of planning. This has encouraged the view of improvisation as a somewhat dysfunctional practice, whose existence was justified only as a late and perhaps satis-factory substitute for planning or as a means for fast imitation (Aram and Walochick, 1997; Dickson, 1997). It is no surprise therefore that the idea of impro-vising action and in fact using the word 'improvisation' itself may be viewed askance by some. This view is echoed in improvised music, where some musicians actually resent the term 'improvisation' because of the connotations that many people, out of ignorance, have come to associate it with. Bailey (1992: xii) makes the following observation:

> There is a noticeable reluctance to use the word and some improvisers express a positive dislike for it. I think this is due to its widely accepted connotations which imply that improvisation is something without preparation and without consideration, a completely *ad hoc* activity, frivolous and inconsequential, lacking in design and method. And they object to that implication because they know from their own experience that it is untrue. They know there is no musical activity which requires greater skill and devotion, preparation, training and commitment.

With this collection, a new perspective on improvisation arises, one that sees impro-visation not merely as a late substitute for planning, or a frivolous and reckless activ-ity, but as an inevitable component of organizational life. The resulting picture has also hopefully captured improvisation as a potentially adaptive tool. Rather than late planning, improvisation assumes the complexion of real-time planning or, better still, as thinking in action (Eden and Ackermann, 1998). As we have dis-cussed in this concluding chapter, much work needs to be done in order to lead this emergent genre of organizational theorizing towards maturity. The seminal chapters collected in this volume can be viewed as pioneering efforts to help organi-zational improvisation mature as a credible scientific field.

Appendix 1

An ad hoc sample of research questions

Theme 1: Improvisation and organizational environments
1.1.   Is improvisation endemic to fast changing environments?
1.2.   Does an increase in competitive intensity influence the rate of organi-zational improvisations?
1.3.   Is there any difference, qualitative or quantitative, between new and tradi-tional industries in terms of improvisational activity and effectiveness?

Theme 2: Improvisation and minimal structures
2.1.   What do minimal structures look like? How are they constituted?
2.2.   How do minimal structures evolve over time? Does minimality evolve towards maximality?
2.3.   Are there any inter-industry differences in terms of how minimal should minimal structures be?

Theme 3: Improvisation and strategy
3.1.   Are prospector organizations more willing to improvise than other strategic types?

3.2.   Are formalized strategies less favourable contexts for improvisation to occur?

3.3.   Can strategizing-by-doing be a source of sustainable competitive advantage?

Theme 4: Improvisation and learning

4.1.   Can improvisational knowledge become standard practice?

4.2.   Who appropriates the knowledge created via improvisation?

4.3.   Can improvisational knowledge be used for both exploratory and exploitative purposes?

Theme 5: Improvisation and innovation

5.1.   Does improvisation have positive impacts on innovation outcomes?

5.2.   Is improvisation more helpful for advancing incremental or radical innovations?

5.3.   Does improvisation increase the speed of innovative processes?

Theme 6: Improvisation and culture

6.1.   Are innovation-oriented cultures more supportive of improvisation than other cultural types?

6.2.   Is improvisational behaviour reinforced by any cultural mechanisms?

6.3.   Are improvisations more acceptable on the informal than on the formal side of the organization?

Theme 7: Improvisation and human resources

7.1.   How can improvising skills be created in individuals and teams?

7.2.   What mechanisms are appropriate for selecting, rewarding and training improvisers?

7.3.   How can managers promote the capacity to improvise while at the same time ensuring quality and customer satisfaction?

References

Aldrich, H. (1999). *Organizations evolving*. Thousand Oaks, CA: Sage.

Anderson, P. (1999). Complexity theory and organization science. *Organization Science*, 10: 216–32.

Ansoff, H.I. (1965). *Corporate strategy*. New York: McGraw-Hill.

Aram, J.D. and Walochik, K. (1997). Improvisation and the Spanish manager. *International Studies of Management and Organization*, 26: 73–89.

Bailey, D. (1992) *Improvisation: its nature and practice in music*. New York: Da Capo Press.

Dickson, P.R. (1997). *Marketing management* (2nd edn). Fort Worth: Dryden Press.

Eden, C. and Ackermann, F. (1998). *Making strategy. The journey of strategic management*. London: Sage.

Eisenhardt, K.M. and Sull, D.N. (2001). Strategy as simple rules. *Harvard Business Review*, January, 107–16.

Goodwin, P. and Wright, G. (2001). Enhancing strategy evaluation in scenario planning: A role for decision analysis. *Journal of Management Studies*, 38, 1–16.

Hamel, G. and Prahalad, C.K. (1994). *Competing for the future. Breakthrough strategies for seizing control of your industry and creating the markets of tomorrow*. Boston: Harvard Business School Press.

Heene, A. and Vermeylen, S. (eds) (1997). Preparing for the future: developing strategic flexibility from a competence-based perspective. *International Studies of Management and Organization*, 27(2).

Hofstede, G. (1978). The poverty of management control philosophy. *Academy of Management Review,* 3: 450–61.

Kamoche, M.P. and Cunha, M.P. (1999). Teamwork, knowledge-creation and improvisation, in M.P. Cunha and C.A. Marques (eds), *Readings in organization science.* Lisbon: ISPA, 435–52.

Kamoche, M.P. and Cunha, M.P. (2001). Minimal structures: from jazz improvisation to product innovation. *Organization Studies,* 22, 5.

Kamoche, K. and Mueller, F. (1998) Human resource management and the appropriation-learning perspective. *Human Relations,* 51: 1033–60.

Martens, R., Bogaert, I. and Van Cauwenbergh, A. (1997). Preparing for the future as a situational puzzle. The fit of strategic assets. *International Studies of Management and Organization,* 27, 7–20.

Mintzberg, H. (1973). *The nature of managerial work.* New York: Harper & Row.

Mintzberg, H. (1994). *The rise and fall of strategic planning.* New York: Prentice-Hall.

Mintzberg, H. and Waters, J. (1982). Tracking strategy in an entrepreneurial firm. *Academy of Management Journal,* 25: 465, 499.

Morgan, G. (1986). *Images of organization.* Beverly Hills: Sage.

Nayak, P.R. and Ketteringham, J. (1997). 3M's Post-it Notes: a managed or accidental innovation? in R. Katz (ed.), *The human side of managing technological innovation.* New York: Oxford University Press, 367–77.

Perry, L.T. (1991). Strategic improvising: how to formulate and implement competitive strategies in concert. *Organizational Dynamics,* 19: 51–64.

Peters, T.J. (1995). *The pursuit of wow! Every person's guide to topsy-turvy times.* London: Macmillan.

Sanchez, R. (1997). Preparing for an uncertain future. *International Studies of Management and Organization,* 27: 71–94.

Semler, R. (1989). Managing without managers. *Harvard Business Review,* Sept–Oct, 68: 76–85.

Semler, R. (1993). *Maverick.* New York: Warner Books.

Semler, R. (1994). Why my former workers still work for me. *Harvard Business Review,* 72(1): 64–74.

Semler, R. (2000). How we went digital without a strategy. *Harvard Business Review,* 78(5): 51–8.

Tatikonda, M. and Rosenthal, S.R. (2000) Successful execution of product development projects: balancing firmness and flexibility in the innovation process. *Journal of Operations Management,* 18: 401–425.

Trist, E. (1997). The next thirty years: concepts, methods and anticipations. *Human Relations,* 50: 885–935.

Valley, K. and Keros, A.T. (2000). It takes two: improvisations in negotiations. Working paper, Harvard Business School.

Wack, P. (1985). Scenarios: uncharted waters ahead. *Harvard Business Review,* 64(1): 72–89.

Weick, K.E. (1979). *The social psychology of organizing* (2nd edn). Reading, MA: Addison-Wesley.

Weick, K.E. (1993). Organizational redesign as improvisation, in G.P. Huber and W.H. Glick (eds), *Organizational change and redesign.* New York: Oxford University Press, 346–79.

Weick, K.E. and Westley, F. (1996). Organizational learning: affirming an oxymoron, in S.R. Clegg, C. Hardy and W.R. Nord (eds), *Handbook of organization studies.* Thousand Oaks: Sage, 440–58.

Whetten, D. (1997). Theory development and the study of corporate reputation. *Corporate Reputation Review,* 1: 26–34.

Index

Aaker, D.A. 262
Abdel, H.T. 146
academic research 64
access control 219–21
action: *ad hoc* 29–30, 148; conception of 106;
  deadlines 117; designing-in-action 188;
  improvisational 29; organizational level
  275; speed of 114; spontaneous 29–31, 36,
  44, 46, 67, 140–2
action events 275
active thinking 144
ad hoc action 29–30, 148
Adams, J.L. 80
adaptation 8, 109, 124, 266, 296
aesthetics of imperfection 147, 148, 176–8
affective resources 107
Agor, W. 32, 39, 40
Albrow, M. 85
alliances 244–5
Allport, F.H. 66
Alvesson, M. 79
Amabile, T.M. 66, 109
ambiguity of structure 82–4
Ancona, D.G. 251
Angle, H.L. 24
anticipatory learning 32
Apple Macintosh 158
approaches to improvisation 35–9
Aram, J.D. 10
architectural metaphor 38
Arendt, H. 148
Argyris, C. 107, 143, 157, 159, 161
Ashforth, B. 85
Asian crisis 8

Bacdayan, P. 66
bad management 257
Bailey, D. 140, 143
Barker, J.R. 5
Barley, S.R. 187–8
Barnard, C. 36, 40

Barney, J. 1
Barrett, F.J. 3, 6, 75, 96–133 *passim*, 138–63
Bastien, Biddy 16, 18
Bastien, D.T. 3–4, 9, 14–27, 60, 75, 96–133
Bateson, M.C. 5, 65
Be-Bop music 80
Becker, H. 11
behavioral improvisation 108
behavioral norms 17–18, 19
behavioral-descriptive approach to
  improvisation 35–6
behavioral-prescriptive approach to
  improvisation 38–9
Behling, O. 30–1, 41
Berkiner, E. 96–133
Berliner, Paul F. 53, 54, 55, 56, 57, 59, 60, 61,
  67, 68, 75, 140, 141, 142, 147, 151
Berry, J.W. 103, 104
Binkhorst, D. 14
blocking 43
blueprint method 172, 173
Blumer, H. 36
Boden, D. 78
Boje, D.M. 74
Bormann, E.G. 16
Boston Consulting Group 34–5
Bosworth, S.L. 36
Bougon, M. 14
Bourdieu, P. 87
Bourgeois, V.W. 37
Boyd, H.W., Jr. 262
breakdowns 147
breakpoint concept 21–2, 23, 25
bricolage 6, 36, 60, 97, 99, 105, 106, 110–11,
  123–4, 154–5, 173; definitions 104
British Airlines 145–6
Brown, J. 96–133 *passim*, 155, 156
Brown, S.L. 96–133 *passim*, 229–58
Bryant, Ray 168
Buckler, S.A. 10–11
Buckley, W. 66